12-07

Fodor's 2008

D0168190

Map in
pocket in
back of book

BOSTON

Where to Stay and Eat
for All Budgets

Must-See Sights
and Local Secrets

Ratings You Can Trust

Fodor's Travel Publications   New York, Toronto, London, Sydney, Auckland
www.fodors.com

FODOR'S BOSTON

Editors: Jacinta O' Halloran, Eric B. Wechter

Editorial Production: Astrid deRidder, Eric B. Wechter
Editorial Contributors: Pam Bair, Louisa Kasdon, Susan MacCallum-Whitcomb, Erin Murray, Sarah Pascarella, Andrew Rimas, Diane Wright
Maps & Illustrations: David Lindroth, *cartographer;* Bob Blake and Rebecca Baer, *map editors*
Design: Fabrizio LaRocca, *creative director*; Guido Caroti, Siobhan O'Hare, *art directors*; Tina Malaney, Chie Ushio, Ann McBride, *designers*; Melanie Marin, *senior picture editor*; Moon Sun Kim, *cover designer*
Cover Photo (Copley Square, Back Bay) James Lemass
Production/Manufacturing: Steve Slawsky

COPYRIGHT

Copyright © 2008 by Fodor's Travel, a division of Random House, Inc.

Fodor's is a registered trademark of Random House, Inc.

ISBN 978–1–4000–1812–3

ISSN 0882–0074

SPECIAL SALES

This book is available at special discounts for bulk purchases for sales promotions or premiums. Special editions, including personalized covers, excerpts of existing books, and corporate imprints, can be created in large quantities for special needs. For more information, write to Special Markets/Premium Sales, 1745 Broadway, MD 6-2, New York, New York 10019, or e-mail specialmarkets@randomhouse.com.

AN IMPORTANT TIP & AN INVITATION

Although all prices, opening times, and other details in this book are based on information supplied to us at press time, changes occur all the time in the travel world, and Fodor's cannot accept responsibility for facts that become outdated or for inadvertent errors or omissions. So **always confirm information when it matters,** especially if you're making a detour to visit a specific place. Your experiences—positive and negative— matter to us. If we have missed or misstated something, **please write to us.** We follow up on all suggestions. Contact the Boston editor at editors@fodors.com or c/o Fodor's at 1745 Broadway, New York, NY 10019.

PRINTED IN THE UNITED STATES OF AMERICA
10 9 8 7 6 5 4 3 2 1

Be a Fodor's Correspondent

Your opinion matters. It matters to us. It matters to your fellow Fodor's travelers, too. And we'd like to hear it. In fact, we need to hear it.

When you share your experiences and opinions, you become an active member of the Fodor's community. That means we'll not only use your feedback to make our books better, but we'll publish your names and comments whenever possible. Throughout our guides, look for "Word of Mouth," excerpts of your unvarnished feedback.

Here's how you can help improve Fodor's for all of us.

Tell us when we're right. We rely on local writers to give you an insider's perspective. But our writers and staff editors—who are the best in the business—depend on you. Your positive feedback is a vote to renew our recommendations for the next edition.

Tell us when we're wrong. We're proud that we update most of our guides every year. But we're not perfect. Things change. Hotels cut services. Museums change hours. Charming cafés lose charm. If our writer didn't quite capture the essence of a place, tell us how you'd do it differently. If any of our descriptions are inaccurate or inadequate, we'll incorporate your changes in the next edition and will correct factual errors at fodors.com immediately.

Tell us what to include. You probably have had fantastic travel experiences that aren't yet in Fodor's. Why not share them with a community of like-minded travelers? Maybe you chanced upon a beach or bistro or B&B that you don't want to keep to yourself. Tell us why we should include it. And share your discoveries and experiences with everyone directly at fodors.com. Your input may lead us to add a new listing or highlight a place we cover with a "Highly Recommended" star or with our highest rating, "Fodor's Choice."

Give us your opinion instantly at our feedback center at www.fodors.com/feedback. You may also e-mail editors@fodors.com with the subject line "Boston Editor." Or send your nominations, comments, and complaints by mail to Boston Editor, Fodor's, 1745 Broadway, New York, NY 10019.

You and travelers like you are the heart of the Fodor's community. Make our community richer by sharing your experiences. Be a Fodor's correspondent.

Happy Traveling!

Tim Jarrell, Publisher

CONTENTS

ABOUT THIS BOOK

Our Ratings

Sometimes you find terrific travel experiences and sometimes they just find you. But usually the burden is on you to select the right combination of experiences. That's where our ratings come in.

As travelers we've all discovered a place so wonderful that its worthiness is obvious. And sometimes that place is so unique that superlatives don't do it justice: you just have to be there to know. These sights, properties, and experiences get our highest rating, **Fodor's Choice**, indicated by orange stars throughout this book.

Black stars highlight sights and properties we deem **Highly Recommended**, places that our writers, editors, and readers praise again and again for consistency and excellence.

By default, there's another category: any place we include in this book is by definition worth your time, unless we say otherwise. And we will.

Disagree with any of our choices? Care to nominate a place or suggest that we rate one more highly? Visit our feedback center at www.fodors.com/feedback.

Budget Well

Hotel and restaurant price categories from ¢ to $$$$ are defined in the opening pages of our restaurant and hotel chapters. For attractions, we always give standard adult admission fees; reductions are usually available for children, students, and senior citizens. Want to pay with plastic? **AE, D, DC, MC, V** following restaurant and hotel listings indicate whether American Express, Discover, Diners Club, MasterCard, and Visa are accepted.

Restaurants

Unless we state otherwise, restaurants are open for lunch and dinner daily. We mention dress only when there's a specific requirement and reservations only when they're essential or not accepted—it's always best to book ahead.

Hotels

Hotels have private bath, phone, TV, and air-conditioning and operate on the European Plan (aka EP, meaning without meals), unless we specify that they use the Continental Plan (CP, with a Continental breakfast), Breakfast Plan (BP, with a full breakfast), or Modified American Plan (MAP, with breakfast and dinner) or are all-inclusive (including all meals and most activities). We always list facilities but not whether you'll be charged an extra fee to use them, so when pricing accommodations, find out what's included.

Many Listings	
★	Fodor's Choice
★	Highly recommended
⊠	Physical address
⊹	Directions
⌂	Mailing address
☎	Telephone
🖶	Fax
⊕	On the Web
✉	E-mail
🖃	Admission fee
☉	Open/closed times
Ⓣ	Subway stations
⊟	Credit cards

Hotels & Restaurants	
🏨	Hotel
⇙	Number of rooms
⚫	Facilities
ⅠⓄⅠ	Meal plans
✕	Restaurant
⚘	Reservations
⊾	Smoking
🆋	BYOB
✕🏨	Hotel with restaurant that warrants a visit

Outdoors	
🏌	Golf
⚠	Camping

Other	
☾	Family-friendly
⇨	See also
⊠	Branch address
☞	Take note

WHAT'S WHERE

Boston, at least north and east of Massachusetts Avenue, is basically comprised of distinctive neighborhoods that seem to share little beyond a passion for the Red Sox and ZIP codes beginning with 02. Diverse as they are, each is worth exploring.

BEACON HILL

If you follow the Freedom Trail (or the Black Heritage Trail, or the Literary Trail, or the Women's Heritage Trail ...) you'll invariably end up on Beacon Hill. The Brahmins' home turf has an enviable collection of local landmarks, including the golden-domed Massachusetts State House. But sites aside, the gaslit streets lined with classic Federal-style town houses make this a wonderful place to walk. Two of the loveliest streets are Chestnut and Mt. Vernon, the latter of which opens onto leafy Louisburg Square, where Louisa May Alcott once wrote and John Kerry now lives. Below them lies Boston Common, a popular public gathering spot since 1634.

THE OLD WEST END

Before urban renewal scattered its residents, the Old West End was a thriving immigrant enclave. Now little remains from the old days save for the imposing Massachusetts General Hospital—and it's unlikely you'll want to visit *that* on your vacation! There are, however, two newer attractions that are definitely worth a look, namely the engaging hands-on Museum of Science and TD Banknorth Garden, known to locals as the "Gah-den" and to sports fans everywhere as the home of Boston's pro hockey and basketball teams.

GOVERNMENT CENTER

Architects wax poetic about the Brutalist and Bauhaus structures that are the focal point of Government Center. Everyone else just seems to think they're ugly. Locals often avert their eyes when scurrying across the sterile plaza to City Hall; out-of-towners tend to avoid it completely, making a beeline instead to Faneuil Hall and the trio of restored market buildings that share its name. Inside Faneuil Hall Marketplace are boutiques, bars, and an affordable food court; outside, exuberant street performers and vendors laden with souvenirs compete for the attention of passersby. On Friday and Saturday nearby Haymarket's open-air stalls offer a less-touristy alternative.

THE NORTH END

Though small in size and hemmed in by water on three sides, Boston's oldest residential neighborhood is crammed full of history. Copp's Hill Burying Ground (which holds the remains of the oh-so-pious Mathers) attests to the North End's Puri-

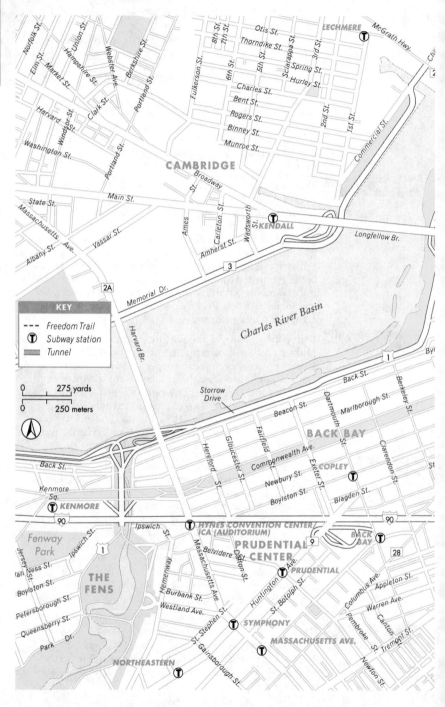

KEY

--- Freedom Trail
Ⓣ Subway station
▨▨ Tunnel

0 — 275 yards
0 — 250 meters

LECHMERE
McGrath Hwy.
Otis St.
Thorndike St.
8th St.
7th St.
6th St.
5th St.
Sciarappa St.
3rd St.
Spring St.
Hurley St.
Charles St.
Bent St.
Rogers St.
2nd St.
Binney St.
1st St.
Munroe St.
Commercial St.
Fulkerson St.

Norfolk St.
Elm St.
Union St.
Hampshire St.
Market St.
Webster Ave.
Berkshire St.
Portland St.
Harvard St.
Clark St.
Windsor St.
Washington St.

CAMBRIDGE
Broadway
Main St.
State St.
Massachusetts Ave.
Vassar St.
Albany St.
Ames St.
Carleton St.
Wadsworth St.
Amherst St.
KENDALL
3
2A
Memorial Dr.
Longfellow Br.

Harvard Br.

Charles River Basin

1

Storrow Drive
Back St.
Beacon St.
Dartmouth St.
Marlborough St.
Berkeley St.
Fairfield
Gloucester St.
Hereford St.
Commonwealth Ave.
Exeter St.
BACK BAY
Clarendon St.
COPLEY
Newbury St.
Boylston St.
Blagden St.
Back St.
Kenmore Sq.
KENMORE
90
Ipswich St.
HYNES CONVENTION CENTER
ICA (AUDITORIUM)
PRUDENTIAL CENTER
9
BACK BAY
28
Fenway Park
Ipswich St.
1
Belvidere St.
Dalton St.
PRUDENTIAL
Jersey St.
Ian St.
Ness St.
Boylston St.
Hemenway St.
Burbank St.
Huntington Ave.
St. Botolph St.
Columbus Ave.
Appleton St.
Warren Ave.
Petersborough St.
Westland Ave.
Canton St.
Pembroke St.
Tremont St.
THE FENS
Queensberry St.
St. Stephen St.
SYMPHONY
Park Dr.
St. Gainsborough St.
MASSACHUSETTS AVE.
NORTHEASTERN
Newton St.

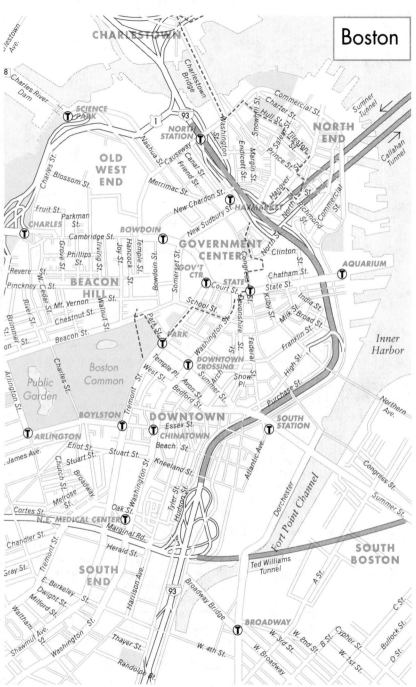

WHAT'S WHERE

	tan past; whereas Paul Revere House and Old North Church evoke the Revolutionary Age. Yet for all the Americana, this often feels more like an Italian village than Main Street U.S.A. because an influx of immigrants, starting in the 19th century, also left their mark here. Alongside salumerias and social clubs are scores of authentic Italian restaurants serving everything from Sicilian comfort food to cutting-edge pasta creations.
CHARLESTOWN	Charlestown's Freedom Trail sites can't be missed—literally or figuratively. The Bunker Hill Monument is a towering tribute to one of the pivotal battles of 1775, and the USS *Constitution,* the oldest commissioned ship in the U.S. fleet, is a towering tangle of masts and rigging. Gentrification began more than three decades ago when Old Ironside's home was transformed from a hardscrabble naval yard into a National Historic Site. Now townies have moved into restored shipbuilders' houses and neighborhood restaurateurs, no longer catering exclusively to the "hardtack-and-grog" crowd, have moved upscale. In fact, ever since Todd English opened Olives in 1989, Charlestown eateries have won a citywide following.
DOWNTOWN BOSTON	Old-timers may be surprised to see the words "Downtown Boston" and "Renaissance" used together. But change is afoot. Historical points of interest—like the Old South Meeting House and Old State House—are still wedged incongruously between office towers. But the Theater District (with vintage venues such as the Opera House and glorious Citi Performing Arts Center) has gotten a face-lift in recent years, and Downtown Crossing (one of the main retail zones, now rebranded as part of the Ladder District) is being cleaned up. So is the waterfront, and HarborWalk.
THE BACK BAY	In the chic Back Bay even landfill looks good. Developed as part of a marsh reclamation project in the mid-1800s, the area contains Boston's most impressive skyscrapers and its single most beautiful building, stunning Trinity Church. Yet the first thing visitors will likely notice is that the streets here are actually laid out in an orderly fashion—which makes it easy to ogle the neighborhood's stylishly dressed denizens. If you've got deep pockets, emulating them is easy, too. The concentration of high-end stores (under "C" alone you'll find Cartier, Chanel, and Christian Dior) have lead some to label Newbury Street the East Coast's Rodeo Drive.

THE SOUTH END	Not to be confused with South Boston, this area hugs the south side of Huntington Avenue southeast of the Back Bay and due south of Chinatown. Although the South End lacks big-ticket attractions, it has enough lavishly embellished bowfront houses to earn a spot in the National Register of Historic Places—and enough style to win the "hippest hood" crown. An active arts community and dynamic multicultural population (including a large gay contingent) are two contributing factors. Innovative restaurants are another.
THE FENWAY	Baseball fans, art aficionados, and aspiring intellectuals meet head-on in the Fens, a meandering green space that's the first link in Frederick Law Olmsted's Emerald Necklace. Fenway Park, a veritable shrine to the Red Sox, stands just northwest of the Fens. To the south are the Museum of Fine Arts and the more-intimate—but nonetheless eclectic—Isabella Stewart Gardner Museum. And all around it are academic institutions, including Boston University and Northeastern University. Nearby Kenmore Square is Boston's nightlife strip. Always popular with the college crowd, it's now in with their parents, too.
SOUTH BOSTON & THE STREETCAR SUBURBS	Thanks to a spate of openings and reopenings in the Seaport District, South Boston is suddenly a magnet for museum hoppers. The Institute of Contemporary Art, the Children's Museum at Fort Point Channel, and the Boston Tea Party Ships & Museum, which is slated to reopen in spring 2008, can all be found here. Outlying neighborhoods traditionally dependent on developments in public transit now offer their own attractions south of "Southie." Chief among these are the Arnold Arboretum in Jamaica Plain and the John F. Kennedy Library & Museum in Dorchester.
CAMBRIDGE	A kissing cousin across the Charles River from Boston, the "People's Republic of Cambridge" has long been a haven for writers, radicals, and iconoclasts of all kinds. Though primarily a working-class city (more than 50 languages are spoken at the local high school), Cambridge is best known as the location of Harvard and MIT. The universities themselves support affiliated museums—most notably the Fogg and the Peabody. Students, meanwhile, support an eclectic mix of stores and services. So, despite creeping gentrification in Harvard Square, the area still has a disproportionately large number of quirky cafés, independent bookshops, funky clothing outlets, and one-of-a-kind craft galleries.

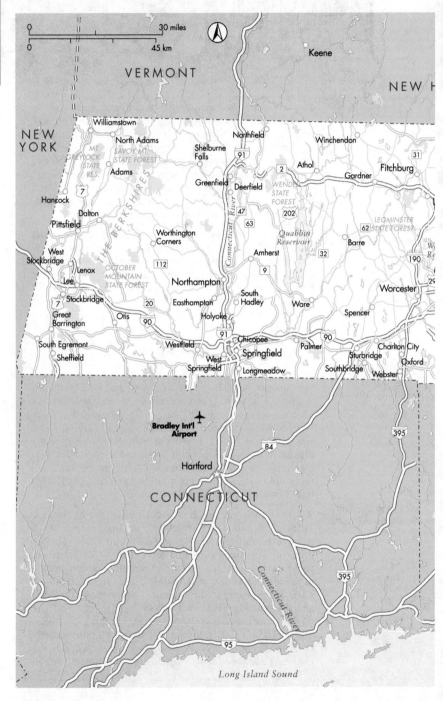

Massachusetts

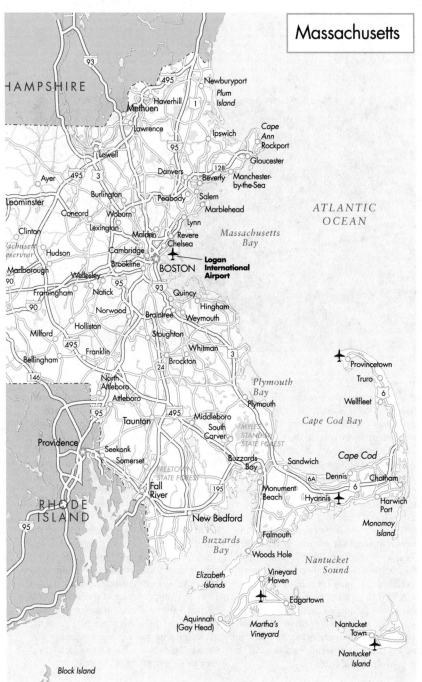

NEW HAMPSHIRE

93
495
Newburyport
Plum Island
Haverhill
Methuen
1
Lawrence
Ipswich
Cape Ann
Rockport
Lowell
95
Gloucester
Ayer
495
3
Danvers
128
Beverly
Manchester-by-the-Sea
Leominster
Burlington
Peabody
Salem
Concord
Woburn
Marblehead
ATLANTIC OCEAN
Clinton
Lexington
Lynn
achusett eservoir
Hudson
Malden
Revere
Massachusetts Bay
Cambridge
Chelsea
Marlborough
Brookline
Logan International Airport
Wellesley
BOSTON
90
95
Framingham
Natick
93
Quincy
90
Norwood
Braintree
Hingham
Milford
Holliston
Weymouth
495
Stoughton
Bellingham
Franklin
Whitman
3
146
Brockton
24
Plymouth Bay
North Attleboro
Attleboro
MYLES STANDISH STATE FOREST
Provincetown
Truro
6
Wellfleet
95
Taunton
495
Middleboro
Plymouth
Cape Cod Bay
Providence
Seekonk
South Carver
FREETOWN STATE FOREST
Cape Cod
Somerset
Buzzards Bay
Sandwich
Fall River
195
6A
Dennis
Chatham
RHODE ISLAND
Monument Beach
6
Hyannis
Harwich Port
New Bedford
Monomoy Island
95
Falmouth
Buzzards Bay
Woods Hole
Nantucket Sound
Elizabeth Islands
Vineyard Haven
Edgartown
Aquinnah (Gay Head)
Martha's Vineyard
Nantucket Town
Nantucket Island
Block Island

QUINTESSENTIAL BOSTON

History 101

Boston may no longer be the "Hub of the Universe," yet it *is* the undisputed epicenter of American history. Much of the political ferment that spawned the nation took place here, and visitors are often awed by the concentration of sites. Locals, on the other hand, take them in stride. Sure, they revere Revere as much as the next guy. But to Bostonians, the past isn't abstract. Rather, it is woven into the fabric of daily life. Families routinely picnic on the same Common where Puritans grazed their cows; and the faithful still worship in Old North Church, where two lanterns were fatefully hung on the night of April 18, 1775. Community activists, similarly, follow Sam Adams's example by debating hot topics in Faneuil Hall, while bookworms continue to gravitate, as Emerson and his transcendentalist buddies did, to the Boston Public Library.

Cultural Encounters

The 17th-century Puritans dubbed Boston "the city on a hill"; 18th-century patriots called it the Cradle of Liberty. To 19th-century arts lovers, however, it was the highly cultured Athens of America. Today Boston still packs quite a cultural punch. For instance, Symphony Hall (a Victorian showpiece with unparalleled acoustics) is widely considered to be one of the world's finest concert venues. And that's just the tip of the artistic iceberg. As part of the Fenway Cultural District, Symphony Hall counts among its neighbors such venerable institutions as the New England Conservatory of Music, the Huntington Theatre Company, the Mary Baker Eddy Library, the Isabella Stewart Gardner Museum, and the Museum of Fine Arts. All offer free public access during the annual "Opening Our Doors Day" and various other points in the year.

Boston is a welcoming city, big on heart and beauty. But fitting in here involves more than dropping your R's and taking the T (as the Massachusetts Bay Transportation Authority is affectionately called). To understand Boston, you must first understand what makes Bostonians tick...

The Red Sox

The "Red Sox Nation" doesn't have a representative at the United Nations, but its citizens couldn't be more fervent if they did. Though Bostonians are wild about their football, hockey, and basketball teams, only the Sox can bring the entire town to its feet—or its knees. Want to see what the fuss is about? The Fenway Park ticket office next to Gate A opens at 10 AM. If you strike out there, a limited number of tickets are sold at Gate C two hours before game time. Alternately, you can sidle up to a guy holding out tickets just after game time, and haggle. Once inside, be prepared to don a Red Sox cap, down a Fenway frank, and sing along to Neil Diamond's "Sweet Caroline," in the eighth inning.

Wicked Good Food

Boston's independent restaurant scene is on par with New York, San Francisco, and Chicago. So while history buffs look back fondly on a certain tea party, foodies simply look forward to dinner. For all the talk of cod and beans, the area lays claim to a long line of "celebrity chefs:" M. Sanzian (remembered largely as the inventor of Boston cream pie) made quite a stir in the mid-1800s and, a century later, Julia Child launched a culinary revolution from her Cambridge kitchen. These days it's Todd "Iron Chef" English, Lydia Shire, Ming Tsai, Gordon Hamersley, and Jasper White who make eating out a gastronomic adventure. The ideal time to taste their wares and try up-and-coming competitors is during Restaurant Week (held in August and March) when more than 100 participating eateries prepare three-course prix-fixe menus for as little as $20.

IF YOU LIKE

City Walks

In a compact place where streets often evolved from cow paths and colonial lanes, driving is no simple task—which may explain why the first U.S. subway was built here in 1897. Still, "America's Walking City" is best seen on foot.

See Red. The logical first step is to follow the red stripe that marks the famed Freedom Trail (⇨ *"Following the Freedom Trail" box in Chapter 1).* Starting in Boston Common, this 2½-mi path winds through the city, connecting 16 Revolutionary-era sites; among them are Paul Revere's home and Samuel Adams's burial place. Join one of the free National Park Service tours or honor the patriots' spirit by doing the route independently.

Go Green. In 1878 renowned landscape architect Frederick Law Olmsted started work on the Emerald Necklace—six jewel-like parks strung together by a greenway. Though the Common and Public Garden predate his designs, they're connected to them by the Commonwealth Avenue Mall, creating an urban oasis that extends 7 mi past meadows, manicured flowerbeds, and marshy ponds from Downtown to Dorchester. ☎617/232-5374 ⊕*www.emeraldnecklace.org.*

Take a Walk on the Waterside. Boston's 47-mi HarborWalk accesses favorite waterfront attractions (like the New England Aquarium), picturesque piers, working wharves, even urban beaches. If you only have an hour, download HarborWalk's free audio guide and stroll from Christopher Columbus Park to the new Institute of Contemporary Art on Fan Pier. ☎617/482-1722 ⊕*www.bostonharborwalk.com.*

Sports

In Beantown, you can mark off the seasons by checking the sports lineup. Avid spectators know that the "Boys of Summer" arrive in spring and that the Head of the Charles Regatta is a harbinger of fall. However, it's easy to get a sports fix in any season.

Touch Base. Small but mighty Fenway, the oldest major-league park, is a pilgrimage site for baseball fans, and year-round tours (☎617/226-6666 ⊕*boston.redsox.mlb.com*) provide the ultimate insider's view. You'll get a first-hand look at the press box, dugout seats, Pesky's Pole, and—when schedules permit—the fabled Green Monster. It's as close as you'll get to this beloved field without being drafted into MLB.

Visit the Secret Garden. Prefer Bobby Orr or Larry Bird over Ted Williams? Seek out the Sports Museum (☎617/624-1237 ⊕*www.sportsmuseum.org*) in TD Banknorth Garden. The Bruins and Celtics get home advantage here (one popular exhibit, for example, is a hockey penalty box). But there's also artwork, equipment, and archival footage relating to the Patriots, the Revolution (Boston's pro soccer team), Boston Marathon winners, and, yes, the Sox.

Row, Row, Row Your Boat. You won't hear fans yelling bloody murder at the Head of the Charles, the world's largest crew regatta held each October. But that doesn't mean they're any less enthusiastic—or that the sport is any less arduous. Try it yourself at any of several local outfitters (⇨ Boating *in* Chapter 6).

Multicultural Experiences

The Brits who founded Boston back in 1630 understandably get a lot of press. Nevertheless, they represent only the first of many immigrant groups who helped shape this city. So don't leave without seeing some of its lively ethnic enclaves.

Get Your Irish Up. All the Boston Celtics aren't basketball players. For proof, simply take the Irish Heritage Trail (☎617/696–9880 ⊕ *www.irishheritagetrail.com*). It's a self-guided, 3-mi walk covering sites associated with prominent Irish-Americans from John Hancock (who knew!?) to JFK, as well as the everyday folks who were forced from their homeland by the 1840s Potato Famine. Afterwards down a pint in their memory at your choice of authentic Irish pubs.

Orient Yourself. Though it covers only a few blocks, Boston's densely populated Chinatown ranks as the country's third largest. To commemorate its 130-year history, Chinatown is developing its own heritage projects, including a trail and youth-led tours. But the best way to experience this colorful quarter is through its equally colorful celebrations. Chinese New Year promises dragon parades and firecrackers, while the August Moon Festival features lion dancing and lanterns.

Chow Bella. Red sauce has been simmering in the North End since the Italian immigrants moved here in the 1880s. The demographic is changing (today only 40% of residents claim Italian descent), but you only have to look at the thriving restaurants to see that *la vita* is still *dolce* in Boston's Little Italy. Have dinner or take a market tour for an inside look at Italian-American cuisine.

Getting Out on the Water

This city has long been defined by its coast and waterways. The original colonists were drawn here largely because of Boston's natural harbor, and local commerce and culture have remained inextricably bound to it. So if you've ever wanted to say "anchors aweigh," this is the place.

Set Sail. June through September, you can relive the Golden Age of Sail aboard the *Liberty Clipper,* a replica two-masted gaff-rigged schooner that operates midday harbor tours and romantic sunset cruises from Long Wharf (⇨ Day Tours & Guides, *in* Boston Essentials). Rather hoist your own jib? In season, several outfitters have sailboat rentals and lessons (⇨ Boating *in* Chapter 6).

Watch Whales. Ahab wannabes might opt for a whale-watching excursion, organized by the **New England Aquarium** (☎617/973–5200 ⊕*www.neaq.org*) from April through October. At Stellwagen Bank (30 mi offshore) an onboard naturalist susses out humpbacks, finbacks, minkes, and more. While these supersize mammals come mainly to feed, some seem happy to perform. If you're lucky, one might breach, blow, or give you a wave with its massive flipper.

Enjoy Ferry Tales. One of the city's top values is the $10 round-trip ride from Long Wharf to Boston Harbor Islands National Park. May to October you can hop the Harbor Express ferry (☎617/222–6999 ⊕*www.harborexpress.com*) for Georges Island, where hiking and beachcombing opportunities abound. Ranger-led tours of the island's pre–Civil War fort are also available and intrepid types can take advantage of a complimentary water shuttle to outlying islets.

WHEN TO GO

Weather-wise, **late spring and fall** are the optimal times to visit Boston. Aside from mild temperatures, the former boasts blooming gardens throughout the city; and the later (specifically from mid-September to early November) sees the surrounding countryside ablaze with brilliantly colored foliage. At both times, however, you should expect crowds.

Autumn, for instance, draws hordes of hopeful leaf-peepers. Students must be factored into the mix as well. More than 250,000 of them flood into Boston and Cambridge each September; then pull out again in May and June. So hotels and restaurants, especially during move-in and move-out weekends, can be packed.

The good news is that this is a four-season destination. Summer brings sailboats to Boston Harbor, concerts to the Esplanade, and café tables to assorted sidewalks. It also brings the most reliable sunshine. If you're dreaming of a classic shore vacation, summer is prime. (Of course, others also know this—which makes advance planning imperative.)

Even winter has its pleasures. The cultural season heats up when it's cold, and Boston sports a festive glow over the holidays, thanks to the thousands of lights strung around the Common, Public Garden, and Commonwealth Avenue Mall. During the post-Christmas period, temperatures continue to fall. But pennypinchers will be pleased to know that lodging prices do, too.

> ### QUICK FORECASTS
>
> Check the coded lights atop the Berkeley Building overlooking Copley Square: *Steady blue means clear view; flashing blue, clouds due; steady red, rain ahead; flashing red, snow instead* . . . except in baseball season when it means the Sox game is canceled!

Climate

Like other northeastern American cities, Boston can be uncomfortably hot and humid in summer and frigid in winter. Yet the saying here is "if you don't like the weather, just wait a moment." A gray, overcast day can quickly turn sunny and warm—or vice versa. Hence, it's best to come prepared for unseasonable spells at anytime of year.

Forecasts Visit the **Weather Channel** (⊕*www.weather.com*) online or call 617/936–1234.

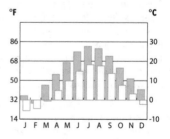

ON THE CALENDAR

There is *always* something happening around Boston. We've rounded up the top annual events. For a fuller selection consult the **Greater Boston Convention & Visitors Bureau** (☎888/733–2678 ⊕*www.bostonusa.com*) or the **Massachusetts Office of Travel & Tourism** (☎800/227–6277 ⊕*www.mass-vacation.com*) Local papers are also reliable resources: the *Boston Globe* (⊕*www.boston.com*), for one, publishes a Thursday "Calendar" section and has searchable listings online.

WINTER November	Winter officially arrives in mid-November when **Boston Common's Frog Pond Rink** (☎617/635–2120 ⊕*www.bostoncommonfrogpond.org*) opens. Ice-skaters have until mid-March to perfect their double axels. Bibliophiles search for treasures among the tomes at the **Boston International Antiquarian Book Fair** (☎617/375–9013 ⊕*www.bostonbookfair.com*), which hosts more than 100 exhibitors. Celebrate Turkey Day the contemporary way by viewing the parade at **America's Hometown Thanksgiving Celebration** (☎508/746–1818 ⊕*www.usathanksgiving.com*) in Plymouth. Or go retro at **Plimoth Plantation** (☎508/746–1622 ⊕*www.plimoth.org*). The re-created Pilgrim village has a themed exhibit and serves a praiseworthy dinner.
Late November– December	Starting in late November, the halls are alive with sound of music as bell ringers, tuba players, and enthusiastic choristers entertain at **Faneuil Hall** (☎617/523–1300 ⊕*www.faneuilhallmarketplace.com*). A literal highlight of the holidays is the **Lighting of the Common's Christmas Tree** (☎617/635–4505 ⊕*www.cityofboston.gov/parks*). An evergreen is draped with 18,000 lights and the switch is flipped with much fanfare.
December	About 100 artisans peddle handmade gifts and holiday treats at the annual **Holly Fair** (☎617/547–6789 ⊕*www.ccae.org*), organized by the Cambridge Center for Adult Education. Dust off your tricorn hat. The **Boston Tea Party Reenactment** (☎617/482–6439 ⊕*www.oldsouthmeetinghouse.org*) kicks off at the Old South Meeting House, and festivities are free to anyone in colonial garb. **Christmas Revels** (☎617/972–8300 ⊕*www.revels.org*) at Harvard's Sanders Theatre mark the winter solstice with music, dance, and folk plays from around the world. Bostonians turn out in force for the city's **First Night**

ON THE CALENDAR

	Celebration (☎ *617/542–1399* ⊕ *www.firstnight.org*), a full day and night of arts-oriented alcohol-free activities. Some 250 performances, held at scores of venues indoors and out, culminate with fireworks over Boston Harbor.
Mid-January–Early April	The long-running **Boston Wine Festival** (☎ *617/439–7000* ⊕ *www.bostonwinefestival.net*), held in the Boston Harbor Hotel at Rowes Wharf, includes seminars, tastings, and decadent vino-themed dinners.
February	Oenophiles have a reason to rejoice when the **Boston Wine Expo** (☎ *877/946–3976* ⊕ *www.wineexpoboston.com*) opens at the World Trade Center. More than 400 wineries from a dozen or so countries pop their corks. Locals honor **Black History Month** with events like concerts, exhibitions, and genealogical workshops, many of them orchestrated by the Museum of Afro American History (☎ *617/725–0022* ⊕ *www.afroammuseum.org*). There's hope for hockey fans. Even if the Bruins let you down (again!) you can still enjoy the annual **Beanpot Hockey Tournament** (☎ *617/624–1000* ⊕ *www.beanpothockey.com*) between area college teams.
SPRING	
March	Gardeners remind themselves that spring really is around the corner by attending the **Annual New England Spring Flower Show** (☎ *617/933–4900* ⊕ *www.masshort.org*) at the Bayside Expo Center. It's easy being green on the closest Sunday to March 17, when all of Boston turns out to watch the **St. Patrick's Day Parade** (☎ *617/268–7955* ⊕ *www.cityofboston.gov/arts*) pass through Southie.
April	Sentimental types sigh contentedly as the **Swan Boats** (☎ *617/522–1966* ⊕ *www.swanboats.com*), floating fixtures since 1877, return to the Public Garden Lagoon. On **Patriots' Day** (the third Monday in April), lanterns are hung in the steeple of Old North Church and costumed celebrants reenact Paul Revere's ride from Hanover Street in Boston's North End to Lexington. Much flag-waving follows. On the same day, the prestigious **Boston Marathon** (☎ *617/236–1652* ⊕ *www.bostonmarathon.org*) fills the streets from rural Hopkinton to the Back Bay. Go to "Heartbreak Hill" and watch competitors sprint, stride, or limp up this make-or-break section of the 26-mi course.

April–May	Step right up! The Children's Museum brings the intimate, one-ring **Big Apple Circus** (☎*800/922–3772* ⊕*www.bigapplecircus.org*) to town. The tent sets up on City Hall Plaza.
May	Everyone "makes way for ducklings" in the Mother's Day **Duckling Parade** (☎*617/723–8144* ⊕*www.friendsofthepublicgarden.org*) as children, many in costume, waddle from Beacon Hill to the Public Garden. The Arnold Arboretum in Jamaica Plain may have more than 4,000 kinds of woody plants, but on **Lilac Sunday** (☎*617/524–1718* ⊕*www.arboretum.harvard.edu*), only one matters. Purple reigns! Over the Memorial Day weekend, musicians, magicians and—you guessed it—mimes do their thing during the **Street Performers Festival** (☎*617/523–1300* ⊕*www.faneuilhallmarketplace.com*) at Faneuil Hall Marketplace.
SUMMER June	Rowing shells are replaced by supersize vessels decorated with dragon heads and tails when the **Hong Kong Dragon Boat Festival** (☎*617/426–6500* ⊕*www.bostondragonboat.org*) takes over the Charles River. The weeklong **Boston Early Music Festival** (☎*617/661–1812* ⊕*www.bemf.org*) takes place in odd-number years, though events and performances celebrating baroque and Renaissance music are scheduled annually. For a quarter-century, the **Rockport Chamber Music Festival** (☎*978/546–7391* ⊕*www.rcmf.org*) has lured music lovers to this picturesque seaside town 45 mi north of Boston.
July	During Boston's weeklong Fourth of July celebration, **Harbor fest** (☎*617/227–1528* ⊕*www.bostonharborfest.com*), hundreds of events—many of them free—take place along the waterfront and Downtown. The celebration includes concerts, walking tours, and the USS *Constitution* Turnaround Cruise, plus a **Chowderfest** on City Hall Plaza where you can sample the recipes from Boston's best restaurants. **Boston Pops Concert & Fireworks Display** (☎*888/484–7677* ⊕*www.July4th.org*) ends Harborfest with a bang on Independence Day. The free star-spangled musical extravaganza at the Hatch Shell draws huge crowds, but you can avoid the worst of them by attending the preview concert on the evening of July 3 instead. Zydeco, fado, raga, rockabilly: you'll hear them all northwest of Boston at the **Lowell Folk Festival** (☎*978/970–5200* ⊕*www.lowellfolkfestival.org*). It's

ON THE CALENDAR

	America's largest free folk event. Marblehead's **Race Week** (☎781/631–2868 ⊕*www.marbleheadracing.org*), usually held the last week of July, has been attracting boaters from all along the eastern seaboard since 1889.
July–August	Cambridge's **Summer in the City Program** (☎617/349–4380 ⊕*www.cambridgeartscouncil.org*) showcases cultural diversity through a series of free family-friendly performances staged in public parks. Throughout the summer, the North End hosts boisterous **Weekend Street Fests** (☎617/720-2283 ⊕*www www.northendboston.com*), honoring Italy's various patron saints with processions, music, and fabulous food.
FALL September	Experience reel life at the **Boston Film Festival** (☎617/523–8388 ⊕*www.bostonfilmfestival.org*). Dozens of independent films premiere, and directors or actors sometimes put in an appearance. Whether you're jazzed up or feeling blue, there's a late-September festival for you. The **Beantown Jazz Festival** (⊕*www.beantownjazz.org*) brings music to the South End; while the **Boston Blues Festival** (⊕*www.bluestrust.com*) caps Blues Week with concerts at the Hatch Shell. New Bedford's commercial fishermen strut their stuff at the **Working Waterfront Festival** (☎508/993–8894 ⊕*www.workingwaterfrontfestival.org*) with skill competitions, seafaring songs, fish tales, and, of course, fresh seafood.
September–October	Essex County remembers its roots at the **Topsfield Fair** (☎978/887–5000 ⊕*www.topsfieldfair.org*), the nation's oldest agricultural fair. Livestock displays, grandstand shows, and midway rides draw 500,000 people. See art in the making: **Boston Open Studios** (⊕*www.bostonopenstudios.org*), scheduled in different neighborhoods throughout autumn, give you the chance to watch demonstrations and buy directly from artists.
October	Columbus Day is also **Opening Our Doors Day** (☎617/437–7544 ⊕*www.fenwayculture.org*) in the Fenway Cultural District. Expect free admissions, concerts, lectures, and tours at some of the city's finest arts institutions. College crew teams—and spectators bearing blankets and beer—come from all over for the **Head of the Charles Regatta** (☎617/868–6200 ⊕*www.hocr.org*). It's the world's largest two-day rowing event. Get bogged down at the **National Cranberry**

Festival (☎508/866–8190 ⊕*www.edaville.com*) in Plymouth County. Wagon pulls, pony rides, and narrow-gauge train tours through a cranberry "plantation" are all on the agenda. You'll see smashing pumpkins at the **Life Is Good Pumpkin Festival** (☎617/635–4505 ⊕*www.cityofboston.gov/parks*). To raise funds for children's charities, carvers cover the Common with more than 30,000 jack-o'-lanterns. Salem is bewitching during **Haunted Happenings** (☎877/725–3662 ⊕*www.hauntedhappenings.com*), a series of candlelit tours, witch trial reenactments, and other themed events climaxing on Halloween.

GREAT ITINERARIES

BOSTON IN 4 DAYS

Clearly every traveler moves at a different pace. One might pass a contented hour in the massive Museum of Fine Arts; another might have to be forcibly removed at closing time. Nevertheless, in four days you should be able to hit the city highlights without feeling rushed. If you're lucky enough to have a few vacation days to spare, you can put them to good use exploring nearby communities.

Day 1: Hit the Trail

About 3 million visitors walk the Freedom Trail every year—and there's a good reason why: taken together, the route's 16 sites offer a crash course in colonial history. That makes the trail a "must" in Bostonian terms, so you might as well tackle it sooner rather than later. Linger wherever you like, leaving time for lunch in bustling Quincy Market. (Its food court is a good place to sample at least one of Boston's edible holy trinity: lobster, clams, and "chowdah.") Next, follow the redbrick road into the North End, where you'll find Old North Church and Paul Revere's former home (Boston's oldest house, it was constructed almost 100 years before he moved in). After wandering the neighborhood's narrow streets, dine in one of Little Italy's many authentic eateries. Or—if you have time and shoe leather left—keep going across the Charlestown Bridge for a look at the USS *Constitution*, then catch the MBTA water shuttle back to Downtown.

Day 2: Head for the Hill

Named for the light that topped it in the 17th century, Beacon Hill originally stood a bit taller until earth was scraped off its peak and used as landfill not far away. What remains—namely gas street lamps, shady trees, brick sidewalks, and stately Brahmin brownstones—evokes old Boston. When soaking up the ambience, don't forget to take in some of Beacon Hill's "official" attractions. After all, major sites from Boston's various themed trails, including the Massachusetts State House, the Boston Athenaeum, the African Meeting House, and the Granary Burying Ground, are located here. Afterwards, stroll over to the Common and the Public Garden (America's oldest public park and oldest botanical garden respectively). Both promise greenery and great people-watching. If shopping is more your bag, cruise for antiques along Charles Street, the thoroughfare that separates them. In the evening, chow down on chow mein in the affordable eateries of Chinatown or go upscale at hot new restaurants in the Theater District.

Day 3: Get an Overview

From the Back Bay, you can cover a lot of Boston's other attractions in a single day. Start at the top (literally) by seeing 360-degree views from the Prudential Center's Skywalk Observatory. Once you understand the lay of the land, just plot a route based on your interests. Architecture aficionados can hit the ground running at the neoclassical Public Library and Romanesque Trinity Church. Shoppers, conversely, can opt for the stores of Newbury Street and Copley Place (a high-end mall anchored by Neiman Marcus). Farther west in the Fens, other choices await. Art connoisseurs might view the collection at the Museum of Fine Arts (with 350,000 *objets d'art* spanning 3,000 years it could take some time!) or the more manageably sized Isabella Stewart Gardner Museum. Quirky, carnival-like Fenway Park beckons baseball fans to the other side of the Fens. Depending on your taste—and the availability of tickets—cap the day with a Symphony Hall concert or a Red Sox game.

Day 4: On the Waterfront

Having spent so much time focusing on the old, why not devote a day to something new? Begin at the Institute of Contemporary Art (ICA) on Fan Pier. Boston's first new art museum in almost a century boasts a bold cantilevered design that makes the most of its waterside location. Next, follow the ever-expanding HarborWalk to the Children's Museum and the Boston Tea Party Ships & Museum, which reopen after major overhauls in 2007 and 2008 respectively. These are all particularly good destinations for kids (even the ICA, thanks to special programming for both little tykes and hard-to-please teens). Also on the waterfront is the New England Aquarium, another family favorite that underwent its own expansion (gaining an IMAX theater in the process) back in 2001. Highlights include the Giant Ocean Tank, hands-on tidal pools, and an engaging sea lion show. Outside you can sign on for a harbor cruise, whale-watching trip, or ferry ride to the Boston Harbor Islands.

BEYOND BOSTON PROPER

Day 1: Explore Cambridge

From pre-Revolutionary days, Boston was the region's commercial center and Cambridge was the "burbs": a place more residential than mercantile, with plenty of room to build the nation's first English-style, redbrick university. Not surprisingly the heart of the community—geographically and otherwise—is still Harvard Square. It would be easy enough to hang here. You could, for instance, simply browse the shops surrounding the square; then wander over to the riverbank to watch crew teams practice. But Harvard Square is also the starting point for free student-led campus tours (details at www.harvard.edu), as well as for strolls along Brattle Street's "Tory Row" (No. 105 was occupied by both Washington *and* Longfellow). If the heady academic atmosphere leaves you hungry for learning, return across the river to see the Science Museum, especially popular with children. Alternately, spend the evening like a true Cantabrigian by taking in a concert or lecture at Sanders Theatre.

Day 2: Step Back in Time

You only have to travel a short distance to visit historic places you read about in grade school. For a side trip to the 17th century, head 35 mi southeast to Plymouth. The famed rock doesn't live up its hype. But Plimoth Plantation (an open-air museum re-creating life among Pilgrims) and *Mayflower II* are worth the trip. A second option is to veer northwest to see Revolutionary-era sites in Lexington (now a well-to-do bedroom community). Start at the National Heritage Museum for a recap of the events that kick-started everything; then proceed to Battle Green where "the shot heard round the world" was fired. After stopping by Minute Man National Historic Park, bookworms may want to continue to Concord to tour the homes of literary luminaries like Ralph Waldo Emerson, Louisa May Alcott, and Nathaniel Hawthorne. Conclude your novel excursion with a walk around Walden Pond, where Henry David Thoreau wrote one of the founding documents of the ecology movement.

Day 3: A Shore Thing

Anyone eager to taste the salt air or feel the surge of the sea should consider a day trip to the North Shore towns of Salem and Gloucester. The former has a Maritime National Historic Site—complete with vintage wharves and warehouses—that proves there's more to the notorious town than just witchcraft; while the latter (America's oldest seaport) demonstrates that men *still* go down to the sea in ships. Prefer to just beach yourself? Nature lovers can flock to Crane Beach in Ipswich, about an hour north of Boston. Part of a 1,200-acre wildlife refuge, it includes 4 mi of sand rimmed by scenic dunes. For a quick sand-in-every-crevice experience take either the MBTA's Harbor Express ferry south to Nantucket Beach in Hull or the commuter train north to Manchester-by-the-Sea's Singing Beach (a high silica content actually causes the sand there to "sing" or squeak when walked on).

TIPS

❶ If walking from one end of town to the other seems too arduous, do as the locals do and take the T. It will put you within a block of almost anywhere you want to go. An MBTA LinkPass ($9 per day, $15 per week) allows for unlimited travel on subways, local buses, and inner-harbor ferries, as well as some commuter trains.

❷ You can usually buy Symphony Hall tickets online or through your hotel concierge. But in-the-know Bostonians get rush seats (unused subscriber tickets put on sale an hour before curtain time). Since the Soxs are in a league of their own, scoring ball tickets is trickier. If you're empty-handed, watch the action at Game On!—a two-story sports bar attached to Fenway Park.

❸ For a traditional lunch "North of Boston," try Longfellow's Wayside Inn in Sudbury (on-site you'll see an 18th-century gristmill and the school "Mary" attended with her "little lamb"). If you don't want to have miles to go before you sleep, book into Concord's Colonial Inn rather than returning to Boston: it was a Thoreau family residence before becoming a hostelry in 1889.

Exploring Boston

WORD OF MOUTH

"Upside: academics, seafood, sports, music, art, access to skiing, sailing, actual trees and ocean, many scenic areas. Downside: long, dark, dreary winter and expensive real estate."

—Daisymae

"Bring your walking shoes!!! It is a perfect-sized city to walk to everything. You can walk over the Mass Ave. Bridge to explore Cambridge and Harvard Square; you can walk the Charles, Comm. Ave., the Public Garden to the Commons to Gov. Center, the Waterfront, and the North End. And if the weather turns, then you can walk to a cab or train! Have a blast. Explore!"

—gyppielou

Updated by
Andrew Rimas

THERE'S HISTORY AND CULTURE AT every turn in Boston, but a down-to-earth attitude can always be found on the edges of its New England pride. The city defies stereotype because it consists of different layers. The deepest layer is the historical base, the place where musket-bearing revolutionaries vowed to hang together or hang separately. The next tier, a dense spread of Brahmin fortune and fortitude, might be labeled the Hub. The Hub saw only journalistic accuracy in the label "the Athens of America" and felt only pride in the slogan "Banned in Boston." Over that layer lies Beantown, home to the Red Sox faithful and the raucous Bruins fans who crowded the old Boston "*Gah*-den"; this is the city whose ethnic loyalties account for its many distinct neighborhoods. Crowning these layers are the students who throng the area's universities and colleges every fall, infuriating some but pleasing many with their infusion of high spirits and money from home.

BEACON HILL & BOSTON COMMON

Past and present home of the old-money elite, contender for the "Most Beautiful" award among the city's neighborhoods, and hallowed address for many literary lights, Beacon Hill is Boston at its most Bostonian. The redbrick elegance of its narrow streets sends you back to the 19th century just as surely as if you had stumbled into a time machine. But Beacon Hill residents would never make the social faux pas of being out of date. The neighborhood is home to hip boutiques and trendy restaurants, frequented by young, affluent professionals rather than D.A.R. matrons.

> ### ANDREW'S TOP 5
>
> ■ **The Museum of Fine Arts** houses one of the country's great art collections.
>
> ■ **The Isabella Stewart Gardner Museum** is the most beautiful spot in the city.
>
> ■ **The Boston Public Garden** is a flowering oasis in our bustling metropolis.
>
> ■ **Fenway Park** is baseball's most hallowed shrine.
>
> ■ **The Children's Museum** is a wonderful, unique place to take tykes.

Once the seat of the Commonwealth's government, Beacon Hill was called "Trimountain" and later "Tremont" by early colonists because of its three summits: Pemberton, Mt. Vernon Hill, and Beacon Hill, named for the warning light set on its peak in 1634. In 1799 settlers leveled out the ground for residences, using it to create what is now Charles Street; by the early 19th century the crests of the other two hills were also lowered.

When the fashionable families decamped for the "new" development of the Back Bay starting in the 1850s, enough residents remained to ensure that the south slope of the Hill never lost its Brahmin character.

By the mid-20th century, most of the multistory single-family dwellings on Beacon Hill were converted to condominiums and apartments, which are today among the most expensive in the city.

Beacon Hill is bounded by Cambridge Street on the north, Beacon Street on the south, the Charles River Esplanade on the west, and Bowdoin Street on the east.

A good place to begin an exploration of Beacon Hill is at the Boston Common Visitor Information Center (⇨ p. 31), where you can buy a map or a complete guide to the Freedom Trail.

Ranger-led tours leave from the **National Park Service Visitor Center** (⊠ *15 State St.* ☎ *617/242–5642* ⊕ *www.nps.gov/bost*) from mid-April through November.

TIMING   Beacon Hill, one of the more-compact areas of Boston, can be easily explored in an afternoon; add an extra few hours if you wish to linger on the Common and in the shops on Charles Street or tour the Black Heritage Trail. In winter the cobblestone streets can be difficult to navigate, but the neighborhood is especially pretty during the holidays—the Common is alive with Christmas lights, and on Christmas Eve carolers and bell ringers fill Louisburg Square. Other seasons bring other pleasures, from cherry blossoms on the Common in spring to free summer concerts on the nearby Esplanade.

> ### HISTORIC BY LAW
>
> The classic face of Beacon Hill comes from its brick row houses, nearly all built between 1800 and 1850. Even the sidewalks are brick and will remain so by public fiat; in the 1940s, residents staged an uncharacteristic sit-in to prevent conventional paving. Since then, public law, the Beacon Hill Civic Association, and the Beacon Hill Architectural Commission have maintained tight control over everything from the gas lamps to the colors of front doors. Beacon Hill was finished quite nicely well over a century ago, and as Yankees say, "If it ain't broke, don't fix it."

Numbers in the margin correspond to numbers on the Beacon Hill & Boston Common map.

TOP ATTRACTIONS

★ ⑭ **Acorn Street.** Surely the most photographed street in the city, Acorn is Ye Olde Colonial Boston at its best. For drivers, the cobblestone street may be Boston's roughest ride (and so narrow that only one car can squeeze through at a time). Delicate row houses line one side, and on the other are the doors to Mt. Vernon's hidden gardens. Once the homes of 19th-century artisans and tradesmen, these little jewels are now every bit as prestigious as their larger neighbors on Chestnut and Mt. Vernon streets.

☾ **Boston Common.** Nothing is more central to Boston than the Common,
Fodor'sChoice   the oldest public park in the United States and undoubtedly the largest
★   and most famous of the town commons around which New England settlements were traditionally arranged. Boston Common is not built on landfill like the adjacent Public Garden, nor is it the result of 19th-century park planning, as are Frederick Law Olmsted's Fens and Franklin Park; it started as 50 acres where the freemen of Boston could graze their cattle. (Cows were banned in 1830.) Dating from 1634, it's as old

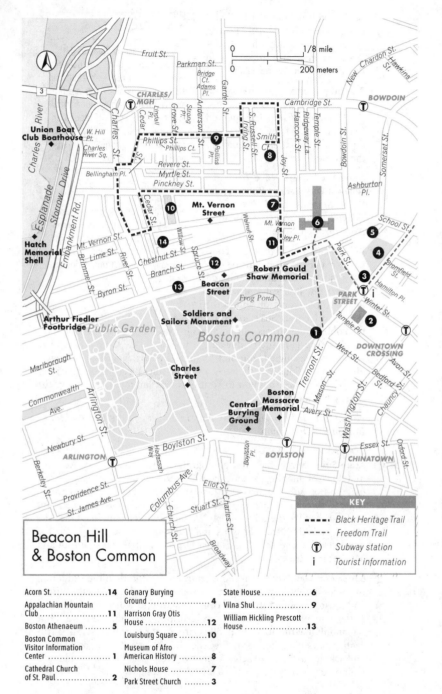

Beacon Hill & Boston Common

KEY

- ▪▪▪▪ *Black Heritage Trail*
- ---- *Freedom Trail*
- ⓣ *Subway station*
- i *Tourist information*

as the city around it. Latin names are affixed to many of the Common's trees; it was once expected that proper Boston schoolchildren be able to translate them.

The **Central Burying Ground** (⊠ *Boylston St. near Tremont, Beacon Hill* T *Park St.*) may seem an odd feature for a public park, but remember that in 1756, when the land was set aside, this was a lonely corner of the Common. It's the final resting place of Tories and Patriots alike, as well as many British casualties of the Battle of Bunker Hill. The most famous person buried here is Gilbert Stuart, the portraitist best known for his likenesses of George and Martha Washington; he died a poor man in 1828. The Burying Ground is open daily 9–5. On Tremont Street near Boylston stands the 1888 **Boston Massacre Memorial**; the sculpted hand of one of the victims has a distinct shine from years of sightseers' caresses. The Common's highest ground, near the park's Parkman Bandstand, was once called Flagstaff Hill. It's now surmounted by the **Soldiers and Sailors Monument,** honoring Civil War troops. The Common's only body of water is the **Frog Pond,** a tame and frog-free concrete depression used as a children's wading pool during steamy summer days and for ice-skating in winter. It marks the original site of a natural pond that inspired Edgar Allan Poe to call Bostonians "Frogpondians." In 1848 a gushing fountain of piped-in water was created to inaugurate Boston's municipal water system.

On the Beacon Street side of the Common sits the splendidly restored **Robert Gould Shaw 54th Regiment Memorial,** executed in deep-relief bronze by Augustus Saint-Gaudens in 1897. It commemorates the 54th Massachusetts Regiment, the first Civil War unit made up of free blacks, led by the young Brahmin Robert Gould Shaw. He and half of his troops died in an assault on South Carolina's Fort Wagner; their story inspired the 1989 movie *Glory.* The monument—first intended to depict only Shaw until his abolitionist family demanded it honor his regiment as well—figures in works by the poets John Berryman and Robert Lowell, both of whom lived on the north slope of Beacon Hill in the 1940s. In Lowell's moving poem "For the Union Dead" he writes, "at the dedication, William James could almost hear the bronze Negroes breathe." This magnificent memorial makes a fitting first stop on the Black Heritage Trail (⇨ *"The Black Heritage Trail" box, below*). ⊠ *Bounded by Beacon, Charles, Tremont, and Park Sts., Beacon Hill* T *Park St.*

❶ **Boston Common Visitor Information Center.** This center, run by the Greater Boston Convention and Visitors Bureau, is on the Tremont Street side of Boston Common. It's well supplied with stacks of free pamphlets about Boston, including a useful guide to the Freedom Trail, which begins in the Common. ⊠ *147 Tremont St., Beacon Hill* ☎ *888/733–2678* ⊕ *www.bostonusa.com* ☉ *Weekdays 8:30–5, weekends 9–5* T *Park St.*

❹ **Granary Burying Ground.** "It is a fine thing to die in Boston," A.C. Lyons, an essayist and old Boston wit, once remarked, alluding to the city's cemeteries, among the most picturesque and historic in America. If you found a resting place here at the Old Granary, as it's called, chances are your headstone would have been impressively ornamented with skeletons and winged skulls. Your neighbors would have been impressive, too: among them Samuel Adams, John Hancock, Benjamin Franklin's parents, and Paul Revere. Note the winged hourglasses carved into the stone gateway of the burial ground; they are a 19th-century addition, made more than 150 years after this small plot began receiving the earthly remains of colonial Bostonians. ⊠*Entrance on Tremont St., Beacon Hill* ☉*Daily 9–5* Ⓣ*Park St.*

★ ⑩ **Louisburg Square.** One of the most charming corners in a neighborhood that epitomizes charm, Louisburg Square was an 1840s model for town-house development that was never repeated on the Hill because of space restrictions. Today, the grassy square—enclosed by a wrought-iron fence and considered the very heart of Beacon Hill—belongs collectively to the owners of the houses facing it. The statue at the north end of the green is of Columbus, the one at the south end of Aristides the Just; both were donated in 1850 by a Greek merchant who lived on the square. The houses, most of which are now divided into apartments and condominiums, have seen their share of famous tenants, including author and critic William Dean Howells at Nos. 4 and 16, and the Alcotts at No. 10 (Louisa May not only lived but died here, on the day of her father's funeral). In 1852 the singer Jenny Lind was married in the parlor of No. 20. Louisburg Square is also the current home of Massachusetts Senator John Kerry.

There's a legend that Louisburg (proper Bostonians always pronounce the "s") Square was the location of the Rev. William Blaxton's spring, although there is no water there today. Blaxton, or Blackstone, was one of the first Bostonians, having come to the Shawmut Peninsula to live with his books and his apple trees in the mid-1620s, after the group with whom he arrived from England disbanded. When the Puritans, who had settled in Charlestown, found their water supply inadequate, Blaxton invited them to move across the river, where he assured them they would find an "excellent spring." Just a few years later, he sold them all but 6 acres of the peninsula he had bought from the Native Americans and left for Rhode Island, seeking greater seclusion; a plaque at 50 Beacon Street commemorates him. ⊠*Between Mt. Vernon and Pickney Sts., Beacon Hill* Ⓣ*Park St.*

☽ ⑧ **Museum of Afro American History.** Ever since runaway slave Crispus
Fodor'sChoice   Attucks became one of the famous victims of the Boston Massacre
★   of 1770, the African-American community of Boston has played an important part in the city's history. Throughout the 19th century, abo-

---

SECRET GARDENS

Strolling through Beacon Hill, you might be sorely tempted to sneak a peek into those glorious private gardens that are just barely visible behind sheltering walls and wrought-iron gates. Rather than risk arrest, time your visit for the third Thursday in May when about a dozen of them open to the public. The self-guided **Hidden Gardens of Beacon Hill tour** (☎617/227–4392 ⊕*www. beaconhillgardenclub.org*), an event that's happened annually since 1929, costs $25 when you purchase tickets in advance.

lition was the cause célèbre for Boston's intellectual elite, and during that time, blacks came to thrive in neighborhoods throughout the city. The Museum of Afro American History was established in 1964 to promote this history. The umbrella organization includes a trio of historic sites: the Abiel Smith School; the African Meeting House; and the African Meeting House on the island of Nantucket, off the coast of Cape Cod. Park Service personnel continue to lead tours of the **Black Heritage Trail** (⇨ *"The Black Heritage Trail" box),* starting from the Shaw Memorial. The museum is the site of activities, including lectures, children's storytelling, and concerts focusing on black composers.

In 2006 the museum honored the 200th anniversary of the **African Meeting House,** the oldest black church building still standing in the United States, with a major restoration that returned the house to its 1855 appearance. The centerpiece of Beacon Hill's African-American community, the Meeting House was constructed almost entirely with African-American labor, using funds raised in both the white and the black communities. The facade is an adaptation of a design for a town house published by the Boston architect Asher Benjamin. In 1832 the New England Anti-Slavery Society was formed here under the leadership of William Lloyd Garrison. When the black community began to migrate at the end of the 19th century to the South End and Roxbury, the building became a synagogue. In 1972 it was purchased by the Museum of Afro American History, but that year a fire destroyed the slate roof and original pulpit. After its reconstruction, it was designated a historic site in 1974 and reopened in 1987.

In keeping with the big anniversary celebration, the **Abiel Smith School** will display the writings of Frederick Douglass, original printings of the poet Phillis Wheatley, and copies of William Lloyd Garrison's antislavery newspaper, the *Liberator.* The two-floor exhibit will also hold the findings of an archaeological dig, including photos, fine china, and a rare pulpit. The school operated from 1835 to 1855, educating a total of about 200 students. ⊠*46 Joy St., Beacon Hill* ☏*617/725–0022* ⊕*www.afroammuseum.org* ✉*Free ($5 suggested donation)* ⊙*Mon.– Sat. 10–4* Ⓣ*Charles/MGH.*

ALSO WORTH SEEING

⑪ **Appalachian Mountain Club.** The bowfront mansion that serves as the headquarters of one of New England's oldest environmental institutions draws nature lovers from all over the world. The club is a reliable source of useful information on outdoor recreation throughout the region, including cross-country skiing and hiking. (You don't have to be a member to use its resources.) Architecturally, the building is notable for its carved cornices and oriel window decorated with vines and gargoyles. ⊠*5 Joy St., Beacon Hill* ☏*617/523–0636* ⊕*www.outdoors.org* ⊙*Weekdays 9–5* Ⓣ*Park St.*

Beacon Street. Some New Englanders believe wealth is a burden to be borne with a minimum of display. Happily, the early residents of Beacon Street were not among them. They erected many fine architectural statements, from the magnificent State House to grand patrician man-

The Black Heritage Trail

Until the end of the 19th century the north side of opulent Beacon Hill contained a vibrant community of free blacks—more than 8,000 at its peak—who built houses, schools, and churches that stand to this day. In the African Meeting House, once called the Black Faneuil Hall, orators rallied against slavery. The streets were lined with black-owned businesses. The black community has since shifted to other parts of Boston, but the 19th-century legacy can be rediscovered on the Black Heritage Trail.

Established in the late 1960s, the self-guiding trail stitches together 14 sites in a 1½-mi walk. Park rangers give tours daily Memorial Day through Labor Day and by special request the rest of the year at 10 AM, noon, and 2 PM, starting from the Shaw Memorial in Boston Common. To tour on your own, pick up brochures from the **Museum of Afro American History** (⊠ 46 Joy St., Beacon Hill) or the **National Park Service Visitor Center** (⊠ 15 State St., Beacon Hill).

Start at the stirring **Robert Gould Shaw 54th Regiment Memorial** in Boston Common. Shaw, a young white officer from a prominent Boston abolitionist family, led the first black regiment to be recruited in the North during the Civil War. From here, walk up Joy Street to 5–7 Pinckney Street to see the 1797 **George Middleton House**, Beacon Hill's oldest existing home built by blacks. Nearby, the **Phillips School** at Anderson and Pinckney streets was one of Boston's first integrated schools. The **John J. Smith House**, 86 Pinckney, was a rendezvous point for abolitionists and escaping slaves, and the **Charles Street Meeting House**, at Mt. Vernon and Charles streets, was once

a white Baptist church and later a black church and community center. In 1876 the building became the site of the **African Methodist Episcopal Church**, which was the last black institution to leave Beacon Hill, in 1939. The **Lewis and Harriet Hayden House** at 66 Phillips Street, the home of freed slaves turned abolitionists, was a stop on the Underground Railroad. Harriet Beecher Stowe, author of *Uncle Tom's Cabin*, visited here in 1853 for her first glimpse of fugitive slaves. The Haydens reportedly kept a barrel of gunpowder under the front step, saying they'd blow up the house before they'd surrender a single slave. At **2 Phillips Street,** John Coburn, cofounder of a black military company, ran a gaming house, described as a "private place for gentlemen."

The five residences on **Smith Court** are typical of African-American Bostonian homes of the 1800s, including No. 3, the 1799 clapboard house where William C. Nell, America's first published black historian and a crusader for school integration, boarded from 1851 to 1865. At the corner of Joy Street and Smith Court is the **Abiel Smith School,** the city's first public school for black children. The school's exhibits interpret the ongoing struggle started in the 1830s for equal school rights. Next door is the venerable **African Meeting House,** which was the community's center of social, educational, and political activity. The ground level houses a gallery; in the airy upstairs, you can imagine the fiery sermons that once rattled the upper pews.

sions. Here are some of the most important buildings of Charles Bulfinch, the ultimate designer of the Federal style in America: dozens of bowfront row houses, the Somerset Club, and the glorious Harrison Gray Otis House.

After the **Boston Athenaeum,** Beacon Street highlights begin at No. 34, originally the Cabot family residence and until 1996 the headquarters of Little, Brown and Company, once a mainstay of Boston's publishing trade. At 33 Beacon Street is the **George Parkman House,** its gracious facade hiding more than a few secrets. One of the first sensational "trials of the century" involved the murder of Dr. George Parkman, a wealthy landlord and Harvard benefactor. He was bludgeoned to death in 1849 by Dr. John Webster, a Harvard medical professor and neighborhood acquaintance who allegedly became enraged by Parkman's demands that he repay a personal loan. At the conclusion of the trial, the professor was hanged; he's buried in an unmarked grave on Copp's Hill in the North End. Parkman's son lived in seclusion in this house overlooking the Common until he died in 1908. The building is now used for civic functions.

Notice the windows of the twin **Appleton-Parker Houses,** built by the pioneering textile merchant Nathan Appleton and a partner at Nos. 39 and 40. These are the celebrated purple panes of Beacon Hill; only a few buildings have them, and they are incredibly valuable. Their amethystine mauve color was the result of the action of the sun's ultraviolet light on the imperfections in a shipment of glass sent to Boston around 1820. The mansions aren't open to the public.

The quintessential snob has always been a Bostonian—and the **Somerset Club,** at 42 Beacon Street, has always been the inner sanctum of blue-nose Cabots, Lowells, and Lodges. The mansion is a rare intrusion of the granite Greek Revival style into Beacon Hill. The older of its two buildings was erected in 1819 by David Sears and designed by Alexander Parris, the architect of Quincy Market. A few doors down is the grandest of the three houses Harrison Gray Otis built for himself during Boston's golden age.

❺ Boston Athenaeum. One of the cofounders of the Boston Athenaeum is credited with coining an expression that has made politicians and newspaper editorialists rejoice ever since: in an 1819 letter, William Tudor first compared Boston with Athens because of its many cultural and educational institutions; Bostonians now jealously guard the title "Athens of America." Tudor, the first editor of the *North American Review,* would surely have cited the athenaeum, one of the oldest libraries in the country, as partial proof. Founded in 1807 from the seeds sown by the Anthology Club (headed by Ralph Waldo Emerson's father), it moved to its present imposing quarters—modeled after Palladio's Palazzo da Porta Festa in Vicenza, Italy—in 1849. Only 1,049 proprietary shares exist for membership in this cathedral of scholarship, and most have been passed down for generations; the athenaeum is, however, open for use by qualified scholars, and yearly memberships are open to all by application.

Following the Freedom Trail

More than a route of historic sites, the Freedom Trail is a 2½-mi walk into history, bringing to life the events that exploded on the world during the Revolution. Its 16 way stations allow you to reach out and touch the very wellsprings of U.S. civilization. (And for those with a pinch of Yankee frugality, only three of the sites charge admission.) Follow the route marked on your maps, and keep an eye on the sidewalk for the red stripe that marks the trail.

It takes a full day to complete the entire route comfortably. The trail lacks the multimedia bells and whistles that are quickly becoming the norm at historic attractions, but on the Freedom Trail, history speaks for itself.

Begin at Boston Common. Get your bearings at the Visitor Information Center on Tremont Street, then head for the **State House,** Boston's finest piece of Federalist architecture. Several blocks away is the **Park Street Church,** whose 217-foot steeple is considered by many to be the most beautiful in all of New England.

Reposing in the church's shadows is the **Granary Burying Ground,** final resting place of Samuel Adams, John Hancock, and Paul Revere. A short stroll to Downtown brings you to **King's Chapel,** built in 1754 and a hotbed of Anglicanism during the colonial period. Follow the trail past the statue of Benjamin Franklin to the **Old Corner Bookstore** site, where Hawthorne, Emerson, and Longfellow were published. Nearby is the **Old**

South Meeting House, where pre-tempest arguments, heard in 1773, led to the Boston Tea Party. Overlooking the site of the Boston Massacre is the earliest-known public building in Boston, the **Old State House,** a Georgian beauty.

Cross the plaza to **Faneuil Hall** and explore its upstairs Assembly Room, where Samuel Adams fired the indignation of Bostonians during those times that tried men's souls. Find your way back to the red stripe and follow it into the North End.

Stepping into the **Paul Revere House** takes you back 200 years—here are the hero's own saddlebags, a toddy warmer, and a pine cradle made from a molasses cask. Nearby Paul Revere Mall is a tranquil rest spot. Next to the Paul Revere House is one of the city's oldest brick buildings, the **Pierce-Hichborn House.**

Next, tackle a place guaranteed to trigger a wave of patriotism: the **Old North Church** of "One if by land, two if by sea" fame—sorry, the 154 creaking stairs leading to the belfry are out-of-bounds for visitors. Then head toward **Copp's Hill Burying Ground,** cross the bridge over the Charles, and check out that revered icon the **USS Constitution,** "Old Ironsides."

The photo finish? A climb to the top of the **Bunker Hill Monument** for the incomparable vistas. Finally, head for the nearby Charlestown water shuttle, which goes directly to the downtown area, and congratulate yourself: you've just completed a unique crash course in American history.

The first floor is open to the public and houses an art gallery with rotating exhibits, marble busts, porcelain vases, lush oil paintings, and books. The children's room is also open for the public to browse or read a story in secluded nooks overlooking the Granary Burying Ground. Take the guided tour to spy one of the most marvelous sights in the world of Boston academe, the fifth-floor Reading Room. With two levels of antique books, comfortable reading chairs, high windows, and assorted art, the room appears straight out of a period movie, rather than a modern scholarly institution. ■ TIP➔ **Only eight people can fit in the tiny elevator to the fifth floor, so call at least 24 hours in advance to reserve your spot on the tour.** Among the athenaeum's holdings are most of George Washington's private library and the King's Chapel Library, sent from England by William III in 1698. With a nod to the Information Age, an online catalog contains records for more than 600,000 volumes. The athenaeum extends into 14 Beacon Street, which you might recognize as the exterior of Ally McBeal's law office on the popular television series that ended in 2002. ⌂ *10½ Beacon St., Beacon Hill* ☎ *617/227–0270* ⊕ *www.bostonathenaeum.org* 🎫 *Free* ◷ *Weekdays 8:30–5:30, Sat. 9–4. Tours Tues. and Thurs. at 3* Ⓣ *Park St.*

➋ **Cathedral Church of St. Paul.** Though it looks a bit like a bank, St. Paul's is actually the first Boston structure built in the Greek Revival style (1820). It was established by a group of wealthy and influential patriots who wanted a wholly American Episcopal parish—the two existing Episcopal churches, Christ Church (Old North) and Trinity, were both founded before the Revolution—that would contrast with the existing colonial and "gothick" structures around town. The building was to be topped with an entablature showing St. Paul preaching to the Corinthians—but the pediment remains uncarved, as Bishop Henry Sherrill instead used the money to start the clergy pension program for the national Episcopal church. ⌂ *138 Tremont St., Beacon Hill* ☎ *617/482–5800* ⊕ *www. stpaulboston.org* ◷ *Weekdays 9–5. Services Sun. at 8 AM and 10 AM; Mon. at 1, Tues., Wed., and Fri. at 12:15; and Thurs. at 6:30. Luncheon concerts Oct.–May, Wed. at 12:15* Ⓣ *Park St.*

▌ DID YOU KNOW?
Beacon Hill's north slope played a key part in African-American history. A community of free blacks lived here in the 1800s; many worshipped at the African Meeting House, established in 1805 and still standing. It came to be known as the "Black Faneuil Hall" for the fervent antislavery activism that started within its walls.

Charles Street. Chockablock with antiques shops, clothing boutiques, small restaurants, and flower shops, Charles Street more than makes up for the general lack of commercial development on Beacon Hill. You won't see any glaring neon; in keeping with the historic character of the area, even the 7-Eleven has been made to conform to the prevailing aesthetic standards. Notice the old-fashioned signs hanging from storefronts—the bakery's loaf of bread, the florist's topiary, the tailor's spool of thread, and the chiropractor's human spine. The contemporary activity would present a curious sight to the elder Oliver Wendell Holmes, the publisher James T. Fields (of the famed Bostonian firm of Ticknor and Fields), and many others who lived here when the neighborhood belonged to establishment literati. Charles Street sparkles at dusk from gas-fueled lamps, making it a romantic place for an evening stroll.

Chestnut Street. Delicacy and grace characterize virtually every structure on this street, from the fanlights above the entryways to the wrought-iron boot scrapers on the steps. Author and explorer Francis Parkman lived here, as did the lawyer Richard Henry Dana (who wrote *Two Years Before the Mast*), and 19th-century actor Edwin Booth, brother of John Wilkes Booth. Edwin Booth's sometime residence, 29A, dates from 1800 and is the oldest house on the south slope of the Hill. Also note the **Swan Houses,** at Nos. 13, 15, and 17, commissioned from Charles Bulfinch by Hepzibah Swan as dowry gifts for her three daughters. Complete with Adam-style entrances, marble columns, and recessed arches, they are Chestnut Street at its most beautiful.

> **THE MAN WHO NEVER RETURNED**
>
> When riding the rails in Boston, look out for Charlie, a poor soul immortalized in the 1950s Kingston Trio hit "M.T.A." He "never returned" from the subway for lack of a nickel needed for his departure fare. Charlie lives on—in odd faceless form—as the mascot of the MBTA's new "CharlieCard" ticket system (metal tokens were phased out in 2006).

⑫ Harrison Gray Otis House. Harrison Gray Otis, a U.S. senator, Boston's third mayor, and one of the Mt. Vernon Proprietors (a group of prosperous Boston investors), built in rapid succession three of the city's most splendidly ostentatious Federal-era houses, all designed by Charles Bulfinch and all still standing. This, the third Harrison Gray Otis House, was the grandest. Now the headquarters of the American Meteorological Society, the house was once freestanding and surrounded by English-style gardens. The second Otis house, built in 1800 at 85 Mt. Vernon Street, is now a private home. The first Otis house, built in 1796 on Cambridge Street, is the only one open to the public. Otis moved into 45 Beacon Street in 1805 and stayed until his death in 1848. His tenure thus extended from the first days of Beacon Hill's residential development almost to the time when many of the Hill's prominent families decamped for the Back Bay, which was just beginning to be filled at the time of Otis's death. ⊠*45 Beacon St., Beacon Hill.*

Mt. Vernon Street. Mt. Vernon Street, along with Chestnut Street, has some of Beacon Hill's most distinguished addresses. Mt. Vernon is the grander of the two, however, with houses set back farther and rising taller; it even has a freestanding mansion, the second Harrison Gray Otis House, at No. 85. Henry James once wrote that Mt. Vernon Street was "the only respectable street in America," and he must have known, as he lived with his brother William at No. 131 in the 1860s. He was just one of many literary luminaries who resided here, including Julia Ward Howe, who composed "The Battle Hymn of the Republic" and lived at No. 32, and the poet Robert Frost, who lived at No. 88.

❼ Nichols House. The only Mt. Vernon Street home open to the public, the Nichols House was built in 1804 and attributed to Charles Bulfinch. It became the lifelong home of Rose Standish Nichols (1872–1960), Beacon Hill eccentric, philanthropist, peace advocate, and one of the first female landscape designers. Although the Victorian furnishings passed to Miss Nichols by descent, she added a number of colonial-style pieces to the mix, such as an American Empire rosewood sideboard and a bonnet-top Chippendale highboy. The result is a delightful mélange of styles. Nichols made arrangements in her will for the house to become a museum, and knowledgeable volunteers from the neighborhood have been playing host since then. To see the house, you must take a tour (included in the price of admission). ⌧*55 Mt. Vernon St., Beacon Hill* ☎*617/227–6993* ⊕*www.nicholshousemuseum.org* ⌧*$7* ☉*May–Oct., Tues.–Sat. noon–4; Nov.–Apr., Thurs.–Sat. noon–4. Tours on the ½ hr; last tour starts at 4* Ⓣ*Park St.*

❸ **Park Street Church.** If this Congregationalist church at the corner of Tremont and Park streets could sing, what a joyful song it would be. Inside the church, which was designed by Peter Banner and erected in 1809–10, Samuel Smith's hymn "America" was first sung on July 4, 1831. The country's oldest musical organization, the Handel & Haydn Society, was founded here in 1815; in 1829 William Lloyd Garrison began his long public campaign for the abolition of slavery here. The distinguished steeple is considered by many critics to be the most beautiful in New England. Just outside the church, at the intersection of Park and Tremont streets (and the main subway crossroads of the city), is **Brimstone Corner.** Does the name refer to the fervent thunder of the church's preachers, the fact that gunpowder was once stored in the church's crypt, or the story that preachers once scattered burning sulfur on the pavement to attract the attention of potential churchgoers? Historians can't agree. ⌧*1 Park St., Beacon Hill* ☎*617/523–3383* ⊕*www.parkstreet.org* ☉*Tours July and Aug., Tues.–Sat. 9:30–3. Sun. services at 8:30, 11, 4, and 6* Ⓣ*Park St.*

Park Street Station. One of the first four stops on the first subway in America, Park Street Station was part of the line that originally ran only as far as the present-day Boylston stop. It was opened for service in 1897 against the warnings of those convinced it would make buildings along Tremont Street collapse. The copper-roof kiosks are National Historic Landmarks—outside them cluster flower vendors, street musicians, and partisans of causes and beliefs ranging from Irish nationalism to Krishna Consciousness. The station is the center of Boston's subway system; "inbound" trains are always traveling toward Park Street. ⌧*Park and Tremont Sts., Beacon Hill.*

NEED A BREAK? There are two Starbucks on the 3/10-mi-long Charles Street—but hold out for Panificio Bakery (⌧**144 Charles St., Beacon Hill** ☎**617/227-4340**), a cozy neighborhood hangout and old-fashioned Italian café. Soups and pizzas are made on the premises; for quick fortification, go for one of the Mediterranean sandwiches, or apply your sweet tooth to a raspberry turnover with a cappuccino.

❻ **State House.** On July 4, 1795, the surviving fathers of the Revolution were on hand to enshrine the ideals of their new Commonwealth in a graceful seat of government designed by Charles Bulfinch. Governor

Samuel Adams and Paul Revere laid the cornerstone; Revere would later roll the copper sheathing for the dome.

Bullfinch's neoclassical design is poised between Georgian and Federal; its finest features are the delicate Corinthian columns of the portico, the graceful pediment and window arches, and the vast yet visually weightless golden dome (gilded in 1874 and again in 1997). During World War II, the dome was painted gray so that it would not reflect moonlight during blackouts and thereby offer a target to anticipated Axis bombers. It's capped with a pinecone, a symbol of the importance of pine wood, which was integral to the construction of Boston's early houses and churches—as well as the State House itself.

Inside the building are Doric Hall, with its statuary and portraits; the Hall of Flags, where an exhibit shows the battle flags from all the wars in which Massachusetts regiments have participated; the Great Hall, an open space used for state functions that houses 351 flags from the cities and towns of Massachusetts; the governor's office; and the chambers of the House and Senate. The Great Hall contains a giant, modernistic clock designed by New York artist R. M. Fischer. Its installation in 1986 at a cost of $100,000 was roundly slammed as a symbol of legislative extravagance. There's also a wealth of statuary, including figures of Horace Mann, Daniel Webster, and a youthful-looking President John F. Kennedy in full stride. Just outside Doric Hall is 1999's "Hear Us," a series of six bronze busts honoring the contributions of women to public life in Massachusetts. But perhaps the best known piece of artwork in the building is the carved wooden *Sacred Cod,* mounted in the Old State House in 1784 as a symbol of the commonwealth's maritime wealth. It was moved, with much fanfare, to Bulfinch's structure in 1798. By 1895, when it was hung in the new House chambers, the representatives had begun to consider the Cod their unofficial mascot—so much so that when *Harvard Lampoon* wags "codnapped" it in 1933, the House refused to sit in session until the fish was returned, three days later. ⊠ *Beacon St. between Hancock and Bowdoin Sts., Beacon Hill* ☎ *617/727–3676* ⊕ *www.state.ma.us/sec/trs/trsidx.htm* ✉ *Free* ☽ *Weekdays 9–5. Tours 10–3:30; call ahead to schedule* Ⓣ *Park St.*

❾ Vilna Shul. As the oldest synagogue in Boston, this historic treasure is the focus of both renovation and research. The two-story brick building was completed in 1919 by Jews from Vilna, in what is now Lithuania. Modeled after the medieval synagogues of Europe, it's the last surviving example of the more than 50 synagogues that once dotted Beacon Hill. The building, abandoned in 1985 after the congregation dropped to a single member, was bought by the Boston Center for Jewish Heritage, which is overseeing its ongoing restoration. Above the doorway gleams renewed gilded Hebrew lettering; the hand-carved ark and the stained-glass Star of David are worth a peek; and murals depicting traditional Sephardic themes are being uncovered from beneath seven layers of paint. Three skylights flood it with natural light. ⊠ *14–18 Phillips St., Beacon Hill* ☎ *617/523–2324* ⊕ *www.bcjh.org* ✉ *Donations accepted* ☽ *Wed., Thurs., and Sun. 11–5* Ⓣ *Charles/MGH.*

⑬ William Hickling Prescott House. A modest but engaging house museum has been installed in this 1808 Federal structure designed by Asher Benjamin. Now the headquarters for the Massachusetts Society of Colonial Dames of America, the house was the home of noted historian William Hickling Prescott from 1845 to 1859. Some rooms are furnished with period furniture, including the former study with Prescott's desk and "noctograph," which helped the nearly blind scholar write. (He was blinded in one eye by a flying crust of bread during a food fight at Harvard.) Ask about Prescott's secret staircase, which allowed him to escape into his study from boring guests in the parlor. The house also has a fine costume collection. ⊠ *55 Beacon St., Beacon Hill* ☎ *617/742–3190*   ⊕ *www.nscda.org/ma/william_hickling_prescott_house.htm* ⊠ *$5* ☉ *Tours May–Oct., Wed., Thurs., and Sat. noon–4* Ⓣ *Park St., Charles/MGH.*

THE OLD WEST END

Just a few decades ago, this district—separated from Beacon Hill by Cambridge Street—resembled a typical medieval city: thoroughfares that twisted and turned, maddening one-way lanes, and streets that were a veritable hive of people. Then, progress—or what passes for progress—all but eliminated the thriving Irish, Italian, Jewish, and Greek communities to make room for a mammoth project of urban renewal, designed in the 1960s by I. M. Pei.

Today little remains of the *Old West End* except for a few brick tenements and a handful of monuments, including the first house built for Harrison Gray Otis. The biggest surviving structures in the Old West End with any real history are two public institutions, Massachusetts General Hospital and the former Suffolk County Jail, which dates from 1849 and was designed by Gridley Bryant. The onetime prison is now part of the luxurious, and wryly named, Liberty Hotel.

> **FRUGAL FUN**
>
> Take a cue from locals and sign up for one of the Boston Park Rangers' programs. Top picks include a visit to the city stables to meet the Mounties and their horses, regularly scheduled readings of Robert McCloskey's *Make Way for Ducklings* in Boston's Public Garden, and city scavenger hunts geared for families. Contact Boston Parks and Recreation ☎ *617/635-7487* ⊕ *www. cityofboston.gov/parks.*

Behind Massachusetts General and the sprawling Charles River Park apartment complex (famous among Storrow Drive commuters as the place with signs reading IF YOU LIVED HERE, YOU'D BE HOME NOW) is a small grid of streets recalling an older Boston. Here are furniture and electric-supply stores, a discount camping-supply house (Hilton's Tent City), and many of the city's most popular watering holes. The main drag here is Causeway Street. North Station and the area around it, on Causeway between Haverhill and Canal streets, provide service to commuters from the northern suburbs and cheap brews to local barflies, and can be jammed when there's a game at the TD Banknorth Garden, the home away from home for loyal Bruins and Celtics fans.

In addition to the Garden, the innovative Museum of Science is one of the more-modern attractions of the Old West End. The newest addition to the area's skyline is the Leonard P. Zakim Bunker Hill Bridge, which spans the Charles River just across from the TD Banknorth Garden.

Numbers in the margin correspond to numbers on the Old West End map.

TOP ATTRACTIONS

6 Museum of Science. With 15-foot lightning bolts in the Theater of Electricity and a 20-foot-long *Tyrannosaurus rex* model, this is just the place to ignite any child's scientific curiosity. Occupying a compound of buildings north of Massachusetts General, the museum sits astride the Charles River Dam. More than 550 exhibits cover astronomy, astrophysics, anthropology, progress in medicine, computers, the organic and inorganic earth sciences, and much more. The emphasis is on hands-on education. For instance, at the "Investigate!" exhibit children explore such scientific principles as gravity by balancing objects—there are no wrong answers here, only discoveries. Children can learn the physics behind everyday play activities such as swinging and bumping up and down on a teeter-totter in the "Science in the Park" exhibit. Other displays include "Light House," where you can experiment with color and light, and the perennial favorite, "Dinosaurs: Modeling the Mesozoic," which lets kids become paleontologists and examine dinosaur bones, fossils, and tracks.

FodorsChoice
★

The Charles Hayden Planetarium (☎617/723–2500), with its sophisticated multimedia system based on a Zeiss planetarium projector, produces exciting programs on astronomical discoveries. Laser light shows, with laser graphics and computer animation, are scheduled Thursday through Sunday evenings. The shows are best for children older than five. Admission to the planetarium is $4 if you paid the admission for the museum and $9 for the planetarium alone. The Museum of Science includes the **Mugar Omni Theater** (☎617/723–2500), a five-story dome screen. The theater's state-of-the-art sound system provides extra-sharp acoustics, and the huge projection allows the audience to practically experience the action on-screen. Try to get tickets in advance online or over the phone. Admission for shows is $9 (or $4 if you paid the admission for the museum). Call or check the museum's Web site for showtimes. Although the museum is usually viewed as a family destination, a more-adult crowd appears on Friday nights from 6 to 10 for the **Science Street Café**, where you can sip a martini and enjoy better-than-usual museum food to the sounds of live music. Afterwards, stroll through near-empty exhibit halls for a late viewing or climb up to the Gilliland Observatory for a romantic up-close glimpse of the nighttime sky. ⊠*Science Park at the Charles River Dam, Old West End* ☎617/723–2500 ⊕*www.mos.org* ⊠$16 ⊙*July 5–Labor Day, Sat.–Thurs. 9–7, Fri. 9–9; Labor Day–July 4, Sat.–Thurs. 9–5, Fri. 9–9* Ⓣ*Science Park.*

ALSO WORTH SEEING

② Harrison Gray Otis House. This is the first of three houses built for and bearing the name of Harrison Gray Otis, Boston's third mayor and a prominent citizen and developer. It's now the headquarters for the Society for the Preservation of New England Antiquities (SPNEA), an organization that owns and maintains dozens of properties throughout the region. The society restored the 1796 house; two of the floors are open as a museum. The furnishings, textiles, wall coverings, and even the interior paint, specially mixed to match old samples, are faithful to the Federal period, circa 1790–1810. You may be surprised to see the bright and vivid colors favored in those days. The dining room is set up as though Harry Otis were about to come in and pour a glass of Madeira. But Otis lived here only four years before moving to more-sumptuous digs, designed by Charles Bulfinch, on Beacon Hill. A corner of the museum details the house's history after Otis moved out. A second-floor room brings to life the home's days as a late-19th-century boardinghouse, and a hallway display describes the "champoo baths" of former resident Mrs. Mott. Thought a quack in her time, she actually promoted the first aromatherapy saunas. A summertime Beacon Hill walking tour originates here. ⊠ *141 Cambridge St., Old West End* ☎*617/227–3956* ⊕*www.historicnewengland.org* ⌨*$8* ☉*Tours on the hr and ½ hr Wed.–Sun. 11–5; last tour at 4:30* Ⓣ*Charles/MGH, Bowdoin.*

> **BOSTON DUCK TOURS...**
>
> Boston Duck Tours is something of an overnight success story. Founded in 1994, the company and its colorful "duck" vehicles are already Boston fixtures, taking more than half a million people a year on unique, amphibious tours of the city: Boylston Street, Tremont Street, and the River Charles, all in one 80-minute trip. Tours depart from the Prudential Center and the Museum of Science, and run seven days a week, rain or shine, from late March to late November (all ducks are heated). Tickets are $27 for adults and $18 for ages 3–11. They sell out fast so reserve early. ☎617/267–3825 ⊕*www.bostonducktours.com.*

⑤ Leonard P. Zakim Bunker Hill Bridge. Dedicated in October 2002, the Zakim Bridge is the newest Boston landmark, part of the "Big Dig" construction project. The 1,432-foot-long bridge, designed by Swiss bridge architect Christian Menn, is the widest cable-stayed hybrid bridge ever built and the first to use an asymmetrical design. The towers evoke the Bunker Hill Monument, and the distinctive fan shape of the cables gives the bridge a modern flair. The bridge was named after Lenny Zakim, a local civil-rights activist who headed the New England Region of the Anti-Defamation League and died of cancer in 1999; and the Battle of Bunker Hill, a defining moment in U.S. history. One of the best spots to view the bridge is from the Charlestown waterfront across the river. The best viewing is at night, when the illuminated bridge glows blue. ⊠ *Old West End.*

① Massachusetts General Hospital. Incorporated in 1811, MGH has traditionally been regarded as the nation's premier general hospital. The domed, gran-

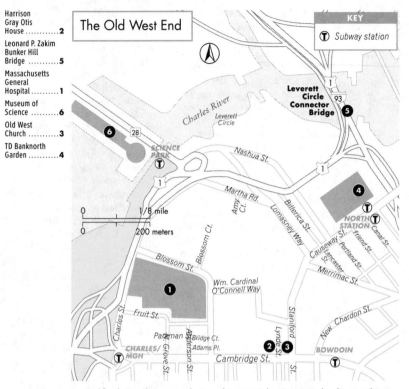

The Old West End

KEY
ⓉSubway station

ite **Bulfinch Pavilion** was designed in 1818 by Boston's leading architect, Charles Bulfinch. It was in the hospital's **amphitheater** (⊠ *Main entrance on N. Grove St.; turn right after coffee shop*) that, on October 16, 1846, Dr. John Collins Warren performed the first operation on a patient anesthetized by ether; the place was promptly nicknamed the "Ether Dome." You may visit the amphitheater today when it's not in use (admission free; open daily 9–5) and see the fourth-floor display describing the procedure that made modern surgery possible. Harvard Medical School was once on the grounds of Massachusetts General, and the hospital is today the school's oldest teaching affiliate. It was in a laboratory here around Thanksgiving 1849 that one of Boston's most notorious murders took place. Dr. George Parkman, a wealthy landlord and Harvard benefactor, was bludgeoned to death by Dr. John Webster after an argument over an unpaid loan. After several days of mystery over Parkman's disappearance, Webster's doom was sealed when part of the victim's jaw was discovered in the laboratory stove. Other grisly evidence turned up in the cesspool beneath Webster's privy. ⊠ *55 Fruit St., Old West End* ☎*617/726–2000* ⊕*www.mgh.harvard.edu* Ⓣ*Charles/MGH.*

NEED A BREAK?

Harvard Gardens (⊠ *316 Cambridge St., Beacon Hill* ☎*617/523-2727*), a Beacon Hill legend, was the first bar in the city to get its liquor license after the repeal of Prohibition. It opened in 1930 and was owned by the same family until the 1990s. Once considered a dive bar, it's become much more upscale with a menu of gourmet pizzas and sandwiches and scrumptious brunch fare, including a spectacular Bloody Mary. The tuna melt on tandoori bread is a solid base for a day's exploring. The place is often packed with doctors and nurses enjoying post-shift drinks.

❸ Old West Church. Built in 1806 to a design of the builder and architect Asher Benjamin, this imposing United Methodist church stands, along with the Harrison Gray Otis House next door, as a reminder of the days when the area was a fashionable district. The church was a stop on the Underground Railroad, and it was the first integrated congregation in the country, giving open seating to blacks and whites alike just before 1820. In the early 1960s, when the church served as a public library and polling place, Congressman John F. Kennedy voted here. Free organ concerts are held here Tuesday at 8 PM in June and July. ⊠ *131 Cambridge St., Old West End* ☎*617/227–5088* ⊕*www. oldwestchurch.org* ⊗ *Mon.–Thurs. 10–2, but call to confirm. Sun. services at 11* AM Ⓣ *Bowdoin, Government Center.*

☾ ❹ TD Banknorth Garden. Diehards still moan about the loss of the old Boston Garden, a much more intimate venue than this mammoth facility, which opened in 1995. Well, now they've got the next best thing. A decade after it opened as the FleetCenter, the home of the Celtics (basketball) and Bruins (hockey) is once again known as the Garden. Okay, so it's got the name of a bank attached now, but to locals it's once again just the good old "Gah-den." The original—which opened in 1928 and was famously the only indoor court in the National Basketball Association where games could be called on account of rain— is fondly remembered as the playing grounds for the likes of Larry Bird and Bobby Orr. Still, the new Garden, with its air-conditioning, comfier seats, improved food selection, a 1,200-vehicle parking garage, and nearly double the number of bathrooms, has won grudging acceptance. After all, the Bruins now play on a regulation-size rink, and there are no obstructed views—though the place is so big you might need binoculars. The Garden occasionally offers public-skating sessions in the winter months; call ahead for hours and prices. The fifth and sixth levels of the TD Banknorth Garden house the **Sports Museum of New England** (⊠ *Use the west premium seating entrance* ☎*617/624– 1234* ⊕*www.sportsmuseum.org*), where displays of memorabilia and photographs showcase the history and the legends behind Boston's obsession with sports. Take a behind-the-scenes tour of locker and interview rooms in the off-season, or test your sports knowledge with interactive games. You can even see how you stand up to life-size statues of sports heroes Carl Yastrzemski and Larry Bird. The museum is open daily 11–5, with admission allowed only on the hour. Last entrance is at 3 PM on most days, 2 PM on game days; admission is $6. ⊠ *Causeway St. at Canal St., Old West End* ☎*617/624–1000* ⊕*www.tdbanknorthgarden.com* Ⓣ *North Station.*

GOVERNMENT CENTER

This is a section of town Bostonians love to hate. Not only does Government Center house what they can't fight—City Hall—but it also contains some of the bleakest architecture since the advent of poured concrete. But though the stark, treeless plain surrounding City Hall has been roundly jeered for its user-unfriendly aura, the expanse is enlivened by feisty political rallies, free summer concerts, and the occasional festival. On the corner of Tremont and Court streets, the bleakness is partly mitigated by the local landmark Steaming Kettle, a gilded kettle cast in 1873 that once boiled around the clock. (It now marks a Starbucks.) More historic buildings are just a little farther on: 18th-century Faneuil Hall and the frenzied Quincy Market.

The curving six-story Center Plaza building, across from the Government Center T stop and the broad brick desert of City Hall Plaza, echoes the much older Sears Crescent, a curved commercial block next to the Government Center T stop. The Center Plaza building separates Tremont Street from the higher ground to the west: Pemberton Square and the old and "new" courthouses.

Although the $14 billion Central Artery/Tunnel project—the Big Dig—is, as of this writing, "98%" complete, construction zones have not yet turned into public parkland as planned, and vacant, fenced-in lots mark the future stretch of the Rose Kennedy Greenway. But after billions of dollars spent and a decade of traffic snarls, Bostonians are finally seeing the good side of the Big Dig. Traffic is flowing better and the roads aren't quite so confusing. The pedestrian ways in this area are also better marked, but don't feel shy about asking a local for help getting where you're going—you may still need it!

Numbers in the box correspond to numbers in the margin and on the Government Center & the North End map.

A GOOD WALK

The modern, stark expanse of Boston's **City Hall ❶** ☞ and the twin towers of the **John F. Kennedy Federal Office Building ❷** are an introduction to Boston in its urban-renewal stage. But just across Congress Street is **Faneuil Hall ❸**, a site of political speech-making since Revolutionary times, and just beyond that is **Quincy Market ❹**, where you can shop (and eat) until you drop. For more Bostonian fare, walk back toward Congress Street to **Blackstone Block ❺** and the city's oldest restaurant, the **Union Oyster House ❻**. (Fashionable ladies take note: The cobblestones are treacherous if you're wearing heels.) Near the restaurant is the **Holocaust Memorial ❼**, a six-tower construction of glass and steel. Follow Marshall Street north and turn right onto Blackstone Street to pass the **Haymarket ❽**, a flurry of activity on Friday and Saturday with open-air stalls selling produce and other foodstuffs. To sample Italian goodies, make your way to the North End via the pedestrian walkways that lead to Salem and Hanover streets.

TIMING You can easily spend several hours hitting the stores, boutiques, and historic sites of the Faneuil Hall and Quincy Market complex. On Friday and Saturday, you can try to forge a path through the packed crowds at the Haymarket farmers' market. Nearly everything is open on Sunday.

TOP ATTRACTIONS

5 Blackstone Block. Between North and Hanover streets, near the Haymarket, lies the Blackstone Block, now visited mostly for its culinary landmark, the **Union Oyster House.** Named for one of Boston's first settlers, William Blaxton, or Blackstone, it's the city's oldest commercial block, for decades dominated by the butcher trade. As a tiny remnant of old Boston, the Blackstone Block remains the city's "family attic"—to use the winning metaphor of critic Donlyn Lyndon: more than three centuries of architecture are on view, ranging from the 18th-century Capen House to the modern Bostonian Hotel. A colonial-period warren of winding lanes surrounds the block.

> **HIGH-TECH HIDE & SEEK**
>
> Geocaching—finding hidden caches using GPS coordinates posted on the Web—is hot, and it turns out that Boston is full of buried treasure with more than 2,200 caches hidden throughout the downtown area alone.
>
> What's in a cache? There's always a logbook with information from the cache's founder, and notes from fellow discoverers. Often the cache contains a small treasure, anything from maps, books, jewelry, games, and more. We know one lucky cache discoverer who found a gift certificate to one of the finest restaurants in Boston. Get coordinates for Boston caches at www.geocaching.com.

Facing the Blackstone Block, in tiny **Union Park,** framed by Congress Street and Dock Square, are two bronze figures, one seated on a bench and the other standing eye to eye with passersby. Both represent James Michael Curley, the quintessential Boston pol and a questionable role model for urban bosses. It's just as well that he has no pedestal. Also known as "the Rascal King" or "the Mayor of the Poor," and dramatized by Spencer Tracy in *The Last Hurrah* (1958), the charismatic Curley was beloved by the city's dominant working-class Irish for bringing them libraries, hospitals, bathhouses, and other public-works projects. His career got off to a promising start in 1903, when he ran—and won—a campaign for alderman from the Charles Street Jail, where he was serving time for taking someone else's civil-service exam. Over the next 50 years he dominated Boston politics, serving four nonconsecutive terms as mayor, one term as governor, and four terms as congressman. No one seemed to mind the slight glitch created when his office moved, in 1946, to the federal penitentiary, where he served five months of a 6- to 18-month sentence for mail fraud: he was pardoned by President Truman and returned to his people a hero.

★ **3 Faneuil Hall.** The single building facing Congress Street is the real Faneuil Hall, though locals often give that name to all five buildings in this shopping complex. Bostonians pronounce it *Fan*-yoo'uhl or *Fan*-yuhl. Like other Boston landmarks, Faneuil Hall has evolved

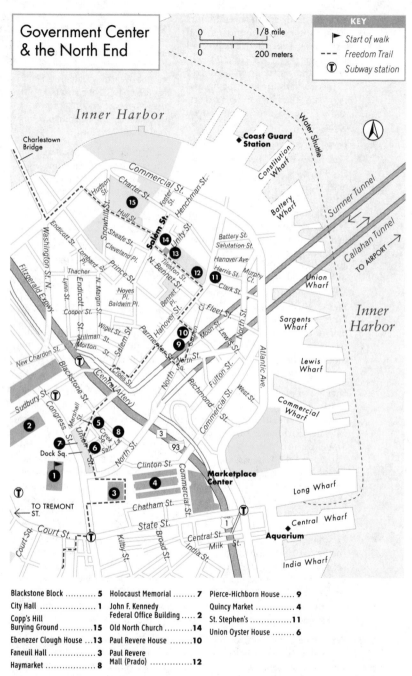

Government Center & the North End

KEY

▶ Start of walk

--- Freedom Trail

Ⓣ Subway station

0 — 1/8 mile

0 — 200 meters

Inner Harbor

Charlestown Bridge

Coast Guard Station

Constitution Wharf

Water Shuttle

Commercial St.

Battery Wharf

Sumner Tunnel

Callahan Tunnel

TO AIRPORT

Hudson St.

Charter St.

Foster St.

Henchman St.

15

Hull St.

Snowhill St.

Sheafe St.

Cleveland Pl.

Salem St.

Unity St.

Battery St.

Salutation St.

Union Wharf

Endicott St.

Lombard St.

Prince St.

N. Bennet St.

Tileston St.

14

13

Hanover Ave

Harris St.

Murphy Ct.

12

11

Clark St.

Inner Harbor

Washington St.

Fitzgerald Expwy.

Thacher

Lynn St.

Endicott St.

N. Margin St.

Noyes Pl.

Baldwin Pl.

Cooper St.

Wiget St.

Bennet Pl.

Hanover St.

Parmenter St.

Fleet St.

Sargents Wharf

Lewis Wharf

Sun Ct.

Stillman St.

Morton

Salem St.

Cross St.

North Sq.

Garden Ct.

Moon St.

Lewis St.

North St.

10

9

Atlantic Ave.

Commercial Wharf

New Chardon St.

Blackstone St.

(Central Artery)

Fulton St.

Richmond St.

Commercial St.

West St.

Sudbury St.

Congress St.

Marshall St.

Union St.

5

Creek Sq.

8

Salt La.

2

7

6

Dock Sq.

North St.

3

93

Commercial St.

Lewis Wharf

1

Clinton St.

4

Marketplace Center

Long Wharf

Ⓣ

3

Chatham St.

TO TREMONT ST.

Court St.

State St.

Ⓣ

1

Central Wharf

Kilby St.

Broad St.

Central St.

Milk St.

India St.

Aquarium

Court Sq.

India Wharf

Blackstone Block **5**	Holocaust Memorial **7**	Pierce-Hichborn House **9**
City Hall **1**	John F. Kennedy Federal Office Building **2**	Quincy Market **4**
Copp's Hill Burying Ground **15**	Old North Church **14**	St. Stephen's **11**
Ebenezer Clough House ...**13**	Paul Revere House **10**	Union Oyster House **6**
Faneuil Hall **3**		
Haymarket **8**	Paul Revere Mall (Prado) **12**	

over many years. It was erected in 1742, the gift of wealthy merchant Peter Faneuil, who wanted the hall to serve as both a place for town meetings and a public market. It burned in 1761 and was immediately reconstructed according to the original plan of its designer, the Scottish portrait painter John Smibert (who lies in the Granary Burying Ground). In 1763 the political leader James Otis helped inaugurate the era that culminated in American independence when he dedicated the rebuilt hall to the cause of liberty.

In 1772 Samuel Adams stood here and first suggested that Massachusetts and the other colonies organize a Committee of Correspondence to maintain semiclandestine lines of communication in the face of hardening British repression. In later years the hall again lived up to Otis's dedication when the abolitionists Wendell Phillips and Charles Sumner pleaded for support from its podium. The tradition continues to this day: in presidential-election years, the hall is the site of debates between contenders in the Massachusetts primary.

> ### THE STORY BEHIND THE GRASSHOPPER
>
> Why is the gold-plated weather vane atop Faneuil Hall's cupola in the shape of a grasshopper? One apocryphal story has it that Sir Thomas Gresham—founder of London's Royal Exchange—was discovered in a field in 1519 as a babe by children chasing grasshoppers. He later placed a gilded metal version of the insect over the Exchange to commemorate his salvation. Years later Peter Faneuil admired the critter (a symbol of good luck) and had a model of it mounted over Faneuil Hall. The 8-pound, 52-inch-long grasshopper is the only unmodified part of the original structure.

Faneuil Hall was substantially enlarged and remodeled in 1805 according to a Greek Revival design of the noted architect Charles Bulfinch; this is the building you see today. Its purposes remain the same: the balconied Great Hall is available to citizens' groups on presentation of a request signed by a required number of responsible parties; it also plays host to regular concerts.

Inside Faneuil Hall are dozens of paintings of famous Americans, including the mural *Webster's Reply to Hayne,* Gilbert Stuart's portrait of Washington at Dorchester Heights. Park rangers give informational talks about the history and importance of Faneuil Hall on the hour and half hour. The rangers are a good resource, as interpretive plaques are few. On the building's top floors are the headquarters and museum of the **Ancient & Honorable Artillery Company of Massachusetts** (☎ *617/227–1638*). Founded in 1638, it's the oldest militia in the Western Hemisphere, and the third oldest in the world, after the Swiss Guard and the Honorable Artillery Company of London. Its status is now strictly ceremonial, but it's justly proud of the arms, uniforms, and other artifacts on display. Admission is free. The museum is open weekdays 9 to 3:30. Brochures about Faneuil Hall's history, distributed by the National Park Service, make lighthearted references to the ongoing commercialism nearby by reprinting a 1958 ditty by Francis Hatch: "Here orators in ages past / Have mounted their attacks / Undaunted by proximity / Of sausage on the racks." Faneuil Hall has always sat in the middle of Boston's main marketplace: when such men as Andrew Jackson and Daniel Webster debated the future of the Republic here, the fragrances of bacon and snuff—sold by merchants in **Quincy Market** across the road—greeted their noses. Today, the aroma of coffee wafts through the hall from a snack bar. The shops at ground level sell New England bric-a-brac. ⊠ *Faneuil Hall Sq., Government Center* ☎ *617/242–5690* ⊕ *www.cityofboston.gov/freedomtrail/faneuilhall.asp* ⊠ *Free* ☉ *Great Hall daily 9–5; informational talks every ½ hr. Shops mid-Apr.–May, Mon.–Sat. 10–7 and Sun. 10–6; June–Christmas, Mon.–Sat. 10–8 and Sun. 10–6* Ⓣ *Government Center, Aquarium, State.*

➐ Holocaust Memorial. At night, its six 50-foot-high glass-and-steel towers glow like ghosts. During the day the monument seems at odds with the 18th-century streetscape of Blackstone Square behind it. Shoehorned into the north end of Union Park, the Holocaust Memorial is the work of Stanley Saitowitz, whose design was selected through an international competition; the finished memorial was dedicated in 1995. Recollections by Holocaust survivors are set into the glass-and-granite walls; the upper levels of the towers are etched with 6 million numbers in random sequence, symbolizing the Jewish victims of the Nazi horror. Manufactured steam from grates in the granite base makes for a particularly haunting scene after dark. ⊠ *Union St. near Hanover St., Government Center.*

FodorśChoice
★

➍ Quincy Market. Not everyone likes Quincy Market, also known as Faneuil Hall Marketplace; some people prefer grit to polish, and disdain the shiny cafés and boutiques. But there's no denying that this pioneer effort at urban recycling set the tone for many similar projects throughout the country, and that it has brought tremendous vitality to a once-tired corner of Boston. Quincy Market continues to attract huge crowds of tourists and locals throughout the year. In the early '70s, demolition was a distinct possibility for the decrepit buildings. Fortunately, the primitive idea that urban renewal was always best accomplished with a bulldozer was beginning to yield to the more-progressive concept of reuse. With the participation of the Boston Redevelopment Authority, architect Benjamin Thompson planned a renovation of Quincy Market, and the Rouse Corporation of Baltimore undertook its restoration, which was completed in 1976. Try to look beyond the shop windows to the grand design of the market buildings themselves; they represent a vision of the market as urban centerpiece, an idea whose time has certainly come again.

The market consists of three block-long annexes: **Quincy market, North market,** and **South market,** each 535 feet long and across a plaza from Faneuil Hall. The structures were designed in 1826 by Alexander Parris as part of a public-works project instituted by Boston's second mayor, Josiah Quincy, to alleviate the cramped conditions of Faneuil Hall and clean up the refuse that collected in Town Dock, the pond behind it. The central structure, made of granite, with a Doric colonnade at either end and topped by a classical dome and rotunda, has kept its tradi-

1

tional market-stall layout, but the stalls now purvey international and specialty foods: sushi, frozen yogurt, bagels, calzones, sausage-on-a-stick, Chinese noodles, barbecue, and baklava, plus all the boutique chocolate-chip cookies your heart desires. This is perhaps Boston's best locale for grazing; the hardest part is choosing what to sample.

Along the arcades on either side of the Central Market are vendors selling sweatshirts, photographs of Boston, and arts and crafts—some schlocky, some not—along with a couple of patioed bars and restaurants. The North and South markets house a mixture of chain stores and specialty boutiques. Quintessential Boston remains here only in Durgin Park, opened in 1826 and known for its plain interior, surly waitresses, and large portions of traditional New England fare.

A greenhouse flower market on the north side of Faneuil Hall provides a splash of color; at Christmastime, trees along the cobblestone walks are strung with thousands of sparkling lights. In summer, up to 50,000 people a day descend on the market; the outdoor cafés are an excellent spot to watch the hordes if you can find a seat. Year-round the pedestrian walkways draw street performers, and rings of strollers form around magicians and musicians. ⊠ *Bordered by Clinton, Commercial, and Chatham Sts., Government Center* ☎ *617/523–1300* ⊕ *www.faneuilhallmarketplace.com* ⊗ *Mon.–Sat. 10–9, Sun. noon–6. Restaurants and bars generally open daily 11 AM–2 AM; food stalls open earlier* Ⓣ *Government Center, Aquarium, State.*

⑥ Union Oyster House. Billed as the oldest restaurant in continuous service in the United States, the Union Oyster House first opened its doors as the Atwood & Bacon Oyster House in 1826. Charles Forster of Maine was the first American to use the curious invention of the toothpick on these premises. And John F. Kennedy was also among its patrons; his favorite booth has been dedicated to his memory. The charming facade is constructed of Flemish bond brick and adorned with Victorian-style signage. With its scallop, clam, and lobster dishes—as well as the de rigueur oyster—the menu hasn't changed much from the restaurant's early days (though the prices have). ⊠ *41 Union St., Government Center* ☎ *617/227–2750* ⊕ *www.unionoysterhouse.com* ⊗ *Sun.–Thurs. 11–9:30, Fri. and Sat. 11–10; bar open until midnight* Ⓣ *Haymarket.*

NEED A BREAK? | If all that snacking has you craving something more substantial, you might want to sample Boston's Irish heritage at the Black Rose (⊠ **160 State St., Government Center** ☎ **617/742-2286** ⊕ **www.irishconnection.com/black-rose.html**); take a right at the far end of the South Market. The bar-restaurant features traditional Irish fare and live music seven nights a week.

ALSO WORTH SEEING

▶ **❶ City Hall.** Over the years, various plans—involving gardens, restaurants, music, and hotels—have been floated to make this a more-people-friendly site. Possibly the only thing that would ameliorate Bostonians' collective distaste for the chilly Government Center is selling it. But for the moment, City Hall, an upside-down ziggurat design on a brutalist redbrick plaza remains in commission. The design, by Kallman,

McKinnell, and Knowles, confines administrative functions to the upper floors and places offices that deal with the public at street level. ✉ *Congress St. at North St., Government Center* Ⓣ *Government Center.*

❽ The Haymarket. Loud, self-promoting vendors pack this exuberant maze of a marketplace at Marshall and Blackstone streets on Friday and Saturday from 7 AM until mid-afternoon (all vendors will likely be gone by 5 at the latest). Pushcart vendors hawk fruits and vegetables against a backdrop of fish, meat, and cheese shops. The accumulation of debris left every evening has been celebrated in a whimsical 1976 public-arts project—Mags Harries's *Asaroton,* a Greek word meaning "unswept floors"—consisting of bronze fruit peels and other detritus smashed into pavement. Another Harries piece, a bronze depiction of a gathering of stray gloves, tumbles down between the escalators in the Porter Square T station in Cambridge.

SCOLLAY SQUARE

The junction of Cambridge and Tremont streets—at one end of the brick plaza that marks City Hall and the John F. Kennedy Federal Office Building—was once known as Scollay Square. A bawdy, raucous place where sailors would prowl when they came into port, Scollay Square was famous for its secondhand bookstores and burlesque houses, including the storied Old Howard Theater, the "Temple of Burlesque," which was built in the mid-1800s and burned under suspicious circumstances in 1961. An ambitious urban-renewal project in the 1960s obliterated the raffish, down-at-the-heels square.

At Creek Square, near the Haymarket, is the **Boston Stone.** Set into the brick wall of the gift shop of the same name, this was a marker long used as milepost zero in measuring distances from Boston.

✉ *Marshall and Blackstone Sts., Government Center* ⊗ *Fri. and Sat. 7 AM–mid-afternoon.*

❷ John F. Kennedy Federal Office Building. Looming up at the northwest edge of City Hall Plaza, these twin towers are noted structures for architecture aficionados: they were designed by the founder of the Bauhaus movement, Walter Gropius, who taught at Harvard toward the end of his illustrious career. Gropius's house, designed by him in textbook Bauhaus style, is in nearby suburban Lincoln.

THE NORTH END

The warren of small streets on the northeast side of Government Center is the North End, Boston's Little Italy. In the 17th century the North End *was* Boston, as much of the rest of the peninsula was still under water or had yet to be cleared. Here the town bustled and grew rich for a century and a half before the birth of American independence. Now visitors can get a glimpse into Revolutionary times while filling up on some of the most scrumptious pastries and pastas to be found in modern Boston.

Today's North End is almost entirely a creation of the late 19th century, when brick tenements began to fill up with European immigrants—first the Irish, then Central European Jews, then the Portuguese, and finally the Italians. For more than 60 years the North End attracted an Italian population base, so much so that one wonders whether wandering Puritan shades might scowl at the concentration of Mediterranean verve, volubility, and Roman Catholicism here. This is Boston's haven not only for Italian restaurants but also for Italian groceries, bakeries, boccie courts, churches, social clubs, cafés, and street-corner debates over home-team soccer games. ■ TIP→ **July and August are highlighted by a series of street festivals, or feste, honoring various saints, and by local community events that draw people from all over the city.** A statue of St. Agrippina di Mineo—which is covered with money when it's paraded through the streets—is a crowd favorite.

Although hordes of tourists follow the redbrick ribbon of the Freedom Trail through the North End, the jumbled streets retain a neighborhood feeling, from the grandmothers gossiping on fire escapes to the laundry strung on back porches. Gentrification diluted the quarter's ethnic character by filling it with yuppies. But linger for a moment along Salem or Hanover streets, and you can still hear people speaking with Abruzzese accents. If you wish to study up on this fascinating district, head for the North End branch of the Boston Public Library on Parmenter Street, where a bust of Dante acknowledges local cultural pride.

TIMING   Allow two hours for a walk through the North End, longer if you plan on dawdling in a café. This part of town is made for strolling, day or night. Many people like to spend part of a day at nearby Quincy Market, then head over to the North End for dinner—the district has an impressive selection of traditional and contemporary Italian restaurants. Families should note that on Saturday afternoons from May through October the Paul Revere House schedules some of the most delightful events for children in the city. And on Sunday, try to catch the ringing of the bells of the Old North Church after the 11 AM service; Paul Revere rang them on Sabbath mornings as a boy.

Numbers in the box correspond to numbers in the margin and on the Government Center & the North End map.

TOP ATTRACTIONS

🕕 **Copp's Hill Burying Ground.** An ancient and melancholy air hovers like a fine mist over this colonial-era burial ground. The North End graveyard incorporates four cemeteries established between 1660 and 1819. Near the Charter Street gate is the tomb of the Mather family, the dynasty of church divines (Cotton and Increase were the most famous sons) who held sway in Boston during the heyday of the old theocracy. Also buried here is Robert Newman, who crept into the steeple of the Old North Church to hang the lanterns warning of the British attack the night of Paul Revere's ride. Look for the tombstone of Captain Daniel Malcolm; it's pockmarked with musket-ball fire from British soldiers, who used the stones for target practice. Across the street at 44 Hull is

A GOOD WALK

Walking is the best way to view the sights of the North End. Parking is for residents only and even then is practically nonexistent, so most people arrive by T (Haymarket or Government Center). ■TIP→ **If you come by car, your best bet is to find a garage near Haymarket and Quincy Market (try the lot at 75 State Street and validate your parking with a purchase at Quincy Market)**; from there you can follow the red stripe of the Freedom Trail to **Salem Street** ➤. Once there, turn right on Cross Street and left on **Hanover Street,** the North End's main thoroughfare. From Hanover, turn right on Parmenter Street and left on North Street, following the Freedom Trail into North Square to reach the venerable brick **Pierce-Hichborn House** ❾ and, beside

it, the contrasting **Paul Revere House** ❿. Take Prince Street back to Hanover Street and continue on Hanover to reach **St. Stephen's** ⓫, the only remaining church designed by the influential architect Charles Bulfinch. Directly across the street is the Prado, or **Paul Revere Mall** ⓬, dominated by a statue of the patriot on horseback. At the end of the mall is the **Old North Church** ⓮, of "one if by land, two if by sea" fame, from which twin lanterns warned of the invading British on the night of Revere's legendary ride. Continue following the Freedom Trail to Hull Street and **Copp's Hill Burying Ground** ⓯, the resting place of many Revolutionary heroes. Then head back to Hanover Street for a well-deserved cappuccino and cannoli.

the **narrowest house in Boston**—it's a mere 10 feet across. ✉*Between Hull and Snowhill Sts., North End* ⊙*Daily 9–5* Ⓣ*North Station.*

Hanover Street. This is the North End's main thoroughfare, along with the smaller and narrower Salem Street. It was named for the ruling dynasty of 18th- and 19th-century England; the label was retained after the Revolution, despite a flurry of patriotic renaming (King Street became State Street, for example). Hanover's business center is thick with restaurants, pastry shops, and Italian cafés; on weekends, Italian immigrants who have moved to the suburbs return to share an espresso with old friends and maybe catch a soccer game broadcast via satellite. Hanover is one of Boston's oldest public roads, once the site of the residences of the Rev. Cotton Mather and the colonial-era patriot Dr. Joseph Warren, as well as a small dry-goods store run by Eben D. Jordan—who went on to launch the Jordan Marsh department stores.

NEED A BREAK?

Caffe Vittoria (✉*290–296 Hanover St., North End* ☎*617/227-7606*) **is rightfully known as Boston's most traditional Italian café. Gleaming brass, marble tabletops, and one of the city's best selections of grappa keep the place packed with locals. Fill a takeaway box with cannolis and other mouthwatering Italian pastries at Mike's Pastry (✉*300 Hanover St., North End* ☎*617/742-3050*). If you're lucky enough to snag a table, linger over the cappuccino or try one of the many flavors of gelato.**

⑭ **Old North Church.** Standing at one end of the **Paul Revere Mall** is a
Fodor'sChoice church famous not only for being the oldest one in Boston (built in
★ 1723) but for housing the two lanterns that glimmered from its steeple
on the night of April 18, 1775. This is Christ Church, or the Old North,
where Paul Revere and the young sexton Robert Newman managed
that night to signal the departure by water of the British regulars to
Lexington and Concord. Newman, carrying the lanterns, ascended the
steeple (the original tower blew down in 1804 and was replaced; the
present one was put up in 1954 after the replacement was destroyed
in a hurricane) while Revere began his clandestine trip by boat across
the Charles.

Although William Price designed the structure after studying Christopher Wren's London churches, the Old North—which still has an active
Episcopal congregation (including descendants of the Reveres)—is an
impressive building in its own right. Inside, note the gallery and the
graceful arrangement of pews (reserved in colonial times for the families that rented them); the bust of George Washington, pronounced by
the Marquis de Lafayette to be the truest likeness of the general he ever
saw; the brass chandeliers, made in Amsterdam in 1700 and installed
here in 1724; and the clock, the oldest still running in an American
public building. The pews—No. 54 was the Revere family pew—are
the highest in the United States because of the little charcoal-burning
foot warmers (used to accommodate parishioners back when). Try to
visit when changes are rung on the bells, after the 11 AM Sunday service; they bear the inscription, WE ARE THE FIRST RING OF BELLS CAST FOR
THE BRITISH EMPIRE IN NORTH AMERICA. On the Sunday closest to April
18, descendants of the patriots reenact the raising of the lanterns in the
church belfry during a special evening service.

Behind the church is the **Washington Memorial Garden,** where volunteers cultivate a plot devoted to plants and flowers favored in the 18th
century. The garden is studded with several unusual commemorative
plaques, including one for the Rev. George Burrough, who was hanged
in the Salem witch trials in 1692; it was his great-grandson, Robert
Newman, who carried the famous pair of lanterns to the steeple. In
another niche hangs the "Third Lantern," dedicated in 1976 to mark
the country's bicentennial celebration. ✉ *193 Salem St., North End*
☎ *617/523–6676* ⊕ *www.oldnorth.com* ⊗ *Daily 9–5. Sun. services at
9 and 11 AM* Ⓣ *Haymarket, North Station.*

DID YOU KNOW?

Longfellow's poem aside, the Old North Church lanterns were not a signal *to*
Paul Revere but *from* him to Charlestown across the harbor.

ALSO WORTH SEEING
Ebenezer Clough House. Built in 1712, this house is now the only local
survivor of its era aside from Old North, which stands nearby. Picture
the streets lined with houses such as this, with an occasional grander
Georgian mansion and some modest wooden-frame survivors of old
Boston's many fires—this is what the North End looked like when Paul
Revere was young. The home is privately owned and not open to the
public. ✉ *21 Unity St., North End.*

⑩ Paul Revere House. It's an interesting coincidence that the oldest house standing in downtown Boston should also have been the home of Paul Revere, patriot activist and silversmith, as many homes of famous Bostonians have burned or been demolished over the years. The Revere house could easily have become one of them back when it was just another makeshift tenement in the heyday of European immigration. It was saved from oblivion in 1902 and restored to an approximation of its original 17th-century appearance.

Originally on the site was the parsonage of the Second Church of Boston, home to the Rev. Increase Mather, the Second Church's minister. Mather's house burned in the great fire of 1676, and the house that Revere was to occupy was built on its location about four years later, nearly a hundred years before Revere's 1775 midnight ride through Middlesex County. Revere owned it from 1770 until 1800, although he lived there for only 10 years and rented it out for the next two decades. Pre-1900 photographs show it as a shabby warren of storefronts and apartments. The clapboard sheathing is a replacement, but 90% of the framework is original; note the Elizabethan-style overhang and leaded windowpanes. A few Revere furnishings are on display here, and just gazing at his silverwork—much more of which is displayed at the Museum of Fine Arts—brings the man alive.

Special events are scheduled throughout the year, many designed with children in mind. During the first weekend in December, the staff dresses in period costume and serves apple-cider cake and other colonial-era goodies. From May through October, you might encounter a silversmith practicing his trade, a dulcimer player entertaining a crowd, or a military-reenactment group in full period regalia. And if you go to the house on Patriots' Day, chances are you'll bump into a fife-and-drum corps.

The immediate neighborhood also has Revere associations. The little park in North Square is named after Rachel Revere, his second wife, and the adjacent brick **Pierce-Hichborn House** once belonged to relatives of Revere. The garden connecting the Revere house and the Pierce-Hichborn House is planted with flowers and medicinal herbs favored in Revere's day. ⊠ *19 North Sq., North End* ☎ *617/523–2338* ⊕ *www.paulreverehouse.org* 🖾 *$3, $4.50 with Pierce-Hichborn House* ☾ *Jan.–Mar., Tues.–Sun. 9:30–4:15; Nov. and Dec., and 1st 2 wks of Apr., daily 9:30–4:15; mid-Apr.–Oct., daily 9:30–5:15* Ⓣ *Haymarket, Aquarium, Government Center.*

⑫ Paul Revere Mall *(Prado).* This makes a perfect time-out spot from the Freedom Trail. Bookended by two landmark churches—Old North and St. Stephen's—the mall is flanked by brick walls lined with bronze plaques bearing the stories of famous North Enders. An appropriate centerpiece for this enchanting cityscape is Cyrus Dallin's equestrian **statue of Paul Revere.** Despite his depictions in such statues as this, the gentle Revere was stocky and of medium height—whatever manly dash he possessed must have been in his eyes rather than his physique. That physique served him well enough, however, for he lived to be 83 and

Paul Revere's Ride

Test: Paul Revere was (1) a patriot whose midnight ride helped ignite the American Revolution; (2) a part-time dentist; (3) a silversmith who crafted tea services; (4) a printer who engraved the first Massachusetts state currency; or (5) a talented metallurgist who cast cannons and bells. The only correct response is "all of the above." But there's much more to this outsize Revolutionary hero—bell ringer for the Old North Church, founder of the copper mills that still bear his name, and father of 16 children.

Although his life spanned eight decades (1734–1818), Revere is most famous for that one night, April 18, 1775, when he became America's most celebrated Pony Express rider. *"Listen, my children, and you shall hear / Of the midnight ride of Paul Revere"* are the opening lines of Henry Wadsworth Longfellow's poem, which placed the event at the center of American folklore. Longfellow may have been an effective evangelist for Revere, but he was an indifferent historian.

Revere wasn't the only midnight rider. As part of the system set in motion by Revere and William Dawes Jr., also dispatched from Boston, there were at least several dozen riders so that the capture of any one of them wouldn't keep the alarm from being sounded. It's also known that Revere never looked for the lantern signal from Charlestown. He told Robert Newman to hang two lanterns from Old North's belfry since the Redcoats were on the move by water, but by that time, Revere was already being rowed across the Charles River to begin his famous ride.

Revere and Dawes set out on separate routes but had the same mission: to warn patriot leaders Samuel Adams and John Hancock that British regular troops were marching to arrest them, and alarm the countryside along the way. The riders didn't risk capture by shouting the news through the streets—and they never uttered the famous cry "The British are coming!," since Bostonians still considered themselves British. When Revere arrived in Lexington a few minutes past midnight and approached the house where Adams and Hancock were lodged, a sentry challenged him, requesting that he not make so much noise. "Noise!" Revere replied. "You'll have noise enough before long."

Despite Longfellow's assertion, Revere never raised the alarm in Concord, for he was captured en route. He was held and questioned by the British patrol, and eventually released, without his horse, to walk back to Lexington in time to witness part of the battle on Lexington Green.

Poetic license aside, this tale has become part of the collective American spirit. Americans dote on hearing that Revere forgot his spurs, only to retrieve them by tying a note to his dog's collar, then awaiting its return with the spurs attached. The resourcefulness he showed in using a lady's petticoat to muffle the sounds of his oars while crossing the Charles is greatly appreciated. Little wonder that these tales resonate in the hearts and imagination of America's citizenry, as well as in Boston's streets on the third Monday of every April, Patriots' Day, when Revere's ride is reenacted—in daylight—to the cheers of thousands of onlookers.

saw nearly all of his Revolutionary comrades buried. ⊠*Bordered by Tileston, Hanover, and Unity Sts., North End* Ⓣ*Haymarket, Aquarium, Government Center.*

⑨ Pierce-Hichborn House. One of the city's oldest brick buildings, this structure, just to the left of the Paul Revere House, was once owned by Nathaniel Hichborn, a boatbuilder and Revere's cousin on his mother's side. Built about 1711 for a window maker named Moses Pierce, the Pierce-Hichborn House is an excellent example of early Georgian architecture. The home's symmetrical style was a radical change from the wood-frame Tudor buildings, such as the Revere House, then common. Its four rooms are furnished with modest 18th-century furniture, providing a peek into typical middle-class life. ⊠*29 North Sq., North End* ☎*617/523–2338* ⊠*$3, $4.50 with Paul Revere House* ☉*Guided tours only; call to schedule* Ⓣ*Haymarket, Aquarium, Government Center.*

⑪ St. Stephen's. Rose Kennedy, matriarch of the Kennedy clan, was christened here; 104 years later, St. Stephen's held mourners at her 1995 funeral. This is the only Charles Bulfinch church still standing in Boston, and a stunning example of the Federal style to boot. Built in 1804, it was first used as a Unitarian Church; since 1862 it has served a Roman Catholic parish. When the belfry was stripped during a major 1960s renovation, the original dome was found beneath a false cap; it was covered with sheet copper and held together with hand-wrought nails, and later authenticated as being the work of Paul Revere. ⊠*401 Hanover St., North End* ☎*617/523–1230* ☉*Daily 7:30–4:30. Sun. Mass at 11, Sat. at 4:30, Tues.–Fri. at 7:30* AM Ⓣ*Haymarket, Aquarium, Government Center.*

Salem Street. This ancient and constricted thoroughfare, one of the two main North End streets, cuts through the heart of the neighborhood and runs parallel to and one block west of Hanover. Between Cross and Prince streets, Salem Street contains several restaurants and shops. One of the best is Dairy Fresh Candies, which carries a huge assortment of nuts, syrups, dried fruits, and packaged candies, as well as by-the-pound truffles, turtles, and marzipan that put Godiva to shame. The rest of Salem Street is mostly residential, but makes a nice walk to the Copp's Hill Burying Ground.

▌ NEED A BREAK?   The allure of Bova's Bakery (⊠*134 Salem St., North End* ☎*617/523–5601*), a neighborhood institution, lies not only in its takeaway Italian breads and pastries, but also in its hours: 24 a day (the deli closes at 1 AM, however).

CHARLESTOWN

Boston started here. Charlestown was a thriving settlement a year before colonials headed across the Charles River at William Blaxton's invitation to found the city proper. Today the district's attractions include two of the most visible—and vertical—monuments in Boston: the Bunker Hill Monument, which commemorates the grisly battle that became a symbol of patriotic resistance against the British, and the USS *Constitution*, whose masts continue to tower over the waterfront where she was built more than 200 years ago.

As a neighborhood, Charlestown remains predominantly Irish-American, although gentrification that began in the 1980s continues. Today, despite the inroads made by trendy restaurants such as Todd English's Olives and chic digs such as the Navy Yard condos, the area still suffers a bit from its reputation as an alleged home turf for Irish-led organized crime. A number of bloody murders that remain unsolved—because of the neighborhood's vaunted "code of silence"—haven't helped. But Townies (as old-time Charlestown residents are called) are fiercely proud of their historic, well-maintained streets.

> **A STICKY SUBJECT**
>
> Boston has had its share of grim historic events, from massacres to stranglers, but on the sheer weirdness scale, nothing beats the Great Molasses Flood. In 1919, a steel container of molasses exploded on the Boston Harbor waterfront, killing 21 people and 20 horses. More than 2.3 million gallons of goo oozed onto unsuspecting citizenry, a veritable tsunami of sweet stuff. Some say you can still smell molasses on the waterfront during steamy weather; smells to us like urban myth!

The blocks around the Bunker Hill Monument are a good illustration of a neighborhood in flux. Along streets lined with gas lamps are impeccably restored Federal and mid-19th-century town houses; cheek by jowl are working-class quarters of similar vintage but more-modest recent pasts. Nearby Winthrop Square also has its share of interesting houses. Near the Navy Yard along Main Street is City Square, the beginning of Charlestown's main commercial district, which includes City Square Park, with brick paths and bronze fish sculptures. On Phipps Street is the grave marker of John Harvard, a young minister who in 1638 bequeathed his small library to the fledgling Cambridge College, thereafter renamed in his honor. The precise location of the grave is uncertain, but a monument of 1828 marks its approximate site.

To get to Charlestown, you can walk across the Charlestown Bridge from the North End, or take Bus 93 from the Haymarket T station; it stops three blocks from the Navy Yard entrance. A more-interesting and speedy way to get here is to take the MBTA water shuttle from Long Wharf in downtown Boston, which runs every 15 or 30 minutes year-round.

Numbers in the box correspond to numbers in the margin and on the Charlestown map.

TOP ATTRACTIONS

④ **Bunker Hill Monument.** Three misunderstandings surround this famous monument. First, the Battle of Bunker Hill was actually fought on Breed's Hill, which is where the monument sits today. (The real Bunker Hill is about ½ mi to the north of the monument; it's slightly taller than Breed's Hill.) Bunker was the original planned locale for the battle, and

Fodor'sChoice
★

A GOOD WALK

If you chose to hoof it to Charlestown, follow Hull Street from Copp's Hill Burying Ground to Commercial Street; turn left on Commercial and, two blocks later, right onto the bridge. The entrance to the **Charlestown Navy Yard** ❶ ☞ is on your right after crossing the bridge. Just ahead is the Charlestown Navy Yard Visitors Information Center; inside the park gate is the **USS *Constitution*** ❷ and the associated **USS *Constitution* Museum** ❸. From here, the red line of the Freedom Trail takes you to the **Bunker Hill Monument** ❹.

TIMING
Give yourself two to three hours for a Charlestown walk; the lengthy Charlestown Bridge calls for endurance in cold weather. You may want to save Charlestown's stretch of the Freedom Trail, which adds considerably to its length, for a second-day outing. You can always save backtracking the historic route by taking the MBTA water shuttle, which ferries back and forth between Charlestown's Navy Yard and downtown Boston's Long Wharf.

for that reason its name stuck. Second, although the battle is generally considered a colonial success, the Americans lost. It was a Pyrrhic victory for the British Redcoats, who sacrificed nearly half of their 2,200 men; American casualties numbered 400–600. And third: the famous war cry "Don't fire until you see the whites of their eyes" may never have been uttered by American Colonel William Prescott or General Israel Putnam, but if either one did shout it, he was quoting an old Prussian command made necessary by the notorious inaccuracy of the musket. No matter. The Americans did employ a deadly delayed-action strategy on June 17, 1775, and conclusively proved themselves worthy fighters, capable of defeating the forces of the British Empire.

Among the dead were the brilliant young American doctor and political activist Joseph Warren, recently commissioned as a major general but fighting as a private, and the British Major John Pitcairn, who two months before had led the Redcoats into Lexington. Pitcairn is believed to be buried in the crypt of the Old North Church.

In 1823 the committee formed to construct a monument on the site of the battle chose the form of an Egyptian obelisk. Architect Solomon Willard designed a 221-foot-tall granite obelisk, a tremendous feat of engineering for its day. The Marquis de Lafayette laid the cornerstone of the monument in 1825, but because of a nagging lack of funds, it wasn't dedicated until 1843. Daniel Webster's stirring words at the ceremony commemorating the laying of its cornerstone have gone down in history: "Let it rise! Let it rise, till it meets the sun in his coming. Let the earliest light of the morning gild it, and parting day linger and play upon its summit."

The monument's zenith is reached by a flight of 294 steps. There's no elevator, but the views from the observatory are worth the effort of the arduous climb. A statue of Colonel Prescott stands guard at the

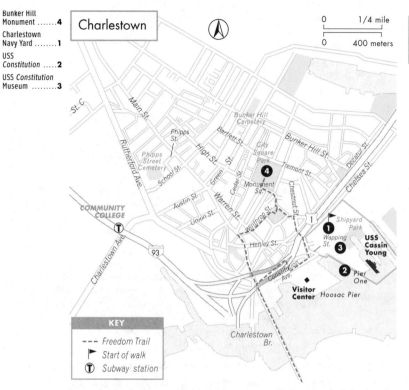

Bunker Hill Monument **4**

Charlestown Navy Yard **1**

USS Constitution **2**

USS Constitution Museum **3**

Charlestown

0   1/4 mile

0   400 meters

KEY

\- - - Freedom Trail

▶ Start of walk

Ⓣ Subway station

base. In the lodge at the base, dioramas tell the story of the battle, and ranger-led talks are given on the hour. ☎ 617/242–5641 ⊕ *www. nps.gov/bost/Bunker_Hill.htm* ☞ *Free* ⊙ *Lodge daily 9–5, monument daily 9–4:30* Ⓣ *Community College.*

DID YOU KNOW?

The country's first commercial railway was built in 1826 for the express purpose of hauling the granite for the Bunker Hill obelisk from a quarry in Quincy.

Ⓒ ❷

Fodor's Choice

★

USS Constitution. Better known as "Old Ironsides," the USS *Constitution* rides proudly at anchor in her berth at the Charlestown Navy Yard. The oldest commissioned ship in the U.S. fleet is a battlewagon of the old school, of the days of "wooden ships and iron men"—when she and her crew of 200 succeeded at the perilous task of asserting the sovereignty of an improbable new nation. Every July 4 and on certain other occasions she's towed out for a turnabout in Boston Harbor, the very place her keel was laid in 1797.

The venerable craft has narrowly escaped the scrap heap several times in her long history. She was launched on October 21, 1797, as part of the nation's fledgling navy. Her hull was made of live oak, the toughest wood grown in North America; her bottom was sheathed in copper, provided by Paul Revere at a nominal cost. Her principal service was during Thomas Jefferson's campaign against the Barbary pirates, off the coast of North Africa, and in the War of 1812. In 42 engagements, her record was 42–0.

The nickname "Old Ironsides" was acquired during the War of 1812, when shots from the British warship *Guerrière* appeared to bounce off her tough oaken hull. Talk of scrapping the ship began as early as 1830, but she was saved by a public campaign sparked by Oliver Wendell Holmes's poem "Old Ironsides." She underwent a major restoration in the early 1990s, and only about 8%–10% of her original wood remains in place. The keel, the heart of the ship, is original. Today she continues, the oldest commissioned warship afloat in the world, to be a part of the U.S. Navy.

The men and women who look after the *Constitution,* regular navy personnel, maintain a 24-hour watch. Sailors show visitors around the ship, guiding them to her top, or spar, deck, and the gun deck below. Another treat when visiting the ship is the spectacular view of Boston across Boston Harbor.

■TIP➔ Instead of taking the T, you can get closer to the ship by taking MBTA Bus 92 to Charlestown City Square or Bus 93 to Chelsea Street from Haymarket. Or you can take the Boston Harbor Cruise water shuttle from Long Wharf to Pier 4. ⊠*Charlestown Navy Yard, 55 Constitution Rd., Charlestown* ☎*617/242–5670* ⊕*www.ussconstitution.navy.mil* 🖭*Free* ⊙*Apr. 7–Oct., Tues.–Sun. 10–4; Nov.–Apr. 6, Thurs.–Sun. 10–4; last tour at 3:30* Ⓣ*North Station.*

NEED A BREAK?

After a blustery walk at the Navy Yard, get a seat by the fireplace and warm yourself with a hearty chowder and Sam Adams draft at the Warren Tavern (⊠*2 Pleasant St., Charlestown* ☎*617/241–8142* ⊕*www.warren-tavern.com*). Built in 1780, this restored colonial neighborhood pub was once frequented by George Washington and Paul Revere. It was one of the first buildings reconstructed after the Battle of Bunker Hill, which leveled Charlestown. For a meal on the waterfront, try the Tavern on the Water (⊠*1 Pier 6, Charlestown* ☎*617/242–8040*) in the Charlestown Navy Yard. It's a neighborhood hangout with outstanding harbor views and the requisite New England seafood dishes.

ALSO WORTH SEEING

▶ ❶ **Charlestown Navy Yard.** A National Park Service Historic Site since it was decommissioned in 1974, the Charlestown Navy Yard was one of six established to build warships. For 174 years, as wooden hulls and muzzle-loading cannons gave way to steel ships and sophisticated electronics, the yard evolved to meet the navy's changing needs. Here are early-19th-century barracks, workshops, and officers' quarters; a ropewalk (an elongated building for making rope, not open to the public), designed in 1834 by the Greek Revival architect Alexander Parris and used by the navy to turn out cordage for more than 125 years; and one of the oldest operational naval dry docks in the United States. The USS *Constitution* was the first to use this dry dock, in 1833.

1

In addition to the ship itself, check out the *Constitution* Museum, the collections of the Boston Marine Society, and the USS *Cassin Young*, a World War II destroyer typical of the ships built here during that era. At the entrance of the Navy Yard is the **Charlestown Navy Yard Visitors Information Center,** which screens "The Whites of Their Eyes," a multimedia presentation about Bunker Hill. Shows ($4) are every half hour from 9:30 to 4:30 March–November, with the last show starting at 4:30. ⊠*55 Constitution Rd., Charlestown* ☎*617/242–5601* ⊕*www.nps.gov/bost/Navy_Yard.htm* ☉ *Visitors Information Center daily 9–5* Ⓣ*North Station; MBTA Bus 92 to Charlestown City Sq. or Bus 93 to Chelsea St. from Haymarket; or Boston Harbor Cruise water shuttle from Long Wharf to Pier 4.*

USS Cassin Young. From a later date than the *Constitution*, this destroyer saw action in Asian waters during World War II. She served the navy until 1960. ⊠*Charlestown Navy Yard, 55 Constitution Rd., Charlestown* ☎*617/242–5601* ☑*Free* ☉*Daily 10–4; tours Apr.–Nov. at 11, 2, and 3; tours Dec.–Mar. at 1 and 2* Ⓣ*North Station; MBTA Bus 92 to Charlestown City Sq. or Bus 93 to Chelsea St. from Haymarket; or Boston Harbor Cruise water shuttle from Long Wharf to Pier 4.*

❸ **USS *Constitution* Museum.** Artifacts and hands-on exhibits pertaining to the USS *Constitution* are on display—firearms, logs, and instruments. One section takes you step-by-step through the ship's most important battles. Old meets new in a video-game battle "fought" at the helm of a ship. ⊠*Adjacent to the USS Constitution, Charlestown Navy Yard, Charlestown* ☎*617/426–1812* ⊕*www.ussconstitutionmuseum.org* ☑*Free* ☉*May–Oct., daily 9–6; Nov.–Apr., daily 10–5* Ⓣ*North Station; MBTA Bus 92 to Charlestown City Sq. or Bus 93 to Chelsea St. from Haymarket; or Boston Harbor Cruise water shuttle from Long Wharf to Pier 4.*

NEED A BREAK? Walking the Freedom Trail is exhausting. Whether Charlestown is your stopping or ending point, take a breather at **Sorelle** (⊠*100 City Sq., Charlestown* ☎*617/242–2125*), a hot little bakery with two locations, delicious sandwiches, and refreshing iced coffees.

DOWNTOWN BOSTON

Boston's commercial and Financial districts—the area commonly called Downtown—are concentrated in a maze of streets that seem to have been laid out with little logic; they are, after all, only village lanes that happen to be lined with modern 40-story office towers. Just as the Great Fire of 1872 swept the old Financial District clear, the Downtown construction in more-recent times has obliterated many of the buildings where 19th-century Boston businessmen sat in front of their rolltop desks. Yet many historic sites remain tucked among the skyscrapers; a number of them have been linked together to make up a fascinating section of the Freedom Trail.

The area is bordered by State Street on the north and by South Station and Chinatown on the south. Tremont Street and the Common form the west boundary, and the harbor wharves the eastern edge. Locals may be able to navigate the tangle of thoroughfares in between, but very few of them manage to give intelligible directions when consulted, so you're better off carrying a map.

Washington Street (aka Downtown Crossing) is the main commercial thoroughfare of downtown Boston. It's a pedestrian street once marked by two venerable anchors of Boston's mercantile district, Filene's (now its discount offspring, Filene's Basement) and Jordan Marsh (now Macy's). The block reeks of history—and sausage carts. Street vendors, flower sellers, and gaggles of teenagers, businesspeople, and shoppers throng the pedestrian mall outside the two buildings.

Downtown is also the place for some of Boston's most idiosyncratic neighborhoods. The Leather District directly abuts Chinatown, which is also bordered by the Theater District (and the buildings of New England Medical Center) farther west, and to the south, the red light of the once-brazen Combat Zone flickers weakly in a pair of adjacent strip clubs. The Massachusetts Turnpike and its junction with the Southeast Expressway cuts a wide swath through the area, isolating Chinatown from the South End.

TIMING   This section of Boston has a generous share of attractions, so it's wise to save a full day, spending the bulk of it at either the New England Aquarium or the Children's Museum. There are optimum times to catch some sights: the only tours to the top of the U.S. Custom House are at 10 and 4 on sunny days, and a stroll along the waterfront at Rowes Wharf is most romantic at dusk. No need to visit the aquarium at a special hour to catch feeding time—there are five of them throughout the day.

Numbers correspond to the Downtown Boston map.

TOP ATTRACTIONS

🌳 ⑮ **Children's Museum.** Most children have so much fun here that they don't
Fodor'sChoice   realize they're actually learning something. Creative hands-on exhib-
★   its demonstrate scientific laws, cultural diversity, and problem solving. After completing a massive 23,000 square-foot expansion in 2007, the museum has updated a lot of its old exhibitions and added new ones, like the aptly named "Adventure Zone." Some of the most popular stops are also the simplest: bubble-making machinery, the two-story climbing maze, and "Boats Afloat," where children can float wooden objects down a 28-foot-long model of the Fort Point Channel. At the Japanese House you're invited to take off your shoes and step inside a two-story silk merchant's home from Kyoto. The "Boston Black" exhibit stimulates dialogue about ethnicity and community while children play in a Cape Verdean restaurant and the "African Queen Beauty Salon." In the toddler "Smith Family PlaySpace," children under three can run free in a safe environment. There's also a full schedule of special exhibits, festivals, and performances. ⊠*300 Congress St., Downtown* ☎*617/426–6500,*

1

617/426–8855 recorded information ⊕*www.bostonkids.org* ☎*$9, Fri. 5–9 $1* ⊙*Sat.–Thurs. 10–5, Fri. 10–9* Ⓣ*South Station.*

☺ **⓫ New England Aquarium.** This aquarium challenges you to really imagine
FodorsChoice life under and around the sea. Seals bark outside the West Wing, its
★ glass-and-steel exterior constructed to mimic fish scales. This facility
has a café, a gift shop, and changing exhibits; one exhibit, "Amazing
Jellies," features thousands of jellyfish, many of which were grown in
the museum's labs. Inside the main facility, you can see penguins, sea
otters, sharks, and other exotic sea creatures—more than 2,000 species
in all. Some make their home in the aquarium's four-story, 200,000-gal-
lon ocean-reef tank, one of the largest of its kind in the world. Ramps
winding around the tank lead to the top level and allow you to view
the inhabitants from many vantage points. Don't miss the five-times-
a-day feedings; each lasts nearly an hour and takes divers 24 feet into
the tank. From outside the glassed-off Aquarium Medical Center, you
can watch veterinarians treat sick animals—here's where you can see
an eel in a "hospital bed." At the "Edge of the Sea" exhibit children
can gingerly pick up starfish and other creatures, while "The Curious
George Discovery Corner" is a fun spot for younger kids. Whale-watch
cruises leave from the aquarium's dock from April to October, and
cost $36.70. Across the plaza is the aquarium's Education Center; it,
too, has changing exhibits. The 6½-story-high IMAX theater takes you
on virtual journeys from the bottom of the sea to the depths of outer
space with its 3-D films. The gift shop seems to have every stuffed
aquatic animal ever made. ⊠*Central Wharf between Central and
Milk Sts., Downtown* ☎*617/973–5200* ⊕*www.neaq.org* ☎*$17.95,
IMAX $9.95, entrance plus IMAX $22.95* ⊙*July–early Sept., weekdays 9–6, weekends 9–7; early Sept.–June, weekdays 9–5, weekends
9–6* Ⓣ*Aquarium, State.*

ALSO WORTH SEEING

❽ Boston Massacre Site. Directly in front of the **Old State House** a circle
of cobblestones (on a traffic island) marks the site of the Boston Massacre. It was on the snowy evening of March 5, 1770, that nine British
regular soldiers fired in panic upon a taunting mob of more than 75
Bostonians. Five townsmen died. In the legal action that followed, the
defense of the accused soldiers was undertaken by John Adams and
Josiah Quincy, both of whom vehemently opposed British oppression
but were devoted to the principle of fair trial. All but two of the nine
regulars charged were acquitted; the others were branded on the hand
for the crime of manslaughter. Paul Revere lost little time in captur-
ing the "massacre" in a dramatic engraving that soon became one of
the Revolution's most potent images of propaganda. ⊠*Congress and
Court Sts., Downtown* Ⓣ*State.*

⓲ Boston Opera House. Originally the B. F. Keith Memorial Theatre in
the days of vaudeville, this venue was designed in beaux arts style by
Thomas Lamb and modeled after the Paris Opera House. The theater
shut its doors in 1991, but a multimillion-dollar restoration completed
in 2004 has brought theater and dance performances back to the Opera

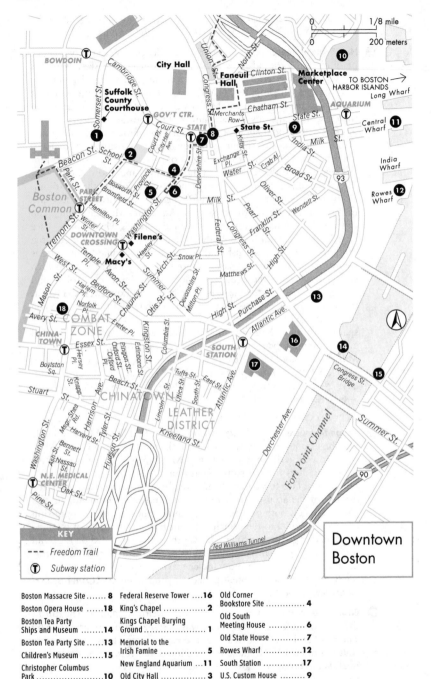

Downtown Boston

KEY

--- Freedom Trail

Ⓣ Subway station

1

House. ✉ *539 Washington St., Downtown* ☎*617/880–2400* ⊕*www.broadwayinboston.com* Ⓣ*Boylston.*

🕐 ⓮ **Boston Tea Party Ships & Museum.** After a lengthy renovation, the museum is, as of this writing, scheduled to reopen in the fall of 2008 (though the opening date has been extended more than once). The *Beaver II,* a reproduction of one of the ships forcibly boarded and unloaded the night Boston Harbor became a teapot, will return to the Fort Point Channel at the Congress Street Bridge and be joined by two tall ships, the *Dartmouth* and the *Eleanor.* Visitors will be able to explore the ships and museum exhibits, meet reenactors, or drink a cup of tea in the new Boston Tea Room. ✉*Fort Point Channel at Congress St. Bridge, Downtown* ☎*617/269–7150* ⊕*www.bostonteapartyship.com* ☉*Daily 9–5; call for updated information* Ⓣ*South Station.*

⓭ **Boston Tea Party Site.** The Boston Tea Party occurred on Atlantic Avenue near Congress Street. The area was once a wharf—further evidence of Boston's relentless expansion into the harbor. There isn't much to see here; a commercial building with a plaque marking the site has been torn down.

Chinatown. Boston's Chinatown may seem small, but it's said to be the third largest in the United States, after those in San Francisco and Manhattan. Beginning in the 1870s, Chinese immigrants started to trickle in, many setting up tents in a strip they called Ping On Alley. The trickle increased to a wave when immigration restrictions were lifted in 1968. As in most other American Chinatowns, the restaurants are a big draw; on Sunday, many Bostonians head to Chinatown for dim sum. Today the many Chinese establishments—most found along Beach and Tyler streets and Harrison Avenue—are interspersed with Vietnamese, Korean, Japanese, Thai, and Malaysian eateries. A three-story pagoda-style arch at the end of Beach Street welcomes you to the district. ✉*Bounded (roughly) by Essex, Washington, Marginal, and Hudson* Ⓣ*Chinatown.*

NEED A BREAK? Never considered bean paste for dessert or eaten a Chinese-style pork bun? Expand your horizons at Eldo Cake House (✉ *36–38 Harrison Ave., Downtown* ☎*617/350–7977*), which has both sweet and savory pastries.

⓾ **Christopher Columbus Park** *(Waterfront Park).* It's a short stroll from the Financial District to a view of Boston Harbor. Once a national symbol of rampant pollution, the harbor is making a gradual comeback. This green space bordering the harbor and several of Boston's restored wharves is a pleasant oasis with benches and an arborlike shelter. Lewis Wharf and Commercial Wharf (north of the park), which long lay nearly derelict, had by the mid-1970s been transformed into condominiums, offices, restaurants, and upscale shops. Long Wharf's Marriott hotel was designed to blend in with the old seaside warehouses. In September, the park is home to the Boston Arts Festival. ✉*Bordered by Atlantic Ave., Commercial Wharf, and Long Wharf, Downtown* Ⓣ*Aquarium.*

Combat Zone. The borders of Chinatown continue to expand, encroaching steadily on the seedy Combat Zone, which has the dubious distinction of being one of the nation's first official red-light districts. It got its name more than 50 years ago when Boston-stationed troops would show up at the local tailor shops for uniform alterations and inevitably tussle with members of other branches of the military here for the same purpose. When the honky-tonk businesses were forced out of what was then Scollay Square to make way for Government Center, they moved into this run-down area. Seeking to contain the spread of vice, city officials created the Lower Washington Street Adult Entertainment District, as Puritan ghosts shuddered. Today the Combat Zone is a shadow of its sleazy self, and the Millennium Place commercial complex on Washington Street has sealed its coffin with Boston's second Ritz-Carlton, a 19-screen Loews theater, a huge spa–fitness center, and luxury condominiums. ⊠ *Roughly Washington St., from Boylston St. to a few blocks north.*

⑯ Federal Reserve Tower. On Atlantic Avenue, across from South Station, is this striking aluminum-clad building, designed in 1976 by Hugh Stubbins and Associates. The tower is mainly used for offices, and is not open to the public. ⊠ *600 Atlantic Ave., Downtown* ☎ *617/973–3000.*

❷ King's Chapel. Both somber and dramatic, King's Chapel looms over the corner of Tremont and School streets. Its distinctive shape wasn't achieved entirely by design; for lack of funds, it was never topped with the steeple that architect Peter Harrison had planned. The first chapel on this site was erected in 1688, when Sir Edmund Andros, the royal governor whose authority temporarily replaced the original colonial charter, appropriated the land for the establishment of an Anglican place of worship. This rankled the Puritans, who had left England to escape Anglicanism and had until then succeeded in keeping it out of the colony.

It took five years to build the solid Quincy-granite structure. As construction proceeded, the old church continued to stand within the rising walls of the new, the plan being to remove and carry it away piece by piece when the outer stone chapel was completed. The builders then went to work on the interior, which remains essentially as they finished it in 1754; it's a masterpiece of proportion and Georgian calm (in fact, its acoustics make the use of a microphone unnecessary for Sunday sermons). The pulpit, built in 1717 by Peter Vintoneau, is the oldest pulpit in continuous use on the same site in the United States. To the right of the main entrance is a special pew once reserved for condemned prisoners, who were trotted in to hear a sermon before being hanged on the Common. The chapel's bell is Paul Revere's largest and, in his judgment, his sweetest sounding. ⊠ *Tremont St. at School St., Downtown* ☎ *617/227–2155* ⊕ *www.kings-chapel.org* ☉ *June–mid-Nov., Mon. and Thurs.–Sat. 10–4; mid-Nov.–May, Sat. 10–3. Year-round music program Tues. 12:15–1; services Sun. at 11, Wed. at 12:15* Ⓣ *Park St., Government Center.*

1

① King's Chapel Burying Ground. Legends linger in this oldest of the city's cemeteries. Glance at the handy map of famous grave sites (posted a short walk down the left path) and then take the path to the right from the entrance and then left by the chapel to the gravestone (1704) of Elizabeth Pain, the model for Hester Prynne in Nathaniel Hawthorne's *The Scarlet Letter.* Note the winged death's head on her stone. Also buried here is William Dawes Jr., who, with Dr. Samuel Prescott, rode out to warn of the British invasion the night of Paul Revere's famous ride (because of Longfellow's stirring poem, Revere is the one who gets all the glory today). Other Boston worthies entombed here—including the first Massachusetts governor, John Winthrop, and several generations of his descendants—were famous for more-conventional reasons. The prominent slate monument between the cemetery and the chapel tells (in French) the story of the Chevalier de Saint-Sauveur, a young officer who was part of the first French contingent that arrived to help the rebel Americans in 1778. He was killed in a riot that began when hungry Bostonians were told they couldn't buy the bread the French were baking for their men, using the Bostonians' own wheat—an awkward situation only aggravated by the language barrier. The chevalier's interment here was probably the occasion for the first Roman Catholic Mass in what has since become a city with a substantial Catholic population. ⊠ *Tremont St. at School St., Downtown* ☎ *617/227–2155* ⊕ *www.cityofboston.gov/freedomtrail/kingschapel. asp* ☉ *Late spring–early fall, daily 9–5; winter, daily 9–3* Ⓣ *Park St., Government Center.*

NEED A BREAK?

Fajitas & 'Ritas (⊠ *25 West St., Downtown* ☎ *617/426–1222*), is a fun stop for a quick dose of Tex-Mex or a liter of frozen margaritas. Service is quick, prices are low, and you can select your nacho toppings.

Leather District. Opposite South Station and inside the angle formed by Kneeland Street and Atlantic Avenue is a corner of Downtown that has been relatively untouched by high-rise development: the old Leather District. It's probably the best place in downtown Boston to get an idea of what the city's business center looked like in the late 19th century. This was the wholesale supply area for raw materials in the days when the shoe industry was a regional economic mainstay; a few leather firms are still here, but most warehouses now contain expensive loft apartments. ⊠ *Bordered by Kneeland St., Atlantic Ave., and Lincoln St.* Ⓣ *South Station.*

⑤ Memorial to the Irish Famine. A reminder of the rich immigrant past of this most Irish of American cities consists of two sculptures by artist Robert Shure, one depicting an anguished family on the shores of Ireland, the other a determined and hopeful Irish family stepping ashore in Boston. ⊠ *Plaza outside Borders, Washington St. near School St., opposite Old South Meeting House* Ⓣ *State, Downtown Crossing.*

③ Old City Hall. Just outside this sight sits Richard S. Greenough's bronze statue (1855) of Benjamin Franklin, Boston's first portrait sculpture. Franklin was born in 1706 just a few blocks from here, on Milk Street, and attended the Boston Latin School, founded in 1635 near the City

Hall site. (The school has long since moved to Louis Pasteur Avenue, near the Fenway.) As a young man, Franklin emigrated to Philadelphia, where he lived most of his long life. Boston's municipal government settled into the new City Hall in 1969, and the old Second Empire building now houses business offices. The remaining nod to the building's political past are the Democratic donkey statue side by side with a plaque containing footsteps decorated with Republican elephants and the slogan "Stand in opposition." ⊠*41–45 School St., Downtown* ⊕*www.oldcityhall.com* Ⓣ*State.*

❹ **Old Corner Bookstore Site.** Through these doors, between 1845 and 1865, passed some of the century's literary lights: Henry David Thoreau, Ralph Waldo Emerson, and Henry Wadsworth Longfellow—even Charles Dickens paid a visit. Many of their works were published here by James T. "Jamie" Fields, who in 1830 had founded the influential firm Ticknor and Fields. In the 19th century the graceful, gambrel-roof early-Georgian structure—built in 1718 on land once owned by religious rebel Anne Hutchinson—also housed the city's leading bookstore. Today, the building has been made over into the Boston Globe Store, selling locally themed memorabilia and offering visitors free use of computers to surf the *Boston Globe* Web site. ⊠*1 School St., Downtown* ☎*617/367–4000* ⊙ *Weekdays 10–6, Sat. 9:30–5, Sun. 11–4* Ⓣ*State.*

❻ **Old South Meeting House.** This is the second-oldest church building in Boston, and were it not for Longfellow's celebration of the Old North in "Paul Revere's Ride," it might well be the most famous. Some of the fieriest of the town meetings that led to the Revolution were held here, culminating in the gathering of December 16, 1773, which was called by Samuel Adams to confront the crisis of three ships, laden with dutiable tea, anchored at Griffin's Wharf. The activists wanted the tea returned to England, the governor would not permit it—and the rest is history. To cries of "Boston Harbor a teapot tonight!" and John Hancock's "Let every man do what is right in his own eyes," the protesters poured out of the Old South, headed to the wharf with their waiting comrades, and dumped 18,000 worth of tea into the water.

One of the earliest members of the congregation was an African slave named Phillis Wheatley, who had been educated by her owners. In 1773 a book of her poems was printed (by a London publisher), making her the first published African-American poet. She later traveled to London, where she was received as a celebrity, but was again overtaken by poverty and died in obscurity at age 31.

The church suffered no small amount of indignity in the Revolution: its pews were ripped out by occupying British troops, and the interior was used for riding exercises by General John Burgoyne's light dragoons. A century later it escaped destruction in the Great Fire of 1872, only to be threatened with demolition by developers. Aside from the windows and doors, the only original interior features surviving today are the tiered galleries above the main floor. The pulpit is a reproduction of the one used by Puritan divines and secular firebrands. Public contributions saved the church.

The exhibition "Voices of Protest" highlights the Old South as a forum for free speech from Revolutionary days to the present, and the 20-minute audio program "If These Walls Could Speak" offers a reenactment of the major events that occurred here. There are also changing exhibits and educational programs, such as the lecture series covering topics from murder cases in Massachusetts to colonial games; it runs Thursday 12:15–1 November to March, and the schedule is available by phone or on the Web. ✉*310 Washington St., Downtown* ☎*617/482–6439* ⊕*www.oldsouthmeetinghouse.org* ▣*$5* ◷*Apr.–Oct., daily 9:30–5; Nov.–Mar., daily 10–4* Ⓣ*State, Downtown Crossing.*

❼ Old State House. This colonial-era landmark has one of the most recognizable facades in Boston, with its State Street gable adorned by a brightly gilded lion and unicorn, symbols of British imperial power. The original figures were pulled down in 1776. For proof that bygones are bygones, consider not only the restoration of the sculptures in 1880 but also that Queen Elizabeth II was greeted by cheering crowds on July 4, 1976, when she stood on the Old State House balcony (from which the Declaration of Independence was first read in public in Boston and which overlooks the site of the Boston Massacre).

This was the seat of the colonial government from 1713 until the Revolution, and after the evacuation of the British from Boston in 1776 it served the independent Commonwealth until its replacement on Beacon Hill was completed in 1798. John Hancock was inaugurated here as the first governor under the new state constitution.

Like many other colonial-era landmarks, it fared poorly in the years that followed. Nineteenth-century photos show the old building with a mansard roof and signs in the windows advertising assorted businesses. In the 1830s the Old State House served as Boston's City Hall. When demolition was threatened in 1880 because the real estate was so valuable, the Bostonian Society organized a restoration, after which the Old State House reopened with a permanent collection that traces Boston's Revolutionary War history and, on the second floor, exhibits that change every few years.

Immediately outside the Old State House, at 15 State Street, is a **visitor center** run by the National Park Service; it offers free brochures and has restrooms. ✉*206 Washington St., at State St., Downtown* ☎*617/720–3290* ⊕*www.bostonhistory.org* ▣*$5* ◷*Daily 9–5* Ⓣ*State.*

⓬ Rowes Wharf. Take a Beacon Hill redbrick town house, blow it up to the *n*th power, and you get this 15-story Skidmore, Owings & Merrill extravaganza from 1987, one of the more-welcome additions to the Boston Harbor skyline. From under the complex's gateway six-story arch, you can get great views of Boston Harbor and the yachts docked at the marina. Water shuttles pull up here from Logan Airport—the most intriguing way to enter the city. A windswept stroll along the HarborWalk waterfront promenade at dusk makes for an unforgettable sunset on clear days. ⊠*Atlantic Ave. south of India Wharf* Ⓣ*Aquarium.*

⑰ South Station. The colonnaded granite structure is the terminal for all Amtrak trains in and out of Boston. Next door on Atlantic Avenue is the terminal for Greyhound, Peter Pan, and other bus lines. Behind the station's grand 1900s facade, a major renovation project has created an airy, modern transit center. Thanks to its eateries, coffee bars, newsstand, flower stand, and other shops, waiting for a train here can actually be a pleasant experience. ⊠*Atlantic Ave. and Summer St., Downtown* Ⓣ*South Station.*

State Street. During the 19th century, State Street was headquarters for banks, brokerages, and insurance firms; although these businesses have spread throughout the Downtown District, "State Street" still connotes much the same thing as "Wall Street" does in New York. The early commercial hegemony of State Street was symbolized by Long Wharf, built in 1710 and extending some 1,700 feet into the harbor. If today's Long Wharf doesn't appear to be that long, it's not because it has been shortened but because the land has crept out toward its end. State Street once met the water at the base of the Custom House; landfill operations were pursued relentlessly through the years, and the old coastline is now as much a memory as such colonial State Street landmarks as Governor Winthrop's 1630 house and the Revolutionary-era Bunch of Grapes Tavern, where Bostonians met to drink and wax indignant at their treatment by King George.

⑨ U.S. Custom House. This 1847 structure resembles a Greek Revival temple that appears to have sprouted a tower. It's just that. This is the work of architects Ammi Young and Isaiah Rogers—at least, the bottom part is. The tower was added in 1915, at which time the Custom House became Boston's tallest building. It remains one of the most visible and best loved in the city's skyline. To appreciate the grafting job, go inside and look at the domed rotunda. The outer surface of that dome was once the roof of the building, but now the dome is embedded in the base of the tower.

The federal government moved out of the Custom House in 1987 and sold it to the city of Boston, which, in turn, sold it to the Marriott Corporation, which has converted the building into hotel space and luxury time-share units, a move that disturbed some historical purists. You can now sip a cocktail in the hotel's Counting Room Lounge, or visit the 26th-floor observation deck. The magnificent Rotunda Room sports maritime prints and antique artifacts, courtesy of the Peabody Essex Museum in Salem. ⊠*3 McKinley Sq., Downtown* 🕾*617/310–6300* Ⓣ*State, Aquarium.*

THE BACK BAY

In the folklore of American neighborhoods, the Back Bay stands with New York's Park Avenue and San Francisco's Nob Hill as a symbol of propriety and high social standing. Before the 1850s it really was a bay,

Tours Worth Trying

1

Boston Movie Tours (☎ *866/668–4345* ⊕ *www.bostonmovietours.net*) takes you to Boston's film and movie hot spots like the South Boston of *The Departed*, the *Ally McBeal* building, the tavern from *Good Will Hunting*, the *Cheers* bar, and Fenway Park, home of the Red Sox and location for movies like *Field of Dreams* and *Fever Pitch*. Guides share filming secrets and trivia from movies like *Legally Blonde* and *Mystic River* along with the best celeb spots in town. Choose between a 90-minute walking tour ($20) or a two- to three-hour theater-on-wheels experience ($35).

Boston Women's Heritage Trail (☎ *617/522–2872* ⊕ *www.bwht.org*) has nine self-guided walks that high-light remarkable women who played an integral role in shaping the history of Boston and the nation as patriots, intellectuals, abolitionists, suffragists, artists, and writers.

The **Literary Trail of Greater Boston** (☎ *617/621–4020* ⊕ *www.literary trailofgreaterboston.org*) offers walking tours of Boston, Cambridge, and Concord, answering questions such as "What inspired Hawthorne to write *The Scarlet Letter*?" and "Where did Charles Dickens hang out when in Beantown?" The Cambridge tour visits the homes of Longfellow, Margaret Fuller, and W. E. B. du Bois, and the Concord one highlights such sites as Louisa May Alcott's Orchard House, Emerson's study at the Concord Museum, and Thoreau's Walden Pond.

---

a tidal flat that formed the south bank of a distended Charles River. The filling in of land along the isthmus that joined Boston to the mainland (the Neck) began in 1850 and resulted in the creation of the South End. To the north, a narrow causeway called the Mill Dam (later Beacon Street) was built in 1814 to separate the Back Bay from the Charles. By the late 1800s, Bostonians had filled in the shallows to as far as the marshland known as the Fenway, and the original 783-acre peninsula had been expanded by about 450 acres. Thus the waters of Back Bay became the neighborhood of Back Bay.

Heavily influenced by the then-recent rebuilding of Paris according to the plans of Baron Georges-Eugène Haussmann, the Back Bay planners created thoroughfares that resemble Parisian boulevards. The thorough planning included service alleys behind the main streets to allow provisioning wagons to drive up to basement kitchens. (Today they're used for waste pickup and parking.)

Almost immediately, fashionable families began to decamp from Beacon Hill and the recently developed South End and establish themselves in the Back Bay's brick and brownstone row houses. By 1900 the streets between the Public Garden and Massachusetts Avenue had become the smartest, most desirable neighborhood in all of Boston. An air of permanence and respectability drifted in as inevitably as the tides once had, and the Back Bay mystique was born.

Today the area retains its posh spirit, but mansions are no longer the main draw. Locals and tourists alike flock to the commercial streets of

Boylston and Newbury to shop at boutiques, galleries, and the usual mall stores. Many of the bars and restaurants have patio seating and bay windows, making the area the perfect spot to see and be seen while indulging in ethnic delicacies or an invigorating coffee. The Boston Public Library, Symphony Hall, and numerous churches ensure that high culture is not lost amid the frenzy of consumerism.

Note: One of the main thoroughfares, Huntington Avenue, which stretches from Copley Square past the Museum of Fine Arts, has technically been renamed the Avenue of the Arts. However, old habits die hard, particularly with Bostonians; everyone still calls it Huntington.

TIMING   If you're not looking to max out your credit cards, then you can hurry past the boutiques and cover the Back Bay in about two hours. Allow at least half a day for a leisurely stroll with frequent stops on Newbury Street and the shops at Copley Place and the Prudential Center. The reflecting pool at the Christian Science Church is a great time-out spot. Around the third week of April, magnolia time arrives, and nowhere do the flowers bloom more magnificently than along Commonwealth Avenue. In May the Public Garden bursts with color, thanks to its flowering dogwood trees and thousands of tulips. Set aside a Sunday to enjoy the district's many historic churches. To stay oriented, remember the north–south streets are arranged in alphabetical order, from Arlington to Hereford.

Numbers in the box and margin correspond to numbers on the Back Bay, the South End & the Fens map.

TOP ATTRACTIONS

❶ Boston Public Garden. Although the Boston Public Garden is often lumped together with Boston Common, the two are separate entities with different histories and purposes and a distinct boundary between them at Charles Street. The Common has been public land since Boston was founded in 1630, whereas the Public Garden belongs to a newer Boston, occupying what had been salt marshes on the edge of the Common. By 1837 the tract was covered with an abundance of ornamental plantings donated by a group of private citizens. The area was defined in 1856 by the building of Arlington Street, and in 1860 the architect George Meacham was commissioned to plan the park.

The central feature of the Public Garden is its irregularly shaped pond, intended to appear, from any vantage point along its banks, much larger than its nearly 4 acres. The pond has been famous since 1877 for its foot-pedal-powered (by a captain) Swan Boats, which make leisurely cruises during warm months. They were invented by one Robert Paget, who was inspired by the swan-drawn boat that carries Lohengrin in the Wagner opera of the same name. (Paget descendants still run the boats.) The pond is favored by ducks and swans, and for the modest price of a few boat rides you can amuse children here for an hour or more. Near the Swan Boat dock is what has been described as the world's smallest suspension bridge, designed in 1867 to cross the pond at its narrowest point.

A GOOD WALK

A walk through the Back Bay properly begins with the **Boston Public Garden ❶** ▶, the oldest botanical garden in the United States. After wandering its meandering pathways, venture into the Back Bay through the gate at Arlington and Commonwealth Avenue. Turn left, and then right on Newbury Street. Ahead are **Emmanuel Church ❺** at No. 15 and the **Church of the Covenant ❻** at No. 67. At the Church of the Covenant, follow Berkeley back to Commonwealth Avenue ("Comm Ave." to natives). One block to your left is the **First Baptist Church ❼**. From here you can continue down the Commonwealth Avenue Mall to view its sumptuous mansions all the way to Massachusetts Avenue. Then, or at any point before you hit Mass Ave. (as the locals refer to it), you can turn south to reach **Newbury Street** and backtrack along Boston's poshest shopping district, browsing all the way. At Dartmouth Street, turn right and head into **Copley**

Square, where the **Old South Church ❽**, the **Boston Public Library ❾**, **Trinity Church ❿**, and the **John Hancock Tower ⓫** all stand. For more shopping, head for the upscale **Copley Place ⓬** complex, reached through the Westin Hotel at the corner of Dartmouth and Huntington Avenue. A walkway takes you over Stuart Street into the shopping galleries. Continue through to the Marriott Hotel, and take another walkway over Huntington to the **Prudential Center ⓭** for more shopping and viewing the city at the Prudential Center Skywalk. Exit onto Boylston Street and turn left walking past the Berklee College of Music, turning left again onto Mass Avenue. Walk several blocks to the reflecting pool and expansive plaza of the **Mary Baker Eddy Library ⓮** and the **First Church of Christ, Scientist ⓯**. Just across Mass Ave. at Huntington Avenue is **Symphony Hall ⓰**.

The Public Garden is America's oldest botanical garden and has the finest formal plantings in central Boston. The beds along the main walkways are replanted for spring and summer. The tulips during the first two weeks of May are especially colorful, and there's a sampling of native and European tree species.

The dominant work among the park's statuary is Thomas Ball's equestrian **George Washington** (1869), which faces the head of Commonwealth Avenue at the Arlington Street gate. This is Washington in a triumphant pose as liberator, surveying a scene that, from where he stood with his cannons at Dorchester Heights, would have included an immense stretch of blue water. Several dozen yards to the north of Washington (to the right if you're facing Commonwealth Avenue) is the granite-and-red-marble **Ether Monument,** donated in 1866 by Thomas Lee to commemorate the advent of anesthesia 20 years earlier at nearby Massachusetts General Hospital. Other Public Garden monuments include statues of the Unitarian preacher and transcendentalist William Ellery Channing, at the corner opposite his Arlington Street Church; Edward Everett Hale, the author (*The Man Without a Country*) and philanthropist, at the Charles Street Gate; and the abolitionist senator Charles Sumner and the Civil War hero Colonel Thomas Cass, along Boylston Street.

The park contains a special delight for the young at heart; follow the children quack-quacking along the pathway between the pond and the park entrance at Charles and Beacon streets to the *Make Way for Ducklings* bronzes sculpted by Nancy Schön, a tribute to the 1941 classic children's story by Robert McCloskey. ⊠ *Bounded by Arlington, Boylston, Charles, and Beacon Sts., Back Bay* ☎ *617/522–1966* ⊕ *www.swanboats.com* ✉ *Swan Boats $2.75* ✆ *Swan Boats mid-Apr.–June 20, daily 10–4; June 21–Labor Day, daily 10–5; Labor Day–mid-Sept., weekdays noon–4, weekends 10–4* Ⓣ *Arlington.*

★ ❾ **Boston Public Library.** This venerable institution is a handsome temple to literature and a valuable research library. When the building was opened in 1895, it confirmed the status of architects McKim, Mead & White as apostles of the Renaissance Revival style while reinforcing Boston's commitment to an enlightened citizenry that goes back 350 years, to the founding of the Public Latin School. Philip Johnson's 1972 addition emulates the mass and proportion of the original, though not its extraordinary detail; this skylighted annex houses the library's circulating collections.

You don't need a library card to enjoy the magnificent art. Charles McKim saw to it that the interior of his building was ornamented by several of the finest painters of the day. The murals at the head of the staircase, depicting the nine muses, are the work of the French artist Puvis de Chavannes; those in the book-request processing room to the right are Edwin Abbey's interpretations of the Holy Grail legend. Upstairs, in the public areas leading to the fine-arts, music, and rare-books collections, is John Singer Sargent's mural series on the *Triumph of Religion,* shining with renewed color after its cleaning and restoration in 2003.

You enter the older part of the library from the Dartmouth Street side, passing under the motto *"Omni lux civium"* (Light of all citizens) through the enormous bronze doors by Daniel Chester French, the sculptor of the Lincoln Memorial. Or you can walk around Boylston Street to enter through the addition. The corridor leading from the annex opens onto the Renaissance-style **courtyard**—an exact copy of the one in Rome's Palazzo della Cancelleria—around which the original library is built. A covered arcade furnished with chairs rings a fountain; you can bring books or lunch into the courtyard, which is open all the hours the library is open, and escape the bustle of the city. Beyond the courtyard is the main entrance hall of the 1895 building, with its immense stone lions by Louis Saint-Gaudens (brother of the more-celebrated Augustus), vaulted ceiling, and marble staircase. The corridor at the top of the stairs leads to **Bates Hall,** one of Boston's most sumptuous interior spaces. This is the main reference reading room, 218 feet long with a barrel-arch ceiling 50 feet high. ⊠ *700 Boylston St., at Copley Sq., Back Bay* ☎ *617/536–5400* ⊕ *www.bpl. org* ✆ *Mon.–Thurs. 9–9, Fri. and Sat. 9–5; Oct.–May, also Sun. 1–5.*

Free guided art and architecture tours Mon. at 2:30, Tues. and Thurs. at 6, Fri. and Sat. at 11, Sun. at 2 ⓣ*Copley.*

NEED A BREAK?

You can take a lunch break at Novel or Sebastians Map Room Café (✉ *700 Boylston St., at Copley Sq., Back Bay* ☎ *617/385–5660*), adjoining restaurants in the Boston Public Library. The café serves breakfast and lunch in the 1895 map room, and the main restaurant, which overlooks the courtyard, is open for lunch and afternoon tea. Enter through the Dartmouth entrance and turn right; the restaurants are at the end of the corridor. Novel is open weekdays 11:30–4:30, and Sebastians Map Room Café is open Monday–Saturday 9–5.

★ ⑩ **Trinity Church.** In his 1877 masterpiece, architect Henry Hobson Richardson brought his Romanesque Revival style to maturity; all the aesthetic elements for which he was famous come together magnificently—bold polychromatic masonry, careful arrangement of masses, sumptuously carved interior woodwork. The Episcopal church remains the crowning centerpiece of Copley Square. A full appreciation of its architecture requires an understanding of the logistical problems of building it here. The Back Bay is a reclaimed wetland with a high water table. Bedrock, or at least stable glacial till, lies far beneath wet clay. Like all older Back Bay buildings, Trinity Church sits on submerged wooden pilings. But its central tower weighs 9,500 tons, and most of the 4,500 pilings beneath the building are under that tremendous central mass. The pilings are checked regularly for sinkage by means of a hatch in the basement.

Richardson engaged some of the best artists of his day—John LaFarge, William Morris, and Edward Burne-Jones among them—to execute the paintings and stained glass that make this a monument to everything that was right about the pre-Raphaelite spirit and the nascent aesthetic of Morris's Arts and Crafts movement. LaFarge's brilliant paintings, including the intricate ornamentation of the vaulted ceilings, received a much-needed overhaul during the extensive renovations that are still wrapping up. It was a mammoth job, but the brilliant LaFarge murals have now been returned to their colorful glory, while his spectacular stained-glass windows (restored to full sparkle) are justly considered among the finest in the country. Along the north side of the church, note the Augustus Saint-Gaudens statue of Phillips Brooks—the most charismatic rector in New England, who almost single-handedly got Trinity built and furnished. Shining light of Harvard's religious community and lyricist of "O Little Town of Bethlehem," Brooks is shown here with Christ touching his shoulder in approval. For a nice respite, try to catch one of the Friday organ concerts beginning at 12:15. ■ TIP→ **The 11:15 Sunday service is followed by a guided tour.** ✉ *206 Clarendon St., Back Bay* ☎ *617/536–0944* ⊕ *www.trinityboston.org* ✉ *Church free, guided and self-guided tours $5* ⊙ *Mon.–Sat. 9–5, Sun. 1–5; services Sun. at 7:45, 9, and 11:15* AM, *and 6* PM; *Tues. and Thurs. at 6* PM; *Wed. at 12:10. Tours take place several times daily; call to confirm times* ⓣ*Copley.*

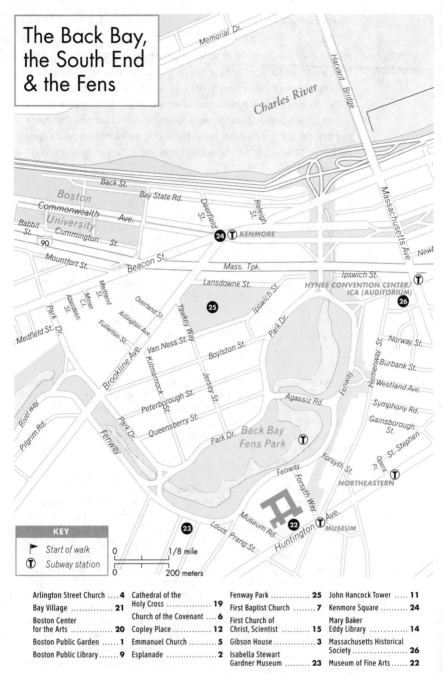

The Back Bay, the South End & the Fens

KEY

► Start of walk

Ⓣ Subway station

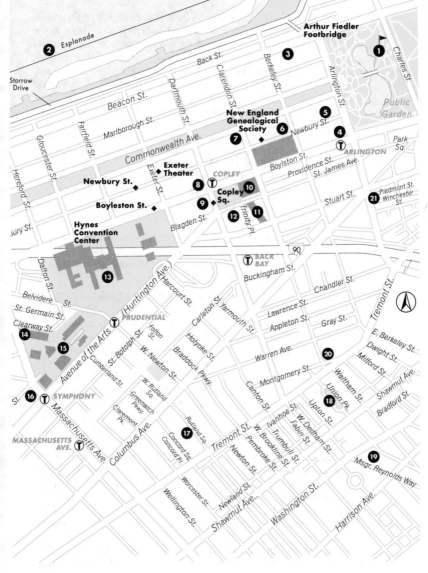

ALSO WORTH SEEING

❹ Arlington Street Church. Opposite the Park Square corner of the Public Garden, this church was erected in 1861—the first to be built in the Back Bay. Following suit, many of the old Downtown congregations relocated to the district's newly filled land and applied their considerable resources to building churches. Often designed in Gothic and Romanesque Revival styles, these churches have aged well and blend harmoniously with the residential blocks, making the Back Bay a great neighborhood for ecclesiastical architecture. Though a classical portico is a keynote and its model was London's St. Martin-in-the-Fields, Arlington Street Church is less picturesque and more Georgian in character. Note the Tiffany stained-glass windows. During the year preceding the Civil War, the church was a hotbed of abolitionist fervor. Later, during the Vietnam War, this Unitarian-Universalist congregation became famous as a center of peace activism. ✉ *351 Boylston St., Back Bay* ☎ *617/536–7050* ⊕ *www.ascboston.org* ⊙ *Call to arrange sanctuary tours. Services Sun. at 11* Ⓣ *Arlington.*

Back Bay Mansions. If you like nothing better than to imagine how the other half lives, you'll suffer no shortage of old homes to sigh over in Boston's Back Bay. Most, unfortunately, are off-limits to visitors, but there's no law against gawking from the outside.

Among the grander Back Bay houses is the **Baylies Mansion** (✉ *5 Commonwealth Ave., Back Bay*) of 1904, now the home of the Boston Center for Adult Education; you can enter to view its first-floor common room. The **Burrage Mansion** (✉ *314 Commonwealth Ave., Back Bay*) is a gem, built in 1899 in an extravagant French-château style, complete with turrets and gargoyles, that reflects a cost-be-damned attitude uncommon even among the wealthiest Back Bay families. It now houses an assisted-living residence for seniors, and walk-in visitors are discouraged. The **Cushing-Endicott House** (✉ *163 Marlborough St., Back Bay*) was built in 1871 and later served as the home of William C. Endicott, secretary of war under President Grover Cleveland; this was dubbed "the handsomest house in the whole Back Bay" by the author Bainbridge Bunting. The opulent **Oliver Ames Mansion** (✉ *55 Commonwealth Ave., corner of Massachusetts Ave., Back Bay*) was built in 1882 for a railroad baron and Massachusetts governor; it's now an office building. The **Ames-Webster House** (✉ *306 Dartmouth St., Back Bay*), built in 1872 and remodeled in 1882 and 1969, is one of the city's finest houses; it's still a private home. Two Back Bay mansions are now used by organizations that promote foreign language and culture: the **French Library and Cultural Center** (✉ *53 Marlborough St., Back Bay* ⊕ *frenchlib.org*) and the German-oriented **Goethe Institute** (✉ *170 Beacon St., Back Bay* ⊕ *www.goethe.de/uk/bos*). See the *Boston Globe*'s "Calendar" section on Thursday or the weekly listings in the free *Boston Phoenix* for details on lectures, films, and other events held in these respected institutions.

Fisher College (✉ *118 Beacon St., Back Bay* ☎ *617/236–8800* ⊕ *www.fisher.edu*) is housed in a 1903 bowfront whose Classical Revival style epitomizes turn-of-the-20th-century elegance. Step inside to see such

CLOSE UP

The Houses of the Back Bay

1

The Back Bay remains a living museum of urban Victorian–residential architecture. The earliest specimens are nearest to the Public Garden (there are exceptions where showier turn-of-the-20th-century mansions replaced 1860s town houses), and the newer examples are out around the Massachusetts Avenue and Fenway extremes of the district. The height of Back Bay residences and their distance from the street are essentially uniform, as are the interior layouts, chosen to accord with lot width. Yet there's a distinct progression of facades, beginning with French academic and Italianate designs and moving through the various "revivals" of the 19th century. By the time of World War I, when development of the Back Bay was virtually complete, architects and their patrons had come full circle to a revival of the Federal period, which had been out of fashion for only 30 years when the building began. If the Back Bay architects had not run out of land, they might have gotten around to a Greek Revival revival.

The Great Depression brought an end to the Back Bay style of living, and today only a few of the houses are single-family residences. Most have been cut up into apartments, then expensive condominiums; during the boom years of the late 1990s some were returned to their original town-house status. Interior details have experienced a mixed fate: they suffered during the years when Victorian fashions were held in low regard, and are undergoing careful restoration now that the aesthetic pendulum has reversed itself and moneyed condo buyers are demanding period authenticity. The original facades have survived on all but Newbury and Boylston streets, so the public face of the Back Bay retains much of the original charm and grandeur.

An outstanding guide to the architecture and history of the Back Bay is Bainbridge Bunting's *Houses of Boston's Back Bay* (Harvard, 1967). A few homes are open to the public.

---

genteel touches as the marble stairway with its gold-plated balustrade, the Circassian walnut–panel dining room, and the library's hand-carved rosewood doors with sterling silver knobs. Admission is free, and it's open on weekdays from 8 to 4.

Boylston Street. Less posh than Newbury Street, this broad thoroughfare is the southern commercial spine of the Back Bay, lined with interesting restaurants and shops.

❻ Church of the Covenant. This 1867 Gothic Revival church at the corner of Newbury and Berkeley streets has one of the largest collections of liturgical windows by Louis Comfort Tiffany in the country. It's crowned by a 236-foot-tall steeple—the tallest in Boston—that Oliver Wendell Holmes called "absolutely perfect." Inside, a 14-foot-high Tiffany lantern hangs from a breathtaking 100-foot ceiling. The church is now Presbyterian and United Church of Christ. ✉ *67 Newbury St., enter at church office, Back Bay* ☎ *617/266–7480* ☾ *Call for hrs; Sun. service at 10* Ⓣ *Arlington.*

Commonwealth Avenue Mall. The mall that extends down the middle of the Back Bay's Commonwealth Avenue is studded with statuary. One of the most interesting memorials, at the Exeter Street intersection, is a portrayal of naval historian and author Samuel Eliot Morison seated on a rock as if he were peering out to sea. The most recent addition was the **Boston Women's Memorial** in 2003 by Meredith Bergmann, between Fairfield and Gloucester streets. Statues of Abigail Adams, Lucy Stone, and Phillis Wheatley celebrate the progressive ideas of these three women and their contributions to Boston's history. The other figures have only tenuous connections to Boston—Viking explorer Leif Eriksson; Domingo F. Sarmiento, president of Argentina; and even Alexander Hamilton, who tried to block Quincy-born John Adams from the presidency.

A dramatic and personal memorial was added to the mall in 1997 near Dartmouth Street: the **Vendome Monument,** dedicated to the nine firemen who died in a 1972 blaze at the Back Bay's Vendome Hotel. Designed by Ted Clausen and Peter White, the curved black-granite block, 29 feet long and waist high, is etched with the names of the dead. A bronze cast of a fireman's coat and hat are draped over the granite as if to say, "The fire is out; we can rest now." Just across the street from the monument, at 160 Commonwealth Avenue, is the **Vendome Hotel** itself, which first opened in 1872 and is now used as office space. ⊠ *Commonwealth Ave. between Arlington St. and Massachusetts Ave.* Ⓣ *Arlington, Copley.*

⓬ **Copley Place.** Two bold intruders dominate Copley Square—the **John Hancock Tower** off the southeast corner, and the even more assertive Copley Place skyscraper on the southwest. An upscale, glass-and-brass urban mall built between 1980 and 1984, Copley Place includes two major hotels: the high-rise Westin and the Marriott Copley Place. Dozens of shops, restaurants, and offices are attractively grouped on several levels, surrounding bright, open indoor spaces. During the long winter months, locals use the mall to escape the elements and take a shortcut between Back Bay Station and points west. ⊠ *100 Huntington Ave., Back Bay* ☎ *617/369–5000* ⊕ *www.shopcopleyplace.com* ☉ *Shopping galleries Mon.–Sat. 10–9, Sun. 11–6* Ⓣ *Copley.*

Copley Square. Every April thousands find a glimpse of Copley Square the most wonderful sight in the world: this is where the runners of the Boston Marathon end their 26-mi race. A square now favored by skateboarders (much to the chagrin of city officials), the civic space is defined by three monumental older buildings. One is the stately, bow-front 1912 **Fairmont Copley Plaza Hotel,** which faces the square on St. James Avenue and serves as a dignified foil to its companions, two of the most important works of architecture in the United States: Trinity Church—Henry Hobson Richardson's masterwork of 1877—and the Boston Public Library, by McKim, Mead & White. The John Hancock Tower looms in the background. To honor the runners who stagger over the marathon's finish line, bronze statues of the Tortoise and the Hare engaged in their mythical race were cast by Nancy Schön, who also did the much-loved *Make Way for Ducklings* group in the Boston

Public Garden. ⊠ *Bounded by Dartmouth, Boylston, and Clarendon Sts. and St. James Ave., Back Bay* Ⓣ *Copley.*

❺ Emmanuel Church. Built in 1860, this Back Bay brownstone Gothic Episcopal church is popular among classical music–loving worshippers—every Sunday at 10 AM from September to May, as part of the liturgy, a Bach cantata is performed by Emmanuel Music with Craig Smith conducting; guest conductors have included Christopher Hogwood and Seiji Ozawa. Inside the church is the Leslie Lindsey Chapel—a neo-Gothic memorial created by parents in memory of their daughter, a young bride who perished with her husband during their 1915 honeymoon voyage on the *Lusitania.* ⊠ *15 Newbury St., Back Bay* ☎ *617/536–3355* ⊕ *www. emmanuel-boston.org* ⊙ *Services Sept.–May, Sun. at 8 AM, 10 AM, and 5 PM, Wed. at noon; June–Aug., Sun. at 10 AM* Ⓣ *Arlington.*

❷ Esplanade. Near the corner of Beacon and Arlington streets, the Arthur Fiedler Footbridge crosses Storrow Drive to the Esplanade and the **Hatch Memorial Shell.** The free concerts here in summer include the Boston Pops' immensely popular televised Fourth of July performance. For shows like this, Bostonians haul lawn chairs and blankets to the lawn in front of the shell; bring a take-out lunch from a nearby restaurant, find an empty spot—no mean feat, so come early—and you'll feel right at home. An impressive stone bust of the late maestro Arthur Fiedler watches over the walkers, joggers, picnickers, and sunbathers who fill the Esplanade's paths on pleasant days. The green is home port for the fleet of small sailboats that dot the Charles River basin; they belong to Community Boating. Here, too, is the turn-of-the-20th-century **Union Boat Club Boathouse,** headquarters for the country's oldest private rowing club.

Exeter Street Theater. This massive Romanesque structure was built in 1884 as a temple for the Working Union of Progressive Spiritualists. Beginning in 1914, it enjoyed a long run as a movie theater; as the *AIA Guide to Boston* points out, "it was the only movie theater a proper Boston woman would enter, probably because of its spiritual overtones." ⊠ *26 Exeter St., at Newbury St., Back Bay* Ⓣ *Copley.*

❼ First Baptist Church. This 1872 structure, at the corner of Clarendon Street and Commonwealth Avenue, was architect Henry Hobson Richardson's first foray into Romanesque Revival. It was originally erected for the Brattle Square Unitarian Society, but Richardson ran over budget and the church went bankrupt and dissolved; in 1882 the building was bought by the Baptists. The figures on each side of its soaring tower were sculpted by Frédéric Auguste Bartholdi, the sculptor who designed the Statue of Liberty. The friezes represent four points at which God enters an individual's life: baptism, communion, marriage, and death. The trumpeting angels at each corner have earned First Baptist its nickname, "Church of the Holy Bean Blowers." If you phone ahead for an appointment on a weekday, you may be surprised by an informal tour. ⊠ *110 Commonwealth Ave., Back Bay* ☎ *617/267– 3148* ⊕ *www.firstbaptistchurchofboston.org* ▧ *Free* ⊙ *Mon., Tues., Thurs., and Fri. 11–3; services Sun. at 11 AM* Ⓣ *Copley.*

CLOSE UP

The Boston Marathon

Though it missed being the first U.S. marathon by one year (the first, in 1896, went from Stamford, Connecticut, to New York City), the Boston Marathon is arguably the nation's most prestigious. Why? It's the only marathon in the world for which runners have to qualify; it's the world's oldest continuously run marathon; it's been run on the same course since it began. Only the New York Marathon compares with it for community involvement. Spectators have returned to the same spot for generations, bringing their lawn chairs and barbecues.

Held every Patriots' Day (the third Monday in April), the marathon passes through Hopkinton, Ashland, Framingham, Natick, Wellesley, Newton, Brookline, and Boston; only the last few miles are run in the city proper. The first marathon was organized by members of the Boston Athletic Association (BAA), who in 1896 had attended the first modern Olympic games in Athens. When they saw that the Olympics ended with a marathon, they decided the same would be a fitting end to their own Spring Sports Festival, begun in the late 1880s.

The first race was run on April 19, 1897, when Olympian Tom Burke drew a line in the dirt in Ashland and began a 24.5-mi dash to Boston with 15 men. For most of its history, the race concluded on Exeter Street outside the BAA's clubhouse. In 1965

the finish was moved to the front of the Prudential Center, and in 1986 it was moved to its current location, Copley Square. The race's guardian spirit is the indefatigable John A. Kelley, who ran his first marathon shortly after Warren G. Harding was sworn in as president. Kelley won twice—in 1935 and 1945—took the second-place spot seven times, and continued to run well into his eighties, finishing 58 Boston Marathons in all. Until his retirement in 1992, his arrival at the finish signaled the official end of the race. A double statue of an older Kelley greeting his younger self stands at the route's most strenuous incline—dubbed "Heartbreak Hill"—on Commonwealth Avenue in Newton.

Women weren't allowed to race until 1972, but in 1966 Roberta Gibb slipped into the throngs under a hooded sweatshirt; she was the first known female participant. In 1967 cameras captured BAA organizer Jock Semple screaming, "Get out of my race," as he tried to rip off the number of Kathrine Switzer, who had registered as K. Switzer. But the marathon's most infamous moment was when 26-year-old Rosie Ruiz came out of nowhere to be the first woman to cross the finish line in the 1980 race. Ruiz apparently started running less than 1 mi from the end of the course, and her title was stripped eight days later. Bostonians still quip about her taking the T to the finish.

NEED A BREAK?

Espresso Royale Caffe (⊠ *286 Newbury St., Back Bay* ☎ *617/859–9515* Ⓣ *Hynes*) is a basement spot with solid coffee and espresso drinks, snacks, and Wi-Fi access. If you want to try the creations of some of the best local chefs but don't want to pay four-star restaurant prices, stop by **Parish Café** (⊠ *361 Boylston St., Back Bay* ☎ *617/247–4777* ⊕ *www.parishcafe.com* Ⓣ *Arlington*). For about $10, you can get a sandwich designed by the top culinary minds in Boston. The bar is open until 2 AM daily, with food service until 1 AM.

⓯ **First Church of Christ, Scientist.** The world headquarters of the Christian Science faith mixes the traditional with the modern—marrying Bernini to Le Corbusier by combining an old-world basilica with a sleek office complex designed by I. M. Pei. Mary Baker Eddy's original granite First Church of Christ, Scientist (1894) has since been enveloped by a domed Renaissance Revival basilica, added to the site in 1906, and both church buildings are now surrounded by the offices of the Christian Science Publishing Society, where the *Christian Science Monitor* is produced, and by Pei's complex of church-administration structures completed in 1973. You can hear all 13,290 pipes of the church's famed Aeolian-Skinner organ during services. ✉ *175 Huntington Ave., Back Bay* ☎ *617/450–3790* ⊕ *www.tfccs.com* 🎟 *Free* ⊙ *Services Sept.– June, Sun. at 10 AM and 7 PM; July and Aug., Sun. at 10 AM, Wed. at noon and 7:30 PM* Ⓣ *Hynes/ICA, Symphony.*

❸ **Gibson House.** Through the foresight of an eccentric bon vivant, this house provides an authentic glimpse into daily life in Boston's Victorian era. One of the first Back Bay residences (1859), the Gibson House is relatively modest in comparison with some of the grand mansions built during the decades that followed; yet its furnishings, from its circa-1790 Willard clock to the raised and gilded wallpaper to the multipiece faux-bamboo bedroom set, seem sumptuous to modern eyes. Unlike other Back Bay houses, the Gibson family home has been preserved with all its Victorian fixtures and furniture intact. That's the legacy of Charles Gibson Jr., a poet, travel writer, and horticulturist who continued to appear in formal attire—morning coat, spats, and a walking stick—well into the 1940s when he dined daily at the Ritz nearby. As early as 1936, Gibson was roping off furniture and envisioning a museum for the house his grandmother built. His dream was realized in 1957, three years after he died. You can see a full-course setting with a China-trade dinner service in the ornate dining room and discover the elaborate system of servants' bells in the 19th-century basement kitchen. The house serves as the meeting place for the New England chapter of the Victorian Society in America; it was also used as an interior for the 1984 Merchant-Ivory film *The Bostonians.* ■ TIP➔ **Though the sign out front instructs visitors not to ring the bell until the stroke of the hour, you will have better luck catching the beginning of the tour if you arrive a few minutes early and ring forcefully.** ✉ *137 Beacon St., Back Bay* ☎ *617/267–6338* ⊕ *www.thegibsonhouse.org* 🎟 *$7* ⊙ *Tours Wed.–Sun. at 1, 2, and 3 and by appointment* Ⓣ *Arlington.*

⓫ **John Hancock Tower.** In the early 1970s, the tallest building in New England became notorious as the monolith that rained glass from time to time. Windows were improperly seated in the sills of the stark and graceful reflective blue rhomboid tower, designed by I. M. Pei. Once the building's 13 acres of glass were replaced and the central core stiffened, the problem was corrected. Bostonians originally feared the Hancock's stark modernism would overwhelm nearby Trinity Church, but its shimmering sides reflect the older structure's image, actually enlarging its presence. The Tower is closed to the public. ⊠*200 Clarendon St., Back Bay* Ⓣ*Copley.*

⑭ **Mary Baker Eddy Library for the Betterment of Humanity.** One of the largest single collections by and about an American woman is housed at this library within Christian Science Plaza, along with two floors of exhibits celebrating the power of ideas and highlighting the link between spirituality and health. The library is home to the fascinating **Mapparium,** a huge stained-glass globe whose 30-foot interior can be traversed on a footbridge. You can experience a sound-and-light show in the Mapparium and learn about the production of the *Christian Science Monitor* in the Monitor Gallery. The Quest Gallery explores Mary Baker Eddy's life and encourages others to think about their own personal quests, and the Hall of Ideas showcases the ideas of the world's greatest thinkers in a virtual fountain. ⊠*200 Massachusetts Ave., Back Bay* ☎*888/222–3711* ⊕*www.marybakereddylibrary.org* ✉*Hall of Ideas and 3rd-fl. library free, exhibits $5* ◷*Tues., Wed., and weekends 10–5, Thurs. and Fri. 10–9.*

㉖ **Massachusetts Historical Society.** The oldest historical society in the United States (founded in 1791) has paintings, a library, and a 10-million-piece manuscript collection from 17th-century New England to the present. Among these manuscripts are the Adams Papers, which comprise more than 300,000 pages from the letters and diaries of generations of the Adams family, including papers from John Adams and John Quincy Adams (the second and sixth American presidents, respectively). Casual visitors are welcome, but if you'd like to examine the papers in depth, call ahead. ⊠*1154 Boylston St., Back Bay* ☎*617/536–1608* ⊕*www.masshist.org* ✉*Free* ◷*Weekdays 9–4:45 (Thurs. until 7:45)* Ⓣ*Hynes/ICA.*

Newbury Street. Eight-block-long Newbury Street has been compared to New York's 5th Avenue, and certainly this is the city's poshest shopping area, with branches of Chanel, Brooks Brothers, Armani, Burberry, and other top names in fashion. But here the pricey boutiques are more intimate than grand, and people live above the trendy restaurants and hair salons, giving the place a neighborhood feel. Toward the Mass Ave. end, cafés proliferate and the stores get funkier, ending with Newbury Comics, Virgin Records, and Urban Outfitters.

New England Historic Genealogical Society. Are you related to Miles Standish or Priscilla Alden? The answer may lie here. If your ancestors were pedigreed New Englanders—or if you're just interested in genealogical research of any kind—you can trace your family tree with the help of the society's collections, which stretch back to the 17th century. An introductory lecture on how to perform your own genealogical study is given every first Wednesday of the month at noon and 6 (the evening lecture is canceled from December through March). The society itself dates from 1845, and is the oldest genealogical organization in the country. ⊠*101 Newbury St., Back Bay* ☎*617/536–5740* ⊕*www.newenglandancestors.org* ✉*$15 fee to use facility* ◷*Tues. and Thurs.–Sat. 9–5, Wed. 9–9* Ⓣ*Copley.*

Care for a read with your caffe latte? Folks gather at the Trident Booksellers & Café (✉ *338 Newbury St., Back Bay* ☎ *617/267–8688* Ⓣ *Hynes/ICA*) to review literary best sellers, thumb through the superb magazine selection, and munch on homemade desserts, sandwiches, and soups. It's open until midnight daily.

❽ Old South Church. Members of the Old South Meeting House, of Tea Party fame, decamped to this new parish in 1875, a move not without controversy for the congregation. In an Italian Gothic style inspired by the sociologist John Ruskin and an interior decorated with Venetian mosaics and stained-glass windows, the "new" structure could hardly be more different from the original plain meetinghouse. Old South's congregation is now part of the United Church of Christ. ✉ *645 Boylston St., Back Bay* ☎ *617/536–1970* ⊕ *www.oldsouth.org* ☉ *Services Sun. at 9 and 11* AM, *jazz services Thurs. at 6.* Ⓣ *Copley.*

⓭ Prudential Center. The only rival to the John Hancock's claim on Boston's upper skyline is the 52-story Prudential Tower, built in the early 1960s when the scale of monumental urban redevelopment projects had yet to be challenged. The Prudential Center, which replaced the railway yards that blocked off the South End, now dominates the acreage between Boylston Street and Huntington Avenue two blocks west of the library, and adds considerably to the area's overabundance of mall-style shops and food courts. Its enclosed shopping mall is connected by a glass bridge to the more-upscale Copley Place. As for the Prudential Tower itself, the architectural historian Bainbridge Bunting made an acute observation when he called it "an apparition so vast in size that it appears to float above the surrounding district without being related to it." Later modifications to the Boylston Street frontage of the Prudential Center effected a better union of the complex with the urban space around it, but the tower itself floats on, vast as ever. The **Hynes Convention Center** (☎ *617/424–8585*) is connected to the Prudential Center; there's also a branch of the Greater Boston Visitors Bureau here, in the center court of the mall. **Prudential Center Skywalk,** a 50th-floor observatory atop the Prudential Tower, offers panoramic vistas of Boston, Cambridge, and the suburbs to the west and south—on clear days, you can even see Cape Cod. You can see sailboats skimming the Charles River, the redbrick expanse of the Back Bay, and a glimpse of the precise abstract geometry of the nearby Christian Science Church's reflecting pool. There are also interactive exhibits on Boston's history; the Skywalk is one of the attractions on the Boston CityPass. ✉ *800 Boylston St., Back Bay* ☎ *617/236–3100, 617/859–0648 for Skywalk* ⊕ *www.prudentialcenter.com* 🎫 *Skywalk $11* ☉ *Mon.–Sat. 10–9, Sun. 11–6; Skywalk daily 10–10* Ⓣ *Hynes/ICA.*

⓰ Symphony Hall. With commerce and religion accounted for in the Back Bay by such monuments as the Prudential Center and the Christian Science headquarters, the neighborhood still has room for a temple to music: Symphony Hall, home of the Boston Symphony Orchestra and the Boston Pops, and frequent host to guest performers. Built in 1900, Symphony Hall was another contribution of McKim, Mead & White to the Boston landscape. But acoustics rather than aesthetics make this hall special for performers and concertgoers. Although acoustical science was a brand-new field of research when Professor Wallace Sabine planned the interior, not one of the 2,500 seats is a bad one—the secret is the box-within-a-box design. ⊠ *301 Massachusetts Ave., Back Bay* ☎ *888/266–1200 box office, 617/638–9392 tours* ⊕ *www.bso.org* ⊗ *Free walk-up tours Oct.–May, Wed. at 4:30 and 1st Sat. of month at 1:30* Ⓣ *Symphony.*

THE SOUTH END

A fashionable neighborhood created with landfill in the mid-1800s, the South End was deserted by the well-to-do for the Back Bay toward the end of the 19th century. Solidly back in fashion today, its redbrick row houses in various states of refurbished splendor now house a mix of ethnic groups, the city's largest gay community, and some excellent shops.

The South End neither rose haphazardly among cow paths and village lanes, like the older sections of the city, nor followed the strict, uniform grid typical of the Back Bay. It's certainly more a sum of random blocks and park-center squares than of bold boulevards and long vistas. An observation often made is that the Back Bay is French-inspired, whereas the South End is English. The houses, too, are noticeably different from those in Back Bay; although they continue the bowfront style, they aspire to a more-florid standard of decoration.

When the Bay Back was established, the South End was relegated to the status of a social backwater, which may have been due to fickle tastes, but likely had something to do with the South End's location. Railroad tracks separated it from the Back Bay, and differences in planning styles and grid patterns never allowed the two districts to comfortably mesh. Even so, in the late 1970s, middle-class professionals began snapping up town houses at bargain prices and restoring them.

Today, a large African-American community resides along Columbus Avenue and Mass Ave., which marks the beginning of the predominantly black neighborhood of Roxbury. Boston's gay community also has a strong presence in the South End, with most of the gay-oriented restaurants and businesses on Columbus Avenue and Tremont Street between East Berkeley Street and Mass Ave. If you like to shop, you'll have a blast in this area, which focuses on home furnishings and accessories, with a heavy accent on the unique and handmade. At the northern tip of the South End, where Harrison Avenue and Washington Street lead to Chinatown, are several Chinese supermarkets, and south of Washington Street is the burgeoning "SoWa" District, home to a growing number of art galleries, many of which have relocated here from pricey Newbury Street.

Numbers in the margin correspond to numbers on the Back Bay, the South End & the Fens map.

TOP ATTRACTIONS

⑰ Rutland Square. Reflecting a time in which the South End was the most prestigious Boston address, this slice of a park is framed by lovely Italianate bowfront houses. ⊠*Rutland Sq. between Columbus Ave. and Tremont St.*

⑱ Union Park. Cast-iron fences, Victorian-era town houses, and a grassy area all add up to one of Boston's most charming mini-escapes. ⊠*Union Park St. between Shawmut Ave. and Tremont St..*

ALSO WORTH SEEING

㉑ Bay Village. It seems improbable that such a fine, mellow neighborhood (Edgar Allan Poe was born here) could remain that way, close as the Village is to the busy Theater District and the Massachusetts Turnpike. Yet here it is, another Boston surprise. This pocket of early-19th-century brick row houses is near Arlington and Piedmont streets. Its window boxes and short, narrow streets make the area seem a toylike reproduction of Beacon Hill. Note that, owing to the street pattern, it's nearly impossible to drive to Bay Village, and it's easy to miss on foot. ⊠*Bounded (roughly) by Arlington, Stuart, Charles, and Marginal Sts.*

⑳ Boston Center for the Arts. Of Boston's multiple arts organizations, this city-sponsored arts-and-culture complex is the one that is closest to "the people." Here you can see the work of budding playwrights, view exhibits on Haitian folk art, or walk through an installation commemorating World AIDS Day. The BCA houses three small theaters, the Mills Art Gallery, and studio space for some 60 Boston-based contemporary artists. It's a bit of a leap from the original purpose of the **Cyclorama Building,** which was built by William Blackall in 1884 to house a 400- by 50-foot circular painting of the Battle of Gettysburg. After the painting was sent to Pennsylvania, the building was used as a boxing ring, a roller-skating rink, and a mechanics garage (Alfred Champion invented the spark plug here). It now is host to frequent antiques shows and fund-raisers. The **Calderwood Pavilion** next door, created when the old National Theater was razed, houses new theaters, along with condos, restaurants, and a furniture store. ⊠*539 Tremont St., South End* ☎*617/426–5000, 617/426–8835 for Mills Gallery* ⊕*www.bcaonline. org* ⊠*Free* ☉*Weekdays 9–5; Mills Gallery Wed., Thurs., and Sun. noon–5, Fri. and Sat. noon–10* Ⓣ*Back Bay/South End.*

⑲ Cathedral of the Holy Cross. This enormous 1875 Gothic cathedral dominates the corner of Washington and Union Park streets. The main church of the Archdiocese of Boston and therefore the seat of Archbishop Sean Patrick O'Malley, Holy Cross is also New England's largest Catholic church. ⊠*1400 Washington St., South End* ☎*617/542–5682* ☉*Mass Sun. at 8 AM and 11 AM, weekdays at 9 AM; in Spanish Sun. at 10 AM, Tues. and Thurs. at 7 PM* Ⓣ*Chinatown, then Bus 49 to Cathedral.*

NEED A BREAK? Although many South End restaurants are intimidatingly pricey, a good spot to refuel on a budget is Flour Bakery and Café (⊠*1595 Washington St., South End* ☎*617/267–4300* Ⓣ*Back Bay/South End*), a perennial candidate

CLOSE UP

Prestige Lost

Not long after its conception in the mid-1800s, the South End, somewhat unfairly, lost its elite status to the Back Bay. The literature of the time documents this exodus: the title character in William Dean Howells's *The Rise of Silas Lapham* abandoned the South End to build a house on the waterside of Beacon as material proof of his arrival in Boston society. In *The Late George Apley*, John P. Marquand's Brahmin hero tells how his father decided, in the early 1870s, to move the family from his South End bowfront to the Back Bay—a consequence of his walking out on the front steps one morning and seeing a man in his shirtsleeves on the porch opposite. Regardless of whether Marquand exaggerated Victorian notions of propriety (if that was possible), the fact is that people such as the Apleys did decamp for the Back Bay, leaving the South End to become what a 1913 guidebook called a "faded quarter."

for Boston's best sandwiches and stuffed bread. Also superb are the fresh pizzas, dinner specials, and shockingly delicious pastries.

THE FENWAY & KENMORE SQUARE

The marshland known as the Back Bay Fens gave this section of Boston its name, but two quirky institutions give it its character: Fenway Park, which in 2004 saw the triumphant reversal of an 86-year dry spell for Boston's beloved Red Sox, and the Isabella Stewart Gardner Museum, the legacy of a high-living Brahmin who attended a concert at Symphony Hall in 1912 wearing a headband that read, OH, YOU RED SOX. Not far from the Gardner is another major cultural magnet: the Museum of Fine Arts. Kenmore Square, a favorite haunt for Boston University students, adds a bit of funky flavor to the mix.

After the outsize job of filling in the bay had been completed, it would have been small trouble to obliterate the Fens with gravel and march row houses straight through to Brookline. But the planners, deciding that enough pavement had been laid between here and the Public Garden, hired vaunted landscape architect Frederick Law Olmsted to turn the Fens into a park. Olmsted applied his genius for heightening natural effects while subtly manicuring their surroundings; today the Fens park consists of irregularly shaped reed-bound pools surrounded by broad meadows, trees, and flower gardens.

The Fens marks the beginning of Boston's Emerald Necklace, a loosely connected chain of parks designed by Olmsted that extends along the Fenway, Riverway, and Jamaicaway to Jamaica Pond, the Arnold Arboretum, and Franklin Park. Farther off, at the Boston–Milton line, the Blue Hills Reservation offers some of the Boston area's best hiking, scenic views, and even a ski lift.

Numbers in the box correspond to numbers in the margin and on the Back Bay, the South End & the Fens map.

A GOOD WALK

With Boston's two major art museums on this itinerary, a case of museum fatigue could set in. Happily, both the Museum of Fine Arts and the Isabella Stewart Gardner Museum are surrounded by the sylvan glades of the Fenway—a perfect oasis and time-out location when you're suffering from gallery gout. From the intersection of Massachusetts and Huntington avenues, with the front entrance of Symphony Hall on your right, walk down Huntington Avenue. On your left is the New England Conservatory of Music and, on Gainsborough Street, its recital center, Jordan Hall. Between Huntington Avenue and the Fenway is the **Museum of Fine Arts (MFA)** ㉒ ⤷ and, just around the corner, the **Isabella Stewart Gardner Museum** ㉓. If you prefer to pay homage to the Red Sox: from Symphony Hall, go north on Mass Ave., turn left on Commonwealth Avenue, and continue until you reach **Kenmore Square** ㉔; from here it's a 10-minute walk down Brookline Avenue to Yawkey Way and **Fenway Park** ㉕.

TIMING   Although this area can be walked through in a couple of hours, art lovers could spend a week here, thanks to the glories of the MFA and the Isabella Stewart Gardner Museum. (If you want to do a museum blowout, avoid Monday, when the Gardner is closed.) To cap off a day of culture, plan for an area dinner, then a concert at nearby Symphony Hall. Another option, if you're visiting between spring and early fall, is to take a tour of Fenway Park—or better yet, catch a game. This district is most easily traveled via branches of the MBTA's Green Line; trains operate aboveground on Commonwealth and Huntington avenues.

■ TIP➔ **Avoid the area around the Fens at night, when it's deserted.**

TOP ATTRACTIONS

㉕   **Fenway Park.** For 86 years, the Boston Red Sox suffered a World Series dry spell, a streak of bad luck that fans attributed to the "Curse of the Bambino," which, stories have it, struck the team in 1920 when they sold Babe Ruth (the "Bambino") to the New York Yankees. All that changed in 2004, when a maverick squad—including Manny Ramirez, Pedro Martinez, and local favorite David Ortiz—broke the curse in a thrilling seven-game series against the team's nemesis in the Series semifinals. This win against the Yankees was followed by a four-game sweep of St. Louis in the finals. Boston, and its citizens' ingrained sense of pessimism, hasn't been the same since. There's a palpable sense of justice being served, and more than a little pride in the way Red Sox caps have become residents' semiofficial uniform.

Fodor'sChoice ★

Fenway may be one of the smallest parks in the major leagues (capacity almost 39,000), but it's one of the most beloved, despite its oddball dimensions and the looming left-field wall, otherwise known as the Green Monster. Parking is expensive and the seats are a bit cramped, but the air is thick with legend. Ruth pitched here when the stadium was new; Ted Williams and Carl Yastrzemski slugged out their entire careers here. ⊠4 *Yawkey Way, between Van Ness and Lansdowne Sts., The Fenway* ☎617/267–1700 box office, 617/226–6666 tours

⊕ *www.boston.redsox.mlb.com* ✉ *Tours $12* ⊙ *Tours Mon.–Sat. 9–4, Sun. noon–4; on game days, last tour is 3 hrs before game time and lasts only ½ hr.*

DID YOU KNOW?

Yawkey Way is named for the late Tom Yawkey, who bought the team in 1933 as a 30th-birthday present for himself and spent the next 43 years pursuing his elusive grail.

㉓ **Isabella Stewart Gardner Museum.** A spirited young society woman, Isa-
Fodor's Choice bella Stewart had come in 1860 from New York—where ladies were
★ more commonly seen *and* heard than in Boston—to marry John Lowell Gardner, one of Boston's leading citizens. Through her flamboy-
ance and energetic acquisition of art, "Mrs. Jack" promptly set about
becoming the most un-Bostonian of the Proper Bostonians. When it
came time finally to settle down with the old master paintings and
Medici treasures she and her husband had acquired in Europe—with
her money (she was heir to the Stewart mining fortune)—she decided
to build the Venetian palazzo of her dreams in an isolated corner of
Boston's newest neighborhood. She built her palace to center on a spacious inner courtyard. On New Year's Day 1903, she threw open the
entrance to Fenway Court (to use the museum's original name)—then
as now, a monument to one woman's individuality and taste. Today, it's
probably America's most idiosyncratic treasure house.

In a city where expensive simplicity was the norm, Gardner's palazzo was amazing: a trove of paintings—including such masterpieces as
Titian's *Rape of Europa,* Giorgione's *Christ Bearing the Cross,* Piero
della Francesca's *Hercules,* and John Singer Sargent's *El Jaleo*—over-
flows rooms bought outright from great European houses. Spanish
leather panels, Renaissance hooded fireplaces, and Gothic tapestries
accent salons; eight balconies adorn the majestic Venetian courtyard.
There's a Raphael Room, a Spanish Cloister, a Gothic Room, a Chinese
Loggia, and a magnificent Tapestry Room for concerts, where Gardner entertained Henry James and Edith Wharton. Throughout the two
decades of her residence, Mrs. Jack continued to build her collection
under the tutelage of the young Bernard Berenson, who became one of
the most respected art connoisseurs and critics of the 20th century.

At one time Gardner lived on the fourth floor of Fenway Court. When
she died, the terms of her will stipulated that the building remain
exactly as she left it—paintings, furniture, everything, down to the
smallest object in a hall cabinet. The courtyard, fully protected from
New England winters by a glass roof, is decorated with fresh poin-
settias at Christmastime, bright orange South African nasturtiums
in spring, and chrysanthemums in autumn—just as when Mrs. Jack
lived here.

Today, with more than 2,500 works in the collection and rates dramati-
cally lower because of increasing recoveries of stolen art, the Gardner
carries insurance. Mrs. Jack never believed in making a contribution
to the Metropolitan Life Insurance Company, putting her faith in her
mansion's entry portal, which carries Renaissance-period figures of

both St. George and St. Florian, the patron saints protecting believers from theft and fire.

An intimate restaurant overlooks the garden, and in spring and summer tables and chairs spill outside. To fully conjure up the spirit of days past, try to attend one of the concerts still held from September to May (with a break for the holidays) in the Tapestry Room. A first-floor gallery has revolving exhibits of historic and contemporary art. ■ TIP → **If you've visited the MFA in the past two days, there's a $2 discount to the admission fee. Also note that a charming quirk of the museum's admission policy waives entrance fees to anyone named Isabella, forever.** ⊠ *280 The Fenway, The Fenway* ☎ *617/566–1401, 617/566–1088 café* ⊕ *www. gardnermuseum.org* ⊡ *$12* ⊙ *Museum Tues.–Sun. 11–5, open some holidays; café Tues.–Fri. 11:30–4, weekends 11–4. Weekend concerts at 1:30* Ⓣ *Museum.*

👪 ▶ 🄾 **Museum of Fine Arts.** Count on staying a while if you have any hope of even beginning to see what's here. Eclecticism and thoroughness, often an incompatible pair, have coexisted agreeably at the MFA since its earliest days. From Renaissance and baroque masters to impressionist marvels to African masks to sublime samples of Native American pottery and contemporary crafts, the collections are happily shorn of both cultural snobbery and shortsighted trendiness.

Fodor'sChoice
★

Founded in 1870, the MFA first resided on the upper floors of the Boston Athenaeum, then a Gothic structure on the site where the Copley Plaza Hotel now stands. As the museum was beginning to outgrow that space, the Fenway area was becoming fashionable, and in 1909 the move was made to Guy Lowell's somewhat severe beaux arts building, to which the West Wing, designed by I. M. Pei, was added in 1981. The move helped cap the half century of expansion of the Back Bay area.

The MFA's collection of approximately 350,000 objects was built from a core of paintings and sculpture from the Boston Athenaeum, historical portraits from the city of Boston, and donations by area universities. The early MFA connoisseurs were as enamored as any cultured Victorians with the great art of European civilizations. Nevertheless, they sought out American works as well; today, the museum's holdings of American art—supplemented by intensive acquisitions in the early 1990s—surpass those of all but two or three U.S. museums. The MFA has more than 60 works by John Singleton Copley; major paintings by Winslow Homer, John Singer Sargent, Fitz Hugh Lane, and Edward Hopper; and a wealth of American works ranging from native New England folk art and colonial portraiture to New York abstract expressionism of the 1950s and 1960s. Also of particular note are the John Singer Sargent paintings adorning the Rotunda. They were specially commissioned for the museum in 1921 and make for a dazzling first impression on visitors coming through the Huntington Street entrance.

American decorative arts are also liberally represented, particularly those of New England in the years before the Civil War. Rooms of period furniture show the progression of taste from the earliest Pilgrim pieces through the 18th-century triumphs of the Queen Anne, Hepplewhite, Sheraton, and Empire styles. Native son Paul Revere, much more than a sounder of alarms, is amply represented as well, with superb silver teapots, sauceboats, and other tableware.

The museum also owns one of the world's most extensive collections of Asian art under one roof. Its Japanese art collection is the finest outside Japan, and Chinese porcelains of the Tang Dynasty are especially well represented. The Egyptian rooms display statuary, furniture, and exquisite gold jewelry; a special funerary-arts gallery exhibits coffins, mummies, and burial treasures. The gathering of classical treasures, including marble busts, jewelry, and glassware, proceeds chronologically from the Cycladic period through the Roman era.

French impressionists abound and are perhaps more comprehensively displayed here than at any other new-world museum outside the Art Institute of Chicago; many of the 38 Monets (the largest collection of his work outside France) vibrate with color. There are canvases by Renoir, Pissarro, Manet, and the American painters Mary Cassatt and Childe Hassam.

Three important galleries explore the art of Africa, Oceania, and the Ancient Americas, expanding the MFA's emphasis on civilizations outside the Western tradition. Highlights include rare examples of the earliest-known figurative sculpture from sub-Saharan Africa, expressive Melanesian works in wood and stone, delicate Olmec jade sculptures, and extraordinary Maya painted ceramics.

The museum has strong collections of textiles, costumes, and prints dating from the 15th century, including many works by Dürer and Goya, and its collection of antique musical instruments is among the finest in the world.

Fifteen second-floor galleries contain the MFA's European painting and sculpture collection, dating from the 11th century to the 20th. Among the standouts are Donatello's marble relief *The Madonna of the Clouds* and J. M. W. Turner's powerful work *The Slave Ship*. Most striking, however, is the **William I. Koch Gallery,** a former tapestry room whose 40-foot-high marble walls are now hung, nearly floor to ceiling, with 53 dramatic Renaissance and baroque paintings by El Greco, Claude Lorraine, Poussin, Rubens, Tintoretto, Titian, Van Dyck, Velázquez, Veronese, and other masters.

The **West Wing,** an airy, well-lighted space, is used primarily to mount special exhibitions, temporary shows drawn from the museum's holdings, and lively contemporary-art and photography exhibits. It also has the Bravo Restaurant, a cafeteria, and a café serving light snacks. From October to April, tea is served from 2:30 to 4 in the second-floor Upper Rotunda, and the year-round cocktail party "MFA Fridays," from 5:30 to 9:30—held weekly in summer and monthly at other times—has become quite the social event. The MFA's Film Program brings new and classic art-house cinema to the museum's theater, often in conjunction with talks with filmmakers. Annual events such as the Boston

French Film Festival and the Boston Jewish Film Festival are also held here. Kids can keep busy with workshops (Tuesday–Sunday) and special programs.

In 2005, the museum broke ground on a massive construction project that the trustees hope will keep it in America's cultural vanguard for the next 100 years. In its first phase, a new **East Wing** will be built to house the Art of the Americas collection, expanding the current gallery space by 50%. The contemporary and 20th-century art collections will move to the Gund Gallery, currently housing temporary exhibitions, and a new special-exhibition space will be built beneath the East Courtyard. Other aspects of the 133-year-old building's enormous face-lift will include a new glass-enclosed courtyard, the reopening of the Fenway entrance, and a "crystal spine" to run the full length of the museum. The first phase of the project is expected to finish in 2009; the museum will remain open during construction. ⊠ *465 Huntington Ave., The Fenway* ☎ *617/267-9300* ⊕ *www.mfa.org* ⊠ *$15, by donation Wed. 4–9:45* ☉ *Sat.–Tues. 10–4:45, Wed.–Fri. 10–9:45. West Wing open Thurs. and Fri. until 9:45. 1-hr tours daily; call for scheduled times* Ⓣ *Museum.*

> ### THE GARDNER HEIST
>
> On March 18, 1990, the Gardner was the target of one of the world's most sensational heists. Thieves disguised as police officers stole 12 works of art with an estimated value of $200–$300 million. Vermeer's *The Concert* was taken, along with works by Rembrandt, Manet, and Degas. To date, none of the art has been recovered, despite a $5 million reward. Because Mrs. Gardner's will prohibited substituting other works for any stolen art, and because of high premiums, the Gardner Museum had chosen not to insure its collections. Empty expanses of wall identify spots where the paintings once hung.

ALSO WORTH SEEING

㉔ **Kenmore Square.** Two blocks north of Fenway Park is Kenmore Square, where you'll find fast-food joints, record stores, and an enormous sign advertising Citgo gasoline. The red, white, and blue neon sign from 1965 is so thoroughly identified with the area that historic preservationists fought, successfully, to save it—proof that Bostonians are an open-minded lot who don't insist that their landmarks be identified with the American Revolution. The old Kenmore Square punk clubs have recently given way to a block-long development of chain stores and pricey restaurants, as well as brick sidewalks, gaslight-style street lamps, and tree plantings. The Hotel Commonwealth, a six-story luxury European-style hotel, sits smack in the middle of Kenmore Square.

In the shadow of Fenway Park between Brookline and Ipswich is **Lansdowne Street,** a nightlife magnet for the young and trendy who have their pick of can't-hear-yourself-think dance clubs such as Avalon and Axis. The urban campus of Boston University begins farther west on Commonwealth Avenue, in blocks thick with dorms, shops, and restaurants. ⊠ *Convergence of Beacon St., Commonwealth Ave., and Brookline Ave.* Ⓣ *Kenmore.*

THE "STREETCAR SUBURBS"

The expansion of Boston in the 1800s was not confined to the Back Bay and the South End. Toward the close of the century, as the working population of the Downtown District swelled and public transportation (first horsecars, then electric trolleys) linked outlying suburbs with the city, development of the "streetcar suburbs" began. These areas answered the housing needs of the rising native-born middle class as well as the second-generation immigrant families already outgrowing the narrow streets of the North and West ends.

The landfill project that became South Boston—known as "Southie" and not to be confused with the South End—isn't a true streetcar suburb; its expansion predates the era of commuting. Some of the brick bowfront residences along East Broadway in City Point date from the 1840s and 1850s, but the neighborhood really came into its own with the influx of Irish around 1900, and Irish-Americans still hold sway here. Southie is a Celtic enclave, as the raucous annual St. Patrick's Day parade attests.

Among the other streetcar suburbs are Dorchester and Jamaica Plain—rural retreats barely more than a century ago that are now thick with tenements and Boston's distinctive three- and six-family triple-decker apartment houses. Dorchester is almost exclusively residential, tricky to navigate by car, and accessible by the T only if you know exactly where you're going. Jamaica Plain is a hip, young neighborhood with a strong lesbian and ecofriendly population; brunch and a wander through the neighborhood's quirky stores or through the Arnold Arboretum makes for a relaxing weekend. Both towns border Franklin Park, an Olmsted creation of more than 500 acres, noted for its zoo. Farther west, Brookline is composed of a mixture of the affluent and students.

Numbers in the margin correspond to numbers on the "Streetcar Suburbs" map.

SOUTH BOSTON

❶ Castle Island Park. South Boston projects farther into the harbor than any other part of Boston except Logan Airport, and the views of the Harbor Islands from along Day Boulevard or Castle Island are expansive. At L Street and Day Boulevard is the L Street Beach, where an intrepid group called the L Street Brownies swims year-round, including a celebratory dip in the icy Atlantic every New Year's Day. Castle Island Park is no longer on an island, but **Fort Independence**, when it was built here in 1801, was separated from the mainland by water. The circular walk from the fort around Pleasure Bay, delightful on a warm summer day, has a stunning view of the city's skyline late at night (South Boston is considered one of the city's safest neighborhoods). The statue near the fort is of Donald McKay, whose clipper ships once sped past this point on their way to California and the Orient. To get here by the T, take the Red Line to Broadway Station. Just outside the station, catch Bus 9 or 11 going east on Broadway, which takes you to within a block of the waterfront. From the waterfront park you can walk the loop, via piers, around the island. ⊠ *Off William J. Day Blvd., South Boston* ☎*617/268–5744* ⊕*www.mass.gov/dcr/parks/metroboston/castle.htm* ⊗ *Tours Memorial Day–Labor Day, weekends noon–3:30, Thurs. 7–dusk; call for specific tour times.*

② **Institute of Contemporary Art.** Housed in a breathtaking cantilevered edifice that juts out over the Boston waterfront, the ICA moved to this site in 2006 as part of a massive reinvention that's seeing the museum grow into one of Boston's most exciting attractions. Since its foundation in 1936, the institute has cultivated its cutting-edge status: it's played host to works by Edvard Munch, Egon Schiele, and Oskar Kokoschka. Andy Warhol, Robert Rauschenberg, and Roy Lichtenstein each mounted pivotal exhibitions here early in their careers. Now the ICA is building a major permanent collection for the first time in its history while continuing to showcase innovative paintings, videos, installations, and multimedia shows. The performing arts get their due in the museum's new theater, and the Water Café features cuisine from Wolfgang Puck. ⊠ *100 Northern Ave., South Boston* ☎*617/478–3100* ⊕*www.icaboston.org* ⊠*$12, free Thurs. 5–9, free for families last Sat. of every month* ⊗ *Tues. and Wed. 10–5, Thurs. and Fri. 10–9, weekends 10–5. Tours on select weekends at 2 and select Thurs. at 6* Ⓣ *Courthouse.*

Fodor's Choice
★

DORCHESTER

③ **Dorchester Heights Monument and National Historic Site.** In 1776 Dorchester Heights hill commanded a clear view of central Boston, where the British had been under siege since the preceding year. Here George Washington set up the cannons that Henry Knox, a Boston bookseller turned soldier, and later secretary of war, had hauled through the wilderness after their capture at Fort Ticonderoga. The artillery did its job of intimidation, and the British troops left Boston, never to return. The view of Boston from the site is magnificent, particularly if you go during the hours the graceful white tower is staffed. Climb its 93 steps and you'll be rewarded with vistas from the Blue Hills to the Harbor Islands, although the lovely park grounds are a destination on their own on a warm day. ⊠ *Thomas Park off Telegraph St., near G St., Dorchester* ☎*617/242–5642* ⊠*Free* ⊗ *Grounds daily. Monument call for schedule.* Ⓣ *Broadway, then City Point Bus (9 or 11) to G St.*

☾ **⑤** **Franklin Park Zoo.** A lion habitat, the Giraffe Savannah, and a 4-acre mixed-species area called the Serengeti Crossing that showcases zebras, ostriches, ibex, and wildebeests keep this zoo roaring. The Tropical Forest, with its renovated Western Lowland Gorilla environment, is a big draw, and wallabies, emus, and kangaroos populate the Australian Outback Trail. From May to September, butterflies flit and flutter at Butterfly Landing, where docents are on hand to answer questions and give advice on attracting the colorful insects to your own garden. The Children's Zoo entices with sheep, goats, and other pet-able beasts. In winter, call in advance to find out which animals are braving the cold.

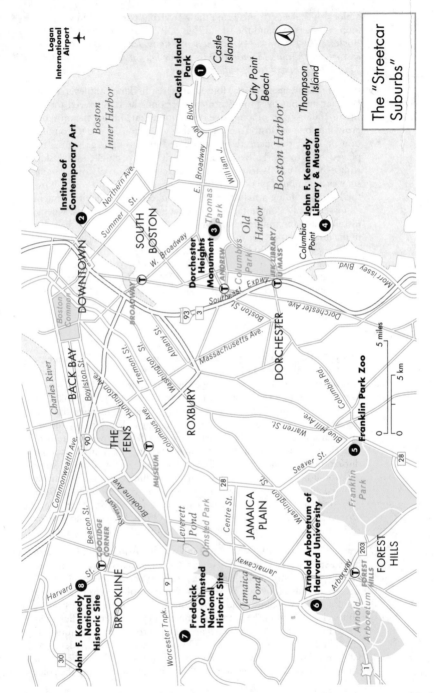

The "Streetcar Suburbs"

Logan International Airport

Castle Island Park ❶
Castle Island
City Point Beach
Thompson Island

Institute of Contemporary Art ❷

Boston Inner Harbor

Boston Harbor

John F. Kennedy Library & Museum ❹
Columbia Point

SOUTH BOSTON

Dorchester Heights Monument ❸
Thomas Park
Old Harbor
Columbus Park

E. Broadway
William J. Day Blvd.
Northern Ave.
Summer St.
W. Broadway
ANDREW

DOWNTOWN
Boston Common
BROADWAY
Tremont St.
Albany St.
Washington St.
Southeast Expwy.
Boston St.
Dorchester Ave.
JFK/LIBRARY/UMASS
Morrissey Blvd.

93
3

DORCHESTER

ROXBURY

Massachusetts Ave.

Columbia Rd.

Blue Hill Ave.

Warren St.

Seaver St.

Franklin Park Zoo ❺
Franklin Park

BACK BAY
Charles River
Boylston St.
Commonwealth Ave.
90
Huntington Ave.
Columbus Ave.

THE FENS
MUSEUM

BROOKLINE
Beacon St.
COOLIDGE CORNER
Brookline Ave.
Harvard St.
9
Worcester Tnpk.

John F. Kennedy National Historic Site ❽

30

Frederick Law Olmsted National Historic Site ❼

Leverett Pond
Olmsted Park
Jamaica Pond
Jamaicaway
Centre St.
28

JAMAICA PLAIN
Washington St.

Arnold Arboretum of Harvard University ❻

Arboway
FOREST HILLS
FOREST HILLS
203
Arnold Arboretum
1

0   5 miles
0   5 km

The park, 4 mi from Downtown, is reached by Bus 16 from the Forest Hills (Orange Line) or Andrew (Red Line) T stops; there's plenty of parking. ⊠ *1 Franklin Park Rd., Dorchester* ☎ *617/541–5466* ⊕ *www. zoonewengland.com* ⊠ *$9.50* ⊗ *Oct.–Mar., daily 10–4; Apr.–Sept., weekdays 10–5, weekends 10–6.*

★ ❹ **John F. Kennedy Library & Museum.** Chronicling a time now passing from memory to history, the library-museum is both a center for serious scholarship and a focus for Boston's nostalgia for her native son. The stark, white, prowlike building (another modernist monument designed by I. M. Pei) at this harbor-enclosed site pays homage to the life and presidency of John F. Kennedy, an Irish-American blessed with charisma, intellect, and passion, and to members of his family, including his wife, Jacqueline, and brother Robert.

The Kennedy Library is the official repository of his presidential papers; the museum displays a trove of Kennedy memorabilia, including re-creations of his desk in the Oval Office and of the television studio in which he debated Richard M. Nixon in the 1960 election. At the entrance, high and dry during the summer months, is the president's 26-foot sailboat; inside, two theaters show a film about his life. The museum exhibits, ranging from the Cuban missile crisis to his assassination, include 20 video presentations. There's also a permanent display on the late Jacqueline Kennedy Onassis, including some samples of her distinctive wardrobe and such personal mementos as a first edition of *One Special Summer,* the book she and her sister wrote and illustrated shortly after a 1951 trip to Paris. A re-creation of the office Robert Kennedy occupied as attorney general from 1961 to 1964 complements "legacy" videos of John's idealistic younger brother. As a somber note in an otherwise gung-ho museum, continuous videos of the first news bulletin of the assassination and the funeral are shown in a darkened hall. Fourth-floor research facilities are open only to serious researchers. The Steven M. Smith Wing provides space for meetings and events; the facility also includes a store and a small café. ⊠ *Columbia Point, Dorchester* ☎ *617/514–1600* ⊕ *www.jfklibrary.org* ⊠ *$10* ⊗ *Daily 9–5* Ⓣ *JFK/UMass, then free shuttle bus every 20 mins.*

JAMAICA PLAIN

❻ **Arnold Arboretum of Harvard University.** This 265-acre living laboratory is
Fodor'sChoice incongruously set in a dense urban area. Established in 1872 in accordance with the terms of a bequest from New Bedford merchant James
★ Arnold, it contains more than 4,000 kinds of woody plants, most from the hardy north temperate zone. The rhododendrons, azaleas, lilacs, magnolias, and fruit trees are eye-popping when in bloom, and something is always in season from early April through September. In October the park puts on a display in blazing colors. Peters Hill has a grand view of the Boston skyline and local surroundings. The Larz Anderson bonsai collection, with individual specimens imported from Japan that are more than 200 years old, includes a 3½-acre Leventritt Shrub and Vine Collection. In the visitor center is a 40-to-1 scale model of

Let Freebies Ring

Freedom may not be free, but Boston's Freedom Trail is—and so are 13 of the 16 attractions that lie along its path, including Faneuil Hall, the USS *Constitution*, and the State House. Better yet, there are free 90-minute tours for visitors who'd like a guided walk, plus free MP3 tours (downloadable at ⊕ *www.boston.com/travel/boston*) for those preferring to go it alone.

Additional themed routes—most notably the Black Heritage Trail, the Irish Heritage Trail, and HarborWalk—can also be enjoyed at no charge. Ditto for outdoor attractions like the city's major monuments, memorials, parks and public gardens. Boston's to-die-for cemeteries (such as the Granary Burying Ground, a preferred resting place for patriots) also have no price tag attached.

Frugal souls can even take complimentary tours of the Boston Athenaeum, the Boston Public Library, and Trinity Church (one of the country's "architectural gems"). October through May, Symphony Hall offers guided tours, too: Boston Pops tickets can be pretty pricey, but every Wednesday afternoon you can see inside their sublime home base without spending a cent.

Other major sites waive admission at set times: among them, the Institute of Contemporary Art (Thursday evening); the Museum of Fine Arts (Wednesday evening); and the Harvard Art Museums (Saturday morning and every day after 4:30). The Isabella Stewart Gardner Museum, meanwhile, is always free for art lovers under 18—as well as for anyone who happens to be named Isabella!

the arboretum (with 4,000 tiny trees), plus an exhibit on "Science in the Pleasure Ground," a kind of "green" history of the landscape. If you visit during May, Lilac Sunday is an annual celebration of blooming trees, Morris dancing, and picnicking. The arboretum, 6 mi from downtown Boston, is accessible by the MBTA Orange Line or Bus 39 from Copley Square to Forest Hills; then follow the signs at the T station. ⊠ *125 Arborway, at Centre St., Jamaica Plain* ☏ *617/524–1718* ⊕ *www.arboretum.harvard.edu* ⊠ *Free* ☉ *Grounds daily dawn–dusk; visitor center weekdays 9–4, Sat. 10–4, Sun. noon–4. Tours Sat. at 10:30, Sun. at 1, and Wed. at 12:15, but not every wk; call to confirm* Ⓣ *Forest Hills.*

BROOKLINE

★ ❼ **Frederick Law Olmsted National Historic Site.** *At this writing, the site was closed for renovation, but it's expected to reopen in late 2009.* Frederick Law Olmsted (1822–1903) is considered the nation's preeminent creator of parks. In 1883 at age 61, while immersed in planning Boston's Emerald Necklace of parks, Olmsted set up his first permanent office at Fairsted, an 18-room farmhouse dating from 1810, to which he added another 18 rooms for his design offices. Plans and drawings on display include projects as the U.S. Capitol grounds, Stanford University, and Mount Royal Park in Montréal. You can also tour the design rooms (some still in use for preservation projects) where Olmsted and staff drew up their plans; highlights include a 1904 "electric blueprint machine," a kind of primitive photocopier. The 1¾-acre site incorporates many trademark Olmstedian designs, including areas of meadow, wild garden, and woodland; Olmsted believed body and spirit could be healed through close association with nature. The site became part of the National Park Service in 1979; Olmsted's office played an influential role in the creation of this federal agency. In 1916 Olmsted's son, who carried on his father's work here, wrote the words that were to serve as a statement of purpose for legislation establishing the Park Service

> **BEER HERE**
>
> Before Prohibition, Jamaica Plain was home to a thriving beer industry, the remnants of which today can be seen in the neighborhood's many 19th-century brick breweries, long since converted to offices and lofts. The **Samuel Adams Brewery** (⊠ *30 Germania St., Jamaica Plain* ☎ *617/368–5080*) is the only hint that the area was once awash in hops, malt, and happy tipplers. Complimentary tastings are the highlight of the brewery's tours.

that same year: "To conserve the scenery and the natural and historic objects and the wildlife therein and to provide for the enjoyment of the same in such manner and by such means as will leave them unimpaired for the enjoyment of future generations." ⊠ *99 Warren St., Brookline* ☎ *617/566–1689* ⊕ *www.nps.gov/frla/home.htm* 🎟 *Free* ☉ *Fri.–Sun. 10–4:30, and by appointment.* Ⓣ *Brookline Hills.*

❽ John F. Kennedy National Historic Site. This was the home of the 35th president from his birth on May 29, 1917, until 1921, when the family moved to nearby Naples and Abbottsford streets. Rose Kennedy provided the furnishings for the restored 2½-story, wood-frame structure. You can pick up a brochure for a walking tour of young Kennedy's school, church, and neighborhood. To get here, take the MBTA Green Line to Coolidge Corner and walk north on Harvard Street four blocks. ⊠ *83 Beals St., Brookline* ☎ *617/566–7937* ⊕ *www.nps.gov/jofi* 🎟 *$3, tours free* ☉ *Mid-May–Nov., Wed.–Sun. 10–4:30, call to confirm; tours every ½ hr 10–3:30, with open house 3:30–4:30* Ⓣ *Coolidge Corner.*

Exploring Cambridge

WORD OF MOUTH

"If the weather's nice, I'd highly recommend walking to or from Harvard Square. You get nice views of Boston across the Charles—you can see the Esplanade, and the view of the Prudential is nice, too. Lots of boathouses as well. For cheap eats near the hotel, check out the Cambridge Brewing Company—great suds and good pub food."

—Rumrita 1

Updated by
Louisa Kasdon

THE CITY OF CAMBRIDGE TAKES a lot of hits—most of them thrown across the Charles River by jealous Bostonians. Cambridge is Boston's Left Bank—an überliberal academic enclave where the city council spends more energy arguing about the regulation of nanotechnologies than on fixing potholes and funding preschools.

The city is punctuated at one end by the funky tech-noids of MIT, and at the other by the soaring—and occasionally seething—rhetoric of the Harvard University community. Civic life connects the two camps into an urban stew of 100,000 residents who represent nearly every nationality in the world, work at every kind of job from tenured professor to taxi driver, and are passionate about living on this side of the river.

The Charles River is Cantabrigians' backyard, running track, and festival ground, and there's virtually no place in Cambridge more than a 10-minute walk from its banks. No visit to Cambridge would be complete without an afternoon (at least) in Harvard Square. It's a hub, a hot spot, and home to every variation of the human condition. A walk down Brattle Street past Henry Wadsworth Longfellow's house is a joy in spring, summer, and fall (you have to be hard core to love Harvard Square in the dead of winter). Farther along Massachusetts Avenue is Central Square, an ethnic melting pot of people and restaurants. Ten minutes more brings you to MIT, with its eclectic architecture, from postwar pedestrian to Frank Gehry's futuristic fantasyland. Take in the best angle for viewing Boston's city skyline, from Smoot's Bridge.

Cambridge dates from 1630, when the Puritan leader John Winthrop chose this meadowland as the site of a carefully planned village he named Newtowne. The Massachusetts Bay Colony chose Newtowne as the site for the country's first college in 1636. Two years later, John Harvard bequeathed half his estate and his private library to the fledgling school, and the college was named in his honor. The town elders changed the name to Cambridge, emulating the university in England where most of the Puritan leaders had been educated.

When Cambridge was incorporated as a city in 1846, the boundaries were drawn to include the university area (today's Harvard Square and Tory Row), and the more-industrial communities of Cambridgeport and East Cambridge. By 1900 the population of these urban industrial and working-class communities, made up of Irish, Polish, Italian, Portuguese, and French Canadian residents, dwarfed the Harvard end of town. Today's city is much more a multiethnic urban community than an academic village. Visitors in search of any kind of ethnic food or music will find it in Cambridge—the local high school educates students who speak more than 40 different languages at home. When MIT, originally Boston Tech, moved to Cambridge in 1916, it was the first educational institution that aimed to be more than a trade school, training engineers but also grounding them in humanities and liberal arts. Many of MIT's postwar graduates remained in the area, and went on to form hundreds of technology-based firms engaged in camera manufacturing, electronics, and space research. By the 1990s, manufacturing had moved to the burbs and software developers, venture capitalists, and robotics and biotech companies claimed the former industrial spaces. This area around Kendall Square is now nicknamed "Intelligence Alley."

GETTING YOUR BEARINGS

Just minutes from Boston, Cambridge is easily reached by taking the Red Line train to any stop past Charles Street. In Cambridge, any commercial area where three or more streets meet in a jumble of traffic and noise has been dubbed a "square." Harvard Square draws the most visitors, but other neighborhood squares exude their own charms. Inman Square, at the intersection of Cambridge and Hampshire streets, has a fine cluster of restaurants and cafés. Central Square, at Massachusetts Avenue (known by locals as "Mass Ave.") and Prospect Street, has Irish pubs, music clubs, and a row of furniture stores. Porter Square, about a mile northwest of Harvard Square on Mass Ave., has several shopping centers and, within the nearby Porter Exchange, a mall filled with Japanese noodle and food shops. Somerville's Davis Square, just over the border of northwest Cambridge and easily accessible on the Red Line, is a hip neighborhood with great eateries, lively bars, and candlepin bowling. At Kendall Square, near the Massachusetts Institute of Technology (MIT) and the heart of the city's thriving biotech industry, an art-house multiplex shows first-run films. The Cambridge Multicultural Arts Center, an intriguing gallery and performance space, is in East Cambridge, near the Cambridgeside Galleria mall and numerous Portuguese cafés and restaurants.

Harvard Square is the best place to begin any visit to Cambridge. The area is notorious for its lack of parking, so consider taking the T. If you insist on driving, avoid endlessly circling the block by pulling into a garage. (The Harvard Square garage is at JFK and Eliot streets, and the University Place garage is behind the Charles Hotel, on University Road at Bennett Street. There's also a small public lot on Church Street.)

HARVARD SQUARE

In Cambridge, all streets point toward Harvard Square. In addition to being the gateway to Harvard University and its various attractions, Harvard Square is home to the tiny yet venerable folk-music club Passim (Bob Dylan played here, and Bonnie Raitt was a regular during her time at Harvard), first-run and vintage movie theaters, concert and lecture venues, and a tempting collection of shops. But real estate is expensive in Harvard Square, and if you are returning after a lapse, you'll notice a shift in the neighborhood's persona. Beloved mom-and-pop shops continue to succumb to proliferating chain-store competitors. The Gap has an outpost in Harvard Square, alongside four Starbucks outlets and three mobile-phone stores. Even the Harvard Coop bookstore is now operated by Barnes & Noble. The good news is that the independent one-of-a-kind shops have migrated north and now line the stretch of Mass Ave. between Harvard and Porter Square.

LOUISA'S TOP 5

- Do the Harvard Museum circuit: the Fogg, the Busch-Reisinger, and the Sackler for art; the Semitic Museum; the Peabody; and the Natural History Museum.

- Visit MIT to wander the halls, visit the museum, and see Frank Gehry's Seuss-like Stata Center.

- Browse the new- and used-book stores, and trawl the artsy boutiques in Harvard Square. Take a break with a hot chocolate at Burdick's (near the Dexter Pratt House), or an espresso at Café Paradiso.

- Breathe the rarefied air of Harvard on an official tour, then return to real life with an ice-cream cone from Herrell's or a burger from Mr. Bartley's Burger Cottage.

- Amble down Brattle Street, visiting the 1700s era homes of Tory Row (Washington really did sleep here.) Have a treat at Hi-Rise bakery in the original Blacksmith House of Longfellow's poem.

Harvard Square is a multicultural microcosm. On a warm day, street musicians coax exotic tones from their Andean pan flutes and Chinese erhus, while cranks and local pessimists pass out pamphlets warning against all sorts of end-of-the-world scenarios. Everyone is on a cell phone, speaking in dozens of languages. In the small plaza atop the main entrance to the Harvard T station known as "the Pit," skaters and punks strut and pose while fresh-faced students impress each other and/or their dates, and quiet clusters study the moves and strategy of the chess players seated outside Au Bon Pain.

TIMING Harvard Square is worth an afternoon, at least—more if you plan to explore Harvard's natural-history or art museums.

➤ A good place to start is the **Cambridge Visitor Information Booth.** Volunteers at this kiosk outside the MBTA station entrance hand out free maps, brochures, and guides about the city. Material available includes a walking tour of historic places, an excellent list of bookstores in the area, and a guide to seasonal events. The booth is supervised by the Cambridge Tourism office at 4 Brattle Street. ⊠*0 Harvard Sq.* ☎*617/497–1630* ⊕*www.cambridge-usa.org* ☉ *Weekdays 9–5, Sat. 10–3, Sun. 1–5* Ⓣ*Harvard.*

Numbers in the box and margin correspond to numbers on the Harvard Square map.

TOP ATTRACTIONS

🔟 **Arthur M. Sackler Museum.** The artistic treasures of the ancient Greeks, Egyptians, and Romans are a major draw here. Make a beeline for the Ancient and Asian art galleries, the permanent installations on the fourth floor, which include Chinese bronzes, Buddhist sculptures, Greek friezes, and Roman marbles. Other exhibits, culled from Harvard's extensive collections, rotate about every other month—it's possible to stumble upon works by Picasso, Klee, Toulouse-Lautrec, or Manet. ⊠*485 Broadway* ☎*617/495–9400* ⊕*www.artmuseums.harvard.edu*

A GOOD WALK

Begin your tour at the **Cambridge Visitor Information Booth** ▶ in **Harvard Square** ❶ near the MBTA station entrance, where you can find maps and information about the entire city, a guide to local bookstores, and brochures that cover walking tours of old Cambridge and seasonal events. Be sure to pick up the MBTA's excellent 25¢ map of the area. If you want to revisit Cambridge's Tory beginnings, walk past the **Wadsworth House** ❷, a clapboard house on Mass Ave. that dates from 1726, and enter the dignified hush of the Yard at **Harvard University** ❸. Stick your nose into **Widener Library** ❹; it houses one of the largest collections of books, historical materials, and journals in the academic world. Then circle back through the yard, crossing Mass Ave. to view the **First Parish in Cambridge and the Old Burying Ground** ❺ on the corner of Church Street. Through the iron railing of the cemetery, you can make out a number of tombstones. Buried here are the remains of 17th- and 18th-century Tory landowners, slaves, and soldiers. Continue up Garden Street to **Christ Church** ❻, designed in 1761 and still an active parish. The Cambridge Common, across Garden Street, has a terrific playground, and is a good spot to take a rest.

Retrace your steps along Mass Ave. and cross the street near the First Parish Church. Cut through Harvard Yard, bearing to your left, pass the

modern Science Center, and look for the striking Victorian architecture of Memorial Hall. If you want to understand what makes Harvard a cultural epicenter, a visit to its museums is advised. It's not just that Harvard has everything, it has the best of everything—from Picassos and Pollacks to Egyptian mummies and Moghul miniatures. Just past Memorial Hall, at the intersection of Quincy and Kirkland streets, turn right onto Kirkland Street and then take a quick left onto Divinity Avenue. At 6 Divinity Avenue is Harvard's **Semitic Museum** ❼. At 11 Divinity Avenue is the entrance to the extensive **Peabody Museum of Archaeology & Ethnology** and the **Harvard Museum of Natural History** ❽ (in the same building).

If you're inclined towards art, cross Harvard Yard to reach Harvard's impressive **Fogg Art Museum** ❾, on Quincy Street at Broadway. The **Arthur M. Sackler Museum** ❿, across Broadway, will show you visions of the ancient world, and the **Carpenter Center for the Visual Arts** ⓫ on Quincy Street offers a strictly contemporary perspective on film and graphic arts. ■TIP➡ **Film lovers: visit the Harvard Web site to find film screenings that coincide with your visit. They are all free.** When you've had your fill of culture, head back to one of the Harvard Square cafés for a snack and serious people-watching.

✉ *$9, includes admission to Fogg Art Museum; free Sat. 10–noon* ⊙ *Mon.–Sat. 10–5, Sun. 1–5* Ⓣ*Harvard.*

❾ **Fogg Art Museum.** Seldom has so much been packed into so small a
FodorśChoice space. Harvard's most famous art museum is a virtual history of art,
★ set in a Gothic interior. It's not overwhelming, rather just the right size to do the collection justice in an hour or two. The more than 80,000

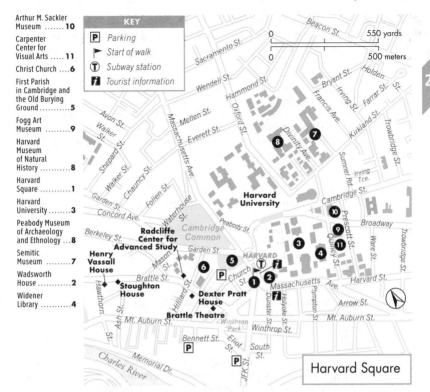

permanent works focus primarily on European, American, and East Asian art. Collections of Italian Renaissance and 19th-century French impressionist paintings include Renoirs and Monets, plus works by van Gogh (*Self-Portrait Dedicated to Paul Gauguin*) and Degas (*The Rehearsal*). There are also works by Gauguin, Whistler, Klee, and Kandinsky. The museum has an impressive collection of decorative arts, including American and English silver, and the curious and distinctly uncomfortable Harvard University "President's Chair," used only at commencement.

Your ticket includes admission to the **Busch-Reisinger Museum,** entered through the Fogg Art Museum. From the serenity of the Fogg's old masters, you step into the jarring and mesmerizing world of German expressionists and other 20th-century artists. The museum was founded in 1902 as the university's Germanic Museum, but its collections now include the modern art considered "degenerate" by the Nazis, and art from central and northern Europe. ⊠*32 Quincy St.* ☎*617/495–9400* ⊕*www.artmuseums.harvard.edu* ☜*$9, includes admission to Arthur M. Sackler Museum; free Sat. 10–noon, daily after 4:30* ☉*Mon.–Sat. 10–5, Sun. 1–5* Ⓣ*Harvard.*

NEED A BREAK?

The Broadway Marketplace (⊠*468 Broadway* ☎*617/547–2334*) is just around the corner from the Fogg Art Museum. Besides the excellent fresh produce, there's a selection of sandwiches and prepared meals; choose one to be heated up and then grab a seat for a quick bite.

8 **Harvard Museum of Natural History.** Many museums promise something for every member of the family; the vast Harvard Museum complex actually delivers. Swiss naturalist Louis Agassiz, who founded the zoology museum, envisioned a museum that would bring under one roof the study of all kinds of life: plants, animals, and humankind. The result is three distinct museums, all accessible for one admission fee.

FodorsChoice ★

The **Museum of Comparative Zoology** traces the evolution of animals and humans. You literally can't miss the 42-foot-long skeleton of the underwater *Kronosaurus.* Dinosaur fossils and a zoo of stuffed exotic animals can occupy young minds for hours. The museum is old-fashioned. You can almost feel the brush of the whiskers of the ardent explorers and the naturalists who combed the world for these treasures. It's also the right size for kids—not jazzy and busy, a good place to ask and answer quiet questions.

Oversize garnets and crystals sparkle at the **Mineralogical and Geological Museum,** founded in 1784. The museum also contains an extensive collection of meteorites.

Perhaps the most famous exhibits of the museum complex are the glass flowers in the **Botanical Museum,** created as teaching tools that would never wither and die. This unique collection holds 3,000 models of 847 plant species. Each one is a masterpiece, meticulously created in glass by a father and son in Dresden, Germany, who worked continuously from 1887 to 1936. Even more amazing than the colorful flower petals are the delicate roots of some plants; numerous signs assure the viewer that everything is, indeed, of glass. ⊠*26 Oxford St.* ☎*617/495–3045* ⊕*www.hmnh.harvard.edu* ☞*$9, includes admission to Peabody Museum of Archaeology & Ethnology, accessible through the museum; free Sun. 9–noon; free Wed. 3–5 Sept.–May* ⊙*Daily 9–5* Ⓣ*Harvard.*

1 **Harvard Square.** Tides of students, tourists, political-cause proponents, and bizarre street creatures are all part of the nonstop pedestrian flow at this most celebrated of Cambridge crossroads.

FodorsChoice ★

Harvard Square is where Mass Ave., coming from Boston, turns and widens into a triangle broad enough to accommodate a brick peninsula (above the T station). The restored 1928 kiosk in the center of the square once served as the entrance to the MBTA station (it's now a newsstand). Harvard Yard, with its lecture halls, residential houses, libraries, and museums, is one long border of the square; the other three are comprised of clusters of banks and a wide variety of restaurants and shops.

On an average afternoon, you'll hear earnest conversations in dozens of foreign languages; see every kind of youthful uniform from Goth to impeccable prep; wander by street musicians playing Andean flutes, singing opera, and doing excellent Stevie Wonder or Edith Piaf imitations; and lean in on a tense outdoor game of pickup chess between a street-tough kid and an older gent wearing a beard and a beret, while you slurp a cappuccino or an ice-cream cone (the two major food groups here). An afternoon in the square is people-watching raised to a high art; the parade of quirkiness never quits.

As entertaining as the locals are, Harvard Square has fine inanimate attractions, too. The historic buildings are worth noting and it's still a thrill to walk though the big brick-and-wrought-iron gates to Harvard Yard, past the residence halls and statues, on up to Widener Library.

Across Garden Street, through an ornamental arch, is **Cambridge Common,** decreed a public pasture in 1631. It's said that under a large tree that once stood in this meadow George Washington took command of the Continental Army on July 3, 1775. A stone memorial now marks the site of the "Washington Elm." Also on the Common is the Irish Famine Memorial by Derry artist Maurice Herron, unveiled in 1997 to coincide with the 150th anniversary of "Black '47," the deadliest year of the potato famine. It depicts a desperate Irish mother sending her child off to America. At the center of the Common, a large memorial commemorates the Union soldiers and sailors who lost their lives in the Civil War. ⊕*www.harvardsquare.com* Ⓣ*Harvard.*

NEED A BREAK?

Herrell's Ice Cream (⊠*15 Dunster St., Harvard Sq.* ☎*617/497–2179*) is a Harvard Square institution: the mix-ins, the hand-rolled cones, nine flavors of chocolate. The friendly scoopers are young, punk Cambridge—their tattoos and body piercings an odd counterpoint to the sweet sundaes.

★ ❸ **Harvard University.** The tree-studded, shady, and redbrick expanse of Harvard Yard—the very center of Harvard University—has weathered the footsteps of Harvard students for more than 300 years. In 1636 the Great and General Court of the Massachusetts Bay Colony voted funds to establish the colony's first college and a year later chose Cambridge as the site. Named in 1639 for John Harvard, a young Charlestown clergyman who died in 1638 and left the college his entire library and half his estate, Harvard remained the only college in the New World until 1693, by which time it was firmly established as a respected center of learning. Local wags refer to Harvard as WGU—World's Greatest University—and it is certainly the oldest and most famous American university. It boasts numerous schools or "faculties," including the Faculty of Arts and Sciences, the Medical School, the Law School, the Business School, and the John F. Kennedy School of Government.

Although the college dates from the 17th century, the oldest buildings in Harvard Yard are of the 18th century; together the buildings chronicle American architecture from the colonial era to the present. **Holden Chapel,** completed in 1744, is a Georgian gem. The graceful **University Hall** was designed in 1815 by Charles Bulfinch. An 1884 statue of John Harvard by Daniel Chester French stands outside; ironically for a school with the motto of "Veritas" ("Truth"), the model for the statue was a member of the class of 1882, as there is no known con-

Cambridge

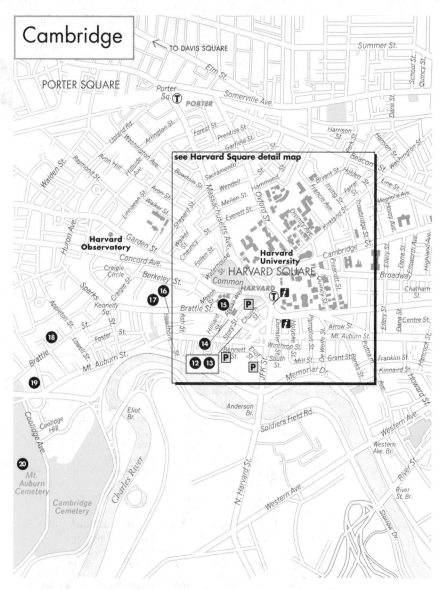

TO DAVIS SQUARE

Summer St.

PORTER SQUARE

Porter Sq. **T** **PORTER**

Elm St.

Somerville Ave.

see Harvard Square detail map

Harvard Observatory

Harvard University

HARVARD SQUARE

Common

T **i**

i

15

16

17

18

19

12 **13**

14

20
Mt. Auburn Cemetery

Cambridge Cemetery

Charles River

Eliot Br.

Anderson Br.

Soldiers Field Rd.

Western Ave.

Memorial Dr.

Western Ave. Br.

River St. Br.

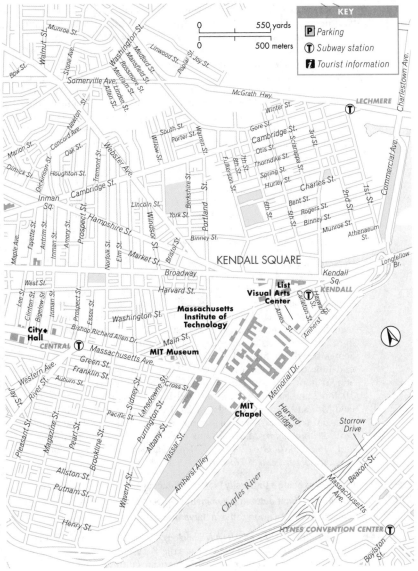

temporary likeness of Harvard himself. **Sever Hall,** completed in 1880 and designed by Henry Hobson Richardson, represents the Romanesque revival that was followed by the neoclassical (note the pillared facade of Widener Library) and the neo-Georgian, represented by the sumptuous brick houses along the Charles River, many of which are now undergraduate residences. **Memorial Church,** a graceful steepled edifice of modified Colonial revival design, was dedicated in 1932. Just north of the Yard is **Memorial Hall,** completed in 1878 as a memorial to Harvard men who died in the Union cause; it's High Victorian both inside and out. It also contains the 1,166-seat Sanders Theatre, site of year-round concerts—student and professional—and the venue for the festive Christmas Revels.

Many of Harvard's cultural and scholarly facilities are important sights in themselves, including the **Arthur M. Sackler Museum,** the **Fogg Art Museum,** the **Harvard Museum of Natural History,** the **Peabody Museum of Archaeology & Ethnology,** and the **Widener Library.** However, be aware that most campus buildings, other than museums and concert halls, are off-limits to the general public.

Harvard University Events & Information Center (⊠ *Holyoke Center, 1350 Massachusetts Ave.* ☎ *617/495–1573* ⊕ *www.harvard.edu*), run by students, includes a small library, a video-viewing area, computer terminals, and an exhibit space. It also distributes maps of the university area and has free student-led tours of Harvard Yard. The tour doesn't include visits to museums, and it doesn't take you into campus buildings, but it provides a fine orientation. The information center is open September through mid-June, Monday through Saturday 9–5; from mid-June through August it's open Monday through Saturday 9–7, Sunday noon–5. During the academic year tours are given weekdays at 10 and 2 and Saturday at 2; from mid-June through August, tours are held Monday through Saturday at 10, 11:15, 2, and 3:15. Call to confirm tour schedules, especially if you are visiting outside the academic year. ⊠ *Bounded by Massachusetts Ave., Mt. Auburn St., Holyoke St., and Dunster St.* ☎ *617/495–1573 for Harvard directory assistance* ⊕ *www.harvard.edu* ⊤ *Harvard.*

DID YOU KNOW?

One perk of being a University Professor (holding an endowed chair)—a title awarded to about a dozen preeminent members of the Harvard faculty—is the official right to graze cattle in Harvard Yard.

❽ Peabody Museum of Archaeology & Ethnology. With one of the world's outstanding anthropological collections, the Peabody focuses on Native American and Central and South American cultures; there are also interesting displays on Africa. The Hall of the North American Indian is particularly outstanding, with art, textiles, and models of traditional dwellings from across the continent. The Mesoamerican room juxtaposes ancient relief carvings and weavings with contemporary works from the Maya and other peoples. ⊠ *11 Divinity Ave.* ☎ *617/496– 1027* ⊕ *www.peabody.harvard.edu* 🎫 *$9, includes admission to Harvard Museum of Natural History, accessible through the museum; free Sun. 9–noon; free Wed. 3–5 Sept.–May* ⊙ *Daily 9–5* ⊤ *Harvard.*

ALSO WORTH SEEING

 Carpenter Center for the Visual Arts. This gravity-defying mass of concrete and glass, built in 1963 to contrast with the more-traditional Fogg Art Museum next door, is the only building in North America designed by the French architect Le Corbusier. The open floor plan provides students with five stories of flexible workspace, and the ramp penetrating the building ensures that the creative process is always visible and public. The center regularly holds free lectures and receptions with artists on Thursday evenings. At the top of the ramp, the **Sert Gallery** plays host to changing exhibits of contemporary works and has a café. The Main Gallery on the ground floor often showcases work by students and faculty. The **Harvard Film Archive** downstairs screens films nightly, often accompanied by discussions with the filmmakers. ⊠*24 Quincy St.* ☎*617/495–3251* ⊕*www.ves.fas.harvard. edu* ☞*Galleries free, film screenings $8* ⊗*Mon.–Sat. 9am–11:30pm, Sun. noon–11:30* Ⓣ*Harvard.*

❻ **Christ Church.** This modest, gray, clapboard structure was designed in 1761 by Peter Harrison, the first architect of note in the Colonies. During the Revolution, members of its mostly Tory congregation fled for their lives. The organ was melted down for bullets and the building was used as a barracks during the Siege of Boston. (Step into the vestibule to look for the bullet hole left during the skirmish.) Martha Washington requested that the church reopen for services on New Year's Eve in 1775. The church's historical significance extends to the 20th century: Teddy Roosevelt was a Sunday school teacher here, and Martin Luther King Jr. spoke from the pulpit to announce his opposition to the Vietnam War. ⊠*0 Garden St.* ☎*617/876–0200* ⊕*www.cccambridge.org* ⊗*Sun.–Fri. 7:30–6, Sat. 7:30–3; Sun. services at 8 AM and 10 AM, with choral evensong at 5; Tues. and Wed. services at 12:10* Ⓣ*Harvard.*

NEED A BREAK? The classic university-town Euro café is Café Paradiso (⊠*1 Eliot St., Harvard Sq.* ☎*617/868–3240*). Stop in for a light lunch of a salad or a panini, an espresso, or an Italian soda. Sip and opine with the rest of Cantabrigia. Bring a journal or a newspaper (preferably one in a foreign language), and you'll be taken for a local.

❺ **First Parish in Cambridge and the Old Burying Ground.** Next to the imposing church on the corner of Church Street and Mass Ave., a spooky-looking colonial graveyard houses 17th- and 18th-century tombstones of ministers, early Harvard presidents, and Revolutionary War soldiers. The wooden Gothic Revival church, known locally as "First Church" or "First Parish," was built in 1833 by Isaiah Rogers. The congregation dates to two centuries earlier, and has been linked to Harvard since the founding of the college. The church sponsors the popular lecture series **"Forum"** (☎*617/495–2727* ⊕*www.cambridgeforum.org*), featuring well-known authors and academics. ⊠*3 Church St.* ☎*617/876–7772* ⊕*www.firstparishcambridge.org* ⊗*Church weekdays 8–4, Sun. 8–1, service at 10:30. Burying ground daily dawn–dusk* Ⓣ*Harvard.*

❼ Semitic Museum. An almost unknown gem, this Harvard institution serves as an exhibit space for Egyptian, Mesopotamian, and ancient Near East artifacts and as a center for archaeological exploration. Who knew that the Sphinx may have had curls? The museum's extensive collection rotates among temporary exhibits. The building also houses the Department of Near Eastern Languages and Civilization, with offices tucked among the artifacts. Note that there are no elevators. ✉*6 Divinity Ave.* ☎*617/495–4631* ⊕*www.fas.harvard.edu/~semitic* ☜*Free* ⊙ *Weekdays 10–4, Sun. 1–4* Ⓣ*Harvard.*

❷ Wadsworth House. On the Harvard University side of Harvard Square stands the Wadsworth House, a yellow clapboard structure built in 1726 as a home for Harvard presidents. It served as the first head-quarters for George Washington, who arrived on July 2, 1775, to take command of the Continental Army, which he did the following day. The house, closed to the public, now houses the Alumni Office and the offices of Harvard's library director. ✉*1341 Massachusetts Ave.* Ⓣ*Harvard.*

❹ Widener Library. Harvard University's Harry Elkins Widener Library was named for a young book lover who went down with the *Titanic*. (It's said that Widener went back to his stateroom to retrieve a first edition of Roger Bacon's *Essays*.) Holding more than 15 million volumes in more than 90 libraries around the world, the Harvard University Library system is second in size in the United States only to the Library of Congress, and Widener Library itself is one of the world's largest individual book repositories. Sixty-five miles of bookshelves snake around six stories above and four stories belowground. The imposing neoclassical structure was designed by the nation's first major African-American architect, Julian Abele. The library isn't open to the public; people with a "scholarly need" can apply for admission at the privileges office inside. ✉*Harvard Yard* ☎*617/495–2411* ⊕*hcl.harvard.edu/widener* Ⓣ*Harvard.*

BRATTLE STREET/TORY ROW

Brattle Street remains one of New England's most elegant thorough-fares. Elaborate mansions line both sides from where it meets JFK Street to Fresh Pond Parkway. Brattle Street was once dubbed Tory Row because during the 1770s its seven mansions, on lands that stretched to the river, were owned by staunch supporters of King George. These properties were appropriated by the patriots when they took over Cambridge in the summer of 1775. Many of the historic houses are marked with blue signs, and although only two (the Hooper-Lee-Nichols House and the Longfellow National Historic Site) are fully open to the public, it's easy to imagine yourself back in the days of Ralph Waldo Emerson and Henry David Thoreau as you stroll the brick sidewalks. Less than 2 mi down Brattle Street from Harvard Square stretches Mt. Auburn Cemetery, an exquisitely landscaped garden cemetery.

A GOOD WALK

Begin your walk in Harvard Square at Winthrop Park, a small open space surrounded by bookstores, music shops, clothing outlets, and restaurants, near the juncture of Mt. Auburn and JFK streets. (Note the sign, a favorite of locals, on the American Express Travel Service office: PLEASE GO AWAY OFTEN.) Walk one block along Mt. Auburn as it curves to your right to reach Brattle Street. Proceeding on Brattle Street past a shopping complex, you pass on your left the **Brattle Theatre** ⑫, followed by the **Brattle House** ⑬, an 18th-century Colonial that now serves as headquarters of the Cambridge Center for Adult Education. Another block farther, past the Crate & Barrel store and two historic apothecaries, you pass on the left the yellow **Dexter Pratt House** ⑭, also known as the Blacksmith House, immortalized in Longfellow's "The Village Blacksmith." Continue up Brattle just past Hilliard Street. On your left is the Loeb Drama Center, at 64 Brattle Street, where the American Repertory Theatre is based. Across Brattle Street on your right is the **Radcliffe Institute for Advanced Study** ⑮, formerly Radcliffe College.

Continue on Brattle to the next corner with Ash Street to **Henry Vassall House** ⑯, at the intersection of Hawthorn Street. Across Brattle Street to your right is **Longfellow National Historic Site** ⑰, a mansion built in 1759 by John Vassall Jr. Continuing along Brattle, you reach No. 159, the **Hooper-Lee-Nichols House** ⑱, one of the few Tory homes open to the public. At No. 175 Brattle stands the Ruggles-Fayerweather House, a white Georgian structure built in 1764 that was taken over by revolutionaries in August 1775 and served as a hospital after the Battle of Bunker Hill. At the next corner turn left onto Elmwood Avenue. At the intersection of Fresh Pond Parkway is **Elmwood** ⑲, another Georgian home and now the official residence of Harvard's president.

Continue west and cross Fresh Pond Parkway and Mt. Auburn Street. Continue slightly uphill and west on Mt. Auburn to **Mt. Auburn Cemetery** ⑳. After exploring the cemetery (maps are provided) you can retrace your steps or catch Bus 71 or 73 just outside the cemetery to get back to the square. Or you can follow Mt. Auburn east, cross over to Memorial Drive on your right, and walk back along the Charles River to JFK Street. This is especially pleasant on summer Sundays, when this section of Memorial Drive is closed to car traffic.

TIMING If you opt to walk all the way to Mt. Auburn Cemetery (it's about 1½ mi from Longfellow National Historic Site), allot two to three hours for a leisurely stroll. In good weather, it's a joy, a kind of country paradise within the borders of the city.

Numbers in the box and margin correspond to the Cambridge map.

★ ⑰ **Longfellow National Historic Site.** Henry Wadsworth Longfellow, the poet whose stirring tales of the Village Blacksmith, Evangeline, Hiawatha, and Paul Revere's midnight ride thrilled 19th-century America, once lived in this elegant mansion. If there's one historic house to visit in

Cambridge, this is it. The house was built in 1759 by John Vassall Jr., and is one of the seven original Tory Row homes on Brattle Street; George Washington lived here during the Siege of Boston from July 1775 to April 1776. Longfellow first boarded here in 1837, and later received the house as a gift from his father-in-law on his marriage to Frances Appleton, who burned to death here in an accident in 1861. For 45 years Longfellow wrote his famous verses here and filled the house with the exuberant spirit of his own work and that of his literary circle, which included Ralph Waldo Emerson, Nathaniel Hawthorne, and Charles Sumner, an abolitionist senator. Upon his death, the poet left the house in trust to his descendants, and every aspect of the house—from the wallpaper to the books on his shelves—has been preserved for future generations. ■TIP→ **Longfellow Park, across the street, is the place to stand to take photos of Longfellow's house.** The park was created to preserve the view immortalized in the poet's "To the River Charles." ⊠ *105 Brattle St.* ☎*617/876–4491* ⊕*www.nps. gov/long* ☜*$3* ☉ *Tours June–Oct., Wed.–Sun. 10:30–4* Ⓣ*Harvard.*

⑬ Brattle House. This 18th-century, gambrel-roof Colonial once belonged to the Loyalist William Brattle. He moved to Boston in 1774 to escape the patriots' anger, then left in 1776 with the British troops. From 1831 to 1833 the house was the residence of Margaret Fuller, feminist author and editor of *The Dial.* Today it's the office of the Cambridge Center for Adult Education and is listed on the National Register of Historic Places. ⊠ *42 Brattle St.* ☎*617/547–6789* ⊕*www.ccae.org* ☉*Mon.– Thurs. 9–9, Fri. 9–7, Sat. 9–2. Summer hrs vary* Ⓣ*Harvard.*

⑫ Brattle Theatre. Occupying a squat, barnlike building from 1890, the Brattle Theatre is set improbably between a modern shopping center and a Colonial mansion. The resident repertory company gained notoriety in the 1950s when it made a practice of hiring actors blacklisted as Communists by the U.S. government. For the last half century it has served as the square's independent movie house, screening indie, foreign, obscure, and classic films, from nouveau to noir. ⊠ *40 Brattle St.* ☎*617/876–6837* ⊕*www.brattlefilm.org* Ⓣ*Harvard.*

▌**NEED A BREAK?**   **Algiers Coffee House** (⊠ *40 Brattle St.* ☎ *617/492–1557*), upstairs from the Brattle Theatre, is a favorite evening hangout for young actors and artists. Linger over your mint tea or plate of hummus, and don't expect rapid service.

⑭ Dexter Pratt House. Also known as the "Blacksmith House," this yellow Colonial is now owned by the Cambridge Center for Adult Education. The tree itself is long gone, but this spot inspired Longfellow's lines: "Under a spreading chestnut tree, the village smithy stands." The blacksmith's shop, today commemorated by a granite marker, was next door, at the corner of Story Street. ⊠ *56 Brattle St.* Ⓣ*Harvard.*

▌**NEED A BREAK?**   The **Hi-Rise Bread Company** in the Blacksmith House (☎*617/492–3003*), on the first floor of the Dexter Pratt House, is the perfect stop for a pick-me-up coffee and fresh-baked treat or fantastic sandwich on their homemade bread.

Snag a table at the outdoor café; it's a choice spot for people-watching. Chocolate lovers may be seduced by the aromas emanating from L. A. Burdick Chocolates (⊠*52 Brattle St.* ☎*617/491-4340* ⊕*www.burdickchocolate. com*); rich confections or elegant hot cocoa may be just the things to restore flagging spirits.

2

⓳ **Elmwood.** Shortly after its construction in 1767, this three-story Georgian house was abandoned by its owner, colonial governor Thomas Oliver. Elmwood House was home to the accomplished Lowell family for two centuries. Elmwood is now the Harvard University president's residence ever since student riots in the 1960s drove President Nathan Pusey from his house in Harvard Yard. ⊠*33 Elmwood Ave.* Ⓣ*Harvard.*

⓰ **Henry Vassall House.** One of Brattle Street's seven Tory houses occupied by wealthy families linked by friendship, if not blood, the house may have been built as early as 1636. In 1737 it was purchased by John Vassall Sr.; four years later he sold it to his younger brother, Henry. It was used as a hospital during the Revolution, and the traitor Dr. Benjamin Church was held here as a prisoner. The house was remodeled during the 19th century. It's now a private residence. ⊠*94 Brattle St.* Ⓣ*Harvard.*

⓲ **Hooper-Lee-Nichols House.** Now headquarters of the Cambridge Historical Society, this is one of two Tory-era homes on Brattle Street fully open to the public. (The Emerson family gave it to the society in 1957.) Built between 1685 and 1690, the house has been remodeled at least six times but has maintained much of the original structure. The downstairs is elegantly, although sparsely, appointed with period books, portraits, and wallpaper. An upstairs bedroom has been furnished with period antiques, some belonging to the original residents. Visits are by tour only; tours run about one hour. ⊠*159 Brattle St.* ☎*617/547–4252* 🎫*$5* 🕐*Tours Tues. and Thurs. at 2, 3, and 4* Ⓣ*Harvard.*

⓴ **Mt. Auburn Cemetery.** A cemetery might not strike you as a first choice for a visit, but this one is a pleasure. Opened in 1831, it was the country's first garden cemetery, and more than 90,000 people have been buried here—among them Henry Wadsworth Longfellow, Mary Baker Eddy, Winslow Homer, Amy Lowell, social reformer Dorothea Dix, and architect Charles Bullfinch. The grave of engineer Buckminster Fuller bears an engraved geodesic dome. In spring, local nature lovers and bird-watchers come out of the woodwork to see the warbler migrations and the glorious blossoms. Brochures, maps, and audio tours are at the entrance. Picnicking, jogging, and bicycling are not permitted. ⊠*580 Mt. Auburn St.* ☎*617/547–7105* 🕐*May–Sept., daily 8–7; Oct.–Apr., daily 8–5* Ⓣ*Harvard; then Watertown (71) or Waverly (73) bus to cemetery.*

⓯ **Radcliffe Institute for Advanced Study.** The famed women's college, situated around a serene yard, was founded in 1879 and wedded to Harvard University in 1977. It was subsumed under Harvard in 1999, when

ALL IN GOOD FUN

Harvard's Hasty Pudding Club is well known for its theatricals—its pun-filled burlesque shows have elicited groans from audiences for over a century. The similarly irreverent Harvard Lampoon has been influencing American comedy since the club's inception; early members wrote for the *New Yorker,* while more recently it has proven fertile ground for television comics and writers: the *National Lampoon, Saturday Night Live,* and *The Simpsons* were all spawned by its alumni. The *Lampoon Castle* (simultaneously located at 44 Bow Street, 14 Linden Street, 17 Plympton Street, and 57 Mt. Auburn Street), replete with hidden doors and secret passages, was built for the club in 1909 by William Randolph Hearst and Boston socialite Isabella Stewart Gardner. The copper ibis on top is reputedly electrified to ward off pranksters from the daily *Harvard Crimson* newspaper, who at the height of the Cold War cut it down and formally presented it to the Soviet Union as a "gift from the students of America." Connections at the State Department had to be called in to retrieve the purloined bird.

its name officially changed from Radcliffe College. ✉ *10 Garden St.* ☎ *617/495–8601* ⊕ *www.radcliffe.edu* Ⓣ *Harvard.*

NEED A BREAK? Once beyond the vicinity of Harvard Square, Brattle Street lacks eateries, so before your walk consider stocking up at Darwin's Ltd. (✉ *148 Mt. Auburn St.* ☎ *617/354–5233*), which carries delectable, Cambridge-inspired sandwiches and other "comestibles and spirituous provisions."

KENDALL SQUARE/MIT

Harvard Square may be the center of the "People's Republic of Cambridge," but the Kendall Square neighborhood is the city's hard-driving capitalist core. Gritty industrial buildings share space with sleek office blocks and the sprawling Massachusetts Institute of Technology. Although the MIT campus may lack the ivied elegance of Harvard Yard, major modern architects, including Alvar Aalto, Frank Gehry, I. M. Pei, and Eero Saarinen, created signature buildings here. To reach MIT, take the Red Line T to Kendall station; if you're headed for the MIT Museum on the western edge of the campus, the Central Square station is more convenient.

TOP ATTRACTIONS

List Visual Arts Center. Local Boston-area artists and art students consider the List Gallery to be the most interesting gallery in town. Founded by Albert and Vera List, pioneer collectors of modern art, this MIT center has three galleries showcasing exhibitions of cutting-edge art and mixed media. Works from the center's collection of contemporary art, such as Thomas Hart Benton's painting *Fluid Catalytic Crackers* and Harry Bertoia's altarpiece for the MIT Chapel, are on view here and around campus. The center's Web site includes a map indicating the locations of more than 25 of these works. ✉ *Wiesner Bldg., 20*

Ames St., off Main St. ☎*617/253–4680* ⊕*web.mit.edu/lvac* ✉*Free* ☽*Sept.–July, Tues.–Thurs. noon–6, Fri. noon–8, weekends noon–6* ⓣ*Kendall/MIT.*

Massachusetts Institute of Technology. Celebrated for both its brains and its cerebral sense of humor, this once-tidy engineering school at right angles to the Charles River is growing like a sprawling adolescent, consuming old industrial buildings and city blocks with every passing year. Once dissed as "the factory," particularly by its Ivy League neighbor, MIT mints graduates that are the sharp blades on the edge of the information revolution.

Founded in 1861, MIT moved to Cambridge from Copley Square in the Back Bay in 1916. It has long since fulfilled the predictions of its founder, the geologist William Barton Rogers, that it would surpass "the universities of the land in the accuracy and the extent of its teachings in all branches of positive science." Its emphasis shifted in the 1930s from practical engineering and mechanics to the outer limits of scientific fields.

Architecture is important at MIT. Although the original buildings were obviously designed by and for scientists, many represent pioneering designs of their times. The **Kresge Auditorium,** designed by Eero Saarinen, with a curving roof and unusual thrust, rests on three, instead of four, points. The nondenominational **MIT Chapel,** a circular Saarinen design, is lighted primarily by a roof oculus that focuses natural light on the altar and by reflections from the water in a small surrounding moat; it's topped by an aluminum sculpture by Theodore Roszak. The serpentine **Baker House,** now a dormitory, was designed in 1947 by the Finnish architect Alvar Aalto in such a way as to provide every room with a view of the Charles River. Sculptures by Henry Moore and other notable artists dot the campus.

The East Campus, which has grown around the university's original neoclassical buildings of 1916, also has outstanding modern architecture and sculpture, including the stark high-rise **Green Building** by I. M. Pei, housing the Earth Science Center. Just outside is Alexander Calder's giant stabile (a stationary mobile) *The Big Sail.* Another Pei work on the East Campus is the **Wiesner Building,** designed in 1985, which houses the **List Visual Arts Center.** Architect Frank Gehry made his mark on the campus with the cockeyed, improbable **Ray & Maria Stata Center,** a complex of

CAMPUS PRANKSTERS

A popular recurring exhibit at the MIT Museum is the "Hall of Hacks," a look at the pranks MIT students have played over the years. Most notable here is a rare photo of Oliver Reed Smoot Jr., a 1958 MIT Lambda Chi Alpha pledge. Smoot's future fraternity brothers used the diminutive freshman to measure the distance of the nearby Harvard Bridge. Every 5 feet and 6 inches became "one Smoot." The markings on the bridge are repainted by the frat every 2 years, and Boston police actually use them to indicate location when filing accident reports. All told, the bridge is "364.4 Smoots plus 1 ear" long.

buildings on Vassar Street. The center houses computer, artificial intelligence, and information systems laboratories, and is reputedly as confusing to navigate on the inside as it is to follow on the outside. East Campus's **Great Dome,** which looms over neoclassical Killian Court, has often been the target of student "hacks," and has at various times supported a telephone booth with a ringing phone, a life-size statue of a cow, and a campus police cruiser. Nearby, the domed **Rogers Building** has earned unusual notoriety as the center of a series of hallways and tunnels dubbed "the infinite corridor." Twice each winter, the sun's path lines up perfectly with the corridor's axis, and at dusk students line the third-floor hallway to watch the sun set through the westernmost window. The phenomenon is known as "MIT-henge."

MIT maintains an information center in the Rogers Building and offers free tours of the campus weekdays at 10:45 and 2:45. General hours for the information center are weekdays 9–5. ⊠*77 Massachusetts Ave.* ☎*617/253–4795* ⊕*web.mit.edu* Ⓣ*Kendall/MIT.*

<table>
<tr><td>▮
NEED A
BREAK?</td><td>**Toscanini's Ice Cream** (⊠*899 Main St.* ☎*617/491–5877*) is a well-loved local spot, specializing in all sorts of creative flavors. Also a good place for coffee, the shop frequently has small art exhibits. From the MIT Museum it's two blocks up Mass Ave. toward Central Square; look for it on the right.</td></tr>
</table>

ALSO WORTH SEEING

☾ **MIT Museum.** A place where art and science meet, the MIT Museum displays photos, paintings, and scientific instruments and memorabilia in a dynamic, hands-on setting. The world's largest collection of holograms is downright eye-popping, though young kids may prefer the moving gestural sculptures of Arthur Ganson. The robot room shows off inventions of MIT's renowned robotics lab and an extensive exhibit on artificial intelligence. ⊠*265 Massachusetts Ave.* ☎*617/253–4444* ⊕*web.mit.edu/museum* ☙*$5* ☾ *Tues.–Fri. 10–5, weekends noon–5* Ⓣ*Kendall/MIT.*

Where to Eat

WORD OF MOUTH

"Absolutely go into the North End of Boston and go hungry. Eat your way through. There are so many wonderful restaurants there. I have never been to a bad one. Some are pricey. Some are not."

—mahs

"Excelsior is amazing. Hamersley's Bistro is fabulous. Les Zygomates can be fun, and at Rialto in the Charles Hotel parking is easy."

—escargot

Updated by
Erin Byers
Murray

WHEN IT COMES TO FOOD, in Boston the Revolution never ended. While Bostonians have proudly clung to their traditional eats (chowders, baked beans, and cream pies can still be found) most diners now choose innovative food without excessive formality. There are still palaces of grand cuisine, but Boston and Cambridge now favor the kind of restaurant overseen by a creative mastermind, often locally born, concocting inspired food served in human surroundings.

Bostonians have caught the passion for artisanal breads, cafés with homemade pastries, and all manner of exquisite and unique specialties. As an example, many high-end restaurants have added uncommon flavors of ice cream—central to Boston living for more than 150 years—to their menus. A young generation of highly trained and well-traveled chefs is reclaiming the regional cuisine. It turns out that the area's wild mushrooms work in a ragout, the cheddar makes a fine quiche, the clambake can be miniaturized, and rabbit fits into a savory ravioli.

A rule of thumb is to seek out what the locals most enjoy—the fish and shellfish abundant from the nearby shores. Although the city has many notable seafood restaurants, almost anyplace you eat will likely have two or three offerings from the sea. Treatments used to be limited to lobsters boiled or baked and fish broiled or fried, but nowadays chefs are more inventive. You may be offered a wood-roasted lobster with vanilla sauce or, in a Chinese restaurant, lobster stir-fried with ginger and scallion. Others are pushing scallops sliced thin and served raw under a dab of olive oil and chickpea puree.

Anything spicy and different has long been popular in the university culture of Cambridge, and the high rate of immigration in recent decades has fueled Bostonians' appetite for foreign cuisines. Variety abounds, evoking the bygone aristocracies of Russia, Persia, Thailand, Ethiopia, or Cambodia, or serving large immigrant communities from Latin America, Asia, Europe, and Africa. In the last few years, an influx of Italian restaurants, both traditional and contemporary, have landed on city corners outside the North End.

The dominant trend today, however, is homegrown—both on the plate and in the kitchen. Because most of Boston's talented chefs have worked their way up the ranks in local kitchens, they prefer to sponsor and cultivate their sous-chefs rather than hire anonymous talent. And while a handful of local chefs have garnered celebrity status, the city has yet to draw (some might say invite) big-name, nationally known chefs into its tight-knit circle.

To find the best around Boston—gustatorily speaking—follow the roads that radiate out from Downtown like the spokes of a giant wheel. Smack inside the hub are the huge, and hugely famous, waterfront seafood restaurants—but go north, west, or south and you're suddenly in the neighborhoods, home to numerous smaller restaurants on the way up.

KNOW-HOW

Like most cities, Boston has its dining dos and don'ts. Here are a few that are good to know.

WHAT TO WEAR

Boston is a notch or two more reserved in its fashion than New York or Los Angeles. Its dining dress code normally hovers at the level of casual chic. Few of the city's most formal restaurants require jackets and even at some of the most expensive places jeans are acceptable as long as they're paired with a dressy top and posh shoes. Shorts are appropriate only in the most casual spots. When in doubt, call and ask.

MEALTIMES

Boston's restaurants close relatively early; most shut their doors by 10 or 11 PM, and a few have bars that stay open until 1 AM. Restaurants that serve breakfast often do so until 11 AM or noon, at which point they start serving lunch.

RESERVATIONS

Reservations generally need to be made at least a few nights in advance, but this is easily done by your concierge or online at www.opentable.com. Tables can be hard to come by if you want to dine between 7 and 9, or on Friday or Saturday night. But most restaurants will get you in if you show up and are willing to wait.

SMOKING

Smoking is prohibited in all enclosed public spaces in Boston and Cambridge, including restaurants and bars.

TIPPING

Never tip the maître d'. In most restaurants, tip the waiter at least 15%–20%. (To figure the amount quickly, just double the tax [8.625%] on the bill and, if you like, add a little more.) Bills for parties of six or more sometimes include service. Tip at least $1 per drink at the bar, and $1 for each coat checked.

WHAT IT COSTS

Entrée prices fluctuate with the state of the economy. Top-tier restaurants remain impervious to market changes, but more restaurants are accommodating every price range with small or half portions at a lower price. Credit cards are widely accepted, but many restaurants (particularly smaller ones Downtown) accept only cash. Our restaurant reviews indicate which credit cards are accepted (if any) at each establishment, but it's a good idea to double-check.

WHAT IT COSTS IN BOSTON				
$$$$	$$$	$$	$	¢
AT DINNER over $32	$25–$32	$15–$24	$8–$14	under $8

Prices are per person for a main course at dinner. Some restaurants are marked with a price range ($$–$$$, for example). This indicates one of two things: either the average cost straddles two categories, or if you order strategically, you can get out for less than most diners spend.

BOSTON

BACK BAY/BEACON HILL

This high-end area encompasses Newbury Street, Commonwealth Avenue, and a slew of enticing restaurants. Toward Beacon Hill, restaurants and the dining rooms of the large hotels tend to be quite dressy. Things are trendier and looser at the newer bistros and espresso bars that predominate around Kenmore Square, the Back Bay's western border.

AMERICAN

$$$$
Fodor'sChoice
★
✕**Excelsior.** Here, at the cream of Boston's culinary crop, Chef Eric Brennan uses his gift for creating exquisite handcrafted American cuisine. His innovative use of fresh local seafood and luxury ingredients serves him well here, especially with his selection of raw-bar items and entrées like seared tuna with beef short-ribs and Macomber-turnip ravioli. Try to finagle a seat near the windows on the second floor for a terrific view of the Public Garden or snag a seat at the bar for one of the incomparable lobster pizzas and a hand-muddled *bajito* (made with rum, sugar, and basil). ⊠*272 Boylston St., Back Bay* ☎*617/426–7878* ⚠*Reservations essential* ▤*AE, D, DC, MC, V* Ⓣ *Arlington.*

$$–$$$
✕**Sonsie.** Café society blossoms along Newbury Street, particularly at Sonsie, where a well-heeled crowd sips coffee up front or angles for places at the bar. Lunch and dinner dishes, such as charcoal duck breast with guava paste and plantains, are basic bistro with an American twist. The restaurant is a terrific place for weekend brunch, when the light pours through the long windows, and is at its most vibrant in warm weather, when the open doors make for colorful people-watching. ⊠*327 Newbury St., Back Bay* ☎*617/351–2500* ▤*AE, D, MC, V* Ⓣ *Hynes/ICA.*

$$
Fodor'sChoice
★
✕**Eastern Standard Kitchen and Drinks.** A vivid red awning beckons those entering this spacious brasserie-style restaurant. The bar area and red banquettes are filled most nights with Boston's power players (members of the Red Sox management are known to stop in) and students from the nearby universities all noshing on raw-bar specialties and comfort dishes such as veal schnitzel, rib eye, and burgers. ⊠*528 Commonwealth Ave., Kenmore Sq.* ☎*617/532–9100* ▤*AE, D, DC, MC, V* Ⓣ *Kenmore.*

CONTINENTAL

$$$$
Fodor'sChoice
★
✕**No. 9 Park.** Chef Barbara Lynch's stellar cuisine draws plenty of well-deserved attention from its place in the shadow of the State House's golden dome. Settle into the plush but unpretentious dining room and indulge in pumpkin risotto with rare lamb or the memorably rich prune-stuffed gnocchi drizzled with bits of foie gras. The wine list bobs and weaves into new territory but is always well chosen and the savvy bartenders are of the classic ilk, so you'll find plenty of classics and very few cloying, dessertlike sips here. ⊠*9 Park St., Beacon Hill* ☎*617/742–9991* ▤*AE, D, DC, MC, V* Ⓣ *Park St.*

$$$–$$$$
✕**The Federalist.** Inside the swanky Fifteen Beacon hotel, the Federalist's modern dining room clearly reflects the attitude around this part

of town: refined, civilized, and all about luxury. Chef David Hutton's menu pushes traditional Boston dishes driven by local ingredients; look for pan-seared foie gras with caramelized quince and duck confit. Be warned, though: the food is as rich as the price tag. The wine list, with more than 1,000 entries, including a few century-old bottles, is an impressive but expensive proposition. ⊠*Fifteen Beacon hotel, 15 Beacon St., Beacon Hill* ☎*617/670–2515* ⌔*Reservations essential* ⊟*AE, D, DC, MC, V* Ⓣ *Park St.*

FRENCH

$$$$ ✕**Aujourd'hui.** Epic renovations to this culinary landmark have yielded an even more elaborate and formal dining room. The New England touches are still there, but the entire space now sports a Continental (and specifically French) vibe. Discreetly located on the second floor of the Four Seasons hotel, Aujourd'hui is a magnet for the city's power brokers and well-heeled travelers who cozy up to the renovated bar and lounge, which serves vodka flights in winter and tasty martinis year-round. The food reflects an inventive approach to regional ingredients and New American cuisine. Some entrées, such as roasted Maine lobster with crabmeat wontons or roast cod with brandade cakes, can be extremely rich, but the menu also offers solid "alternative cuisine." Window tables overlook the Public Garden. ⊠*Four Seasons, 200 Boylston St., Back Bay* ☎*617/351–2071* ⌔*Reservations essential* ⊟*AE, D, DC, MC, V* Ⓣ *Arlington.*

$$$$ ✕**Clio.** Years ago when Ken Oringer opened his snazzy leopard skin–
Fodor's Choice lined hot spot in the tasteful boutique Eliot Hotel, the hordes were
★ fighting over reservations. Things have quieted down since then, but the food hasn't. Luxury ingredients pack the menu, from foie gras and tiny eels called elvers to the octopus sashimi and Kobe beef Oringer serves at Uni, the small but adventurous sushi bar set up in a side room off the main dining room. ⊠*Eliot Hotel, 370 Commonwealth Ave., Back Bay* ☎*617/536–7200* ⌔*Reservations essential* ⊟*AE, D, MC, V* Ⓣ *Hynes/ICA.*

$$$$ ✕**L'Espalier.** From sole with black truffles to foie gras with quince, chef-
Fodor's Choice owner Frank McClelland's masterpieces are every bit as impeccable
★ and elegant as the Victorian town house in which they are served. You can skip the opulent menu by choosing a prix-fixe tasting, such as the innovative and flat-out fabulous vegetarian degustation, or try the Saturday-afternoon tea, one of the city's hidden treasures, for bite-size sandwiches with flair. With two fireplaces and subtle decor in earthy

ERIN'S TOP 5

■ The chef's tasting menu at Craigie Street Bistrot is out of this world, so arrive hungry.

■ Summer dining on the patio at Oleana. It's the most romantic place in the city.

■ Lobster rolls on the outdoor deck at Barking Crab Restaurant.

■ A Palmyra martini (vodka, lime juice, and mint simple syrup) and prune-stuffed gnocchi at No. 9 Park.

■ Tapas from Taberna de Haro where the owners, a husband-and-wife team, tell great stories about living in Spain.

3

colors, this is known as one of Boston's most romantic places, with consistently reliable service and cuisine. ⊠ *30 Gloucester St., Back Bay* ☎ *617/262–3023* ♠ *Reservations essential* ⊟ *AE, D, DC, MC, V* ⊗ *Closed Sun. No lunch* Ⓣ *Hynes/ICA.*

$$$
Fodor's Choice
★

✕ **Pigalle.** A quaint, 20-table spot, Pigalle is a romantic destination to hit before taking in a show in the neighboring Theater District. Chef Marc Orfaly spices up basic French fare (steak frites, cassoulet) by throwing in the occasional Asian-inspired special. He plays around with global flavors so don't be alarmed to find spicy Szechuan pork on the nightly specials. For a delicious, cozy meal, this spot consistently has some of the best service in town. ⊠ *75 Charles St. S, Theater District* ☎ *617/423–4944* ♠ *Reservations essential* ⊟ *AE, D, DC, MC, V* ⊗ *No lunch* Ⓣ *Arlington.*

> ### STAR-GRAZING
>
> Boston may not attract A-list celebrities that often, but when they're here, you'll spot them dining at **Via Matta**. Chef Michael Schlow takes a quiet pride in having Mick Jagger and Billy Joel on his speed dial. Another celeb hot spot is **Blu** (⊠ *4 Avery St., 4th fl., Downtown,* ☎ *617/375–8550*), the restaurant and café connected to the Sports Club/LA inside the Ritz-Carlton Hotel.

ITALIAN

$$$$ ✕ **Sorellina.** A roar of approval went up when this cavernous Back Bay space opened. It's faded into a loving hum but the noise remains. This is a sexy space filled with well-heeled locals (some live in the gorgeous apartment building above it) who come for the modern twist on basic Italian dishes. Crudo, carpaccio, and arancini dot the list of starters while handmade ravioli with toasted chestnuts and pappardelle (wide, flat noodles) with braised rabbit take the spotlight. Desserts are a highlight, especially the orange panna cotta, a silky, eggless Italian custard. ⊠ *1 Huntington Ave, Back Bay* ☎ *617/412–4600* ⊟ *AE, DC, MC, V* Ⓣ *Copley, Back Bay.*

$$$ ✕ **Davio's.** Eating here is like sitting at the grown-ups' table for the first time. Comfy armchairs and a grand, high-ceilinged dining room give diners a sense of self-importance. Come at lunch, like the rest of the city's power elite, for great pastas (half portions are available) and oversize salads. For dinner, those rushing off to the theater grab a quick bite at the bar—others are in for a lengthy meal, since the kitchen's focus on sophisticated Italian cuisine makes every meal a special occasion. ⊠ *75 Arlington St., Back Bay* ☎ *617/357–4810* ⊟ *AE, DC, MC, V* Ⓣ *Arlington.*

$$$ ✕ **Via Matta.** Abuzz with well-heeled locals every night, the city's most stylish Italian spot is paradoxically one of its simplest on the culinary front. The kitchen's emphasis is on fresh, intensely flavored ingredients in traditional dishes like pappardelle with rabbit, chestnuts, dates, and olives. The abutting *enoteca* (café)—all mosaic tile and dim lighting—serves daily pizzas and is the perfect spot for a rendezvous or a nightcap. ⊠ *79 Park Plaza, Back Bay* ☎ *617/422–0008* ⊟ *AE, DC, MC, V* Ⓣ *Arlington.*

$-$$ ✗**Croma.** Of all the sidewalk patios on Newbury, Croma's has the best view. The easy pasta dishes and somewhat inventive pizzas make it an ideal refueling spot if you're trolling the street for deals. Grab a seat in the shade and order a glass of wine from the varied list before tucking into the fluffy dough balls and a Peking duck pizza. ⊠*269 Newbury St., Back Bay* ☎*617/247–3200* ⊟*AE, MC, V* Ⓣ *Copley.*

PERSIAN

★ $$ ✗**Lala Rokh.** Persian miniatures and medieval maps cover the walls of this beautifully detailed fantasy of food and art. The focus is on the Azerbaijanian corner of what is now northwest Iran, including exotically flavored specialties and dishes such as familiar (and superb here) eggplant puree, pilaf, kebabs, *fesanjoon* (the classic pomegranate-walnut sauce), and lamb stews. The staff obviously enjoys explaining the menu, and the wine list is well selected for foods that often defy wine matches. ⊠*97 Mt. Vernon St., Beacon Hill* ☎*617/720–5511* ⊟*AE, DC, MC, V* Ⓣ *Charles/MGH.*

SEAFOOD

$$-$$$$ ✗**Turner Fisheries of Boston.** On the first floor of the Westin hotel in Copley Square, Turner Fisheries is second only to Legal Sea Foods in its traditional appeal. Turner broils, grills, bakes, fries, and steams everything in the ocean but also prepares classic and modern sauces, vegetables, and pasta with panache. Any meal should begin with the creamy chowder—the restaurant has won Boston's yearly Chowderfest competition too many times to contend any more. Round it out with one of the city's best-looking lobster rolls. ⊠ *Westin Copley Place Boston, 10 Huntington Ave., Back Bay* ☎*617/424–7425* ⌂*Reservations essential* ⊟*AE, D, DC, MC, V* Ⓣ *Copley.*

$$$ ✗**Great Bay.** The dining experience you have at this house of modern seafood all depends on where you sit. Settle in at the casual "island" in the cavernous front room and you'll tuck into tiny plates such as slivered scallops over chickpea puree while watching as a sous-chef displays his finest knife skills. Grab a table by the sweeping staircase and tall windows, and expect remade New England specialties such as clam chowder teeming with nearly whole clams. Or head into the more-formal dining room to sup on a multicourse dinner of modern fish dishes. ⊠*Hotel Commonwealth, 500 Commonwealth Ave., Kenmore Sq.* ☎*617/532–5300* ⊟*AE, D, MC, V* Ⓣ *Kenmore.*

$$-$$$ ✗**Legal Sea Foods.** What began as a tiny restaurant upstairs over a Cambridge fish market has grown to important regional status, with more than 20 East Coast locations, plus a handful of national ones. The hallmark is the freshest possible seafood, whether you have it wood grilled, in New England chowder, or doused with an Asia-inspired sauce. The smoked-bluefish pâté is delectable, and the clam chowder is so good it has become a menu staple at presidential inaugurations. A preferred-seating list allows calls ahead, and this location has private dining inside its beautiful, bottle-lined wine cellar. ⊠*26 Park Sq., Theater District* ☎*617/426–4444* ⌂*Reservations not accepted* ⊟*AE, D, DC, MC, V* Ⓣ *Arlington.*

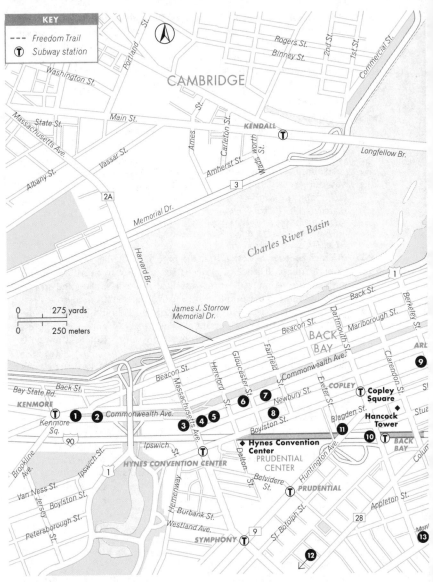

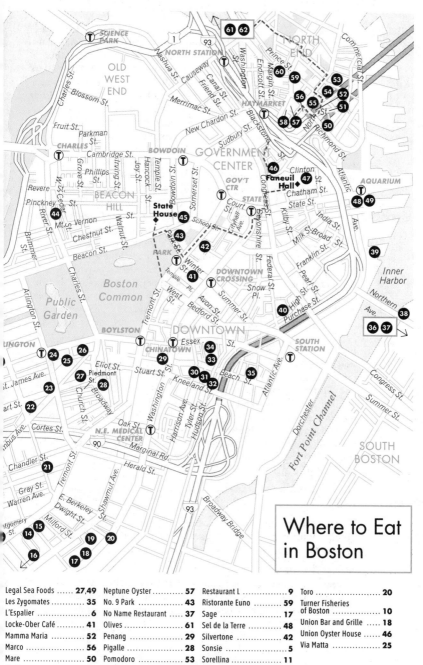

Where to Eat in Boston

STEAK

$$$–$$$$ ✕**Abe & Louis.** Go ahead: live the fantasy of the robber baron feasting among cavernous fireplaces and deep-textured, plush mahogany booths. Abe & Louis may be a tad Disney-esque in its decor, but its menu lives up to the promise with gorgeous, two-tiered raw platters and juicy rib-eye steaks under velvety hollandaise. Even the linen napkins have little buttonholes for the perfect collar hold. ⊠*793 Boylston St., Back Bay* ☎*617/536–6300* ▤*AE, D, DC, MC, V* Ⓣ *Copley.*

$$–$$$$ ✕**Capital Grille.** A carnivore's utopia awaits within these clubby, dark-wood walls. Steak-house staples such as cottage fries and a plump order of shrimp cocktail start things nicely, followed by succulent meats such as the 24-ounce dry-aged porterhouse. The crowd-watching is as tasty as the food: VIPs in striped suits make deals over dessert, and wives in Manolo Blahnik heels sip martinis. ⊠*359 Newbury St., Back Bay* ☎*617/262–8900* ▤*AE, D, DC, MC, V* ☾*No lunch* Ⓣ *Hynes/ICA.*

★ $$–$$$$ ✕**Grill 23 & Bar.** Pinstriped suits, dark paneling, Persian rugs, and waiters in white jackets give this steak house a posh demeanor. The food is anything but predictable, with dishes such as Kobe beef carpaccio with smoked onion compote and rotisserie tenderloin with Roquefort mashed potatoes. Seafood specialties such as tuna au poivre give beef sales a run for their money. Chef Jay Murray gets his beef supply from organic and all-natural farms. Desserts, such as the wonderful apple-blackberry potpie and the sticky toffee pudding, are far above those of the average steak house. ⊠*161 Berkeley St., Back Bay* ☎*617/542–2255* ⌕*Reservations essential* ▤*AE, D, DC, MC, V* ☾*No lunch* Ⓣ *Back Bay/South End.*

★ $$$ ✕**Restaurant L.** Ultrachic fashion house Louis Boston is the setting for this renovated spot, where Chef Pino Maffeo elegantly fuses Asian and Western flavors into a modern steak-house concept. Maffeo has a deft hand with meats and seafood, and a whimsical touch with *amuse bouches* (small bites)—one is barbecued baby back ribs piled atop one another and served with a mouth-puckering green Thai chili sauce. Cocktails and desserts also tend more towards fun than serious cuisine. ⊠*234 Berkeley St., Back Bay* ☎*617/266–4680* ▤*AE, MC, V* Ⓣ *Copley.*

CHARLESTOWN

This little neighborhood across Boston Harbor contains the Bunker Hill Monument, the USS *Constitution,* and one culinary landmark, the famous Olives, a standout among the local taverns.

MEDITERRANEAN

$$–$$$ ✕**Copia.** This Mediterranean grill covers almost all the gustatorial bases with mix-n-match antipasti, pizzas, grilled and roasted meats, pastas, and even a Greek dish or two. A wood-burning oven produces a fine smoky aroma that wafts over the round dining room. Picture windows fill the room with light, but unfortunately they don't face the city's harbor, which lies to the back of the restaurant. ⊠*100 City Sq., Charlestown* ☎*617/242–6742* ▤*AE, D, DC, MC, V* ☾*No lunch* Ⓣ *Community College.*

★ $$–$$$ ✕ **Olives.** No longer will you see chef Todd English tending the wood-fire brick oven here—these days he's too busy watching over his many restaurants in New York and elsewhere. But don't worry, English's recipes are in good hands. Witness smart signature offerings such as the house Caesar, with anchovy-caper dressing and jumbo lump crab, or a number of wood-grilled fish and meat dishes. Crowded seating, noise, long lines, and abrupt service only add to the excitement. If you can't secure a reservation, come early or late or be prepared for an extended wait. ⊠ *10 City Sq., Charlestown* ☎ *617/242–1999* ▤ *AE, D, DC, MC, V* ☉ *No lunch* Ⓣ *Community College.*

CHINATOWN

Boston's Chinatown is the focal point for Asian cuisines of all types, from authentic Cantonese and Vietnamese to Malaysian, Japanese, and Mandarin. Many places are open after midnight, while the rest of the city sleeps or lurks. It's definitely worth the trek, especially if you're tracking down live-tank seafood prepared in Hong Kong or Chiu Chow style.

CHINESE

$$–$$$ ✕ **Chau Chow City.** Spread across three floors, this is the largest, glitziest, and most versatile production yet of the Chau Chow dynasty, with dim sum by day and live-tank seafood by night. Overwhelmed? Order the clams in black-bean sauce, the sautéed pea-pod stems with garlic, or the honey-glazed shrimp with walnuts. ⊠ *83 Essex St., Chinatown* ☎ *617/338–8158* ▤ *AE, D, MC, V* Ⓣ *Chinatown.*

$$–$$$ ✕ **Grand Chau Chow.** Chau Chow (or Chaozhou, in China) is the term for people from Shantou (formerly Swatow). They and their wonderful seafood cuisine—served here—migrated all over Southeast Asia and around the world, introducing other cultures to clams in black-bean sauce, steamed sea bass, or any dish with their famous ginger sauce. Your best bet is not to order from the menu per se but to look around at what others are eating and order that way. It's not as rude as it sounds since everyone else does it, too. ⊠ *41–45 Beach St., Chinatown* ☎ *617/292–5166 or 617/426–6266* ▤ *AE, D, DC, MC, V* Ⓣ *Chinatown.*

$$–$$$ ✕ **Jumbo Seafood.** Although this Cantonese/Hong Kong–style restaurant has much to be proud of, it's happily unpretentious. Have a whole sea bass with ginger and scallion to see what all the fuss is about. Non-oceanic offerings are equally outstanding—even such simple dishes as stir-fried sugar-snap-pea tendrils with white rice. The Hong Kong influence results in a lot of fried food; crispy fried calamari with salted pepper is a standout. The waiters are very patient with newcomers' questions, though some don't speak English fluently. ⊠ *7 Hudson St., Chinatown* ☎ *617/542–2823* ▤ *AE, MC, V* Ⓣ *Chinatown.*

$$ ✕ **Imperial Seafood House.** On the first floor is a wonderful (and seldom crowded) Cantonese restaurant specializing in seafood. The livelier second floor is a large, airy dining room with the most extensive dim sum selection in Chinatown. Dim sum denotes both the meal (a veritable Chinese brunch, served daily 8:30–3:30) and the variety of

On the Menu

Not for nothing did Boston become known as the home of the bean and the cod: simple Yankee specialties—many of them of English origin—and traditional seafood abound.

Boston baked beans are a thick, syrupy mixture of navy beans, salt pork, and molasses that is cooked for hours. They were originally made by Puritan women on Saturday so that the leftovers could be eaten on Sunday without breaking the Sabbath by cooking.

You may also want to keep an eye out for Parker House rolls, yeast-bread dinner rolls first concocted at the Parker House Hotel in the 1870s.

Boston cream pie is an addictive simple yellow vanilla cake filled with a creamy custard and iced with chocolate frosting. Many traditional New England eateries (and some steak houses and hotel restaurants) serve a house version. Occasionally you'll find a modernized version, with some creative new element added at trendier restaurants.

The city's beer-drinking enthusiasm is older than the Declaration of Independence—which, incidentally, was signed by Samuel Adams, an instigator of the Boston Tea Party and the man whose name graces the bottles of the country's best-selling craft-brew beer.

---

dumplings and buns, tiny spareribs, morsels of pork, chicken, clams, shrimp, and other foods that you select from roving carts and pay for by the item. Pointing is fine. The selection is wider when the restaurant is more crowded with weekend shoppers, mostly suburban Chinese-Americans. ⊠ *70 Beach St., Chinatown* ☎*617/426–8543* ⊟*AE, MC, V* **T** *Chinatown.*

JAPANESE

★ **$-$$** ✕ **Ginza.** One of Chinatown's best restaurants—and one of Boston's best sushi spots—turns out a remarkably fresh and creative raw-fish menu. The *kmeeks* maki is a roll of crab-stick tempura, grilled eel, cucumber, avocado, and roe. For something equally fresh but much simpler, opt for the sashimi appetizer—small, gleaming slabs of maguro (bluefin) tuna, salmon, and yellowtail. Cooked foods are also available, but sushi is the real star. Late night, the room feels even more like Tokyo: waitresses in kimonos flit from the sushi bar to tables at top speed, and Japanese-American club kids table-hop and flirt. There's another location in Brookline (⇨ *below*). ⊠ *16 Hudson St., Chinatown* ☎*617/338–2261* ⊟*AE, DC, MC, V* **T** *Chinatown.*

MALAYSIAN

$-$$ ✕ **Penang.** Penang is a resort island with a history like that of nearby Singapore and a cuisine of many influences—Malaysian, Chinese, Indian, Thai, and a bit of British Trader Vic. It all comes together here in favorites such as the "yam pot" stir-fry (vegetables arrive in a shaped, fried taro root), the house-special squid with a dark and spicy sauce, an Indonesian beef curry called *rendang,* and enormous fried coconut shrimp, all paired with umbrella drinks. The loud, open kitchen adds drama. Reservations are accepted for six or more. ⊠ *685–691 Washington St., Chinatown* ☎*617/451–6372* ⊟*MC, V* **T** *Chinatown.*

DOWNTOWN

Boston's downtown scene revs up at lunchtime, but the streets get quiet after 5 PM, when everyone goes back to the suburbs. The city center is great for after-hours dining, though, especially in the hideaway restaurants around the former Leather District.

AMERICAN

$–$$ ✕ **Silvertone.** Devotees of this hip basement restaurant swear by the no-fuss options such as a truly addictive macaroni and cheese, meat loaf, and steak tips. Among the more-interesting offerings are the appetizers, such as the spicy Caesar salad, and the fish of the day, which might be trout amandine or locally caught bluefish. The wine list is compact but varied. ⊠ *69 Bromfield St., Downtown* ☎ *617/338–7887* ⚠ *Reservations not accepted* ⊟ *AE, D, DC, MC, V* Ⓣ *Park St.*

CONTINENTAL

$$$–$$$$ ✕ **Locke-Ober Café.** Chef-owner Lydia Shire gave this old Boston spot a much-needed update when she took the reins in 2001. The ornate woodwork gleams again, and the once-stodgy kitchen is turning out classics with flair—and a slightly lighter touch. Traditionalists needn't worry, though; many favorites remain on the menu, including Shire's signature finnan haddie (smoked haddock) stew; Indian pudding, which has never been better; and clams casino. There is valet parking after 6 PM. ⊠ *3 Winter Pl., Downtown* ☎ *617/542–1340* ⚠ *Reservations essential* ⊟ *AE, D, DC, MC, V* ☉ *No lunch weekends* Ⓣ *Downtown Crossing.*

FRENCH

$$$–$$$$
Fodor'sChoice
★
✕ **Radius.** Acclaimed chef Michael Schlow's notable contemporary French cooking lures scores of designer-clad diners to the Financial District. The decor and menu are minimalist at first glance, but closer inspection reveals equal shares of luxury, complexity, and whimsy. Peruse the menu for such choices as roasted beet salad, a selection of ceviches, buttery Scottish salmon, or coconut panna cotta for dessert. It's a meal made for special occasions and business dinners alike. ⊠ *8 High St., Downtown* ☎ *617/426–1234* ⚠ *Reservations essential* ⊟ *AE, DC, MC, V* Ⓣ *South Station.*

★ **$$–$$$** ✕ **Les Zygomates.** *Les zygomates* is the French expression for the muscles on the human face that make you smile—and this combination wine bar–bistro inarguably lives up to its name, with quintessential French bistro fare that is both simple and simply delicious. The menu beautifully matches the ever-changing wine list, with all wines served by the 2-ounce taste, 6-ounce glass, or bottle. Prix-fixe menus are available at lunch and dinner, and could include oysters by the half dozen or pancetta-wrapped venison with roasted pears. There's live jazz several nights a week. ⊠ *129 South St., Downtown* ☎ *617/542–5108* ⚠ *Reservations essential* ⊟ *AE, D, DC, MC, V* ☉ *Closed Sun. No lunch Sat.* Ⓣ *South Station.*

FANEUIL HALL

A perfect refueling stop before hitting the Freedom Trail, Faneuil Hall is a tourist magnet, packed with fast-food concessions as well as some more-serious alternatives. If you're not on a schedule, and if you've seen enough of Faneuil Hall and want a change of scene, you shouldn't rule out a walk to the North End.

AMERICAN

¢–$$ ✕ **Durgin Park Market Dining Room.** You should be hungry enough to cope with enormous portions, yet not so hungry you can't tolerate a long wait. Durgin Park was serving its same hearty New England fare (Indian pudding, baked beans, corned beef and cabbage, and a prime rib that hangs over the edge of the plate) back when Faneuil Hall was a working market instead of a tourist attraction. The service is as brusque as it was when fishmongers and boat captains dined here. ✉ *340 Faneuil Hall Market Pl., North Market Bldg., Government Center* ☎ *617/227–2038* ▤ *AE, D, DC, MC, V* Ⓣ *Government Center.*

NORTH END

The North End is Boston's oldest immigrant neighborhood. At the end of the 19th century, Paul Revere's house was a crowded tenement, and at the beginning of this one, black-clad Italian grandmothers continue to push past suburban foodies to get the best of the local groceries. Since the late 1990s, small storefront restaurants have been converting from red-sauce tourist traps to innovative trattorias. And some of Boston's most authentic old-country restaurants are still here (as you might guess, the smaller the place, the better the kitchen), along with charming cafés serving to-die-for espresso and cannoli. Many of the restaurants don't take credit cards or reservations, but because they're so close to each other, it's easy to scout among them for a table.

ITALIAN

$$–$$$$ ✕ **Mamma Maria.** Don't let the clichéd name fool you: Mamma Maria is far from a typical red-sauce joint, although some locals think it can feel stuffy. From the Maine lobster–filled tortellini to the innovative sauces and entrées to some of the best desserts in the North End, you can't go wrong here. The view, meanwhile, is lovely; gaze out onto cobblestone-lined North Square as you finish your pappardelle layered with braised rabbit and a finale of *limoncello* (an Italian lemon-flavored liquor). ✉ *3 North Sq., North End* ☎ *617/523–0077* ▤ *AE, D, DC, MC, V* Ⓣ *Haymarket.*

★ $$–$$$ ✕ **Bricco.** A sophisticated but unpretentious enclave of nouveau Italian, Bricco has carved out quite a following. And no wonder: the velvety butternut-squash soup alone is argument for a reservation. Simple but well-balanced main courses such as melt-in-your-mouth pistachio-crusted Kobe beef and rabbit loin wrapped in pancetta have a sweet smokiness that lingers. You're likely to want to linger in the warm room, too, gazing through the floor-to-ceiling windows while sipping a glass of Sangiovese. ✉ *241 Hanover St., North End* ☎ *617/248–6800* ⌃ *Reservations essential* ▤ *AE, D, MC, V* Ⓣ *Haymarket.*

$$–$$$ ✕**Mare.** Anchoring a tucked-away corner on Richmond Street, this organic Italian seafood restaurant has stepped out of tradition and moved into nouveau Italian. Ignore the distraction of the color-changing walls, lighted by fluorescent neon, and scope out the menu: the chefs here prefer the simplicity of grilling and poaching seafood and meat dishes rather than dousing them in seasonings, which presents a simple but delicious option among its red-sauce-heavy neighbors. Go for a plate of tagliatelle tossed with fresh tomatoes, slivers of basil, and shaved Parmesan.

> **TOP PICKS FOR BREAKFAST**
>
> ■ **Zaftigs,** Coolidge Corner, for casual
>
> ■ **Aujourd'hui,** Back Bay, for power breakfasts
>
> ■ **Bob's Southern Bistro,** South End, for soul or jazz with your eggs
>
> ■ **Union Bar and Grille,** South End, for see-and-be-scene

And don't miss the mixed grill—a selection of fresh-caught fish prepared with a touch of seasoning. ⊠*135 Richmond St., North End* ☎*617/723–6273* ⊟*AE, D, MC, V* Ⓣ *Haymarket.*

$–$$$ ✕**Carmen.** Here's the kind of undeniably friendly, downright cute hole-in-the-wall that keeps the neighborhood real. Packed with a mere 15-odd tables, Carmen keeps its crowds happy with glasses of wine and small tapas-style plates of roasted red pepper and olives at the up-front bar. At tables, meanwhile, diners tuck into clean-flavored specials such as creamy homemade salmon lasagna and braised rabbit. ⊠*33 North Sq., North End* ☎*617/742–6421* ⊟*AE, DC, MC, V* ⊗*No lunch* Ⓣ *Haymarket.*

$–$$$ ✕**Marco.** The second-story dining room is meant to evoke a charming Italian bistro and succeeds with its warm tones and roaring fireplace. Your best bet here is to go for a family-style selection of antipasti, pastas (handmade gnocchi with brown butter is a must), and grilled meats. Plates are meant to be shared and grazed over while enjoying a bottle or two from the all-Italian wine list. This is an unpretentious spot where candlelight and laughter usually fill the room. ⊠*253 Hanover St., 2nd fl., North End* ☎*617/742–1276* ⚑*Reservations essential* ⊟*AE, D, MC, V* ⊗*Closed Mon.* Ⓣ *Haymarket.*

$$ ✕**Terramia.** Nearly everything this little autumnal-color restaurant kicks out tastes home cooked and authentic. The simple, largely southern Italian cuisine is full of game (look for boar, venison, and quail specials) and rich, fresh pastas tossed with equally fresh ingredients. The risottos come perfectly cooked and powerfully flavored. Dessert and coffee aren't on the menu, though. Lines can get long on weekends. ⊠*98 Salem St., North End* ☎*617/523–3112* ⊟*AE, DC, MC, V* Ⓣ *Haymarket.*

$–$$ ✕**Antico Forno.** Many of the menu choices come from the eponymous wood-burning brick oven, which turns out surprisingly delicate pizzas simply topped with tomato and fresh mozzarella. Don't overlook the handmade pastas; the specialty, gnocchi, is rich and creamy but light. The room is cramped and noisy, but the hubbub is part of the fun. ⊠*93*

Fodor's Choice
★

Salem St., North End ☎*617/723–6733* ▤*MC, V* ⓣ *Haymarket.*

$–$$ ✕**Pomodoro.** This teeny trattoria—just eight tables—is worth the wait, with excellent country Italian favorites such as white beans with pasta, roasted vegetables, and a fine salad of field greens. The best choice could well be the clam-and-tomato stew with herbed flat bread, accompanied by a bottle of Vernaccia. Pomodoro doesn't serve dessert, but it's easy to find great espresso and pastries in the cafés on Hanover Street. ✉*319 Hanover St., North End* ☎*617/367–4348* ⚠*Reservations essential* ▤*No credit cards* ⓣ *Haymarket.*

$–$$ ✕**Ristorante Euno.** Tiny and friendly, Euno is the North End's culinary mouse that roars. The rustic room used to be a butcher shop, and meat hooks still stud the wall, doubling as coat hangers. Everything from start (a bowl of the buttery olives) to middle (handmade pastas and risottos) to finish (duck ragout with pumpkin tortellini) explains why this postage-stamp gem is a neighborhood favorite. ✉*119 Salem St., North End* ☎*617/573–9406* ▤*AE, DC, MC, V* ⓣ *Haymarket.*

SEAFOOD

★ **$$–$$$** ✕**Neptune Oyster.** This tiny oyster bar, the first of its kind in the neighborhood, has only six tables, but the long marble bar has extra seating for a dozen more and mirrors hang over the bar with handwritten menus. From there, watch the oyster shuckers as they deftly undo handfuls of bivalves. The *plateau di frutti di mare* is a gleaming tower of oysters and other raw-bar items piled over ice that you can order from the slip of paper they pass out listing each day's crustacean options. And the lobster roll, hot or cold, overflows with meat. Service is prompt even when it gets busy (as it is most of the time). Go early to avoid a long wait. ✉*63 Salem St., North End* ☎*617/742–3474* ⚠*Reservations not accepted* ▤*AE, DC, MC, V* ⓣ *Haymarket.*

$$–$$$ ✕**Union Oyster House.** Established in 1826, this is Boston's oldest continuing restaurant, and almost every tourist considers it a must-see. If you like, you can have what Daniel Webster had—oysters on the half shell at the ground-floor raw bar, which is the oldest part of the restaurant and still the best. The rooms at the top of the narrow staircase are dark and have low ceilings—very Ye Olde New England—and plenty of nonrestaurant history. The small tables and chairs (as well as the endless lines and kitschy nostalgia) are as much a part of the charm as the simple and decent (albeit pricey) food. One cautionary note: locals hardly ever eat here. There is valet parking after 5:30 PM. ✉*41 Union St., Government Center* ☎*617/227–2750* ▤*AE, D, DC, MC, V* ⓣ *Haymarket.*

$–$$ ✕**Daily Catch.** You've just got to love this place—for the noise, the intimacy, and, above all, the food. Shoulder-crowdingly small, the storefront restaurant specializes in calamari dishes, black-squid-ink fettuccine, and linguine with clam sauce. There's something about a big skillet of linguine and calamari that would seem less perfect if served on fine white china. ✉*323 Hanover St., North End* ☎*617/523–8567 or 617/734–5696* ⌖*Reservations not accepted* ⊟*No credit cards* Ⓣ *Haymarket.*

SOUTH END

Boston's South End is a highly diverse neighborhood, these days home to many of the city's gay professionals, hip straight couples, and young families. Barely a month seems to go by when a hot restaurant doesn't open—either at the restaurant row at the bend of Tremont Street or up and down the length of Washington Street.

AMERICAN

$$$–$$$$ ✕**Icarus.** Be ready for an exotic menu of real intensity. Inventive touchstones such as red-kuri squash ravioli with Gorgonzola and heirloom apples form the basis of the seasonal menu. The romantic two-tier dining room offers excellent service, and an extensive wine list complements the fare. Friday nights are spiked with live jazz. To get even cozier, reserve a private dining room. ✉*3 Appleton St., South End* ☎*617/426–1790* ⌖*Reservations essential* ⊟*AE, D, DC, MC, V* ☾*No lunch* Ⓣ *Back Bay/South End.*

$$–$$$$ ✕**Union Bar and Grille.** There's rarely a quiet night at Union, where the bar buzzes with the neighborhood's coolest residents and couples on dates fill the darkly lighted dining room's leather banquettes. Despite all the show, the menu keeps things relatively down-to-earth with tender-as-can-be burgers, spice-rubbed grilled steak, and thick, crispy fries. ✉*1357 Washington St., South End* ☎*617/423–0555* ⊟*AE, MC, V* ☾*No lunch* Ⓣ *Back Bay/South End.*

$–$$ ✕**Butcher Shop.** Chef Barbara Lynch has remade the classic meat market as a polished wine bar–cum–hangout, and it's just the kind of high-quality, low-pretense spot every neighborhood could use. Stop in for a glass of wine, chat with any of the friendly but cosmopolitan clientele, and grab a casual, quick snack of homemade prosciutto and salami, daily pasta and sandwich specials, or a plate of artisanal cheeses. ✉*552 Tremont St., South End* ☎*617/423–4800* ⊟*AE, D, DC, MC, V* Ⓣ *Back Bay/South End.*

$–$$ ✕**Franklin Café.** This place has jumped to the head of the class by keeping things simple yet effective. (Its litmus: local chefs gather here to wind down after work.) Try anything with the great chive mashed potatoes and don't miss the double-thick brined pork chops. The vibe is generally more bar than restaurant, so be forewarned: it can get loud. Desserts are not served. ✉*278 Shawmut Ave., South End* ☎*617/350–0010* ⌖*Reservations not accepted* ⊟*AE, D, DC, MC, V* Ⓣ *Back Bay/South End.*

¢–$ ✕**Flour Bakery Café.** When the neighbors need coffee, or a sandwich, or a muffin, or just a place to sit and chat, they come here. A communal table in the middle acts as a gathering spot around which diners enjoy classic sandwiches and a few specialties, like the grilled chicken with Brie and arugula or the BLT with applewood-smoked bacon. Take-out dinner is available in the form of Asian-inspired entrées. ✉*1595 Washington St., South End* ☎*617/267–4300* ⌖*Reservations not accepted* ⊟*MC, V* Ⓣ *Massachusetts Ave.*

FRENCH

$$$–$$$$ ✕ **Hamersley's Bistro.** Gordon Hamersley has earned a national reputation, thanks to such signature dishes as a grilled mushroom-and-garlic sandwich, roast chicken, and souffléed lemon custard. He's one of Boston's great chefs and is famous for sporting a Red Sox cap instead of his white chef's hat. His place has a full bar, a café area with 10 tables for walk-ins, and a larger dining room that's a little more formal and decorative than the bar and café, though nowhere near as stuffy as it looks. ⊠ *553 Tremont St., South End* ☎ *617/423–2700* ⊟ *AE, D, DC, MC, V* Ⓣ *Back Bay/South End.*

ITALIAN

$$–$$$ ✕ **Sage.** Intensely fragrant Italian specialties and a pretty dining room are the draws here. Local chef Anthony Susi has a steady hand with pastas and gnocchis, but can also render seared salmon feather light and sweet next to garlic-laden polenta. ⊠ *1395 Washington St., South End* ☎ *617/867–0707* ⊟ *AE, D, MC, V* Ⓣ *Back Bay/South End.*

SEAFOOD

$–$$ ✕ **B & G Oysters, Ltd.** Chef Barbara Lynch (of No. 9 Park fame) has made **Fodor's**Choice yet another fabulous mark on Boston with a style-conscious seafood ★ restaurant that updates New England's traditional bounty with flair. Designed to imitate the inside of an oyster shell, the iridescent bar glows with silvery, candlelit tiles and a sophisticated crowd. They're in for the lobster roll, no doubt—an expensive proposition at $24, but worth every cent for its decadent chunks of meat in a perfectly textured dressing. If you're sans reservation, be prepared to wait: the line for a seat can be epic. ⊠ *550 Tremont St., South End* ☎ *617/423–0550* ⊟ *AE, D, MC, V* Ⓣ *Back Bay/South End.*

SOUL FOOD

$–$$ ✕ **Bob's Southern Bistro.** Boston's home of genteel soul food and jazz attracts a mellow mix of yuppies and neighborhood families. Take the crab cakes, catfish fingers, chitterlings, and "glorifried" chicken over ribs or chicken wings, which are baked, not smoked or fried. The all-you-can-eat Sunday brunch is a surefire way to lift your spirits, especially when there's live jazz or gospel music. ⊠ *604 Columbus Ave., South End* ☎ *617/536–6204* ⊟ *AE, D, MC, V* ☉ *Closed Mon.* Ⓣ *Massachusetts Ave.*

SPANISH

$$–$$$ ✕ **Toro.** The buzz from chef Ken Oringer's tapas joint still hasn't qui- **Fodor's**Choice eted down—for good reason. Small plates of saffron-and-garlic shrimp ★ and crusty bread smothered in tomato paste are hefty enough to make a meal out of many, or share the regular or vegetarian paella with a group. An all-Spanish wine list complements the plates. Crowds have been known to wait it out for more than an hour. ⊠ *1704 Washington St., South End* ☎ *617/536–4300* ⌂ *Reservations not accepted* ⊟ *AE, D, MC, V* Ⓣ *Massachusetts Ave.*

WATERFRONT

Tourists flock to Faneuil Hall and the Marketplace almost year-round, so tried-and-true cuisine tends to dominate there. However, some of Boston's most famous seafood restaurants are on the waterfront.

AMERICAN

$$–$$$ ✗**Aura.** Simplicity and seasonality are the keys to this waterfront restaurant. Local farmers and anglers make daily drops at the kitchen's back door, and the menu changes accordingly. In spring look for asparagus; in fall order squash. Dishes can be rich, such as foie gras with maple-braised shallots, or light, such as a tart of morel, asparagus, and goat cheese. The ingredients are impeccable, and though the presentations are at times overly capricious, in the end the cuisine glows. Note that the service is included in the bill. ⊠*Seaport Hotel, 1 Seaport La., Waterfront* ☎*617/385–4300* ☰*AE, D, DC, MC, V* Ⓣ *Aquarium.*

CONTINENTAL

$$$ ✗**Meritage.** Set inside the stately Boston Harbor Hotel, Meritage stays focused with its astounding wine list. Chef Daniel Bruce creates scintillating menus to match the cellar's treasures between the field trips on which he takes his staff to hunt wild mushrooms—his personal passion. With the stunning Rowes Wharf as its backdrop, Meritage has, perhaps, the city's finest waterfront view. *Jacket required.* ⊠*Boston Harbor Hotel at Rowes Wharf, 70 Rowes Wharf, Waterfront* ☎*617/439–3995 or 617/439–7000* ☰*AE, D, DC, MC, V* Ⓣ *Aquarium.*

FRENCH

★ $$$ ✗**Sel de la Terre.** Sitting between the waterfront and what used to be the Central Artery, this is a hot spot to hit before the theater, after sightseeing, or for a simple lunch Downtown. The rustic, country-French menu is brilliantly priced so that all entrées cost the same. Dinner mates can choose between braised beef short ribs with rosemary-infused mashed potatoes or a hazelnut-crusted rack of lamb. Stop by the *boulangerie* (bread shop) to take home fresh, homemade loaves, which are some of the best in the city. ⊠*255 State St., Downtown* ☎*617/227–1579* ⌲*Reservations essential* ☰*AE, D, DC, MC, V* Ⓣ *Aquarium.*

SEAFOOD

¢–$$$ ✗**Legal Sea Foods.** What better place than the waterfront to build one of the snazziest branches of the local Legal Sea Foods chain? The classic and contemporary seafood preparations mirror those of the other locations, but this one's dining room is full of colorful tiles and sea-inspired sculpture. A preferred-seating list allows calls ahead. ⊠*255 State St., Downtown* ☎*617/227–3115* ☰*AE, D, DC, MC, V* Ⓣ *Aquarium.*

Refueling

If you're on the go, you might want to try a local chain restaurant where you can stop for a quick bite or get some takeout. The ones listed below are fairly priced and committed to quality, and use decent, fresh ingredients.

Au Bon Pain. The locally based chain whips up quick salads and sandwiches, fresh-daily croissants, and muffins, and has plenty of fruit and juices.

Bertucci's. Thin-crust pizzas fly fast from the brick ovens here, along with pastas and a decent tiramisu.

BoLoCo. For quick, cheap, healthful, and high-quality wraps and burritos, this is easily the city's most dependable (and also locally based) chain.

Finagle AA Bagel. Find fresh, doughy bagels in flavors from jalapeño cheddar to triple chocolate, plus sandwiches and salads. Service is swift and efficient.

¢–$$ ✗**Barking Crab Restaurant.** It is, believe it or not, a seaside clam shack plunk in the middle of Boston, with a stunning view of the downtown skyscrapers. An outdoor lobster tent in summer, in winter it retreats indoors to a warmhearted version of a waterfront dive, with chestnuts roasting on a cozy woodstove. Look for the classic New England clambake—chowder, lobster, steamed clams, corn on the cob—or the spicier crab boil. ✉ *88 Sleeper St., Northern Ave. Bridge, Waterfront* ☎ *617/426–2722* ▭ *AE, DC, MC, V* Ⓣ *South Station.*

★ ¢–$ ✗**No Name Restaurant.** Famous for not being famous, the No Name has been serving fresh seafood, simply broiled or fried, since 1917. Once you find it, tucked off of New Northern Avenue (as opposed to Old Northern Avenue) between the World Trade Center and the Bank of America Pavilion, you can close your eyes and pretend you're in a little fishing village—it's not much of a stretch. ✉ *15½ Fish Pier, off New Northern Ave., Waterfront* ☎ *617/338–7539 or 617/423–2705* ▭ *AE, D, MC, V* Ⓣ *Courthouse.*

CAMBRIDGE

Among other collegiate enthusiasms, Cambridge has a long-standing fascination with ethnic restaurants. A certain kind of great restaurant has also evolved here, mixing world-class cooking with a studied informality. Famous chefs, attired in flannel shirts, cook with wood fires and borrow flavors from every continent. For posher tastes and the annual celebrations that come with college life (or the end of it), Cambridge also has its share of linen-cloth tables.

AFGHAN

$–$$ ✗**The Helmand.** The area's first Afghan restaurant is named after a province of Afghanistan south of Kabul. Try any of the three kinds of great rice, some fine sour soups, terrific *aushak* (ravioli stuffed with leeks), the various kebabs you might expect, and an excellent vegetarian menu you might not, with a number of choices grilled and stewed in novel ways. ✉ *143 1st St., Cambridge* ☎ *617/492–4646* ⊲ *Reservations essential* ⊟ *AE, MC, V* ⊗ *No lunch* Ⓣ *Lechmere.*

AMERICAN

$$$–$$$$ ✕ **Harvest.** The New England–inspired menu of up-to-date dishes is hedged with traditional regional favorites made with locally sourced ingredients. Starters include raw seafood and a salad of braised rabbit on arugula; grilled Block Island swordfish and honey-lacquered duck breast are among the recommended main plates. The open kitchen makes some noise, but customers at the ever-popular bar don't seem to mind. Warm weather brings the opening of a lush outdoor patio. ✉ *44 Brattle St., 1 Mifflin Pl., Cambridge* ☎ *617/868–2255* ⊲ *Reservations essential* ⊟ *AE, D, DC, MC, V* Ⓣ *Harvard.*

$$–$$$ ✕ **Blue Room.** Totally hip, funky, and Cambridge, the Blue Room blends a host of cuisines from Southwestern to Mediterranean with fresh, local ingredients. Brightly colored furnishings, counters where you can meet others while you eat, and a friendly staff add up to a good-time place that's serious about food. Try the seared scallops grilled over French green lentils, or perhaps a cassoulet brimming with braised pork and wild-boar sausage. An extraordinary buffet brunch with grilled meats and vegetables, as well as regular breakfast fare and a gorgeous array of desserts, is served on Sunday. ✉ *1 Kendall Sq., Cambridge* ☎ *617/494–9034* ⊟ *AE, D, DC, MC, V* ⊗ *No lunch* Ⓣ *Kendall/MIT.*

★ **$$–$$$** ✕ **Green Street.** The tables are small and the service is casual, but the relatively inexpensive New England menu speaks to the young, artistic community that now claims the neighborhood. Clambakes, pot roast, and Boston baked beans are mixed in with more-modern takes like duck breast with cranberry relish. With an emphasis on microbrews and cocktails (the latest owner is a wiz of a bartender) the restaurant has a relaxed and neighborly bar scene. ✉ *280 Green St., Cambridge* ☎ *617/876–1655* ⊟ *AE, MC, V* Ⓣ *Central.*

$–$$$ ✕ **East Coast Grill and Raw Bar.** Owner-chef-author Chris Schlesinger built
Fodor's Choice his national reputation on grilled foods and red-hot condiments. The
★ Jamaican jerk, North Carolina pulled pork, and habañero-laced "pasta from Hell" are still here, but this restaurant has made an extraordinary play to establish itself in the front ranks of fish restaurants. Spices and condiments are more restrained, and Schlesinger has compiled a wine list bold and flavorful enough to match the highly spiced food. The dining space is completely informal. A killer brunch (complete with a do-it-yourself Bloody Mary bar) is served on Sunday. ✉ *1271 Cambridge St., Cambridge* ☎ *617/491–6568* ⊟ *AE, D, MC, V* ⊗ *No lunch* Ⓣ *Central.*

★ **$$** ✕ **West Side Lounge.** *Understated* is the buzzword at this relaxed but suave bistro, where the food is as comfortable as the setting. A homey, rotating menu complements the room's earthy tones and cushy banquette seating. The crispy seasoned fries are a justified hit—they all but fly out of the kitchen—and the black-pepper mussels release an aromatic cloud of steam when they arrive. Couples on first dates and groups of regulars gather nightly for the well-priced specials. ✉ *1680 Massachusetts Ave., Cambridge* ☎ *617/441–5566* ⊟ *AE, D, DC, MC, V* Ⓣ *Porter.*

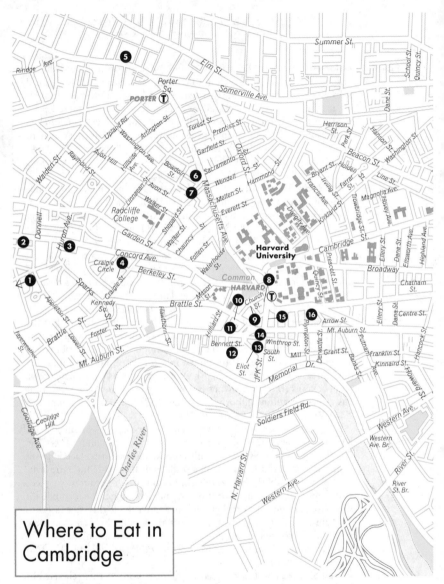

Where to Eat in Cambridge

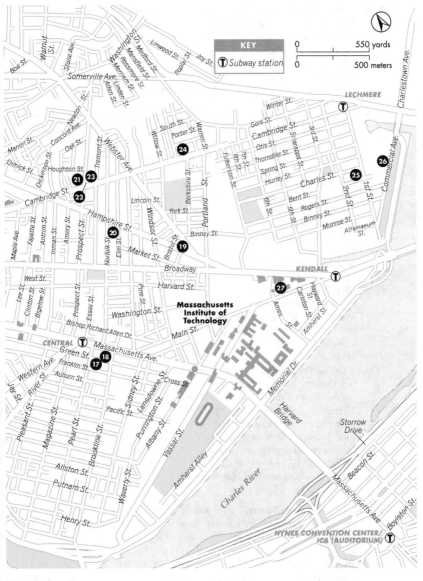

⏱ $–$$ ✕ **Full Moon.** Here's a happy reminder that dinner with children doesn't have to mean hamburgers. Choices include child pleasers such as pasta as well as grown-up entrées that include grilled sirloin with blue-cheese butter, arugula, and fries. Youngsters can spread out with plenty of play space and juice-filled sippy cups while adults weigh the substantial menu and a well-paired wine list. ⊠*344 Huron Ave., Cambridge* ☎*617/354–6699* ⌘*Reservations not accepted* ▭*MC, V* Ⓣ *Harvard.*

¢–$ ✕ **All Star Sandwich Bar.** Chris Schlesinger has a strict definition of what makes a sandwich: no wraps. He's put together a list of classics, like crispy, overstuffed Reubens and beef on weck, which are served quickly from an open kitchen. The only nonsandwich item on the board is a hot dog. Bathed in primary colors, the space has about a dozen tables that fill up at lunchtime. At dinner burgers are also served, along with a small selection of beer and wine. ⊠*1245 Cambridge St., Cambridge* ☎*617/868–3065* ⌘*Reservations not accepted* ▭*MC, V* Ⓣ *Central/Inmand.*

Fodor's Choice
★

⏱ ¢–$ ✕ **Hi-Rise Bread Company.** The best sandwiches start with stellar bread. Here, a range of breads are made on-site and sandwiches are given odd names like Bill's Seoul Show (chicken, bacon, and tarragon mayo on corn bread). The service matches the noontime rush: brusque and slightly harried. But once you get through the line with your daily soup and a Mahatma Gloves (curried-chicken salad with cashews) you can join the neighborhood regulars at wooden, communal tables and take in a noisy but comforting slice of Cambridge life. ⊠*208 Concord Ave., Cambridge* ☎*617/876–8766* ⌘*Reservations not accepted* ▭*MC, V* Ⓣ *Harvard.*

¢–$ ✕ **Mr. Bartley's Burger Cottage.** It may be perfect cuisine for the student metabolism: a huge variety of variously garnished thick burgers, deliciously crispy French fries (regular and sweet potato), and onion rings. There's also a competent veggie burger. The nonalcoholic "raspberry lime rickey," made with fresh limes, raspberry juice, sweetener, and soda water, is the must-try classic drink. Tiny tables in a crowded space make eavesdropping unavoidable. ⊠*1246 Massachusetts Ave., Cambridge* ☎*617/354–6559* ⌘*Reservations not accepted* ▭*No credit cards* ⊘*Closed Sun.* Ⓣ *Harvard.*

CHINESE

$$$–$$$$ ✕ **Upstairs on the Square.** In the middle of Harvard Square, this restaurant strikes just the right balance between funky and urbane, with pink linens and fringes tempering the dining room's old-boy look. The Monday Club Bar offers a more casual, yet still chic, spot to nosh. Entrées aren't too straitlaced either; you might try a crispy skate wing with seared foie gras or a charcoaled lamb sirloin with Japanese eggplant on the side. Finish with an apple custard tart. ⊠*91 Winthrop St., Cambridge* ☎*617/864–1933* ▭*AE, DC, MC, V* Ⓣ *Harvard.*

$–$$ ✕ **Lucky Garden.** A modest holdover from the first golden period of Szechuan food in Cambridge, Lucky Garden still serves excellent hot-and-sour soup, *yu hsiang* scallops (with garlic, hot pepper, and ginger), chicken and peanuts, and fried dumplings, in a pleasant, comfortable atmosphere. Liquor isn't served. ⊠*282 Concord Ave., Cambridge* ☎*617/354–9514* ⊟*D, MC, V* ⊤ *Harvard.*

ECLECTIC

$$–$$$
Fodor'sChoice
★

✕**Chez Henri.** French with a Cuban twist—odd bedfellows, but it works for this sexy, confident restaurant. The dinner menu gets serious with rabbit paella and saffron rice, veal stew with buttered egg noodles, and sinfully sweet rum-laced pineapple cake. At the cozy bar you can sample spiced fries, clam fritters, and the best grilled three-pork Cuban sandwich in Boston. The place fills quickly with Cantabrigian locals— an interesting mix of students, professors, and sundry intelligentsia. ⊠*1 Shepard St., Cambridge* ☎*617/354–8980* ⊟*AE, DC, MC, V* ⊗*No lunch* ⊤ *Harvard.*

$$–$$$
✕**Conundrum.** Hidden down a narrow alley, this tiny, red-hued space sports a hodgepodge of cuisines from Italy, France, even the Southwest as well as cute touches like puzzle-piece-shape bread plates. Try mixing and matching: pair sizzling chipotle-laced shrimp with a stuffed poblano pepper for a Southwestern theme. Bananas "Conundrum" is a decadent finish: crepes filled with bananas and smothered in chocolate ice cream. A tiny patio out back has super-cushiony chairs and just six tables. ⊠*56 JFK St., Cambridge* ☎*617/868–0335* ⊟*AE, D, MC, V.*

★ **$–$$$**
✕**Elephant Walk.** The chef of this popular Cambodian-French fusion house, Langtaine de Monteiro, learned to manage a Cambodian kitchen as the wife of a diplomat and for a time ran a restaurant in Provence. Her daughter, Nadsa, now runs the kitchen. The common element in both cuisines (which are listed separately on the menu) is garlic, from appetizers such as *moules* (mussels) swimming in butter infused with the stuff to superb Cambodian spring rolls, delicate salads, and a red curry of surpassingly fresh flavor. Vegetarians and diners suffering food allergies are easily accommodated. ⊠*2067 Massachusetts Ave., Cambridge* ☎*617/492–6900* ⊟*AE, D, DC, MC, V* ⊤ *Porter.*

FRENCH

★ **$$$–$$$$**
✕**Craigie Street Bistrot.** Buried away on a residential street, this tiny bistro churns out outstanding dishes. Chef-owner Tony Maws is fanatical about fresh, local, and organic so he's in the kitchen every morning, prepping ingredients (which most likely came from the Harvard Square farmers' market or another local purveyor). His menu changes daily so options can range from a Spanish-style octopus to tender beef short ribs to pork done three ways. Sunday is Chef's Whim night, meaning you'll eat (and most likely love) whatever he feels like cooking for a discounted price. The mostly organic wine list focuses on France. ⊠*5 Craigie Circle, Cambridge* ☎*617/497–5511* ⊟*AE, DC, MC, V* ⊗ *Closed Mon. No lunch* ⊤ *Harvard.*

INDIAN

$–$$
✕**Tamarind Bay.** This tiny, subterranean space is brick lined and warm— a cozy place to try dishes from all over India. The owners, longtime Cambridge residents, decided to open a restaurant that truly represented their homeland cuisine, hence the *chat* (warm vegetarian or chicken salads) dishes aren't filled with creamy yogurt, but marinated lightly with fresh ingredients, and all of the dishes are made to order.

Lamb chops *bhunna* masala are a sweet, spicy trio of chops served on a crescent-shape plate. A small selection of Indian wines is also available. ⊠*75 Winthrop St., Cambridge* ☎*617/491–4552* ▤*AE, MC, V* Ⓣ *Harvard.*

★ $ ✕**Tanjore.** The menu at this fully regional restaurant, from the owners of Rangoli in Allston, reaches from Sindh to Bengal, with some strength in the western provincial foods (Gujarat, Bombay) and their interesting sweet-hot flavors. An extra menu of *nashta,* or Indian tapas, adds to the confusion—or the fun, depending on how adventurous you're feeling. The *bhel* is a Bombay nashta of fried goodies in a sweet-hot curry; the rice dishes, chais, and breads are all excellent. The spicing starts mild, so don't be afraid to order "medium." ⊠*18 Eliot St., Cambridge* ☎*617/868–1900* ⌕*Reservations essential* ▤*AE, D, MC, V* Ⓣ *Harvard.*

ITALIAN

$$$–$$$$ ✕**Rialto.** The ultraposh dining room and its bar continue a pleasant drift from its Italian beginnings toward more-French techniques and New England ingredients, such as grilled local clams and Macomber turnips (a local, sweet, white turnip). An updated menu encourages ordering an appetizer, midcourse, and entrée with each dish layered with deeper and richer flavors. Or try the signature dishes like Tuscan-style sirloin steak with portobello-and-arugula salad, from chef Jody Adams, one of Boston's most admired kitchen wizards. ⊠*Charles Hotel, 1 Bennett St., Harvard Sq., Cambridge* ☎*617/661–5050* ▤*AE, DC, MC, V* ◷*No lunch* Ⓣ *Harvard.*

MEDITERRANEAN

$$–$$$$ ✕**Dante.** With one of the best patio views of the Charles River, Dante almost resembles a seaside café on the Amalfi coast. Almost. Chef-owner Dante DeMagistris culls flavors from that region, and a few others, to present a seafood- and pasta-heavy menu with entrées that focus on hearty portions of protein like porcini-basted scallops and basil-roasted guinea hen. Try the chef's tasting menu for seven to nine courses that might include a number of specialties not on the daily menu. ⊠*40 Edwin H. Land Blvd., Cambridge* ☎*617/497–4200* ▤*AE, D, MC, V.*

$$–$$$ ✕**Oleana.** Chef and owner Ana Sortun is one of the city's culinary treasures—and so is Oleana. Here, flavors from all over the Middle Eastern Mediterranean sing loud and clear, in the hot, crispy fried mussels starter, and in the smoky eggplant puree beside tamarind-glazed beef. Fish gets jacked up with Turkish spices, then grilled until it just barely caramelizes. In warm weather, the back patio is a hidden piece of utopia—a homey garden that hits the perfect note of casual refinement. ⊠*134 Hampshire St., Cambridge* ☎*617/661–0505* ⌕*Reservations essential* ▤*AE, MC, V* ◷*No lunch* Ⓣ *Central.*
FodorsChoice ★

★ $$ ✕**Casablanca.** Long before *The Rocky Horror Picture Show,* Harvard and Radcliffe types would put on trench coats and head to the Brattle Theatre to see *Casablanca,* rising to recite the Bogart and Bergman lines in unison. Then it was on to this restaurant, where the walls are painted with scenes from the film, for more of the same. The path to this local institution is still well worn, thanks to velvety, deep-flavored braised beef ribs and grilled quail with almond-honey butter. The bar still attracts a worldly graduate student crowd with its range of local beers and classic cocktails. ✉ *40 Brattle St., Cambridge* ☎ *617/876–0999* 🖃 *AE, D, DC, MC, V* Ⓣ *Harvard.*

$-$$ ✕**Baraka Café.** Tiny Baraka may be atmospherically challenged, but after a few bites you won't care. Chef-owner Alia Rejeb was born in France and raised in Tunisia—a fact reflected sharply in her menu. Imagine a smoky, creamy dish of peppers awakened with mint, oregano, and cheese (*mechouia*) or a spice-laden deep-chocolate cake, redolent of star anise. Make a meal from the selection of small plates or try an entrée of couscous or marinated vegetables. No alcohol is served. ✉ *80 Pearl St., Cambridge* ☎ *617/868–3951* ⌚ *Reservations essential* 🖃 *No credit cards* ☾ *Closed Mon.* Ⓣ *Central.*

MEXICAN

¢–$ ✕**Border Café.** Reasonably priced Sunbelt fare—Tex-Mex with Cajun and Caribbean influences—and a tightly packed Margaritaville bar scene have the Harvard Square throngs here on weekends. The Cajun shrimp is a favorite, as is the *burro* (a burrito with enchilada sauce). ✉ *32 Church St., Cambridge* ☎ *617/864–6100* 🖃 *AE, MC, V* Ⓣ *Harvard.*

PORTUGUESE

$-$$ ✕**Sunset Café.** The lively atmosphere here may make you feel as though you're attending a giant Portuguese wedding. Entire families come, and on a Friday or Saturday night (when the café has guitarists and singers), it's not unusual to see little girls in frilly dresses and boys in jackets and ties. Specialties include kale soup thickened with potatoes, *mariscada a chefe* (seafood casserole with fine spices), and shrimp Ana María (panfried shrimp in seafood stock). The bargain-price wines on the list include some of the best Dão reds available outside Portugal. ✉ *851 Cambridge St., Cambridge* ☎ *617/547–2938* 🖃 *AE, D, DC, MC, V* Ⓣ *Central.*

SEAFOOD

$$-$$$ ✕**Legal Sea Foods.** All the regional seafood classics, from famed New England chowder to a sumptuous raw bar, can be found here, in the Cambridge outpost of the Legal chain. Just as worthwhile are the more-modern takes: seafood stew with Indian spices, for example, and grilled swordfish with mango salsa. A preferred-seating list allows calls ahead. ✉ *5 Cambridge Center, Kendall Sq.* ☎ *617/864–3400* ⌚ *Reservations not accepted* 🖃 *AE, D, DC, MC, V* Ⓣ *Kendall/MIT.*

SOUTHERN

★ $-$$ ✕**Magnolia.** The heady scent of sizzling hush puppies mixes with the spice of jambalaya in Inman Square's Southern outpost. Flavors are matched by the bright setting—from the primary-color decor to the prompt and friendly service. Catch any of the delectable fish dishes such as meaty crab cakes or grilled swordfish. ✉ *1193 Cambridge St., Cambridge* ☎ *617/576–1971* 🖃 *AE, D, DC, MC, V* ☾ *Closed Mon.* Ⓣ *Central.*

VIETNAMESE

★ ¢–$$ ✕**Le's.** Vietnamese noodle soup called *pho* is the name of the game in this quick-and-casual eatery. At less than $10, it's a meal unto itself. Get it filled with chicken, shrimp, or beef, steaming hot in a big bowl. Fresh salads and stir-fries are offered as well. It's all notably fresh fare, and, even better, it's healthy, without gloppy sauces, and many of the dishes are steamed. ✉ *36 JFK St., Cambridge* ☎ *617/864–4100* 🚫 *AE, MC, V* Ⓣ *Harvard.*

BROOKLINE

Going to Brookline is a nice way to get out of the city without really leaving town. Although it's surrounded by Boston on three sides, Brookline has its own suburban flavor, seasoned with a multitude of historic—and expensive—houses and garnished with a diverse ethnic population that supports a string of sushi bars and an expanding list of kosher restaurants. Most Brookline eateries are clustered in the town's commercial centers: Brookline Village, Washington Square, Longwood, and bustling Coolidge Corner.

AMERICAN

$–$$ ✕**Publick House.** What started as a simple neighborhood beer bar has reached cultlike status for Brookline-ites and beyond. Serving more than 175 out-of-the-ordinary and artisanal beers, the bar also offers extraordinarily tasty sandwiches, smaller entrées, and main dishes, most of which have beer incorporated into them. A Smuttynose grilled chicken sandwich, for example, is marinated in IPA, and fried shrimp are battered with Japanese bread crumbs and Whale's Tale pale ale. There are even beer recommendations to match. Weekend nights find long lines, but one taste of the city's only "cuisine à la bier" is absolutely worth it. ✉ *1648 Beacon St., Brookline* ☎ *617/277–2880* 🚫 *AE, D, DC, MC, V* Ⓣ *Washington Square.*

DELICATESSENS

$ ✕**Rubin's.** The last kosher Jewish delicatessen in the Boston area serves a hand-cut pastrami sandwich a New Yorker can respect. There are *kasha varnishkes* (buckwheat with bow-tie noodles), hot brisket, and many other high-cholesterol classics but, of course, no real cream for your coffee or dairy desserts. ✉ *500 Harvard St., Brookline* ☎ *617/731–8787* 🚫 *AE, DC, MC, V* ⊙ *Closed Sat. No dinner Fri.* Ⓣ *Coolidge Corner.*

$ ✕**Zaftigs.** Here's something different: a contemporary version of a Jewish delicatessen. How refreshing to have genuinely lean corned beef, a modest slice of cheesecake, low-sugar homemade borscht, and a lovely whitefish-salad sandwich. Weekend brunch time can bring hour-long waits for a plate of the area's best pancakes, though. ✉ *335 Harvard St., Brookline* ☎ *617/975–0075* 🚫 *AE, D, DC, MC, V* Ⓣ *Coolidge Corner.*

Best Bets with Kids

Though it's unusual to see children in Boston's most elite restaurants, eating out with youngsters does not have to mean culinary exile. The vast majority of restaurants are happy to accommodate kids with simplified dishes and an out-of-the-way booth. Here are some particularly family-friendly options.

Charley's Saloon. Saloons may be no place for kids, but this is no real saloon. Charley's doles out American classics (grilled cheese, steaks, and apple pies) in a fun retro setting. Kids can color and people-watch. ✉ *284 Newbury St., Back Bay* ☎ *617/266–3000.* **Full Moon.** Kids will delight in the play kitchen and dollhouse, and parents can cheer that they get to tuck into lovelies such as grilled salmon with bok choy. Meanwhile there's plenty of macaroni and cheese or burgers for the young ones. ✉ *344 Huron Ave., Cambridge* ☎ *617/354–6699.* **Joe's American Bar & Grille.** So what if the restaurant looks as if it has been decorated by a raving mob at a Fourth of July parade? Next to an oversize burger and a slice of apple pie, the red, white, and blue overload is kind of fun. The clam chowder is almost always a hit with all generations. ✉ *279 Dartmouth St., Back Bay* ☎ *617/536–4200.* **King-fish.** Parents can dig into the fresh raw bar and junior can sup on clam chowder while watching the grill in the open kitchen. ✉ *1 S. Market St., Downtown* ☎ *617/523–8860.* **Legal Sea Foods.** Smack between Faneuil Hall and the New England Aquarium, Legal is a great break after a long day on your feet. The children's meals, extra rolls, and playful menus don't hurt matters either. ✉ *255 State St., Downtown* ☎ *617/227–3115.* **Mr. Bartley's Burger Cottage.** Maybe it's the frappés (thick milk shakes), silly cartoons all over the walls, or just the fun, high-energy vibe. Whatever it is, Bartley's is a hit with kids. ✉ *1246 Massachusetts Ave., Cambridge* ☎ *617/354–6559.* **P. F. Chang's China Bistro.** Straightforward, Americanized, and inexpensive Chinese food makes the rounds in this theatrically decorated spot. Kids love the lemon chicken and the fake Imperial sculptures and screens; parents love the prices and the accommodating staff. ✉ *8 Park Plaza, Back Bay* ☎ *617/573–0822.* **Stephanie's on Newbury.** Here's comfort food at its best—sophisticated enough for parents, simple enough for kids. The place is pretty but homey, and has plenty of booths for spreading out. ✉ *190 Newbury St., Back Bay* ☎ *617/236–0990.* **Summer Shack.** Boston überchef Jasper White has given New England seafood an urban tweak in his laid-back, loud, and fun spot next to the Prudential Center. The colors are bright, and the entire affair is like one big indoor clambake. ✉ *10 Scotia St., Back Bay* ☎ *617/867–9955.* **Zaftigs.** Fill up on huge plates of deli fixings such as matzo-ball soup, first-rate knishes, and heaping plates of grilled chicken, thick-cut onion rings, and three-cheese macaroni. Families cram the place regularly, so servers are used to kids' requests. ✉ *335 Harvard St., Brookline* ☎ *617/975–0075.*

ECLECTIC

★ $$-$$$ ✕**Elephant Walk.** Technically this outpost of Elephant Walk (the other is in Cambridge) is in Boston, but psychologically it's the gateway to Brookline. The French-Cambodian menu is separated by region, so you get the best of both worlds. Tease your palate with an exotic assortment of dumpling appetizers, spring rolls that you wrap in fresh lettuce leaves, and mouthwatering coq au vin. The airy atmosphere evokes a British Colonial hotel; the food reminds you of why Phnom Penh was "the Paris of Asia." The desserts, though, are pure Paris. ✉*900 Beacon St., Brookline* ☎*617/247–1500* ▤*AE, D, DC, MC, V* Ⓣ *St. Mary's.*

> ### BEST BANG FOR YOUR BUCK
>
> ▪ **Ginza** (Chinatown, Brookline) for sushi
>
> ▪ **Matt Murphy's Pub** (Brookline) for hearty, heartwarming Irish food
>
> ▪ **Silvertone** (Downtown) for burgers and beer
>
> ▪ **Rubin's** (Brookline) for deli sandwiches which are piled with almost a full pound of meat
>
> ▪ **Magnolia** (Cambridge) for soulful Southern food

INDIAN

$-$$ ✕**Rani.** One of Brookline's more-unusual restaurants serves excellent Indian cuisine in the Hyderabadi style, which incorporates northern and southern flavors. Dishes are complex, rich, and layered with sweet and salty. *Murg musalam,* a roasted chicken in a fragrant brown sauce, is tender and juicy, and any of the tandoori dishes (meats cooked in a clay oven) are designed for beginners. The variety of specialty breads is impressive, and the sleek interior fills up nightly with locals looking for a change of pace from Downtown's more-casual Indian buffet. ✉*1353 Beacon St., Brookline* ☎*617/734–0400* ▤*AE, D, DC, MC, V* Ⓣ *Coolidge Corner.*

IRISH

$-$$ ✕**Matt Murphy's Pub.** Boston has dozens of Irish pubs, but very few are notable for food—this being a welcome exception. Matt Murphy's makes real poetry out of thick slabs of bread and butter, giant servings of soup, fish-and-chips presented in a twist of newspaper, shepherd's pie, and hot rabbit pie. Don't miss the housemade ketchup with your French fries or the nightly jam sessions with local rock bands who crowd into one tiny corner of the bar after 10 PM. ✉*14 Harvard St., Brookline* ☎*617/232–0188* ⚊*Reservations not accepted* ▤*No credit cards* Ⓣ *Brookline Village.*

JAPANESE

$$-$$$ ✕**Fugakyu.** The name sounds vaguely offensive in English, but in Japanese it means "house of elegance." The interior hits the mark, with tatami mats, rice-paper partitions, and wooden ships circling a moat around the sushi bar. The menu is both elegant and novel, with Boston's first live-tank sashimi, the rare Japanese *matsutake* mushrooms in a vegetarian stir-fry, and appetizers such as *ikura tanzaku* (an orange-on-orange combination of salmon, salmon eggs, and Japanese yam)

served in a martini glass. Bento boxes and noodle soups are available at lunch only. ✉*1280 Beacon St., Brookline* ☎*617/734–1268* 🖃*AE, D, DC, MC, V* Ⓣ *Coolidge Corner.*

★ **$$** ✕**Ginza.** The two Ginzas (there's one in Chinatown) are thought to have the most advanced sushi in town, but this spot gains extra points for its selection of 15 types of hot sake. Avant-sushi these days includes hot spices, fried morsels, boozy marinades, and presentations with such props as a martini glass. A quick anthology is the "Ginza Surprise," consisting of a daily assortment of chef's eccentricities, such as "caterpillar" maki with avocado scales. There are lots of good appetizers and hot dinners as well, including teriyaki, tempura, and *nabemono* (one-pot meals). ✉*1002 Beacon St., Brookline* ☎*617/566–9688* 🖃*AE, DC, MC, V* Ⓣ *Brookline.*

SEAFOOD

★ **$–$$$** ✕**Lineage.** Downtown is saturated with decent seafood options but few hit the mark on inventive fare quite like Lineage. Chef-owner Jeremy Sewell puts the restaurants central wood-burning stove to good use and roasts everything from halibut to pork chops. His cousin Mark is a lobsterman and provides a fresh catch now and then. A number of seats at the bar, along with ample dining room space, allow diners the option of a casual meal or a comfortable fine-dining experience. ✉*242 Harvard St., Brookline* ☎*617/232–0065* 🖃*AE, MC, V* ☽*Closed Mon. No lunch* Ⓣ *Brookline Village.*

$–$$ ✕**Village Fish.** With one of the few raw bars west of Boston's waterfront, Village Fish serves nothing but classic seafood, including light and crispy fried calamari and the freshest grilled shrimp around. The best seats in the house are either at the bar or at a handful of tables on the bar side. ✉*22 Harvard St., Brookline* ☎*617/566–3474* 🖃*AE, MC, V* ☽*No lunch weekends* Ⓣ *Brookline Village.*

SPANISH

★ **$–$$** ✕**Taberna de Haro.** Although Bostonians have already fallen for tapas, this is the first tapas bar to fully capture the spirit of this Spanish cuisine. At dinner, along with a few entrées, you have a choice of about 30 tapas, including classics such as an enormous cheese platter or *pollo en pepitoria,* chicken legs with enough almond-garlic sauce to necessitate a huge hunk of bread. A well-planned and inexpensive all-Spanish wine list is hand-selected by the owners, and an outdoor patio fills up throughout the summer. ✉*999 Beacon St., Brookline* ☎*617/277–8272* 🖃*DC, MC, V* Ⓣ *Coolidge Corner.*

ALLSTON

More or less northwest of Downtown, this densely packed little enclave of grunge mixes twentysomething college students with immigrants from four continents. In general, the restaurants are homey and cheap, but the best offer a culinary world tour. A number of places allow low-key BYOB (Blanchard's and Marty's on Harvard Avenue are both great wine stores). For cheap eats and a young vibe, the neighborhood can't be beat.

BRAZILIAN

$ ✕ **Café Brazil.** Terrific meaty entrées from Brazil's Minas Gerais region fill the menu, including a fine mixed grill and a couple of fish stews from the neighboring province of Bahia. This little place also turns out a great version of the fried yucca appetizer called *mandioca*. The decor is basic travel posters, but the down-home Brazilian cooking itself could almost transport you to Brazil. ✉ *421 Cambridge St., Allston* ☎ *617/789–5980* ▤ *AE, D, DC, MC, V* Ⓣ *Harvard.*

INDIAN

$-$$ ✕ **Rangoli.** Most of what Americans think of as Indian food is decidedly northern Indian, so Rangoli offers a nice alternative journey into the hotter and spicier (and relatively vegetarian) world of southern Indian cooking. Specialties include curries wrapped in *dosa* (sourdough pancakes) and *idli sambar,* a fiery vegetable soup with soothing dumplings. ✉ *129 Brighton Ave., Allston* ☎ *617/562–0200* ▤ *AE, D, DC, MC, V* Ⓣ *Harvard.*

KOREAN

$-$$ ✕ **Choe's Café.** The food here is outstanding—kept honest by Korean students who drift up from Boston University. Winners include seafood-scallion pancake and hot, spicy squid. ✉ *957 Commonwealth Ave., Allston* ☎ *617/783–8702* ▤ *MC, V* ⊘ *No lunch Sun.* Ⓣ *Babcock St.*

SOUTHERN

¢-$ ✕ **Soul Fire Barbecue.** What this neighborhood needed most took a long time to get here, but there's finally a quick stop for barbecue, complete with a range of sauces and styles. The pit resides in the kitchen but the enticing, smoky aroma fills the whole high-ceiling space. Everything from pulled pork to spare- and baby back ribs to hickory-roasted chicken can be smothered in the sauce of your choice, including a North Carolina vinegar and spicy mustard. It's counter service only but there's also a bar to sit at that's covered with old soul and blues album covers. ✉ *182 Harvard Ave., Allston* ☎ *617/787–3003* ▤ *AE, MC, V* Ⓣ *Harvard.*

JAMAICA PLAIN

This neighborhood is a kind of mini-Cambridge: multiethnic and filled with cutting-edge artists, graduate students, political idealists, and yuppie families. Recently, the area, known for its affordable and unusual ethnic spots, has seen a swell of a more gentrified—but no less creative—sort.

AMERICAN

★ $$ ✕ **Centre Street Café.** It's impossible not to love J.P.'s funky and fun hangout, where neighborhood residents pack the tables and local artwork fills the walls. The eclectic menu veers from ethnic inspirations like spicy cream-sauced shrimp and rice to super-fresh salads brimming with local produce. Lines snake around the block every Sunday for

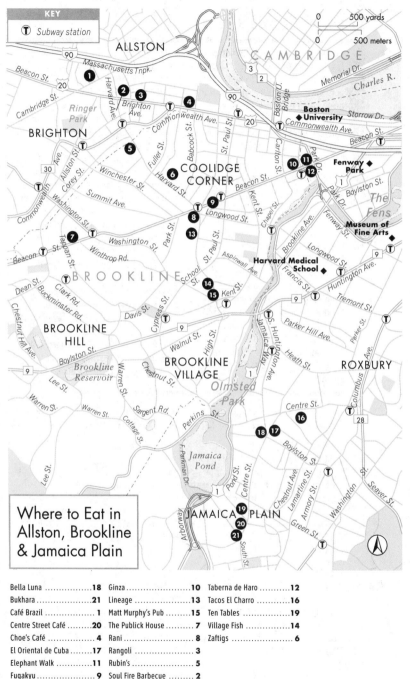

Where to Eat in Allston, Brookline & Jamaica Plain

KEY

ⓣ *Subway station*

I Scream, You Scream

Come snow, sleet, or horrendous humidity, Boston's appetite for ice cream remains undiminished. Flavors far exceed basic vanilla with burnt caramel, honey-anise, or cinnamon that could bring tears to your eyes (and not due to an "ice-cream headache").

Christina's (⊠ 1255 Cambridge St., Cambridge ☎ 617/492–7021), Inman Square's dessert mecca, serves such creatively flavored scoops as Wild Turkey–walnut and an amazingly addictive chocolate mousse. Dieting meets decadence at **Emack & Bolio's** (⊠ 290 Newbury St., Back Bay ☎ 617/247–8772), a pint-size parlor that's half juice bar, half ice-cream counter. You can lap up the delicious handiwork of ice-cream maestro Steve Herrell, pioneer of the "smoosh-in" (candy and nuts mixed into the cold stuff), at **Herrell's** (⊠ 15 Dunster St., Cambridge ☎ 617/497–2179). Simple but sublime cones have

addicted many a Bostonian to the fun and funky likes of **J. P. Licks** (⊠ 659 Centre St., Jamaica Plain ☎ 617/524–6740). Don't miss J. P. Licks' ice-cream floats—equal parts cream and fizz. If you're looking for serious ice cream, look no further than **Toscanini's** (⊠ 899 Main St., Cambridge ☎ 617/491–5877 ⊠ 1310 Massachusetts Ave., Cambridge ☎ 617/354–9350). With such exotic flavors as cardamom and burnt caramel, and textures that range from refreshing to truly rich, Toscanini's has few (if any) equals. If it's quantity or a good cause that you're after, nothing beats the **Scooper Bowl** (☎ 800/525–4669 ⊕ www.scooper-bowl.org), an annual all-you-can-eat extravaganza held in early June at City Hall Plaza. Organizers serve up 10 tons of brand-name ice-cream (including Baskin-Robbins, Ben & Jerry's, and Häagen-Dazs). Proceeds benefit the Dana-Farber Cancer Institute.

the spectacular (and spectacularly filling) brunch. ⊠ 669A Centre St., Jamaica Plain ☎ 617/524–9217 ☐ MC, V ☉ No lunch Ⓣ Green St.

CARIBBEAN
¢–$ ✕ **El Oriental de Cuba.** This small haven, which was refurbished into a bigger, better space after a fire, serves a large variety of excellent Cuban food, including a restorative chicken soup, a classic Cuban sub, superb rice and beans (opt for the red beans over the black), and sweet "tropical shakes." The *tostones* (twice-fried plantains) are beloved during cold New England winters by the city's many Cuban transplants. *Breakfast also served* ⊠ 416 Centre St., Jamaica Plain ☎ 617/524–6464 ☐ MC, V Ⓣ Stony Brook.

FRENCH
★ $–$$ ✕ **Ten Tables.** Jamaica Plain's postage-stamp-size, candlelit boîte is an enchanting mix of Gallic elegance and chummy neighborhood revelry. So, too, the food. Simple but high-quality dishes such as pumpkin soufflé and seared diver scallops—followed by a carefully chosen international cheese plate—seamlessly seal the deal. ⊠ 597 Centre St., Jamaica Plain ☎ 617/524–8810 ☐ AE, D, DC, MC, V Ⓣ Stony Brook.

INDIAN

$–$$ ✗**Bukhara.** The helpful staff here guides you through a menu that spans the cuisines of several Indian regions. The condiments alone could keep you satiated, but check out the dosas, curries, and anything from the tandoor oven. The spice quotient varies from mild to incendiary. ✉ *701 Centre St., Jamaica Plain* ☎*617/522–2195* ▤*AE, D, DC, MC, V* Ⓣ *Forest Hills.*

ITALIAN

$–$$ ✗**Bella Luna.** Sci-fi jokes are sprinkled across this spot's spaced-out menu of eccentric pizzas, calzones, and Italian standards. The "Brendan Behan" pizza is topped with goat cheese and roasted red peppers, and the "Diedre Delux" mixes dried cranberries, caramelized onions, and Gorgonzola cheese. Work by local artists lines the walls, and local musicians provide the music. (The weekly schedule ranges from jazz to salsa.) ✉*405 Centre St., Jamaica Plain* ☎*617/524–6060* ▤*AE, MC, V* Ⓣ *Green St.*

MEXICAN

★ **$–$$** ✗**Tacos El Charro.** Drag naysayers who claim that "Boston has no *real* Mexican restaurants" to this authentic hole-in-the-wall. Order them one of the delectable soft tacos crammed with chicken or pineapple-flavored pork, or tempt them with a rich enchilada or savory goat stew. Wash it all down with a thickly blended *horchata* (a cold, frappé-like drink made with rice, milk, and ground almonds). Soon the guilty offenders will be thanking you while eating their words—along with everything else. Odds are they won't even comment on the perfunctory decor. ✉*349 Centre St., Jamaica Plain* ☎*617/522–2578* ▤*AE, D, DC, MC, V* Ⓣ *Jackson Sq.*

WORTH A SPECIAL TRIP

ASIAN

★ **$$$** ✗**Blue Ginger.** Chef Ming Tsai's nimble maneuvers in the kitchen have caught the nation's eye via a cable-TV cooking program, *Simply Ming*, and his many cookbooks, including the first, *Blue Ginger: East Meets West Cooking with Ming Tsai (1999)*. Plan ahead (and make sure Tsai is there) to savor his Occident-meets-Asian cuisine. Top choices include roast-duck pot stickers with fresh pea salad and *sambal* (an Indonesian condiment of red chilies, onion, and lime) and tangerine-teriyaki wild salmon. There's no T stop anywhere nearby, but the 15-mi trip from downtown Boston is an easy jaunt west on the Massachusetts Turnpike to Route 16/Washington Street. ✉*583 Washington St., Wellesley* ☎*781/283–5790* ▤*AE, MC, V* ⊙*Closed Sun. No lunch Sat.*

Where to Stay

WORD OF MOUTH

"We love the Marriott Long Wharf. Stay on the Concierge Level on the top floor. Great view of the Harbor, kids can enjoy the breakfasts and snacks, and it is in a great location. It's a block from Faneuil Hall, Quincy Market and across from the Aquarium, etc."

–MBnancy

Updated by
Diane Bair
and Pamela
Wright

BUH-BYE, RITZ-CARLTON! BOSTON'S OLD GUARD is still shaking its head in disbelief, but it's true. Boston's grande dame, built in 1927 and host to Winston Churchill, British royalty, and rooftop soirees for the city's high society, has gone the way of Jordan Marsh and the Bailey's sundae. The Taj chain is the new owner of the property (though the Ritz flag still flies over the nearby Ritz-Carlton Boston Common), staking its claim as Boston's ultimate luxury property. Want proof? The Taj Boston recently offered a $1 million Valentine's Day package that included a new Bentley. (A *Bentley!* So ... Hollywood! So ... *not* Boston!) Meanwhile, across the Public Garden, the Four Seasons celebrates 20-plus years in Boston with a top-to-bottom makeover, all the better to take on competition from new properties like the InterContinental. As is true of Boston in general, the lodgings scene is a hodgepodge of old and new. For every gilded old historic hotel, there's a brash newcomer, tarted up in red leather and black lacquer. There's the place you'd send you mother, the place you'd meet your lover, and a whole bunch of places that fall somewhere in the middle.

If it's luxury you seek—300-thread-count linens, MP3 players with surround sound, private bars, and nationally renowned restaurants—you can certainly find it. Expensive they may be, but many hotels have been plumping up their amenities, giving you more perks for the price. Even less-expensive establishments are adding pillow-top mattresses, down duvets, and, in a nod to the business traveler, high-speed Internet access and wireless connections. Be sure to ■ TIP→ **check out promotional packages.** Weekend rates at some of the city's best hotels, especially those that cater to a business crowd on weekdays, can be far below standard "rack" rates and often include free perks such as parking, breakfast, or cocktails to entice leisure travelers.

On the other hand, there are abundant options at the smaller and older hotels, and bed-and-breakfast inns that give you cleanliness and convenience, and a few nice perks to boot. Cheaper than most hotels, and more stylish than most HoJos, B&Bs are good bases from which to experience Boston's famous neighborhoods, from the hip and gastronomically diverse South End to the hallowed, gaslit streets of Beacon Hill or slightly out-of-town enclaves such as Brookline and Cambridge.

BOSTON

BACK BAY

$$$$
Fodor's Choice
★

Fairmont Copley Plaza. For those who believe that too much of a good thing is just about right, the deliciously decadent, unabashedly romantic Fairmont lures. Richly decorated, and very ornate—we're talking cherubs on the ceiling here—this favors romance and tradition over sleek and modern. (Really love pampering? Stay on the Fairmont Gold floor, an ultradeluxe club level offering a dedicated staff, lounge, dining room, and library.) Shopping fanatics adore the close proximity to Newbury Street, the Prudential Center, and Copley Place. This

KNOW-HOW

BOOKING TIPS

With the many educational institutions in Boston and Cambridge, commencement weekends in May and June can book months—sometimes even a year—in advance, and beginning-of-term is also a busy time as parents enter town to drop their children off at school for the year. Expect to pay top dollar at these times, sometimes more than triple the price of an off-season rate.

Leaf-peepers arrive in early October during foliage season. Fall is also a popular time for conventions, which brings waves of business travelers. Keep in mind that many hotels in the Back Bay area receive a large portion of their business from conference attendees to the Hynes Convention Center. Check which events are happening before you reserve a room in the area. Other special events such as the Boston Marathon in April and the Head of the Charles in October are busy times for large hotels and small inns alike.

PRICES

The lodgings we list are the cream of the crop in each price category. We always list the facilities that are available, but we don't specify whether they cost extra. Assume that all rooms have private baths, phones, cable TV (we note when cable TV comes with DVD), and air-conditioning unless otherwise noted.

Assume that hotels operate on the European Plan (EP, with no meals) unless we specify that they use the Continental Plan (CP, with a Continental breakfast daily) or Breakfast Plan (BP, with full breakfast daily).

HOW TO SAVE

Business-oriented hotels will often lower their rates on weekends in an attempt to draw in tourists, and small and large hotels alike have value-saving packages involving sights and special events happening throughout the city. Outlying areas often have some of the best deals. If you don't need to be right Downtown, look toward Cambridge, Brookline, and Dorchester, where rates are almost always lower and parking is easier. During the winter months, the Back Bay is a good option, because large hotels here try to draw leisure travelers (as opposed to business travelers) with competitive packages and rates, especially on weekends.

If you're traveling as a family, keep in mind that children often stay free (or at a discounted rate) in their parents' room. The cutoff age ranges from 12 to 18.

WHAT IT COSTS					
	$$$$	$$$	$$	$	¢
FOR 2 PEOPLE	over $325	$225–$325	$150–$224	$75–$149	under $75

Prices are for two people in a standard double room in high season, excluding 12.45% tax and service charges.

1912 landmark underwent a $34 million renovation in 2004, updating rooms with new classically inspired decor, marble bathrooms, and high-speed Internet access. The grand public spaces have mosaic floors, marble pillars, and high gilded ceilings hung with glittering chandeliers. The Oak Room restaurant matches its mahogany-panel twin in New York's Plaza Hotel; the equally stately—and tryst-worthy—Oak Bar has live music and one of the longest martini menus in town. **Pros:** Very elegant, great Copley Square location, cozy bar. **Cons:** Small closets and bathrooms; charge for Internet access (no charge on Fairmont Gold level); not much shelving or storage. ⊠*138 St. James Ave., Back Bay, 02116* ☏*617/267–5300 or 800/441–1414* 🖷*617/375–9648* ⊕*www.fairmont.com/copleyplaza* ⬅*366 rooms, 17 suites* ⚷*In-room: safe, refrigerator, ethernet. In-hotel: restaurant, room service, bar, gym, laundry service, concierge, executive floor, public Wi-Fi, parking (fee), some pets allowed* ⊟*AE, D, DC, MC, V* Ⓣ*Copley, Back Bay/South End.*

★ $$$$ ⬚**Four Seasons.** Jeans-clad billionaires and assorted business types cluster in the glossy lobby of the Four Seasons, while TV anchorfolk diss the competition over 'tinis and Bristol Burgers in the Bristol Lounge. (Visiting celebs are whisked to the 2,000-square-foot, $6,000-per-night Presidential Suite—no waiting in the lobby for them!) Thanks to a recent face-lift, the Four Seasons retains its perch as Boston's go-to hotel for luxury with a *soupçon* of hip. Designers resisted the trend of soothing taupe for bright shots of citron and apricot in public spaces; guest rooms sport black-and-cream toile with gold and lemon accents, large bay windows, and oversize work areas. Luxury amenities include DVD players, 42-inch plasma TVs, and L'Occitane toiletries. (Celebrities stash the full-size soaps in their luggage, we're told.) Even if you spring for the basic city-view room (as low as $295 on weekends in January and February), you can enjoy fab views of the Public Garden from the pool and whirlpool on the eighth floor, or from Aujourd'hui, the hotel's top-rated contemporary French restaurant, or the Bristol Lounge. **Pros:** Great location, overlooking the Public Garden and a short walk to Newbury Street shops and the Theater District; Mercedes courtesy car makes short trips around town; excellent gym. **Cons:** Front entrance can get busy (you might have to wait for your valet-parked car), restaurants are pricey. ⊠*200 Boylston St., Back Bay, 02116* ☏*617/338–4400 or 800/819–5053* 🖷*617/423–0154* ⊕*www. fourseasons.com/boston* ⬅*197 rooms, 76 suites* ⚷*In-room: safe, refrigerator, dial-up, Wi-Fi. In-hotel: 2 restaurants, room service, bar, pool, gym, laundry service, concierge, public Wi-Fi, parking (fee), some pets allowed* ⊟*AE, D, DC, MC, V* Ⓣ*Arlington.*

$$$$ ⬚**Taj Boston Hotel.** Formerly the Ritz-Carlton Boston (not to be confused with the Ritz-Carlton Boston Common), this landmark hotel is now owned by Taj Hotels. Standing guard at the corner of fashionable Newbury Street and the Public Garden, it has long been a symbol of gracious opulence. So far, the cobalt-blue-and-crystal chandeliers, lavish fabrics, and gilded sconces remain, as do many of the former Ritz's staff members. Small changes include plush new robes and towels in guest rooms, and Molton Brown bath amenities instead of Bulgari. The

Fodor'sChoice
★

Taj has added vibrant floral displays in the lobby, and offers three meals daily in The Café, plus high tea in the Lounge. It's too soon to predict any major changes but, for now, if you liked the old Ritz—with its cozy luxury, wood-burning fireplaces (and fireplace butlers), afternoon tea (with a harpist), and glorious views—you'll be as happy as one of the swans in the Public Garden's lagoon at the "new" Taj. ⊠ *15 Arlington St., Back Bay, 02116* ☎*617/536–5700* 🖷*617/536–1335* ⊕*www.tajhotels.com* ↪*228 rooms, 45 suites* ⚐*In-room: safe, refrigerator, ethernet. In-hotel: restaurant, room service, bar, gym, laundry service, concierge, executive floor, parking (fee), some pets allowed* ⊟*AE, D, DC, MC, V* Ⓣ*Arlington.*

★ **$$$–$$$$**   🏨**Colonnade Hotel.** Whoa. Did the stylists at Saks Fifth Avenue, across the street at the Pru, sneak in and give the Colonnade an extreme makeover? The hotel has gone from so-*over* '80s brass-and-mahogany to a clean, modern look with tones of espresso, khaki, chocolate, and chrome. All this would be mere window dressing if it weren't for new, guest-friendly touches like flat-panel TVs, DVD players, and alarm clock/MP3 players, plus extendable reading lights and fab high-tech coffeemakers. Even the minibar goodies got an upgrade, with fresh shortbread cookies and the like. The look is slightly masculine but quite comfy, with pillow-top mattresses, high-thread-count sheets, and a round worktable (replacing the typical desk) so guests can eat or work comfortably. Floor-to-ceiling windows (these actually open) have been triple glazed to keep out the traffic noise of Huntington Avenue. Alas, the downside of all this is, rates have gone up a bit. In summer, the roof deck pool is a huge draw. Open to hotel guests only, the pool area has great views of the neighborhood, and live music. For your gustatory needs, Brasserie Jo is an authentic French brasserie. **Pros:** Roof deck pool; T stop a few steps away; across the street from Prudential Center for shopping and restaurants. Con: Prices have gone up since hotel was renovated. ⊠*120 Huntington Ave., Back Bay, 02116* ☎*617/424–7000 or 800/962–3030* 🖷*617/424–1717* ⊕*www.colonnadehotel.com* ↪*276 rooms, 9 suites* ⚐*In-room: safe, Wi-Fi. In-hotel: restaurant, room service, bar, pool, gym, laundry service, concierge, public Wi-Fi, parking (fee), some pets allowed* ⊟*AE, D, DC, MC, V* Ⓣ*Prudential Center.*

$$$–$$$$ 🏨**Courtyard by Marriott Boston Copley Square.** Oops. You *meant* to book the big Marriott Copley Place across the street, and you mistakenly chose this one? No worries. Some call this the best Courtyard by Marriott they've ever seen, praising its modern, upscale, and large-for-Boston rooms. They don't mind that the lobby isn't grand, breakfast is a self-serve affair, and room service consists of a handful of menus to nearby eateries. This property opened in 2004 after extensive renovations to a turn-of-the-19th-century historic building. Rooms in the 10-floor tower are spacious and filled with traditional, unfussy furnishings. Small niceties include cookies and fruit in the lobby. You can't beat the location: Prudential Center and Copley Plaza shops and Back Bay restaurants, galleries, and boutiques are all within walking distance. **Pros:** Good-size modern rooms (nicer than the "big" Marriott, some say), great location, free Internet. **Cons:** Restaurant is fairly lame (reader tip: get the cheapest room available and eat elsewhere); no room service. ✉*88 Exeter St., Back Bay, 02116* ☎*617/437–9300 or 800/321–2211* 🖷*617/437–9330* ⊕*www.courtyardboston.com* ◌*77 rooms, 4 suites* ⚘*In-room: refrigerator (some), ethernet. In-hotel: restaurant, gym, laundry service, public Wi-Fi, some pets allowed (fee)* ☰*AE, D, DC, MC, V* Ⓣ*Copley.*

ROOMS WITH A VIEW

If grand vistas are high on your list, check into one of these: Boston Harbor Hotel at Rowes Wharf for sweeping waterfront and harbor views; Nine Zero, where some rooms overlook the gold dome of the State House and Longfellow Bridge; Boston Yacht Haven for gazing at sailboats and pleasure craft; Westin Copley Plaza (top floors) for unbeatable Boston skyline views; and the Hyatt Regency Cambridge for a look up the Charles River.

★ **$$$–$$$$**   ⊞**Eliot Hotel.** The luxury of this plush boutique hotel extends from the split-level marble lobby with its vast chandelier to the taupe-toile- or chocolate-silk-accented rooms, each with an Italian marble bathroom and two televisions. The majority of the rooms are one- or two-bedroom suites; all have marble-topped bar areas (with sink). The award-winning Clio restaurant, helmed by rising star–chef Ken Oringer, garners raves for its contemporary French-American cuisine. Or you can dine at the Uni Sashimi Bar, a less-expensive option. The Eliot is close to Newbury Street and a short walk from Kenmore Square. Fenway Park is within walking distance as well. A sweet perk for fitness buffs: free passes to the nearby Boston Sports Club. This property has popped up on several "best" lists lately, but there are a couple of caveats. Readers warn that rooms near elevators are noisy, and complain of lapses in service. **Pros:** Good location, great restaurants, pet-friendly. **Cons:** Very small bathrooms, elevator noise, lapses in service by young staff. ✉*370 Commonwealth Ave., Back Bay, 02215* ☎*617/267–1607 or 800/443–5468* 🖷*617/536–9114* ⊕*www.eliothotel.com* ◌*16 rooms, 79 suites* ⚘*In-room: refrigerator, dial-up, Wi-Fi. In-hotel: 2 restaurants, room service, bar, laundry service, concierge, public Wi-Fi, parking (fee), some pets allowed* ☰*AE, DC, MC, V* Ⓣ*Hynes/ICA.*

$$$–$$$$ ⊞**Jurys Boston Hotel.** "The staff is great." "The lobby bar is great." "The location is great." Sense a theme going on here? Readers rave about this hotel, one of the few in the city where you can nip into the bar for a beverage and actually chat with a friendly local or two. There's something about this place that thaws even the frostiest Bostonian—and it's not just the Irish coffee talking. Part of a Dublin-based hotel chain, Jurys may remind you more of Iceland than Ireland, design-wise. There's a fire-and-ice thing going on, from the bed of icy glass shards in the igloolike gas fireplace on the lower level to the puffs of steam coming from the staircase waterfall. Eye-catching blown-glass chandeliers add to the cool appeal. Rooms are decorated with warm taupes and golds, and Ireland-themed artwork adorns the walls. The hotel gets the small touches right, such as the Aveda products in the sleek, modern bathrooms; free bottled water in the fridge; toasty down comforters; and heated towel racks. **Pros:** Lively, friendly bar; great amenities, like large-screen TVs, at a good price point; friendly staff. **Cons:** Not the prettiest location in the city, but close to the

Choosing a Neighborhood

Location, location, location! It can make or break a trip. Are you looking for a hotel in the heart of the city? An intimate inn on a tree-lined street in a quieter area? Maybe you want the nightlife and shopping found across the river in Cambridge?

Some of the city's most luxurious hotels are clustered near the Boston Common and Public Garden (in **Beacon Hill, Back Bay,** and **Downtown**). These prime locations offer access to the Theater District, Chinatown, the stylish shopping meccas of Newbury and Boylston streets, and the Downtown Crossing shopping district.

Boston's "downtown" hotels in the Theater District, the South End, Chinatown, Government Center, and the Waterfront are convenient bases for exploration. Stay close to the theaters at the Boston Park Plaza Hotel & Towers or the Radisson Hotel Boston, or near the water at the Boston Harbor Hotel at Rowes Wharf or Marriott Long Wharf. The Hyatt Regency Boston Financial District and the Omni Parker House, meanwhile, give you easy access to the shops of Downtown Crossing and the seasonal perks of the Common.

The **Kenmore Square** area has a distinct student vibe but it's also convenient to several major attractions. Here, at the epicenter of Fenway Park, the surrounding streets are hopping during baseball season. Adjacent to Fenway Park is Lansdowne Street, a strip of bars and nightclubs catering to college students and young adults. The Fenway offers beautiful parks and community gardens, and a walk through

to the other side will bring you to the Museum of Fine Arts. A short trolley ride east will bring you to the heart of Boston, and a short ride west will bring you to the suburbs of Brookline, Brighton, and Newton. Consider the Hotel Commonwealth in this area.

Cozy B&Bs are your best bet in the **South End,** well known as a gay-friendly area and strewn with beautiful boutiques and excellent restaurants and cafés. These inns, including the hip and stylish Clarendon Square Inn and the bargain-priced 82 Chandler Street B&B, blend perfectly with the neighborhood's charming brownstone- and tree-lined streets.

If your vacation style leans toward physical activity, stay at a riverside property in **Cambridge.** Several larger hotels here give you easy access to Memorial Drive and the Charles. Memorial Drive is closed to traffic on Sunday in summer and becomes an excellent venue for biking, running, and in-line skating. Many of these properties have bike rentals for guest use. Boston and Cambridge hot spots in Harvard and Central squares are minutes away.

The suburb of **Brookline** is a largely residential neighborhood with lovely homes and parks and tree-lined streets, but there are still several bustling areas such as Coolidge Corner and Washington Square that give you plenty of shopping, dining, and recreation options. Most of the lodging selections in this area are B&Bs. The subway offers quick access to downtown Boston.

T (subway). ✉*350 Stuart St., Back Bay, 02116* ☎*617/266–7200* 📠*617/266–7203* ⊕*www.jurysdoyle.com* ⤵*220 rooms, 3 suites* ⚒*In-room: refrigerator, DVD, Wi-Fi. In-hotel: restaurant, room service, bar, laundry service, concierge, public Wi-Fi, parking (fee)* ▤*AE, D, DC, MC, V* Ⓣ*Back Bay/South End.*

$$$–$$$$

Fodor'sChoice

★

🏨**Lenox Hotel.** Brits and business travelers especially appreciate the charms of this gracious, older hotel set in the bustling shopping and dining zone of Back Bay. Family-owned, it's a pleasing alternative to the nearby big-box hotels and it's a good option if you need more services, like room service, a business center, and a fitness room, than the more-basic Charlesmark Hotel (across the street) can deliver. There's no need to have a car here, since so much is within walking distance and a T stop is nearby; plus, overnight parking costs a bundle. (Skip the hotel's garage and use a city parking facility to save some cash.) Wide, blue-tone hallways have archways, elaborate moldings, and other period details of this 1901 building. A jazz pianist plays on weekdays, adding to the ambience. This longtime Back Bay landmark won several awards for restoration work on it's grand brick-and-granite facade. The smallish size of this hotel lends a feeling of personalized service, although some say the staff can be chilly. Guest rooms have custom-made furnishings and marble baths. Of the 24 airily spacious corner rooms, 12 have working wood-burning fireplaces. The sophisticated City Bar is a popular evening destination for its infused vodka martinis. Sólás pub is a more-casual option. ■TIP➜ **Book your reservation from the hotel's Web site; they guarantee the best price. Pros:** Fantastic location, historic/architectural charm. **Cons:** Some call the rooms a little faded; bathrooms are small; no minibar/mini-fridge, safe, or coffeemaker (though available upon request). ✉*61 Exeter St., Back Bay, 02116* ☎*617/536–5300 or 800/225–7676* 📠*617/267–1237* ⊕*www.lenoxhotel.com* ⤵*187 rooms, 27 suites* ⚒*In-room: Wi-Fi. In-hotel: 3 restaurants, room service, bars, gym, laundry service, concierge, public Wi-Fi, parking (fee)* ▤*AE, D, DC, MC, V* Ⓣ*Copley.*

$$$–$$$$

🏨**Radisson Hotel Boston.** Looking to cram four bodies into one room to save a little cash? They've got no problem with that at the Radisson. The welcome mat is rolled out to price-sensitive students and families. The abundant oversize rooms with queen-size beds sleep four comfortably and get extra points for private balconies and luxurious beds with adjustable-firmness mattresses, goose-down quilts, and 250-thread-count sheets. In Park Square at the edge of the Theater District, this 1970s concrete high-rise is home to a small off-Broadway theater, the Stuart Street Playhouse. (If this appeals, ask about theater packages.) Another good feature here: a pleasant on-property restaurant, Rustic Kitchen, which hosts a cooking show on Friday nights. **Pros:** Free wireless Internet throughout the property; corner rooms, like 24 and 25, have great city views; indoor pool. **Cons:** No minibars; $20 fee to rent a refrigerator or microwave. ✉*200 Stuart St., Back Bay, 02116* ☎*617/482–1800 or 800/333–3333* 📠*617/451–2750* ⊕*www.radisson.com/bostonma* ⤵*326 rooms, 30 suites* ⚒*In-room: safe, Wi-Fi. In-hotel: 2 restaurants, room service, pool, gym, laundry service, concierge, public Wi-Fi, parking (fee)* ▤*AE, D, DC, MC, V* Ⓣ*Arlington, Boylston.*

4

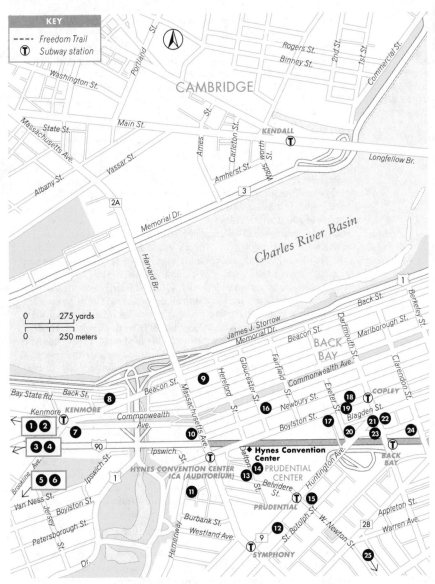

KEY
- - - - *Freedom Trail*
Ⓣ *Subway station*

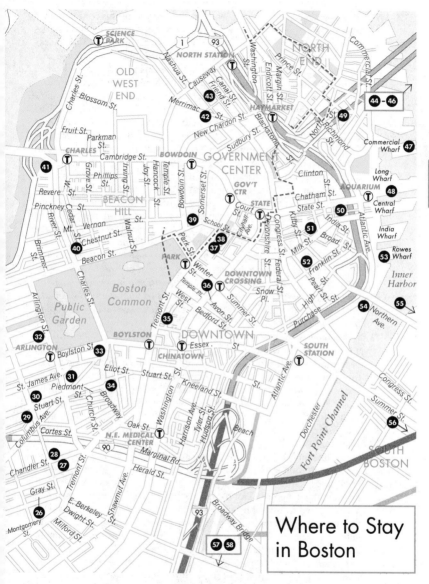

Where to Stay in Boston

$$$–$$$$ 🖼 **Westin Copley Place Boston.** The top-floor rooms of this contemporary 36-story hotel have some of the best views in Boston—of the Charles River, Copley Square, the South End, the Back Bay, and Boston skylines (especially gorgeous when a-twinkle at night). No surprise that business travelers and visiting families love this place, especially when you factor in the bright, modern pool and fitness center and the fabulous Copley Square location. Guest rooms are awash in beiges, dark greens, and blues, with wildly comfortable beds and plush linens. The Westin is in the thick of Back Bay activity and connected by a covered skywalk to the Hynes Convention Center and Copley Place shopping mall. (Great for wintertime visits; you can walk for blocks and eat and shop without venturing outside.) For dining, you can't go wrong with a meal at Turner Fisheries Bar and Restaurant (don't miss the award-winning clam chowder). **Pros:** Great location, connected by skywalk to Copley Place; great views; clean, spacious rooms. **Cons:** Decor varies, with some rooms more recently renovated than others; bathroom fittings could use updating; some say it's overpriced. ■ **TIP→ Check the Starwood Web site for promotional rates.** ⊠ *10 Huntington Ave., Back Bay, 02116* ☎*617/262–9600 or 800/937–8461* 🖷*617/424–7483* ⊕*www.westin.com/copleyplace* ⬤*753 rooms, 50 suites* ⬥*In-room: safe, refrigerator, Wi-Fi. In-hotel: 4 restaurants, room service, bar, pool, gym, spa, laundry service, concierge, executive floor, public Wi-Fi, airport shuttle, some pets allowed (fee)* ⊟*AE, D, DC, MC, V* Ⓣ*Copley, Back Bay/South End.*

★ $$–$$$$ 🖼 **Boston Park Plaza Hotel & Towers.** "She may be old, but she still has a lot of class," a reader wrote of this Boston classic. Indeed. You can bemoan the small rooms, but you can't deny the lush, historic feel of this grand hotel, created in 1927 by renowned hotelier E.M. Statler. Original plaster moldings and a chandeliered gilt-and-cream lobby grace this property; guest rooms are decorated in taupes and pastels with dark cherrywood furnishings. Tiny though they are, the rooms are comfy, with beds topped by puffy down comforters and lush linens. The less said about the bathrooms, however, the better. On the top floor, the concierge level, rooms are slightly larger and have access to the Towers lounge. Todd English's Bonfire is a Latin American–style steak house, and Whiskey Park is a staple in the chic bar scene; don't miss Finale, the go-to place for decadent desserts. Elaborate afternoon tea is offered in the lobby café, and room service is available around the clock. **Pros:** Pretty lobby, great restaurants on the Park Plaza block, helpful concierge. **Cons:** Rooms are cramped, bathrooms are small, hotel's breakfast buffet is "expensive and mediocre," some say. ⊠*64 Arlington St., Back Bay, 02116* ☎*617/426–2000 or 800/225–2008* 🖷*617/426–5545* ⊕*www.bostonparkplaza.com* ⬤*941 rooms, 22 suites* ⬥*In-room: refrigerator, Wi-Fi (some). In-hotel: 8 restaurants, room service, bars, gym, laundry service, concierge, executive floor, public Wi-Fi, parking (fee)* ⊟*AE, D, DC, MC, V* Ⓣ*Arlington.*

$$–$$$$ 🖼 **Copley Square Hotel.** To some, it's shabby-chic; to others, it's just plain shabby, but you can't deny that the Copley Square Hotel is unique. This property has a quirky turn-of-the-20th-century vibe—and its convenient Back Bay location is an all-around plus. The circa-1891 hotel, one

of the city's oldest, is busy and comfortable, with winding corridors and repro-antique furniture. Chintz and cabbage roses rule. The idiosyncratic rooms have a few common denominators, such as coffeemakers, and some have couches. Complimentary afternoon tea is served daily in the lobby. The property is a favorite with international travelers (and lovers of vintage everything, we'd surmise). Pros: Good location, next door to a large supermarket, a bit of character. Cons: Worn around the edges, some rooms overlook brick walls, readers complain about the indifferent (some say rude) staff. ⊠*47 Huntington Ave., Back Bay, 02116* ☎*617/536–9000 or 800/225–7062* 🖷*617/267–3547* ⊕*www. copleysquarehotel.com* ↩*148 rooms, 5 suites* ⚭*In-room: safe, dial-up, Wi-Fi. In-hotel: 2 restaurants, room service, bar, concierge, public Wi-Fi, parking (fee)* ▤*AE, D, DC, MC, V* Ⓣ*Copley.*

$$$ 🖼**Hilton Boston Back Bay.** It's perfect, if you like the anonymity of a large hotel and a location that's convenient to everything. And you can't beat the oversize rooms, the big, comfy beds, and the availability of a pool and hot tub. This 26-story hotel occupies a corner pocket between the Prudential Center and the Christian Science Church complex. Deluxe rooms with contemporary furnishings are done in blues, golds, and burnished maple and have wall-to-wall windows overlooking the Back Bay and Fenway Park. (Views vary from room to room. You might have a great view of Boston's iconic neon Citgo sign! Bostonians would consider this a *good* thing, as the Citgo sign is a beloved—if odd—landmark.) Generally, rooms above the ninth floor have the best views. Bathrooms have oversize showers. Try one of the older rooms, which have windows that open (some even have balconies). Pros: Large rooms and bathrooms, nice views, better-than-expected restaurant. Cons: Somewhat oddly situated; no VIP floor. ⊠*40 Dalton St., Back Bay, 02115* ☎*617/236–1100 or 800/874–0663* 🖷*617/867–6104* ⊕*www. hilton.com* ↩*385 rooms, 5 suites* ⚭*In-room: refrigerator, ethernet. In-hotel: restaurant, room service, bar, pool, gym, laundry service, concierge, public Wi-Fi, parking (fee)* ▤*AE, D, DC, MC, V* ⦿*CP* Ⓣ*Hynes/ICA.*

$$–$$$ 🖼**Marriott Hotel at Copley Place.** You can access this 38-story "megahotel" from any of three impressive entrances: the street-level lobby, a glass sky bridge from the Prudential Center–Hynes Auditorium complex, or the Copley Place shopping mall. Rooms have French Colonial–style dark-wood furniture and are decorated in burgundy and green. Some rooms overlook Boston Harbor or the Charles River. This hotel gets high marks for doing things right, such as employing a happy, professional staff and filling the place with a good vibe, a great sports bar, and a cool pool, but it loses fans with a nickel-and-dime-y approach to little things: guests pay for the Internet and bottled water, and there are too few creams and sugars for the in-room coffee. Small stuff, but annoying nonetheless, especially when there's so much competition (and another hotel, the Westin, that connects to the same two malls). One person's "lively buzz" is another one's "too crowded," and some complain about the crowded pool and long waits for the elevator. Pros: Exceptional service, plush beds, great location between two shopping malls. Cons: Extra charges for small things, crowded pool area, crowded lobby, housekeeping not always up to par. ⊠*110 Huntington Ave., Back Bay, 02116* ☏*617/236–5800 or 800/228–9290* 📠*617/236–5885* ⊕*www.marriott.com* ⇄*1,100 rooms, 47 suites* ⌂*In-room: safe, refrigerator, ethernet. In-hotel: 3 restaurants, room service, bars, gym, laundry facilities, laundry service, concierge, executive floor, public Wi-Fi, parking (fee)* ⊟*AE, D, DC, MC, V* ⊤*Copley, Back Bay/South End.*

$$–$$$ 🖥**Midtown Hotel.** If you're coming to Boston by car, get ready for a shock: the parking here is cheap—$14 per day—and easy. (Most hotels charge around $40 a day.) The convenient location, near Prudential Center, Symphony Hall, and the Christian Science Center, and reasonable rates enable this motel-style property to hold its own against its large, expensive neighbors. If it's been a while since you visited, you'll be surprised to discover that the '60s rec-room look of the place has been updated with new wallpaper, carpet, and furnishings. High-speed Internet is available in each guest room for a small fee. The Midtown is owned by the Christian Science Church, whose visitors wouldn't think of staying anywhere else. **Pros:** Good value for the money, friendly staff, cheap parking. **Cons:** Uninviting pool area, no restaurant on-site. ⊠*220 Huntington Ave., Back Bay, 02115* ☏*617/369–6286* 📠*617/369–6299* ⊕*www.midtownhotel.com* ⇄*159 rooms* ⌂*In-room: ethernet. In-hotel: pool, laundry service, concierge, public Wi-Fi, parking (fee), some pets allowed* ⊟*AE, D, DC, MC, V* ⊤*Symphony.*

$$–$$$ 🖥**Sheraton Boston Hotel.** Some call it cookie-cutter bland, but those who have lucked into good deals via the Internet praise this hotel's location and convenience. Get similar online deals and you won't mind sharing the parking garage with Prudential Center shoppers or drinking from paper cups in the Club Floor lounge. The two 29-story towers, topped with the bright Sheraton sign, can be seen from just about anywhere in Back Bay. The property sheds the stuffy Boston historical look for a more-contemporary style. Open public spaces are decorated with modern artwork. Rooms have large work areas and wide windows with panoramic city views (those facing the Christian Science Center or the Charles River have the best). Book a room in the South Tower, if you can, since these rooms were among those recently renovated. All rooms have sleigh beds with pillow-top mattresses, elegant white cotton linens, feather pillows, down comforters, and large mirrors. The health club's pool, one of the largest in Boston, is a real bonus with its light-filled atrium and retractable roof. **Pros:** Free Internet in the lobby, nice rooms in South Tower, location is handy to restaurants and shopping. **Cons:** Rooms near Club Floor lounge are noisy, some say porters are surly and unhelpful. ⊠*39 Dalton St., Back Bay, 02199* ☏*617/236–2000 or 800/325–3535* 📠*617/236–1702* ⊕*www.starwoodhotels.com/boston* ⇄*1,066 rooms, 150 suites* ⌂*In-room: ethernet. In-hotel: restaurant, room service, bar, pool, gym, laundry service, concierge, executive floor, public Internet, airport shuttle, parking (fee), some pets allowed* ⊟*AE, D, DC, MC, V* ⊤*Hynes/ICA.*

$–$$$ 🖥**Charlesmark Hotel.** Hipsters and romantics who'd rather spend their
Fodor'sChoice cash on a great meal than a hotel bill have put this skinny little bou-
★ tique hotel on the map. You can typically grab a room for around

$139, an amazing value considering the Copley Square location: the shops and restaurants of Boylston and Newbury streets are at the doorstep. An outdoor patio is a great place to watch the passing parade (or the Boston Marathon—this hotel is right on the finish line). Guest rooms, rather smallish, have contemporary custom-made furnishings with surround-sound stereo and wireless throughout. Free Continental breakfast and Wi-Fi are examples of how the hotel provides cost-saving incidentals. It doesn't do room service, but the Thai place next door is quite good. The Charlesmark doubles as a gallery, with the work of local artists lining the winding brick corridors. **Pros:** Great price point for what you get; great location near T, shopping, and dining; free Wi-Fi and water bottles. **Cons:** Hot-air heating system is noisy, not much storage area, rooms at the front of the house can be noisy due to lounge and traffic. ⊠655 Boylston St., Back Bay, 02116 ☎617/247–1212 ☐617/247–1224 ⊕www.thecharlesmarkhotel.com ✑33 rooms ♨In-room: refrigerator, VCR, Wi-Fi. In-hotel: laundry service, public Wi-Fi, some pets allowed ⊟AE, D, DC, MC, V ⓧCP Ⓣ Copley.

$–$$ ⌂**Newbury Guest House.** Visitors rave about the wonderful accommodations, friendly staff, and fabulous breakfast at this elegant red-brick-and-brownstone 1882 row house. On Boston's most fashionable shopping street, the inn looks the part, with natural pine flooring, elegant reproduction Victorian furnishings, and prints from the Museum of Fine Arts. Some rooms have bay windows; others have decorative fireplaces. Limited parking is available at $15 for 24 hours—a good deal for the area. **Pros:** Cozy, homey, great location. **Cons:** Some say that rooms don't look as nice as the Web site indicates; furnishings and carpets are OK but look a little tired. ⊠261 Newbury St., Back Bay, 02116 ☎617/670–6100 or 800/437–7668 ☐617/262–4243 ⊕www.newburyguesthouse.com ✑32 rooms ♨In-room: Wi-Fi. In-hotel: no elevator, concierge, public Wi-Fi, parking (fee) ⊟AE, D, DC, MC, V ⓧBP ⓉHynes/ICA, Copley.

$ ⌂**463 Beacon Street Guest House.** There's not even a sign on the door of this handsome brownstone—that's how much it blends in with its residential neighbors. International visitors and college students have discovered this place, warming to its slightly quirky, visiting-an-old-auntie charm. Check out the old black-and-white photos of Boston in the hallways as you head to your guest room (each is slightly different, as befits an old house). The antiques-filled sitting room functions as a guest room in summertime. Digs are tidy but basic, with hardwood floors; those on the fifth floor are loft-style. Some rooms are small and share a bath. No meals are served, but some of the rooms have kitchenettes. Several restaurants are within walking distance, too. Each room has a two-person occupancy limit, and because of the layout, the house isn't appropriate for children. ⊠463 Beacon St., Back Bay, 02115 ☎617/536–1302 ☐617/247–8876 ⊕www.463beacon.com ✑20 rooms, 17 with bath ♨In-room: no a/c (some), kitchen (some), Wi-Fi. In-hotel: no elevator, laundry facilities, parking (fee), no kids under 7 ⊟D, MC, V ⓉKenmore.

BEACON HILL

$$$–$$$$ **Fifteen Beacon.** Although it's
Fodor'sChoice housed in a an old (1903) beaux
★ arts building, this boutique hotel
is anything but stodgy. The tiny
lobby is all black lacquer with bold
splashes of red, brightened with
recessed lighting and abstract art.
Even the cage elevator is paneled
in red leather. Just when you're
thinking, "Hmm," you enter a
guest room and go, "Ahh!" Rooms
are done up in soothing-but-manly
shades of cinnamon, taupe, and
black, and each has a canopy bed, a
gas fireplace, and surround-sound
stereo. Fab little touches abound,
like bath amenities from Newbury
Street's Fresh, and little flat-screen
TVs in the bathroom, plus huge
mirrors and heated towel bars. A
nearby health club is available to
hotel guests, and the hotel's res-

taurant, the Federalist, is a favorite for fine dining. Tip: This is *the*
place to be for Boston's Harborfest (July 4th) celebration, when guests
can watch fireworks from the roof deck (open from Memorial Day to
Labor Day). **Pros:** Courtesy car service, friendly concierge, you can
charge your laptop in your in-room safe. **Cons:** Mattresses are just
average. ⊠ *15 Beacon St., Beacon Hill, 02108* ☎ *617/670–1500 or
877/982–3226* 🖷 *617/670–2525* ⊕ *www.xvbeacon.com* 🛏 *58 rooms,
2 suites* ⚲ *In-room: safe, refrigerator, ethernet. In-hotel: restaurant,
room service, bar, gym, laundry service, concierge, parking (fee), some
pets allowed* ☰ *AE, D, DC, MC, V* Ⓣ *Government Center, Park St.*

★ **$$$**   **Beacon Hill Hotel & Bistro.** Two 19th-century town houses have been
meticulously renovated to house this intimate boutique hotel on Bea-
con Hill. You can't beat the location on Charles Street, one of the city's
premier addresses, within walking distance of the Public Garden, Back
Bay, and Government Center. Minimalist-style rooms are individually
decorated with soft neutral colors and plush bed linens. Rooms have
plenty of natural light filtering through the large windows overlooking city streets. There's a rooftop deck for lounging and a popular
street-side bistro with fireplace and bar that's open for breakfast, lunch,
and dinner. **Pros:** Beacon Hill location, with boutiques and restaurants
within walking distance, parking available at nearby Boston Common
garage. **Cons:** Rooms are small. ⊠ *25 Charles St., Beacon Hill, 02114*
☎ *617/723–7575 or 888/959–2442* 🖷 *617/723–7525* ⊕ *www.beacon-
hillhotel.com* 🛏 *12 rooms, 1 suite* ⚲ *In-room: Wi-Fi. In-hotel: restaurant, laundry service* ☰ *AE, D, DC, MC, V* ⏀❘*BP* Ⓣ *Arlington.*

★ **$**   **John Jeffries House.** It's devilishly tricky to locate, especially if you're
driving, but once you do, you'll discover the JJH is a real find. This

turn-of-the-20th-century building, across from Massachusetts General Hospital, was once a housing facility for nurses. Now, it's a sedate four-story inn, and one of the best values in town. The Federal-style double parlor has a cluster of floral-pattern chairs and sofas where you can relax with afternoon tea or coffee. Guest rooms are furnished with handsome upholstered pieces, and nearly all have kitchenettes. Triple-glazed windows block much noise from busy Charles Circle; many rooms have views of the Charles River. The inn is adjacent to Charles Street, home to lovely cafés, specialty boutiques, and antiques shops. **Pros:** Close to Beacon Hill, free Wi-Fi, good value. **Cons:** Continental breakfast is small and uninspired, inn is hard to find, it's near a hospital so you might hear ambulance sirens. ✉ *14 David G. Mugar Way, Beacon Hill, 02114* ☎ *617/367–1866* 📠 *617/742–0313* 🌐 *www.johnjeffrieshouse.com* *23 rooms, 23 suites* *In-room: kitchen, Wi-Fi. In-hotel: public Wi-Fi, parking (fee)* 💳 *AE, D, DC, MC, V* 🍽 *CP* Ⓣ *Charles/MGH.*

4

DOWNTOWN

$$$$ Fodor's Choice ★ **Boston Harbor Hotel at Rowes Wharf.** Red Sox owner John Henry parks his yacht here in summertime. The rest of us can arrive by boat in a less-grand fashion—the water shuttle runs from Logan Airport to the back door of this deluxe harborside hotel. The hotel's dramatic entryway is an 80-foot archway topped by a rotunda, so eye-catching that it qualifies as a local landmark. The lobby, too, is stunningly elegant, with marble arches, antique maps, and a huge tumble of fresh flowers. Guest rooms have marble bathrooms, custom-made desks, 300-thread-count sheets, and down comforters. Many have views of the harbor. Meritage restaurant has a unique, wine-inspired menu that pairs small plates with appropriate vintages, under light fixtures that mimic a starry sky. Want to work out in the hotel's health club, but forgot your exercise duds? Not to worry—they provide them for their guests. Now if only they would exercise for you. ✉ *70 Rowes Wharf, Downtown, 02110* ☎ *617/439–7000 or 800/752–7077* 📠 *617/330–9450* 🌐 *www.bhh.com* *206 rooms, 24 suites* *In-room: refrigerator, Wi-Fi. In-hotel: 2 restaurants, room service, bar, pool, gym, spa, laundry service, concierge, public Wi-Fi, airport shuttle, parking (fee), some pets allowed* 💳 *AE, D, DC, MC, V* Ⓣ *Aquarium, South Station.*

$$$$ Fodor's Choice ★ **InterContinental Boston.** Call it the anti-boutique hotel. Boston's new (2007), 424-room InterContinental Hotel, facing the harbor and the as-yet-unfinished Rose Kennedy Greenway—is housed in two opulent, 22-story towers wrapped in blue glass. In a nod to the city's history, the towers equal the height of the masts of the old tall ships, and the pewter bar in RumBa, the hotel's rum bar, would surely delight metalsmith Paul Revere. (It also harks back to Boston's connection with the rum trade.) Miel, the hotel's organic Provencal brasserie, is open 24/7. (Elsewhere in the city, good luck finding dinner after 9 PM.) Hallways are lined with Texan limestone, and lobbies are gleaming with Italian marble and leather—there's not a red brick in the place. Guest rooms are oversize, wired with the latest technology, and have wide-screen TVs, but best, perhaps, are the spalike bathrooms, done in mosaic tile

HOTELS TO DINE FOR

Hotel dining has come a long way since the clam-strip plate at HoJo's (great though it was!)

■ **Boston Harbor Hotel.** The wine-pairing dinner at Meritage is seriously wow-worthy.

■ **Boston Park Plaza Hotel & Towers.** Todd English's Bonfire has fire and spice.

■ **Colonnade Hotel.** Thanks to Brasserie Jo, we no longer have to go to Montréal for our favorite *moules et frites. Merci!*

■ **Eliot Hotel.** Clio dishes up fab French food with a contemporary tilt.

■ **Four Seasons.** Splurge-worthy neo-French cuisine is paired with stunning views of the Public Garden at Aujourd'hui.

■ **Ritz-Carlton Boston Common.** Forget the gimmicky name (JER-NE? Journey! We get it) and the fact that *Stuff@Night* named it "Boston's Sexiest Bar." Just enjoy the good food.

■ **Westin Copley Place Boston.** Pop downstairs to Turner Fisheries for (at least) a quick bowl of award-winning clam chowder and some oysters.

and granite, with separate tubs and showers. Another drawing card here is the 6,600-square-foot spa and health club, and a pool that overlooks Atlantic Avenue and the Boston Fire Department. (Views on this side of the building will improve once they finish the Greenway.) Other features include a posh retail store and Sushi-Teq, a sushi-tequila restaurant with salsa dancers. Movers and shakers from local financial, real estate, and law firms of the Financial District make for a lively after-work scene in the bars. **Pros:** Rooms have great views and great bathrooms, close to Financial District and South Station, brasserie open 24 hours. **Cons:** Pool and front of house currently overlook construction, huge function rooms mean lots of conventioneers, far from Newbury Street and museums, fee for wireless. ⊠*510 Atlantic Ave., Downtown, 02210* ☎*617/747–1000* 🖷*617/217–5020* ⊕*www.intercontinentalboston.com* ➷*424 rooms, 38 suites* ⚹*In-room: safe, refrigerator, DVD, Wi-Fi. In-hotel: 2 restaurants, room service, bar, pool, gym, spa, laundry service, concierge, executive floor, public Wi-Fi, parking (fee)* ▤*AE, D, DC, MC, V.*

$$$$

Fodor'sChoice

★

🖳 **Nine Zero.** The little doggie dish outside the entrance is a tip-off—this isn't an ordinary hotel. Owned by Kimpton Hotels since 2006, this property is stylish and swank. The lobby is a knockout, with copper metallic draperies and high-backed leather chairs. Giant suspended glass globes stand in for chandeliers. It all adds up to a spare feel, the better to compliment the cool threads of the youngish, style-conscious crowd. Guest rooms, updated in 2006 and 2007, have bold patterns, curvy black armoires, and full martini bars; some have floor-to-ceiling windows. Unexpected features include in-room yoga (turn on their yoga channel, and ask them to bring you a yoga basket) and "guppy love" (they'll lend you a goldfish bowl if you get lonely). Corner rooms (ending in 05) have awesome views of the Longfellow Bridge and the gold dome of the State House, but they'll cost you $80 over the room rate.

The gym is really small, but they'll give you a pass to a local fitness club. **Pros:** Great style; lobby wine-tasting every evening (from 5 to 6); Mario Russo (Newbury Street) bath products; KO Prime, a new-in-2007 steak house (replacing Spire restaurant) run by überchef Ken Oringer. **Cons:** Smallish rooms, overlooks a cemetery. ⊠ *90 Tremont St., Downtown, 02108* ☎*617/772–5800 or 866/646–3937* 🖷*617/772–5810* ⊕*www. ninezero.com* ➮*185 rooms, 5 suites* ⚴*In-room: safe, refrigerator, dial-up, Wi-Fi. In-hotel: restaurant, room service, bar, gym, laundry service, concierge, public Wi-Fi, parking (fee), some pets allowed* ⊟*AE, D, DC, MC, V* Ⓣ*Park St., Government Center.*

★ $$$$ 🏨 **Ritz-Carlton Boston Common.** You're likely to see famous bodies (the hotel won't say who) sweating next to you at the LA Sports Club, the Ritz's mega–fitness center. It's the go-to gym for pop stars are performing in Boston, so you might feel a bit more fabulous—or a whole lot fatter—simply by hanging out here. While the hotel gets compared, often unfavorably, to the late, lamented Ritz-Carlton Boston, it's only fair to judge it for what it is: a sleek, contemporary hotel that speaks more to rock stars than royalty. Warm wood walls and trim complement an extensive art collection, dramatic lighting, and fresh flowers and plants. Guest rooms, fitted with luxurious golden spreads and featherbeds, all have separate marble showers and deep tubs. Some rooms have spectacular views of Boston Common. A short walk will get you to Filene's Basement, the Theater District, and Newbury Street. Besides the fitness center, the hotel complex houses a movie theater. **Pros:** Killer gym, central location. **Cons:** Lacks the "wow" factor you'd expect from a Ritz property, some say. ⊠ *10 Avery St., Downtown, 02111* ☎*617/574–7100 or 800/241–3333* 🖷*617/574–7200* ⊕*www. ritzcarlton.com* ➮*150 rooms, 43 suites* ⚴*In-room: safe, refrigerator, dial-up, Wi-Fi. In-hotel: restaurant, room service, bar, pool, gym, laundry service, concierge, executive floor, public Wi-Fi, parking (fee)* ⊟*AE, D, DC, MC, V* Ⓣ*Boylston St.*

★ $$$$ 🏨 **Seaport Hotel.** Wearing a badge on your lapel? You'll be among your own kind here, where the hotel is part of the Seaport World Trade Center, a mammoth conference complex. If you need to keep your mind on business, you won't mind at all that your hotel is a bit distant from the heart of the city. (You'll have a hard time resisting the great pool and fitness center, though.) Inside this gleaming waterfront property is a crisply elegant lobby in hues of hunter green, mustard, and carrot. The huge rooms have handcrafted cherry furniture and marble bathrooms as well as state-of-the-art conveniences such as wireless Internet and (in some rooms), Seaportal, a touch-screen Web portal for phone calls, hotel and meeting updates, and Boston tourism info. A complimentary shuttle runs throughout the day to State Street (the Financial District) and North Station. Bug out of your meeting early to swim in the heated lap pool, or get a facial, at the luxurious Wave Health & Fitness Club. **Pros:** No-tipping policy, fabulous gym, free shuttle to other parts of Boston. **Cons:** Located away from city center; no breakfast available before 6 AM; room service is expensive (good, though). ⊠ *World Trade Center, 1 Seaport La., Downtown, 02210* ☎*617/385–4000 or 877/732–7678* 🖷*617/385–4001* ⊕*www.seaportboston.com* ➮*402* rooms, 24 suites ⅃In-room: safe, refrigerator (upon request), dial-up, Wi-Fi. In-hotel: restaurant, room service, bar, pool, gym, laundry service, concierge, executive floor, public Wi-Fi, airport shuttle, parking (fee), some pets allowed ▤AE, D, DC, MC, V ⓣSilver Line.

★ $$$–$$$$ 🏨**Hilton Boston Financial District.** If you're looking for sleek, comfortable, and quiet, you'll find it at this luxury hotel. And if you're looking for the old Wyndham hotel, this is it, now a Hilton property. The place has been freshened up some, with stylish teal and taupe carpeting and new linens. The 1928 building was not only the first art deco building in the city, but also the first skyscraper. The lobby's mahogany paneling and soft gold lighting complement the restored bronze elevators and original let-

JUST OFF ROUTE 128

In town for business in the high-tech 'hood of Route 128? Avoid rush hour traffic and stay at the **Doubletree Guest Suites Boston/Waltham** (☎ 781/890–6767 ⊕www.bostonwalthamsuites.doubletree.com). It's easily accessible from the highway. Parking is free and food is served in the lounge day and night. Squeeze in a workout in the fitness center, a swim in the indoor pool, or a soak in the crescent-shape hot tub. When it comes to smoothing the rough edges of business travel, these folks have it down. Runner up: The **Westin Hotel Waltham-Boston** (☎ 781/290–5601 ⊕www.starwoodhotels.com/westin).

terbox. Guest rooms are spacious, with high ceilings and crown moldings; some overlook the waterfront. (For extra space, ask for a room at the end of the hallway.) Comforting touches include terry robes, feather pillows, and nightly turndown service. Night owls can take advantage of the 24-hour health club and business center. **Pros:** Well-maintained, clean, and quiet; friendly, helpful staff. **Cons:** Poor-quality breakfast buffet (try the nearby Bean Leaf Café, instead); expensive food in general (lots of options in the neighborhood, though); daily fee for Wi-Fi; hard to find. ✉89 Broad St., Downtown, 02110 ☎617/556–0006 ☏617/556–0053 ⊕www.hilton.com ⤶362 rooms, 66 suites ⅃In-room: refrigerator, safe, Wi-Fi. In-hotel: restaurant, room service, bar, gym, laundry service, concierge, public Wi-Fi, parking (fee) ▤AE, D, DC, MC, V ⓣState.

★ $$$–$$$$ 🏨**Langham Hotel.** The red awnings of this 1922 Renaissance Revival landmark (the former Federal Reserve Building) lead to a gleaming lobby of honeyed gold, deep red, and creamy marble, a stark contrast to the ubiquitous gray suits of Financial District types who gather here. Crystal chandeliers light the hallways, and jewel-tone fabrics swath guest rooms—it's not daring, but it works. While the place is all business during the week (except for the luncheon crowd at Café Fleuri), families and couples drop in on weekends for the lower—by as much as 50%—room rates and for the specialty packages like the Very Important Baby package, which includes luxury baby bedding, unlimited disposable diapers, preordered baby food, and top-of-the-line baby bath products. It's a bit of a hike to Newbury Street and Boston's museums from here, but there are good reasons to stay put: Café Fleuri is the site of a seasonal all-chocolate buffet Saturday afternoon and a wonderful jazz brunch on Sunday. **Pros:** Fabulous Sunday brunch; thick, fluffy towels and robes; good discounts on weekends. **Cons:** Extra charge for Internet use, a bit pricey, expensive valet parking—■ TIP➜ **use a public parking lot, where rates are cheaper on weekends.** ✉*250 Franklin St., Downtown, 02110* ☎*617/451–1900 or 800/543–4300* 📠*617/423–2844* ⊕*www.langhamhotels.com/langham/boston* ⟋*325 rooms, 17 suites* ⟐*In-room: safe, refrigerator, Wi-Fi. In-hotel: 2 restaurants, room service, bar, pool, gym, laundry service, concierge, public Wi-Fi, parking (fee), some pets allowed* ⊟*AE, D, DC, MC, V* Ⓣ*State.*

$$$–$$$$ ⊡**Marriott Long Wharf.** Families can't resist this waterfront hotel, thanks to its close proximity to New England Aquarium (and its IMAX theater), whale-watch tours, and the shops and restaurants of Quincy Market. Even the Italian-flavored North End isn't far, if you're willing to walk a bit. Cute Christopher Columbus Park is right outside the door, with brick walkways and wisteria-covered archways. And then there's the Marriott's great swimming pool, overlooking the harbor, plus a huge gym and an itty-bitty game room, a Starbucks … convenience is the name of the game here. Jutting out into the bay, this airy, multitiered redbrick hotel resembles a ship. Most of the rooms, pleasantly decorated with cherry furnishings and pillow-top mattresses, open onto a five-story atrium. Some rooms have views of the park or New England Aquarium. Clean-freak alert: Plush feather duvets on the beds are changed every night. There's no excuse to avoid the gym here—it's open 24 hours a day. **Pros:** Waterfront location, good weekend rates (check the Web for deals), convenience store close by. **Cons:** Standard guest rooms are small for families, so you'll need adjoining rooms or a suite; restaurant is pricey—■ TIP➜ **head to Quincy Market instead of eating on-site, even for breakfast.** ✉*296 State St., Downtown, 02109* ☎*617/227–0800 or 800/228–9290* 📠*617/227–2867* ⊕*www.marriott.com/boslw* ⟋*399 rooms, 3 suites* ⟐*In-room: refrigerator, dial-up, Wi-Fi. In-hotel: 2 restaurants, room service, bar, pool, gym, laundry facilities, laundry service, concierge, executive floor, parking (fee)* ⊟*AE, D, DC, MC, V* Ⓣ*Aquarium.*

$$$–$$$$ ⊡**Onyx Hotel.** Sexy, supper-club atmosphere oozes from this contemporary boutique hotel a block from North Station. Sip an ice-cold martini and nibble some tapas in the intimate Ruby Room, with its flashy velvet-padded chairs and black-granite bar lighted with fiber optics. The crowd in the Ruby Room varies. If there's a concert going on at nearby TD Banknorth Garden, you might party with band members and assorted fans. If the Celtics or the Bruins are playing at home in the Garden, you'll get a lively, sports-loving crowd (unless somebody's having a terrible season). Later, head upstairs to slip into your leopard-print bathrobe and cushy socks. Rooms are done in black and taupe with checkerboard carpeting and colorful accents, including red suede chairs. (The exception here is the Britney Spears suite, all white and cream like Brit's childhood room, with platinum records and photos, designed by the pop tart's mom.) All have plush linens, flat-screen TVs, DVD players, surround sound, free Wi-Fi, and Aveda bath products. Included in the rate is a weekday morning car service to the Financial District and evening wine hour. They've also got a ski/stay deal with the Wachusett Mountain ski train. **Pros:** Good location for catching a sporting event or concert at the Garden, near North Station commuter rail and T stop, near several inexpensive restaurants and bars. **Cons:** Smallish rooms and bathrooms, small gym (but they do offer free passes to the Boston Sports Club). ⊠ *155 Portland St., Downtown, 02114* ☎ *617/557–9955 or 866/660–6699* 🖷 *617/557–0005* ⊕ *www.onyxhotel.com* ⇶ *110 rooms, 2 suites* ⚷ *In-room: safe, refrigerator, DVD, Wi-Fi. In-hotel: restaurant, room service, bar, gym, laundry service, concierge, public Wi-Fi, some pets allowed* ⊟ *AE, D, DC, MC, V* ¹⁰¹ *CP* Ⓣ *North Station.*

$$$–$$$$ Ⓣ **Westin Boston Waterfront.** A modern, 17-story tower of gleaming glass and steel, this new (2007) South Boston waterfront property is connected to the megasize Boston Convention & Exhibition Center and is predictably a magnet for the men and women in suits. Rooms are handsome with a neutral palette of whites, tans, and pastels, punctuated with cherrywood furnishings. Most—some 85%—have water or skyline views. When you're not in meetings, work out the kinks at the state-of-the-art fitness center, with a slew of up-to-date machines, an indoor pool, and steam and sauna rooms. **Pros:** Lobby stations with wireless check-in, Silver Line from Logan takes you directly to hotel, heavenly beds. **Cons:** Clusters of conventioneers and meeting-goers crowd the place, too new and too sterile for some tastes, South Boston waterfront neighborhood is still up-and-coming, rooms are pricey during top conventions. ⊠ *425 Summer St., Downtown, 02210* ☎ *617/532–4600* ⊕ *www.starwood.com* ⇶ *759 rooms, 31 suites* ⚷ *In-room: ethernet, Wi-Fi. In-hotel: restaurant, room service, bar, pool, gym, laundry service, concierge, public Internet, public Wi-Fi, parking (fee)* ⊟ *AE, D, DC, MC, V* Ⓣ *South Station.*

$$–$$$$ Ⓣ **Boston Yacht Haven.** The high-ceilinged, post-and-beam boathouse sits on steel pilings jutting out into Boston Harbor, giving the lucky guests who stay here some of the largest rooms and the best views in Boston. The supersize rooms, at value-packed prices, have king or queen beds, cathedral ceilings, cozy sitting areas (some with pull-out leather couches), and remarkable views. Though it's a stone's throw from Faneuil Hall and the North End, you may not want to leave. Grab a room with a balcony—worth the extra pennies—and watch the luxury yachts and sailboats cruise into the harbor. The No. 210 penthouse has a huge wraparound deck; look one way to see the Boston skyline and city lights, turn the other for harbor and ocean views. **Pros:** Outside waterfront terrace is a great sitting area, airport water taxi picks up and

---

PET-FRIENDLY PADS

It's Fido's birthday? **Hotel Marlowe** will order a special cake from Polka Dog Bakery. And, the pet ambassadors at the **Fairmont Copley** will be happy to take your pets out for a scenic stroll around the city. At the **Onyx Hotel,** Lassie can have her own bed, fleece blanket, and gourmet dog biscuits; fine felines get a scratching post, too. The **Ritz-Carlton Boston Common** Pampered Pet package includes a welcome fruit-and-cheese platter, dog biscuits, a ceramic water bowl, customized dog tag, and a purr-fect one-hour pampering session for you and your pet—one of you gets a massage and the other gets groomed.

drops off at the hotel dock, the 75-slip marina plays summer host to the opulent yachts of the visiting rich and famous—makes for a good show. **Cons:** Bathrooms are basic, bedding and furnishings are moderate. ✉ *87 Commercial Wharf, Downtown, 02110* ☎ *617/367–5050* ⊕ *www.byhonline.com* ➫ *10 rooms* ⚒ *In-room: refrigerator, DVD, Wi-Fi. In-hotel: laundry facilities, public Wi-Fi, parking (fee)* ▭ *AE, D, DC, MC, V* ⦿*CP* Ⓣ *Aquarium.*

\$\$–\$\$\$\$ ⚏ **Hyatt Regency Boston.** Aromatherapy wafts through the halls of the former Swissôtel at Downtown Crossing—perhaps an energizing citrus scent in the am to get you going and a calming lavender essence to relax you in your room. If it's been a while since you visited this 22-story hotel, you'll likely notice some changes. High-end amenities are standard in guest rooms here and include Sony Dream Machines, pillow-top mattresses and featherbeds (with foam beds upon request), bathrobes, cordless phones, and bath products from Newbury Street's Portico. A favorite among business travelers, the hotel is a short walk from the Financial District, not to mention Boston Common and Chinatown. Savvy vacationers find weekend bargains and good package deals with theater tickets and shopping discounts at Macy's and Filene's Basement. The sleek lobby has marble floors and columns, dark woods, and bold, geometric rugs. Spacious guest rooms, set around four atriums, are decorated with mahogany furnishings, taupe linen walls, and soothing earth tones. **Pros:** Outdoor terraces off atriums on each floor, good package deals, saunas and whirlpools. **Cons:** Views of neighboring office buildings from guest rooms, few chairs around indoor pool, small gym. ✉ *1 Ave. de Lafayette, Chinatown, 02111* ☎ *617/912–1234 or 800/233–1234* ⊟ *617/451–2198* ⊕ *www.bostonfinancial. hyatt.com* ➫ *474 rooms, 26 suites* ⚒ *In-room: refrigerator, dial-up, Wi-Fi. In-hotel: restaurant, room service, bar, pool, gym, laundry service, concierge, executive floors, public Wi-Fi, parking (fee), some pets allowed* ▭ *AE, D, DC, MC, V* Ⓣ *Chinatown, Downtown Crossing.*

\$\$–\$\$\$\$ ⚏ **Millennium Bostonian Hotel.** As of this writing, the Millennium hotel was undergoing a \$14 million transformation. The circular front entrance will feature stone floors, polished wood, and two fireplaces, plus a miniwaterfall. The old Seasons restaurant will become a function space, and the hotel will add a new eatery. The working fireplaces and balconies will remain (hooray!) and guest rooms will be punched up with stone entryways, wood paneling, crown moldings and earth-toned hues, accented with Boston-themed photography and artwork. Rooms will be updated with duvets and 300-thread-count sheets, flat-screen TVs, and safes large enough for laptops, and Wi-Fi will be available in public spaces. Windows will get additional soundproofing—a welcome feature for a hotel in a busy area like Quincy Market. ✉ *Faneuil Hall Marketplace, 26 North St., Downtown, 02109* ☎ *617/523–3600 or 866/866–8086* ⊟ *617/523–2454* ⊕ *www.millenniumhotels.com* ➫ *187 rooms, 14 suites* ⚒ *In-room: safe, Wi-Fi. In-hotel: restaurant, room service, bar, gym, laundry service, concierge, public Wi-Fi, parking (fee)* ▭ *AE, D, DC, MC, V* Ⓣ *Government Center, Haymarket.*

★ **\$\$–\$\$\$\$** ⚏ **Omni Parker House.** Any place that serves dessert for breakfast is quite okay with us, and it's even better that the Parker House dishes up the treat invented here at the hotel: Boston cream pie. Should cupid's arrow strike, the place to propose is Table 40 at Parker's restaurant, where JFK popped the question to Jackie. (JFK also gave his first speech here, in the press room at age six.) Other famous names on the "slept here" list include Charles Dickens, whose first reading of *A Christmas Carol* occurred at the hotel. The Parker House, the oldest continuously operating hotel in the United States, opened in 1855. You'll be transported in time the moment you enter the lobby, with its glossy wood paneling and ornately carved ceilings. All of this gives the Parker House a genuinely Boston appeal, which helps offset the fact that guest rooms are small. (The furnishings were custom-built to fit.) At least they're nicely turned out, in shades of blue and taupe with ivory wall coverings and cushy mattress covers. Another plus: rooms are extremely quiet—a claim that can't be made by some of the Parker House's newer neighbors. The hotel stands opposite old City Hall, on the Freedom Trail. **Pros:** Historical element, uniquely Boston feel, location near Downtown Crossing (Filene's Basement) on Freedom Trail. **Cons:** Small rooms, some say that staff could be friendlier. ⊠ *60 School St., Downtown, 02108* ☎ *617/227–8600 or 800/843–6664* 🖷 *617/742–5729* ⊕ *www.omniparkerhouse.com* ⤺ *551 rooms, 21 suites* ♿ *In-room: Wi-Fi. In-hotel: 2 restaurants, room service, bars, gym, laundry service, concierge, public Wi-Fi, parking (fee), some pets allowed* ⊟ *AE, D, DC, MC, V* Ⓣ *Government Center, Park St.*

★ **$$–$$$** 🏨 **Bulfinch Hotel.** The clean, crisp, contemporary look of this boutique hotel is simplicity at its best. Steps from TD Banknorth Garden (forever known as Boston Garden) and an easy walk to Government Center, Faneuil Hall, and the North End, this unique nine-floor flat-iron (triangular) property offers one of the best values in town, if you don't mind tiny digs. The immaculate, minimalist rooms have honey-hue walnut furnishings, gunmetal light fixtures, marble-tiled baths, and high-end mattresses, plus flat-screen TVs, CD players, and work desks. The neutral and white-on-white color scheme adds additional serenity—a welcome oasis from the maddening Garden crowds just outside the door. **Pros:** Modern, spotless rooms; great staff; lots of restaurants and bars in the area (also North Station commuter rail and T). **Cons:** Small guest rooms and lobby; parking garage is across the street. ⊠ *107 Merrimac St., Downtown, 02109* ☎ *617/624–0202* 🖷 *617/624–0211* ⊕ *www.bulfinchhotel.com* ⤺ *80 rooms* ♿ *In-room: ethernet. In-hotel: restaurant, bar, gym, laundry service, concierge, parking (fee), some pets allowed* ⊟ *AE, D, DC, MC, V* Ⓣ *North Station.*

★ **$$–$$$** 🏨 **Harborside Inn.** One of the best values in the neighborhood, this former 19th-century mercantile warehouse is now a plush, sedate inn with exposed brick-and-granite walls, hardwood floors, Turkish rugs, and Federal-style furnishings. Walk to popular Faneuil Hall, Quincy Market, and the North End, then return to the quiet and calm of this inn. Many of the snug, variously shaped rooms (no two are alike) have windows overlooking the small, open lobby, which extends eight stories up to the roof. If an outdoor view is important to you, request a room overlooking the city, but if you value quiet even more, book a room that faces the interior atrium. **Pros:** Good value for the area; close to Quincy

Market, North End, New England Aquarium, water taxi; good reading lights. **Cons:** Nearby nightclubs can be noisy, rooms differ in terms of size and configuration, some say rooms could be cleaner. ✉ *185 State St., Downtown, 02109* ☎ *617/723–7500 or 888/723–7565* 📠 *617/670–6015* 🌐 *www.harborsideinnboston.com* *52 rooms, 2 suites* *In-room: dial-up, Wi-Fi. In-hotel: laundry service, concierge, public Wi-Fi, parking (fee)* *AE, D, DC, MC, V* Ⓣ *Aquarium.*

KENMORE SQUARE

★ $$$–$$$$ **Hotel Commonwealth.** The Hotel Commonwealth is anything but common, blending old-world charm with modern conveniences for a sophisticated, boutiquey feel. Rich color schemes enhance the elegant rooms, and king- or queen-size beds are piled with down pillows and Italian linens. Choose rooms with views of bustling Commonwealth Avenue or Fenway Park. All rooms have marble baths and floor-to-ceiling windows. The much-acclaimed seafood restaurant, Great Bay, makes you feel like you're sitting by the ocean, with diffused lighting, a sandy color scheme, and a vast, shiplike room. **Pros:** Luscious bedding and bath products; great service; Red Sox fans will love the views of Fenway Park from some of the rooms (request these when booking); on-site restaurant is one of the best in the city for fresh fish. **Cons:** Hotel and surroundings can be mobbed during a Red Sox game. ✉ *500 Commonwealth Ave., Kenmore Sq., 02215* ☎ *617/933–5000 or 866/784–4000* 🌐 *www.hotelcommonwealth.com* *149 rooms, 1 suite* *In-room: safe, refrigerator, DVD, ethernet, Wi-Fi. In-hotel: 2 restaurants, room service, bar, gym, laundry service, concierge, public Wi-Fi, parking (fee)* *AE, D, DC, MC, V* Ⓣ *Kenmore.*

$$–$$$ Fodor's Choice ★ **Gryphon House.** Many of the suites in this four-story, 19th-century brownstone are thematically decorated; one evokes rustic Italy, another is inspired by neo-Gothic art. Among the many amenities—including gas fireplaces, wet bars, VCRs, CD players, and private voice mail—the enormous bathrooms with oversize tubs and separate showers are the most appealing. Even the staircase (there is no elevator) is extraordinary: a 19th-century wallpaper mural, *El Dorado,* wraps along the walls. Trompe-l'oeil paintings and murals by local artist Michael Ernest Kirk decorate the common spaces. Another nice touch: free passes to the Museum of Fine Arts and Isabella Stewart Gardner Museum. **Pros:** Elegant suites are lush and spacious; gas fireplaces are in all the rooms; helpful, friendly staff. **Cons:** May be too fussy for some; there's no elevator or handicapped access. ✉ *9 Bay State Rd., Kenmore Sq., 02215* ☎ *617/375–9003 or 877/375–9003* 📠 *617/425–0716* 🌐 *www.gryphonhouseboston.com* *8 suites* *In-room: refrigerator, VCR, ethernet, Wi-Fi. In-hotel: no elevator, public Internet, parking (no fee)* *AE, D, MC, V* *CP* Ⓣ *Kenmore.*

¢–$ **Hostelling International Boston.** This low-cost option near the Museum of Fine Arts is ideal if you don't mind sharing one of the six-person dormitories. (Private rooms are available for a higher price.) Bright purple paint enlivens the rather drab decor. Linens are provided, and there's a full kitchen and TV room for guests to use. Discounted tickets are often available to cultural events, and Continental breakfast is included. Run by American Youth Hostels, the lodging does not require membership but does suggest reservations. Travelers under 18 must be accompanied by parent or guardian. **Pros:** Facilities are clean and up-to-date; it's open 24 hours a day; can't beat the price. **Cons:** You'll feel like you're back in the college dorm; don't expect a lot of privacy; it gets noisy during busy times. ⊠*12 Hemenway St., Kenmore Sq., 02115* ☎*617/536–9455 or 800/909–4776 Ext. 07* 🖷*617/424–6558* ⊕*www.bostonhostel.org* 🛏*10 rooms without bath* ♿*In-room: no a/c, no phone, no TV. In-hotel: restaurant, laundry facilities, public Internet,* ⊟*MC, V* Ⓣ*Hynes/ICA.*

¢–$ 🏨 **Hostelling International Fenway.** Dying to see the boys of summer play in legendary Fenway Park, but don't want to pay big bucks for lodging? (And who has money left over after dishing it out for the hard-to-come-by Red Sox tickets?) This clean and convenient hostel offers low-cost dormitory rooms ($35–$38 per person) and private rooms for one to three people ($89 per night) in the Fenway 'hood. You'll have use of kitchen and laundry facilities, too. Open June through mid-August only. **Pros:** Cheap digs in the Fenway 'hood, kitchen and laundry facilities add to the convenience. **Cons:** Rooms are small and basic, not a lot of privacy. ⊠*575 Commonwealth Ave., Kenmore Sq., 02115* ☎*617/267–8599 or 800/909–4776 Ext. 07* 🖷*617/424–6558* ⊕*www. bostonhostel.org/fenway* 🛏*10 rooms without bath* ♿*In-room: no a/c, no phone, no TV. In-hotel: restaurant, bar, laundry facilities, public Internet* ⊟*MC, V* Ⓣ*Kenmore.*

SOUTH END

★ $$–$$$$ 🏨 **Clarendon Square Inn.** Tucked into a quiet South End neighborhood, this hip property is popular with travelers who appreciate the intimacy of a B&B and the style and sophistication of an upscale hotel. A massive renovation blended original 1860 Victorian touches, including hardwood floors, marble fireplaces, and decorative moldings, with modern art and up-to-date amenities. All rooms have queen-size beds and baths with limestone floors, tile walls, and whirlpools or two-person showers; some even have skylights. The fifth floor has a roof deck and hot tub with a view of the Boston skyline. **Pros:** Stylish decor, free parking, more boutique than B&B. **Cons:** Only three rooms means reservations are often tough to come by; families or party-hardy visitors may find it too refined ⊠*198 W. Brookline St., South End, 02118* ☎*617/536–2229* 🖷*617/2–2993* ⊕*www.clarendonsquare.com* 🛏*3 rooms* ♿*In-room: DVD, Wi-Fi. In-hotel: no elevator, public Wi-Fi, parking (no fee)* ⊟*AE, D, MC, V* ⦿*CP* Ⓣ*Back Bay/South End.*

$$ 🏨 **Chandler Inn.** The rooms are small, the bathrooms are minuscule, and the in-window air conditioners are noisy, but if money is an object, this cozy hotel is a contender. At the end of one of the South End's prettiest streets, the gay-friendly lodging is an easy walk to the T, the Amtrak station, or any of Tremont Street's trendy restaurants. Try to snag a room whose number ends in 08, as these are larger corner rooms with views of the Back Bay, or one of the eight deluxe rooms. Fritz, a popular sports bar, moonlights as a brunch spot on weekends. The inn often hosts huge crowds during June's Gay Pride celebrations. **Pros:**

Can't beat the price; friendly, bend-over-backwards staff. **Cons:** Some rooms are quite dingy, parking is tough in this area and expensive, thin-walled rooms can be noisy, expect more hostel than hotel. ⊠*26 Chandler St., South End, 02116* ☎*617/482–3450 or 800/842–3450* 🖷*617/542–3428* ⊕*www.chandlerinn.com* ⤸*56 rooms* ⚟*In-room: dial-up (some), Wi-Fi (some). In-hotel: restaurant, bar, public Wi-Fi, some pets allowed* ⊟*AE, D, DC, MC, V* Ⓣ*Arlington.*

★ $$ ⌂ **82 Chandler Street Bed & Breakfast.** Location and price are the selling points of this 1863 redbrick row house, a five-minute walk from Copley Square and Amtrak's Back Bay station. Each room is individually decorated in shades of green, red, blue, or yellow and is accessible via the four-story main staircase; all are no-frills but are white-glove clean. Standard rooms have a discreetly placed kitchen area. The best room, with wide bay windows overlooking downtown, is on the top floor and has a working fireplace and a skylight. **Pros:** Lots of historic charm, good price point. **Cons:** Minimum two-night stays, rooms are tiny, paper-thin walls. ⊠*82 Chandler St., South End, 02116* ☎*617/482–0408 or 888/482–0408* 🖷*617/482–0659* ⊕*www.82chandler.com* ⤸*3 rooms, 2 studios* ⚟*In-room: kitchen (some), refrigerator (some), ethernet. In-hotel: no elevator, no kids under 12* ⊟*No credit cards* ⦿*CP* Ⓣ*Back Bay/South End.*

$$ ⌂ **Encore.** What happens when talented architect Reinhold Mahler and creative set designer David Miller pool their energies and talents? You get this stylish, sophisticated converted town house, within easy walking distance to trendy South End shops and restaurants, and the Prudential Center. Sun-filled rooms, each named after a famous playwright (Sondheim, Albee, Bernstein), are spacious and spotless, decked out with modern Italian furnishings, contemporary rugs, brushed-steel and chrome touches, and brick accent walls. The Albee room has a private deck (the playwright has stayed in the room, too!); all rooms have ultramodern baths with glossy tiles, steel sinks and deluxe amenities. All this for a value-packed price. **Pros:** Trendy South End location; high-end, remote-control radio systems and CD players in rooms; lush linens; David and Reinhold are gracious hosts. **Cons:** Small breakfast nook; in season, room reservations are becoming harder to get as the word on this place gets out! ⊠*116 W. Newton St., South End, 02118* ☎*617/247–3425* ⊕*www.encorebandb.com* ⤸*3 rooms* ⚟*In-room: DVD, Wi-Fi. In-hotel: no elevator, public Wi-Fi, parking (no fee)* ⊟*AE, D, DC, MC, V* ⦿*CP* Ⓣ*Back Bay.*

$$ ⌂ **Hotel 140.** That old standby, the Y, got cranked up a notch. Once the province of gloves-wearing young ladies looking for a safe place to stay in the Big City, this historic 1929 brownstone now fills another practical niche: it offers cheap digs, a great locale—and boys are allowed. The Y headquarters are still here, at the site of the first YWCA in the United States, but three floors of the restored building are devoted to this hotel. Done up in soothing sage green and Easter-egg yellow, the property is a bunny-hop away from the John Hancock Tower and Back Bay shopping and dining hot spots. Although the hotel can't quite escape an institutional feel, nice touches such as a complimentary Continental breakfast soften the edges. The off-Broadway Lyric

Stage is on the second floor of the building, and if that appeals, you might consider a discount package that includes a room, tickets, and a light supper. **Pros:** Bargain-basement off-season prices, free use of computer and Internet, good base for single travelers on a budget. **Cons:** Cramped quarters, small beds, can't shake the YWCA/youth hostel feel. ☒ *140 Clarendon St., South End, 02116* ☎*617/585–5600 or 800/714–0140* ᗕ*617/585–5699* ⊕*www.hotel140.com* ⤿*54 rooms, 1 suite* ♿*In-room: ethernet. In-hotel: restaurant, gym, laundry facilities, public Internet, parking (fee), some pets allowed* ⊟*AE, MC, V* ⫯⃝⃝*CP* ⓣ*Back Bay/South End.*

$ ⊞**Berkeley Residence YWCA Boston.** This bare-bones facility has single ($60), double ($90), and triple ($105) rooms within walking distance of Back Bay and South End restaurants and shops. A dining room serves inexpensive meals. The Back Bay T station (which also serves Amtrak) is just three blocks away. For stays of more than a few nights, you must apply at least a week in advance. Long-term stays are $195 per week, which includes breakfast and dinner. Men, housed on a separate floor, can stay up to 13 nights; women can stay longer. **Pros:** Cheapest stay in town, economical long-term option for women traveling alone. **Cons:** Not a lot of privacy, rooms can be hot and stuffy in dog days of summer. ☒ *40 Berkeley St., South End, 02116* ☎*617/375–2524* ᗕ*617/375–2525* ⊕*www.ywcaboston.org* ⤿*200 rooms without bath* ♿*In-room: no a/c, no phone, no TV. In-hotel: restaurant, laundry service, public Internet* ⊟*MC, V* ⫯⃝⃝*BP* ⓣ*Back Bay/South End.*

BOSTON OUTSKIRTS

BRIGHTON

$$ ⊞**Best Western Terrace Inn.** In a residential neighborhood between Boston University and Boston College, on the line that divides Boston from Brookline, this motel is well priced and well maintained, if unremarkable. Most rooms have kitchenettes, and there's a supermarket two blocks away. The T is less than a block away, but with its ethnic shops, cafés, and Olmsted and Kennedy sights, Brookline itself is worth exploring. **Pros:** Close to neighborhood shops and restaurants, economical option for parents visiting BU or BC students. **Cons:** Slow T ride to downtown, dated decor, marginal breakfast. ☒*1650 Commonwealth Ave., Brighton, 02135* ☎*617/566–6260 or 800/937–8376* ᗕ*617/731–3543* ⊕*www.bostonbw.com* ⤿*68 rooms, 6 suites* ♿*In-room: kitchen (some), refrigerator, Wi-Fi. In-hotel: no elevator, public Internet, parking (no fee)* ⊟*AE, D, DC, MC, V* ⫯⃝⃝*CP* ⓣ*Washington St.*

BROOKLINE

$$$ ⊞**Inn at Longwood Medical.** Within walking distance of Fenway Park and the Museum of Fine Arts, this modern Best Western affiliate is also near six hospitals. Many hotel guests are patients or relations of patients (there's a discount medical rate, even on the busiest weekends). In the

Lodging Alternatives

APARTMENT RENTALS

If you want a home base that's roomy enough for a family and comes with cooking facilities, consider a furnished rental. Home-exchange directories sometimes list rentals as well as exchanges, and many of the B&B agencies below also handle apartment, cottage, and house rentals.

BED-AND-BREAKFASTS

Bed & Breakfast Agency of Boston (☎617/720–3540 or 800/248–9262 🖶617/523–5761 ⊕ www.boston-bnbagency.com). **Bed & Breakfast Associates** (☎781/449–5302 or 888/486–6018 🖶781/455–6745 ⊕ www.bnbboston.com). **Bed and Breakfast Reservations: North Shore/Greater Boston/Cape Cod** (☎617/964–1606, 978/281–9505, 800/832–2632 outside MA 🖶978/281–9426 ⊕ www.bbreserve.com). **Greater Boston Hospitality Bed & Breakfast Service** (☎617/393–1548 🖶617/227–0021 ⊕ www.bostonbedandbreakfast.com). **Host Homes of Boston** (☎617/244–1308 or 800/600–1308 🖶617/244–5156 ⊕ www.hosthomesofboston.com).

HOME EXCHANGES

A home-exchange organization will send you its updated listings of available exchanges via either e-mail or printed brochure. It's up to you to make specific arrangements.

HomeLink International (☎956/566–2687 or 800/638–3841 🖶954/566–2786 ⊕ www.homelink.org). **Intervac U.S** (☎800/756–4663 🖶415/435–7440 ⊕ www.intervacus.com).

HOSTELS

Hostelling International (HI), the umbrella group for a number of national youth-hostel associations, offers single-sex, dorm-style beds and, at many hostels, rooms for couples and family accommodations. Membership in any HI national hostel association, open to travelers of all ages, allows you to stay in HI-affiliated hostels at member rates; one-year membership is about $28 for adults (C$35 for a two-year minimum membership in Canada, £16 in the United Kingdom, A$52 in Australia, and NZ$40 in New Zealand); hostels charge about $10–$30 per night. Members have priority if the hostel is full; they're also eligible for discounts around the world, even on rail and bus travel in some countries.

Eastern New England Council of Hostelling International–American Youth Hostels (☎617/779–0900 Ext. 10 🖶617/779–0904 ⊕ www.usahostels.org) provides information on membership and on hostels in the Boston area. **Hostelling International Australia** (☎02/9565–1699 🖶02/9565–1325 ⊕ www.yha.com.au). **Hostelling International Canada** (☎613/237–7884 or 800/663–5777 🖶613/237–7868 ⊕ www.hihostels.ca). **Hostelling International New Zealand** (☎03/379–9970 or 0/800/278–299 🖶03/365–4476 ⊕ www.yha.org.nz). **Hostelling International UK** (☎0870/770–8868 🖶0870/770–6127 ⊕ www.yha.org.uk). **Hostelling International US** (☎301/495–1240 🖶301/495–6697 ⊕ www.hiusa.org).

4

summer, expect Sox fans to crowd the halls and lobby. Rooms are Best Western cookie-cutter, but nicely appointed with desks and updated linens and bed coverings. **Pros:** Superfriendly, helpful staff, medical rate packages are hard to beat, attached to Longwood Galleria Mall and food court. **Cons:** Many guests are here for medical treatments or visiting family members in nearby hospitals. ⊠*342 Longwood Ave., Brookline 02215* ☎*617/731–4700 or 800/468–2378* ⊟*617/731–4870* ⊕*www.innatlongwood.com* ⇋*140 rooms, 15 suites* ⌂*In-room: kitchen (some), Wi-Fi. In-hotel: restaurant, room service, bar, laundry service, public Internet, public Wi-Fi, parking (fee)* ⊟*AE, D, DC, MC, V* Ⓣ*Longwood.*

\$\$–\$\$\$ 📷**Beacon Inn at 1087 Beacon Street.** A B&B budget option, this inn comprises two separate locations in the "streetcar suburb" of Brookline. This Victorian brick town house could use a little TLC—the garish blue floral wallpaper and blah beige carpeting in the hallway are begging to be updated—but period detailing gives the place a genteel charm. The T stops just outside and gets you to downtown Boston in 15 minutes. Most rooms are spacious, with hardwood floors, antique furniture, and free local calls. The Fenway Room has three beds (two queens, one full), and room enough for six die-hard Sox fans. The second of the two guesthouses is a turn-of-the-20th-century town house, slightly farther outside the city toward Boston College, though still directly on the C branch of the Green Line, not far from the restaurants and shops of Washington Square. **Pros:** There's a large refrigerator in the lobby for guest use; wallet-pleasing slow-time rates; quiet setting. **Cons:** Off the beaten track; only two parking spaces for guests; fireplaces are nonworking; tiny baths, some detached from rooms (though still private). ⊠*1087 Beacon St., Brookline 02446* ☎*617/566–0088 or 888/575–0088* ⊟*617/278–9736* ⊕*www.beaconinn.com* ⇋*11 rooms* ⌂*In-room: refrigerator (some), ethernet. In-hotel: no elevator, laundry service, public Internet, parking (fee)* ⊟*AE, D, MC, V* ⦿❙*CP* Ⓣ*Hawes St.*

\$\$–\$\$\$ 📷**Brookline Courtyard by Marriott.** Prefer the comforts of a full-service hotel to the coziness of an old inn? This hotel, opened in 2002, has been discovered by families of students at nearby colleges—there are about a dozen schools within 5 mi of here, including Boston University and Boston College—who like the fact that they can treat the kids to dinner at one of several funky Coolidge Corner eateries, then unwind in the indoor pool and hot tub or hit the gym. The T is right outside the door, as are 15 or so restaurants. (An on-site eatery is open for breakfast only.) And in the Stuff You Won't Find Everywhere Department: rooms with Sabbath locks on the door for Jewish guests. This property is also more child-friendly than some, with babysitting (they can hook you up) and several connecting rooms. **Pros:** Indoor pool, close to T station. **Cons:** Don't expect rollicking nightlife nearby, staff can be indifferent. ⊠*40 Webster, Brookline 02446* ☎*617/734–1393 or 866/296–2296* ⊟*617/734–1392* ⊕*www.brooklinecourtyard.com* ⇋*180 rooms, 8 suites* ⌂*In-room: safe, ethernet. In-hotel: restaurant, pool, gym, laundry facilities, public Internet, public Wi-Fi, parking (fee)* ⊟*AE, D, DC, MC, V* Ⓣ*Beacon St.*

$$ ⊡**Bertram Inn.** If you prefer quiet and old-fashioned, you'll feel right at home in this historic, antiques-laden inn, within walking distance to lively Cleveland Circle. Built in 1907 as a wedding present for a wealthy Boston merchant's daughter, the Victorian-style building retains some original elements, like wood floors, paneled walls, and marble fireplaces. Each room is unique; one has hummingbird wallpaper, another a high canopy bed with steps. The room off the large living room is a favorite, with a four-poster bed, Oriental rug, cherry paneling, and working fireplace. **Pros:** Fresh fruit, pastries, snacks, and drinks are available all day; large living room with fireplace, leather couches, and porch with wicker cushioned rockers, are nice places to relax; two rooms have ultradeluxe (and superexpensive) Dux mattresses. **Cons:** Dust balls in the corners and ashes in the fireplaces—just like home; it's a walk and a T ride to downtown Boston. ⊠*92 Sewall Ave., Brookline 02446* ☏*617/566–2234 or 800/295–3822* 📠*617/277–1887* ⊕*www. bertraminn.com* ⇆*14 rooms* ♿*In-room: DVD, ethernet, Wi-Fi. In-hotel: no elevator, public Wi-Fi, parking (fee), some pets allowed, no kids under 7* ▭*AE, D, DC, MC, V* ⭤*BP* Ⓣ*St. Paul St.*

DORCHESTER

$$ ⊡**Courtyard by Marriott South Boston.** Tucked behind the Fortress, a behemoth storage facility, this property is a higher-end option to the neighboring Holiday Inn Express (⇨*below*). What this hotel has going for it will hit you in the face, figuratively speaking, as soon as you enter. Standing in front of the crescent-shape cherry reception desk (topped by a big flat-screen TV), you can easily take it all in: there's the grocery store (open 24 hours), the business center (with a neat two-sided fireplace), the lobby lounge, and the breakfast bar, all done up in coral and green, with leather chairs and cherry pillars. Guest rooms are pleasant enough, with two queen beds in a standard room. It's all brighter than the drab surroundings. The T station is just two blocks away, and free shuttles will get you to Downtown, the airport, Faneuil Hall, and the convention center. Fun feature: the Beantown Trolley shows up every morning at 8:30 sharp; join 'em for a day of sightseeing 'round town. **Pros:** Free parking, city skyline views from some rooms, family-friendly with weekend package deals. **Cons:** Not much going on in this area. ⊠*63R Boston St., Dorchester, 02125* ☏*617/436–8200 or 800/642–0303* 📠*617/436–0866* ⊕*www.marriott.com/property/ propertypage/BOSSO* ⇆*161 rooms, 5 suites* ♿*In-room: refrigerator, ethernet. In-hotel: bar, pool, gym, laundry service, public Internet, airport shuttle, parking (no fee), some pets allowed* ▭*AE, D, DC, MC, V* ⭤*CP* Ⓣ*Andrew.*

$ ⊡**Holiday Inn Express.** Just off the Southeast Expressway, this may be a convenient option if you're in town for business and don't need the ambience (or price tag) of downtown digs. Lower floors overlook a car wash and Dorchester's triple-deckers, but sixth-floor suites have views of the Boston skyline. Recently refurbished guest rooms are decorated in navy and taupe with Danish maple furnishings and cool chrome lamps. It's a five-minute walk to public transportation into the city; shuttles to the airport, Faneuil Hall, Downtown, and the Hynes

Convention Center are free. **Pros:** Price is right, lobby is comfy place to hang out and has free Internet access. **Cons:** Some rooms have crummy industrial views, not the best area in town, have to reserve the shuttle to Downtown or walk to the T. ✉ *69 Boston St., Dorchester, 02125* ☎ *617/288–3030 or 800/315–2621* 📠 *617/265–6543* ⊕ *www.HIExpress.com* 🛏 *112 rooms, 6 suites* 🛍 *In-room: refrigerator, dial-up (some), ethernet (some). In-hotel: gym, laundry service, concierge, executive floor, public Internet, airport shuttle, parking (no fee)* 🚫 *AE, D, DC, MC, V* 🍴 *CP* Ⓣ *Andrew.*

LOGAN AIRPORT (EAST BOSTON)

$$–$$$$ 🏨 **Hyatt Harborside at Boston Logan International Airport.** A 15-story glass structure punctuates this luxury hotel, on a point of land separating the inner and outer sections of Boston Harbor. Half of the rooms have sweeping views of either the city skyline or the ocean; the others overlook planes taking off and landing at the airport. The Hyatt operates its own 24-hour shuttle to all Logan Airport terminals and the airport T stop, and you'll get a discount on the water shuttle that runs between the airport and Downtown. Rooms, all decorated in soothing taupes and beiges, are soundproof. **Pros:** Convenient base for early flights out of Boston; pool area has skyline views; competent, can-do staff. **Cons:** Overpriced restaurant (skip it), airport shuttle service can be frustratingly slow. ✉ *101 Harborside Dr., East Boston, 02128* ☎ *617/568–1234 or 800/233–1234* 📠 *617/567–8856* ⊕ *www.harborside.hyatt.com* 🛏 *273 rooms, 6 suites* 🛍 *In-room: ethernet, Wi-Fi. In-hotel: restaurant, room service, bar, pool, gym, spa, laundry service, concierge, public Wi-Fi, airport shuttle, parking (fee)* 🚫 *AE, D, DC, MC, V* Ⓣ *Airport.*

$$$ 🏨 **Hilton Boston Logan Airport.** They know they've got a captive audience, so maybe that's why they've got a bit of an attitude at this soaring Hilton hotel. If you can get past the indifferent-bordering-on-rude service, you'll do fine here. The location is good if you're looking for proximity to Logan Airport—there's a skywalk to terminals A and E. Rooms have granite countertops in the baths and desks with ergonomic chairs. There's an unremarkable restaurant and an Irish pub on the premises, along with a gym where a security guard presides. **Pros:** Easy access to Logan Airport, competitive prices, health club with steam room is a great place to unwind. **Cons:** Uninterested staff, extras like Internet access and parking can add up. ✉ *1 Hotel Dr., East Boston, 02128* ☎ *617/568–6700* 📠 *617/568–6800* ⊕ *www.hilton.com* 🛏 *595 rooms, 4 suites* 🛍 *In-room: refrigerator, ethernet (some), Wi-Fi (some). In-hotel: restaurant, room service, bar, pool, gym, spa, executive floor, public Internet, public Wi-Fi, parking (fee)* 🚫 *AE, D, DC, MC, V* Ⓣ *Silver Line.*

$$ 🏨 **Holiday Inn Boston-Logan Airport.** "Get 'em in and get 'em out" is the philosophy at this airport hotel, but it does have some pleasant extras. The hotel's park-and-fly package, for example, allows you to leave your car for up to 10 days after staying just one night. There's a free airport shuttle, too. A baby grand is the centerpiece of the lobby, and the copper-ceiling pub is a cozy spot for a late-night bite. **Pros:** Cheap one-night stay for anyone parking and flying in and out of Boston, free airport shuttle. **Cons:** Shabby rooms need TLC, out-of-the-way location. ✉225 McClellan Hwy., East Boston, 02128 ☎617/569–5250 or 800/798–5849 🖶617/569–5159 ⊕www.ichotelsgroup.com ↩356 rooms ⚡In-room: ethernet. In-hotel: restaurant, room service, bar, pool, gym, executive floor, public Internet, airport shuttle, parking (fee) ▭AE, D, DC, MC, V ⓣOrient Heights.

CAMBRIDGE

$$$–$$$$
Fodor'sChoice
★
🖼**Charles Hotel.** Gracious service, top-notch amenities, and a great location on Harvard Square keeps this first-class hotel in high demand. The New England Shaker interior is contemporary yet homey; antique quilts and art by nationally recognized artists hang throughout. Relax in the lobby library, chock-full of titles, some autographed by authors who frequent the hotel; also sign up for a guided art tour of the hotel or pick up a self-guided map. Guest rooms come with lots of nice touches, like terry robes, quilted down comforters, flat-screen TVs (plus LCD mirror TVs in the bathroom), and Bose radios. If you're looking for a river or skyline view, ask for something above the seventh floor. Both of the hotel's restaurants—Rialto and Henrietta's Table—are excellent. **Pros:** Your wish is their command; on-site spa, health club, premier jazz club, and two of the area's top restaurants; Harvard Square is out the door; outdoor skating rink is a fun gathering spot for families during the winter months. **Cons:** Luxury comes with a price, great for visiting Cambridge sites, less convenient to downtown Boston (though Red Line T is two blocks away). ✉1 Bennett St., Cambridge 02138 ☎617/864–1200 or 800/882–1818 🖶617/864–5715 ⊕www.charleshotel.com ↩249 rooms, 45 suites ⚡In-room: safe, refrigerator, ethernet, Wi-Fi. In-hotel: 2 restaurants, room service, bars, pool, gym, spa, laundry service, concierge, public Internet, public Wi-Fi, parking (fee), some pets allowed ▭AE, DC, MC, V ⓣHarvard.

★ **$$$–$$$$**
🖼**Inn at Harvard.** You don't have to be an alumnus to enjoy the handsome, hushed elegance of this hotel, which borders Harvard Yard and has a Georgian-style brick exterior that mirrors many of those on campus. The skylighted atrium, used as a lobby, restaurant, and meeting space, is studded with sculptures and fine woodwork, and a comfy hangout for Harvard executives and visiting parents and profs. Rooms have classic furnishings, with understated black, brown, and neutral fabric and wall colors. Oversize windows frame views of Harvard Square or Harvard Yard and help give rooms a bright, cheerful feel; many rooms have tiny balconies, and others have window seats. **Pros:** Quiet oasis in midst of bustling Cambridge/Harvard University, rooms all have flat-screen TVs. **Cons:** Smallish bathrooms, tiny gym with four machines in a converted room, might be a bit stuffy for some. ✉1201 Massachusetts Ave., Cambridge 02138 ☎617/491–2222 or 800/458–5886 🖶617/520–3711 ⊕www.theinnatharvard.com ↩109 rooms, 4 suites ⚡In-room: ethernet, Wi-Fi. In-hotel: restaurant, room service, gym, laundry service, concierge, public Internet, public Wi-Fi, parking (fee) ▭AE, D, DC, MC, V ⓣHarvard.

A+ AMENITIES

Ritz-Carlton Boston Common. The Sports Club/LA, on property, offers 100,000 square feet of the latest fitness equipment. The Ritz has a fireplace butler to fetch wood for your hearth and a bath butler to cater to your bubble needs.

Marriott Long Wharf. Awesome pool-with-a-view, arguably the best in Boston, and the New England Aquarium (and IMAX theater) is right next door.

Fairmont Copley Plaza. Guests of culturally themed suites receive benefits like backstage passes to the Boston Symphony Orchestra.

Seaport Hotel. Don't leave town without getting a "margarita pedi-cure" or a massage at Wave Health & Fitness.

Beacon Hill Hotel & Bistro. Stroll the shops on Charles Street, wander the Public Garden, and come back to the hotel for a drink on the rooftop deck.

Onyx Hotel. Pampered pop-loving teens may croon for the Britney Spears Suite, designed by the diva's mother to replicate her daughter's bedroom.

Charles Hotel. The hotel's lending library is stuffed with titles, many autographed by authors who frequent the hotel. Art experts conduct tours of the hotel's extensive art collection.

$$–$$$$ 🏨**Kendall Hotel.** You might expect a hotel in a techno-zone such as Kendall Square to be all stainless steel and chrome, but this one is quite homey and ultrafriendly. In the former home of Engine House 7, it is stuffed with firehouse memorabilia. Owner Charlotte Forsythe loves collectibles, so an antique Chinese checkerboard and a ceramic dalmation add to the whimsical mix. Rooms are done up in Easter-egg hues. The small dining area serves local favorites such as Iggy's bread and Dave's Pasta. A seven-story addition in the works will include an enclosed rooftop lounge, eight deluxe rooms, and four suites with kitchens. **Pros:** Super-accommodating staff make guests feel right at home; extended, tasty breakfast is included; quiet rooms. **Cons:** May be too tchotchke-filled for some tastes. ✉*350 Main St., Cambridge 02142* ☎*617/577–1300 or 866/566–1300* 🖷*617/577–1377* ⊕*www. kendallhotel.com* 🛏*65 rooms* ⚿*In-room: ethernet, Wi-Fi. In-hotel: restaurant, room service, bar, laundry service, public Internet, public Wi-Fi, parking (fee)* ⊟*AE, DC, MC, V* ⦿|*BP* Ⓣ*Kendall/MIT.*

$$$ 🏨**Sheraton Commander.** The beloved, aging Harvard Square Hotel, with its signature neon light, finally got a face-lift. Rooms and most public areas have been updated with classic furnishings and handsome, jewel colors. It's got great bones and a fab location, minutes from Harvard Square. History buffs will appreciate the lovely arches found throughout the building and elegant touches, such as the bi-level ballroom, with a carved ceiling and gilt mirrors. Colonial-style rooms, some with four-poster or canopy beds, rocking chairs, and fireplaces, add to the historic flavor. **Pros:** Historical landmark with period architecture and detailing; helpful, knowledgeable staff. **Cons:** Small bathrooms, some rooms have views of the parking lot, extra charges for news-

paper, in-room Internet access, and local calls add up. ⊠*16 Garden St., Cambridge 02138* ☎*617/547–4800* ☏*617/868–8322* ⊕*www. starwoodhotels.com/sheraton* ⤙*175 rooms, 24 suites* ⌂*In-room: ethernet. In-hotel: restaurant, room service, bar, gym, laundry service, concierge, executive floor, public Internet, public Wi-Fi, parking (fee)* ▭*AE, D, DC, MC, V* Ⓣ*Harvard.*

$$–$$$
Fodor'sChoice
★

A Cambridge House Bed & Breakfast. A gracious 1892 Greek Revival home listed on the National Register of Historic Places, A Cambridge House has richly carved cherry paneling, a grand fireplace, elegant Victorian antiques, and polished wood floors overlaid with Oriental rugs. One of the antiques-filled guest rooms has fabric-covered walls, and many have four-poster canopy beds. Rooms in the adjacent carriage house are smaller, but all have fireplaces. Harvard Square isn't terribly close, but public transportation is available nearby. **Pros:** Pretty public sitting areas with fireplaces are cozy places to relax; free parking; complimentary coffee, tea, and hot chocolate served all day. **Cons:** Not a lot happening in the area, the removed-from-it-all setting is not for everyone. ⊠*2218 Massachusetts Ave., Cambridge 02140* ☎*617/491–6300 or 800/232–9989* ☏*617/868–2848* ⊕*www.acambridgehouse.com* ⤙*15 rooms* ⌂*In-room: ethernet, Wi-Fi. In-hotel: no elevator, public Internet, public Wi-Fi, parking (no fee), some pets allowed* ▭*AE, D, MC, V* ⃝*CP* Ⓣ*Davis.*

$$–$$$
Boston Marriott Cambridge. Businesspeople and vacationing families like the sleek, modern look and efficiency of this 26-story, high-rise hotel in Kendall Square, Cambridge's high-tech district, just steps from the subway and MIT. It's also a prime location for viewing Fourth of July fireworks. Rooms are done in the Marriott chain's signature greens, with floral spreads and drapes. A room on one of the two concierge floors nets you complimentary breakfast, hors d'oeuvres, and desserts in the lounge. **Pros:** Top-floor rooms have stunning skyline and river views; luxe bed linens; family-friendly; decent cost-saving packages. **Cons:** High-rise chain doesn't have a lot of charm, tiny pool, parking is expensive. ⊠*2 Cambridge Center, Cambridge 02142* ☎*617/494–6600 or 800/228–9290* ☏*617/494–0036* ⊕*www.marriotthotels.com* ⤙*431 rooms, 12 suites* ⌂*In-room: ethernet (some), Wi-Fi (some). In-hotel: 2 restaurants, room service, bar, pool, gym, laundry service, executive floor, public Wi-Fi, parking (fee)* ▭*AE, D, DC, MC, V* Ⓣ*Kendall/MIT.*

$$–$$$
Doubletree Guest Suites. The best things about this place: the very excellent, on-site Sculler's Jazz Club, one of the best places in town to catch a national act, and the extra-spacious two-room suites that cost no more than a single room elsewhere. The worst thing: it's a long walk to the subway and not really within walking distance of anywhere you want to go. A courtesy shuttle van is offered, but requires a bit of planning on your part. Each unit has a living room (with refrigerator and sofa bed), a bedroom with a king-size bed or two oversize twin beds, and a bathroom with a phone. Most suites have views of the Charles River or the Cambridge or Boston skyline—along with the traffic skirting Storrow Drive. **Pros:** After listening to top-notch jazz acts, your room is steps away; value-packed dinner, jazz, and room packages.

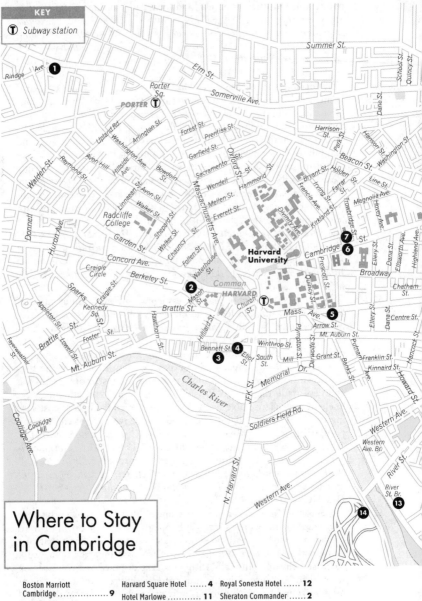

Where to Stay in Cambridge

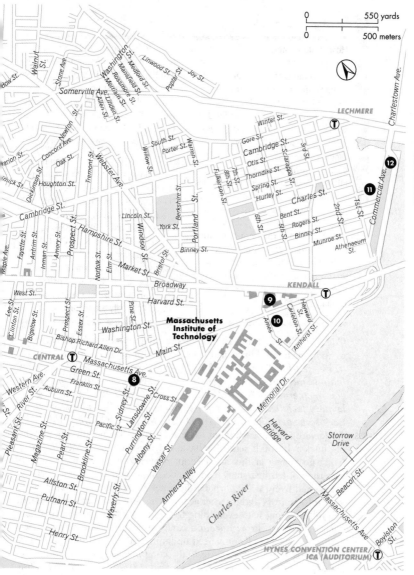

Bring the Kids

Most Boston hotels allow kids, but a few go out of their way to make them feel welcome with a slew of special features and packages. **Fairmont Copley Plaza** offers a Just Ducky package that includes tickets for Boston Public Garden Swan Boat rides, a copy of Robert McCloskey's *Make Way for Ducklings,* and a free plush duck. **The University Park Hotel at MIT** has value-priced family packages that include museum discounts, trolley passes, and "techie treats" (cookies shaped like elemental symbols). Traveling with baby? **The Langham Hotel** offers a Very Important Baby package, including unlimited diapers during your stay, baby bedding and nursery items, preordered baby food, valet parking, and more.

If you're looking for a place for kids to splash around, **the Seaport Hotel** and the **Sheraton Boston Hotel** have two of the largest pools in the city. When only the best for your little one will do: the children's suite at the **Taj** was outfitted in part by FAO Schwarz and has its own private playroom.

Many city hotels allow children under a certain age to stay in their parents' room at no extra charge. Request a "Kids Love Boston" brochure from the **Greater Boston Convention & Visitors Bureau** (☎ *617/536–4100, 888/733–2678 [888/SEE BOSTON] ⊕ www.bostonusa.com*). The Web site lists a variety of family-friendly packages that include such extras as complimentary use of strollers and discounts to city attractions.

Cons: You'll spend time driving or shuttling if you stay here, you have to book the hotel shuttle in advance. ⊠ *400 Soldiers Field Rd., Allston, 02134* ☎ *617/783–0090 or 800/222–8733* 🖷 *617/783–0897* ⊕ *www.hiltonfamilyboston.com* ⬦ *22 rooms, 286 suites* ⬦ *In-room: refrigerator, ethernet. In-hotel: 2 restaurants, room service, bar, pool, gym, laundry facilities, laundry service, concierge, public Internet, parking (fee), some pets allowed* ⊟ *AE, D, DC, MC, V* Ⓣ *Central.*

$$–$$$ 🏨 **Harvard Square Hotel.** Want to be in Harvard Square and not pay the big bucks? If you'll settle for basic lodgings in a great location, you won't go wrong at this nondescript property that feels more dormitory than hotel. Just steps from the neighborhood's many restaurants, shops, and lively street corners, the hotel has simple but clean rooms, with refrigerators and Internet access. The desk clerks are particularly helpful, assisting with everything from sending faxes to securing dinner reservations. **Pros:** Location can't be beat, some windows open for fresh air. **Cons:** Rooms need updating and baths are small (many with exposed pipes); Wi-Fi, in-lobby computer use, and parking cost extra. ⊠ *110 Mt. Auburn St., Cambridge 02138* ☎ *617/864–5200 or 800/458–5886* 🖷 *617/864–2409* ⊕ *www.harvardsquarehotel.com* ⬦ *73 rooms* ⬦ *In-room: safe, refrigerator, ethernet, Wi-Fi. In-hotel: laundry service, concierge, public Wi-Fi, parking (fee)* ⊟ *AE, D, DC, MC, V* Ⓣ *Harvard.*

★ $$–$$$ 🏨 **Hotel at MIT.** Witty and stylish, without going overboard, this modern hotel plays off its high-tech Cambridge location. Art on loan from the MIT collection playfully introduces guests to the world of artificial intelligence; early robotic specimens act as sculptures. Rooms are simple and sleek with maple armoires, inlaid with computer circuit boards. Whimsical touches abound, such as the pattern of the elevator's carpeting that uses stylized molecules and bed coverings with scientific-equation fabric. Rooms have floor-to-ceiling windows behind wood shutters, ergonomically designed furniture, and luxurious bedding. In the lobby and the large, open-kitchen restaurant, cool metal highlights are mixed with burnished maple, redwood, and oak. It's a hub for techie business travelers and a real bargain for weekend vacationers. **Pros:** Unique, tech-savvy rooms and surroundings; fitness center is open 24 hours, great off-season, Internet rates. **Cons:** A bit out of the way, with a 10-minute or so walk to the T; may be too sleek for some tastes. ⊠*20 Sidney St., Cambridge 02139* ☎*617/577–0200 or 800/222–8733* ⊟*617/494–8366* ⊕*www.hotelatmit.com* ⋑*196 rooms, 14 suites* ⌂*In-room: safe, ethernet, Wi-Fi. In-hotel: restaurant, room service, bar, gym, laundry service, concierge, public Internet, public Wi-Fi, parking (fee)* ⊟*AE, D, DC, MC, V* Ⓣ*Central, Kendall/MIT.*

4

$$–$$$ ▥**Hotel Marlowe.** Understated it's not! Vivid stripes, swirls, and other patterns punctuate this slightly over-the-top, lively boutique hotel, which expertly combines luxury, unique stylish flair, and unpretentious service. Leopard-print pillows and fake-fur throws add whimsy to the spacious rooms; many overlook the Charles River. Nice touches abound, like luscious linens, complimentary coffee and tea each morning, popular complimentary wine receptions each evening, and use of bikes and kayaks in summer. **Pros:** Luxury with below-market price tag, free use of business center, super family- and pet-friendly, great money-saving packages available throughout the year; free book readings and other literary events are held weekly in the hotel lobby. **Cons:** It's a cab ride or a walk and T ride into Boston; the wild colors and decor may not be for everyone. ⊠*25 Edwin H. Land Blvd., Cambridge 02141* ☎*617/868–8000 or 800/825–7140* ⊟*617/868–8001* ⊕*www.hotelmarlowe.com* ⋑*222 rooms, 14 suites* ⌂*In-room: safe, refrigerator, ethernet, Wi-Fi. In-hotel: restaurant, room service, bar, gym, bicycles, laundry service, concierge, public Internet, public Wi-Fi, parking (fee), some pets allowed* ⊟*AE, D, DC, MC, V* Ⓣ*Lechmere.*

$$–$$$ ▥**Hyatt Regency.** A dramatic ziggurat, this aging Hyatt is built around a central 16-story atrium. It's a magnet for wedding parties and group functions and the location is a bit out of the way; long walks or taxis are required to get around to top sites and attractions. But you can't beat the stunning views of the Charles River and the Boston skyline. Rooms that end in 06 have a river view and an interior balcony overlooking the atrium. For a small additional fee, add a large external private sundeck. **Pros:** Nice views from most rooms, look for bargain-basement Internet rates, large pool area. **Cons:** It's time to put some money into this has-been property, rooms need major freshening and updating, some bathrooms are shabby and out-of-date. ⊠*575 Memorial Dr., Cambridge 02139* ☎*617/492–1234 or 800/233–1234* ⊟*617/491–6906* ⊕*www.cambridge.hyatt.com* ⋑*459 rooms, 10 suites* ⌂*In-room: ethernet, Wi-Fi. In-hotel: 2 restaurants, room service, bar, pool, gym, bicycles, laundry service, concierge, public Internet, public Wi-Fi, parking (fee), some pets allowed* ⊟*AE, DC, MC, V* Ⓣ*Kendall/MIT.*

★ $$-$$$ 🏨**Royal Sonesta Hotel.** An impressive collection of modern art, spread throughout the hotel, makes this otherwise cookie-cutter property a bit of a surprise. Its location next to the Museum of Science and Galleria shopping center, and an attractive indoor/outdoor pool add to its appeal. Some rooms have superb views of Beacon Hill and the Boston skyline. Guest rooms are done in neutral earth tones, with modern amenities such as Sony PlayStation consoles, high-speed Internet, and CD clock radios. The hotel has great family excursion packages. **Pros:** kids feel welcome here; rooms are spacious; nice pool. **Cons:** Lacks personality, a bit sterile ⊠*40 Edwin Land Blvd., off Memorial Dr., Cambridge 02142* ☎*617/806–4200 or 800/766–3782* 🖷*617/806–4232* ⊕*www.royalsonestaboston.com* 📞*379 rooms, 21 suites* 🔑*In-room: safe, refrigerator, ethernet, Wi-Fi. In-hotel: 2 restaurants, room service, bars, pool, gym, bicycles, laundry service, concierge, public Internet, public Wi-Fi, parking (fee)* ▤*AE, D, DC, MC, V* Ⓣ*Lechmere.*

$-$$ 🏨**A Friendly Inn.** For a basic room and friendly service, this wallet-pleasing inn, within short walking distance to Harvard Square, can't be beat. It's a popular choice for visiting University professors and parents, who appreciate the homey, boardinghouse feel, great location, and value-packed price point. The simple, white-glove-clean rooms have plain furnishings, small, private baths, and comfy-enough queen beds. A few nice touches, like free Internet, 24-hour coffee and tea, and free parking, make this one of the best lodging deals in the area. **Pros:** Location; free parking; and low rates. **Cons:** Bathrooms are small, with stall showers (no tubs); furniture and furnishings are a bit used and worn. ⊠*1673 Cambridge St., Cambridge 02138* ☎*617/547–7851* ⊕*www.afinow.com* 📞*17 rooms* 🔑*In-room: Wi-Fi. In-hotel: no elevator, public Internet, public Wi-Fi, parking (no fee)* ▤*AE, D, DC, MC, V* ⓞ*CP* Ⓣ*Harvard.*

$-$$ 🏨**Irving House.** Tucked away on a residential street three blocks from Harvard Square, this four-story gray clapboard B&B is still a bargain. It has two small porches, hardwood floors, and Oriental carpets, making it homier than a hotel; there's a real sense of conviviality among guests, who are mostly European visitors and visiting parents and profs. Rooms are small but superclean. The limited off-street parking is a real coup in car-clogged Cambridge. **Pros:** Location and price; large downstairs sitting area has microwave, ice, and guest refrigerator; coffee, tea, and pastries are available until 10 PM. **Cons:** Parking spaces are first-come, first served; small baths, most with only showers. ⊠*24 Irving St., Cambridge 02138* ☎*617/547–4600 or 877/547–4600* 🖷*617/576–2814* ⊕*www.irvinghouse.com* 📞*44 rooms, 29 with bath* 🔑*In-room: no TV (some), ethernet, Wi-Fi (some). In-hotel: no elevator, laundry facilities, concierge, public Internet, public Wi-Fi, parking (no fee)* ▤*AE, D, MC, V* ⓞ*CP* Ⓣ*Harvard.*

Nightlife & the Arts

WORD OF MOUTH

"The Burren in Somerville is the real deal. Nothing fancy, just a dark, crowded pub—usually with some very authentic Irish music, and lots of interesting ales and beers."

—zootsi

"Try to pick up a copy of the Improper Bostonian (free on street corners). They have listings/reviews that will also tell you the type of people that are usually found at any given place—their annual favorite bartender issue is usually a good start."

—milemarker0

Updated
by Sarah
Pascarella

WHEN VISITORS COME TO BOSTON, the must-list for culture often includes visits to the Museum of Fine Arts, Isabella Stewart Gardner Museum, and the Boston Symphony Orchestra. Many also enjoy Boston's lively theater scene, which usually features traveling Broadway shows, national comedy acts, or previews of new plays soon headed to New York.

Those liking their entertainment a bit less upper-crust (and more budget-friendly) will still find plenty to do. Quincy Jones, Aimee Mann, and Branford Marsalis all got started at Berklee College of Music, and you may see tomorrow's big stars by taking in a local rock or jazz show around town. Star athletes and celebrities can often be spotted at nightclubs such as Felt, and Boston's award-winning restaurants (and their famous chefs) have brought a national focus to the city's dining scene. Whether it's an indie rock show at a local club, the finest martini at a hip lounge, or sports and beers at a college bar, Boston has cultural amusements for all types.

NIGHTLIFE

First and foremost, Boston is a Cinderella city. With public transportation shutting down each night between midnight and 1 AM, most nightspots follow accordingly, with last call typically around 2 AM. While true night owls may be disappointed at the late-night options, there are plenty of possibilities for those open to stepping out on the earlier side. The martini crowd may want to stroll Newbury and Boylston streets in the Back Bay, selecting from the neighborhood's swank restaurants, lounges, and clubs. Coffee- and tea-drinkers can find numerous cafés in Cambridge and Somerville, particularly Harvard and Davis squares. And beer swillers—well, there's pretty much an option on every corner. If you're having trouble finding a place to down a pint, you must have wandered out of Boston. For dancing, Lansdowne Street near Fenway Park has a mix of student-oriented clubs, sports bars, techno clubs, and a bar where dueling pianists take requests from the crowd at a fever pitch. There's also a thriving "lounge" scene in Downtown's coolest hybrid bar-restaurant-clubs, providing a mellower, more-mature alternative to the student-focused club scene. Tourists crowd Faneuil Hall for its pubs, comedy club, and dance spots. The South and North ends, as well as Cambridge and Somerville, cater to the "dinner-and-drinks" set, while those seeking great rock clubs should look no further than Allston, Jamaica Plain, and Cambridge.

BARS

BOSTON

ALLSTON

The **Sports Depot** has televisions visible from any vantage point, and if there's a game on, you'll be able to see it here. The menu includes a wide variety of greasy favorites, from burgers and wings to chili and fries, quesadillas and tacos to pizza and steak tips. ⊠ *353 Cambridge St., Allston* ☎ *617/783–2300* ⊕ *www.sportsdepotboston.com* Ⓣ *Harvard.*

KNOW-HOW

5

GETTING INFORMED

The best source of arts and nightlife information is the *Boston Globe*'s "Sidekick" section, available Monday through Saturday in the paper and on www.boston.com/ae/sidekick. Also worth checking are the Thursday "Calendar" section of the *Boston Globe;* the Friday "Scene" section of the *Boston Herald;* the free entertainment guide *Stuff@Night,* which is available in drop boxes around town; and the listings in the *Boston Phoenix,* a free weekly that comes out on Thursday. The Friday and Sunday "Arts" sections in the *Boston Globe* and the Saturday and Sunday "Arts" sections in the *Boston Herald* also contain recommendations for the week's top events. *Boston* magazine's arts section gives a more-selective, but less-detailed, overview. The listings at www.bostonphoenix.com, www.weeklydig.com, and at www.boston.com (a Web site affiliated with the *Boston Globe*) provide up-to-the-minute information online. Comprehensive theater listings can be found at www.theatermirror.com.

GETTING TICKETS

Boston's supporters of the arts are an avid group; tickets often sell out well in advance, particularly for the increasing number of shows making pre-Broadway stops. Buy tickets when you make your hotel reservations if possible. Most theaters take telephone orders and charge them to a major credit card, generally with a small service fee.

BosTix is a full-price Ticketmaster outlet that sells half-price tickets for same-day performances. The "menu board" in front of the booth (corner of Boylston & Dartmouth streets) and on the Web site (⊕www.bostix.com) announces the available events. Only cash and traveler's checks are accepted. On Friday, Saturday, or Sunday show up at least a half hour early. There is a booth in Quincy Market (◷10–6 Tuesday through Saturday and 11–4 on Sunday) and a booth in Copley Square (◷10–6 Monday through Saturday and 11–4 on Sunday).

Broadway Across America—Boston (☎617/880–2400 ⊕www.broadwayacrossamerica.com) brings Broadway shows to Boston and serves as a pre–New York testing ground for Broadway shows. Productions usually take place at the Colonial and Wilbur theaters, the Charles Playhouse, and the Opera House.

Live Nation/NEXT Ticketing (☎617/423–6000 [NEXT] ⊕www.livenation.com), a Boston-based outlet, handles tickets for shows at the Orpheum Theatre, Paradise Rock Club, and other nightclubs. Visit the Web site for ticket purchases anytime, or sales reps are available Monday through Saturday 10–5..

Ticketmaster (☎617/931–2000 or 617/931–2787 ⊕www.ticketmaster.com) allows phone charges, weekdays 9 AM–10 PM and weekends 9–8, with no refunds or exchanges. It also has outlets in local stores; call for locations.

Sunset Grill & Tap is a bit off the beaten path and looks at first glance like any other unpretentious neighborhood hangout. But venture inside and choose from more than 500 varieties of beer, 112 of which are on tap. Forget about pale domestic brews; try something unpronounceable

THE SKINNY ON…

WHAT'S PLAYING

Check the listings in a local weekly such as *The Improper Bostonian* or *The Weekly Dig.*

COVERS

Cover charges for local acts and club bands generally run $5–$15; big-name acts can be double that. Dance clubs usually charge a cover of $5–$10.

LAST CALL

Because Boston retains some vestiges of its puritanical "blue laws," the only places open after the official 2 AM closing time for bars and clubs are a few restaurants in Chinatown (at some you can ask for "cold tea" and still get a beer), and the city's few all-night diners, which won't serve alcohol. Bars may also close up shop early if business is slow or the weather is bad. Blue laws also prohibit bars from offering happy-hour drink specials, although happy-hour food specials abound.

SMOKING

Boston and Cambridge's tough anti-cigarette laws ban smoking in all bars and restaurants.

PAYING

Nearly all nightlife spots accept major credit cards; cash-only places are noted.

from a faraway country—and if you're really thirsty, get a yard of it. ⊠ *130 Brighton Ave., Allston* ☎ *617/254–1331* ⊕ *www.allstonsfinest. com* Ⓣ *Harvard.*

BACK BAY/BEACON HILL

★ **The Alley,** just off Boston Common, packs several watering holes onto one cozy street for those wanting a late night without having to crisscross the city. With a mechanical bull and loud music, the **Liquor Store** (⊠ *25 Boylston Pl.* ☎ *617/357–6800* ⊕ *www.liquorstoreboston.com*) is a place to check your inhibitions at the door. **Sweetwater Café** (⊠ *3 Boylston Pl.* ☎ *617/351–2515* ⊕ *www.sweetwatercafeboston.com*) has a booming sound system and plenty of drink options. ⊠ *Boylston Pl. off Boylston St., Theater District* Ⓣ *Boylston.*

Bukowski Tavern is a narrow barroom with a literary flair and more than 100 beers on the menu. The burgers are cheap, the draught selection is original, and the sound track is loud and very cool. ⊠ *50 Dalton St., Back Bay* ☎ *617/437–9999* ▭ *No credit cards* Ⓣ *Hynes/ICA.*

The Cactus Club is one of the few places in Boston that makes a decent margarita. In summer months, the restaurant's street-side outdoor patio is popular for kicking back, sipping frozen drinks, and watching the stylish Back Bay crowds pass by. ⊠ *939 Boylston St., Back Bay* ☎ *617/236–0200* ⊕ *www. bestmargaritas.com* Ⓣ *Hynes/ICA.*

Champions Sports Bar welcomes sports fans—the more rabid, the better. Visiting-team fans may be welcome, but

TOP-SCORING SPORTS BARS

Champions, Back Bay
The Fours, Old West End
Fritz Lounge, South End
Sports Depot, Allston
Sports Grille Boston, Old West End

expect to be drowned out by cheers for the home team. ⊠*Marriott Hotel at Copley Place, 110 Huntington Ave., Back Bay* ☎*617/279–6996* ⊕*www.championsboston.com* Ⓣ*Prudential Center.*

Cheers, formerly known as the Bull & Finch Pub, was dismantled in England, shipped to Boston, and reassembled here. Though it was the inspiration for the TV series *Cheers,* it doesn't look anything like the bar in the show. Addressing that complaint, however, a branch in Faneuil Hall that opened in 2001 is an exact reproduction of the TV set. ⊠*Hampshire House, 84 Beacon St., Beacon Hill* ☎*617/227–9605* ⊕*www.cheersboston.com* Ⓣ*Park St., Arlington, Charles/MGH.*

5

Fodor'sChoice
★ **Gypsy Bar** is the place to go if you're on the prowl. Expect scantily clad, well-imbibed club cats here. It's a great option for singles who want to dance the night away. ⊠*116 Boylston St., Theater District* ☎*617/482–7799* ⊕*www.gypsybarboston.com* Ⓣ*Boylston.*

Jacque's Cabaret, an institution for more than 60 years, is anything but traditional. Nightly female-impersonator shows draw everyone from drag queens to bachelorette parties to watch while swilling cocktails from paper cups. Downstairs, Jacque's Underground features indie rock bands and cabaret acts on Friday and Saturday. Because of a long-running licensing dispute, the whole carnival shuts down nightly at midnight. ⊠*79 Broadway, Beacon Hill* ☎*617/426–8902* ⊕*www.jacquescabaret.com* ⊟*No credit cards* Ⓣ*Arlington.*

Oak Bar has an elegant backdrop of whirring ceiling fans and marble that evokes cricket matches under the Bombay sun and duels fought over illicit love affairs. The old-world atmosphere is perfect for perusing a generous menu of signature martinis, single malts, and desserts. ⊠*Fairmont Copley Plaza hotel, 138 St. James Ave., Back Bay* ☎*617/267–5300* ⊕*www.fairmont.com/copleyplaza/* Ⓣ*Copley.*

The Rattlesnake lures in Back Bay shoppers and the post-work crowd. Located a few blocks off the Public Garden, the restaurant/bar has pool tables, televised sports, and (in-season) an open-air rooftop patio. ⊠*384 Boylston St., Back Bay* ☎*617/859–7772* ⊕*rattlesnakebar.com* Ⓣ*Arlington.*

Fodor'sChoice
★ **Saint,** despite its name, draws patrons who are anything but. The spacious underground lounge consists of two rooms: an airy main space is decorated in blue and silver, with long couches to lounge on over appetizers while making eyes across the room. A more-devilish "bordello room" is all plush red velvet and tasseled light fixtures, and has private alcoves for more-intimate conversation. ⊠*Courtyard by Marriott Boston Copley Square hotel, 90 Exeter St., Back Bay* ☎*617/236–1134* ⊕*www.saintnitery.com* Ⓣ*Copley.*

The Sevens is a laid-back alternative to the tony atmosphere of Beacon Hill. There's nothing stuffy or pretentious here, just good pints and old-fashioned mixed drinks, plus darts and the televised game of the night. ✉ *77 Charles St., Beacon Hill* ☎*617/523–9074* Ⓣ*Charles/MGH.*

MAKE IT A DATE

Bristol Lounge (for dessert), Back Bay
Casablanca, Cambridge
Oak Bar, Back Bay
RumBa, Downtown
Top of the Hub, Back Bay

Sonsie keeps the stereo volume at a manageable level. The bar crowd, which spills through the French doors onto a sidewalk café in warm weather, is full of young, trendy, cosmopolitan types and professionals. ✉*327 Newbury St., Back Bay* ☎*617/351–2500* ⊕*www.sonsieboston. com* Ⓣ*Hynes/ICA.*

Top of the Hub is a lounge with a wonderful view over the city; that and the hip jazz help to ease the sting of pricey drinks. ✉*Prudential Tower, 800 Boylston St., 52nd fl., Back Bay* ☎*617/536–1775* ⊕*www. selectrestaurants.com/tophub/* Ⓣ*Prudential Center, Hynes/ICA.*

21st Amendment, named after the amendment that ended Prohibition, is a convivial pub across from the State House that draws state legislators and lobbyists as well as neighborhood regulars. They all trade gossip (and favors) at notched wooden tables over beer and barbecue chicken salad. ✉*150 Bowdoin St., Beacon Hill* ☎*617/227–7100* ⊕*http://21stboston.com* Ⓣ*Park St.*

CHARLESTOWN

Massachusetts' oldest watering hole is Charlestown's **Warren Tavern,** more than 200 years old and once frequented by Paul Revere. Today it caters mostly to tourists and Charlestown professionals. It's an easy stop for a pint en route to the Bunker Hill Monument or historic Navy Yard. ✉*2 Pleasant St., Charlestown* ☎*617/241–8142* ⊕*www. warrentavern.com* Ⓣ*Community College.*

DOWNTOWN

Beantown Pub, right on the Freedom Trail, is the only pub in Boston where you can enjoy a Sam Adams lager while overlooking the grave of Adams himself. It's a great place to watch the game or get a snapshot of the throngs of tourists, professionals, and students going by. The menu—also available late-night—includes burgers, sandwiches, and other traditional pub fare. ✉*100 Tremont St., Downtown* ☎*617/426–0111* ⊕*www.beantownpub.com* Ⓣ*Park St., Downtown Crossing.*

Felt is *the* place to see and be seen. Dress to impress; once past the velvet ropes, you may spot a celebrity here at a pool table, on the dance floor, or just enjoying a cocktail. ✉*533 Washington St., Downtown* ☎*617/350–5555* ⊕*http://feltclubboston.com* Ⓣ*Chinatown, Downtown Crossing, Boylston, Park Street.*

The Good Life is a creative martini bar, with such exotic varieties as cucumber, strawberry-basil, and caramel macchiato. On the basement level is the Afterlife Lounge, with more than 150 frozen vodka options on the menu. ✉*28 Kingston St., Downtown* ☎*617/451–2622* ⊕*www.goodlifebar.com* Ⓣ*Downtown Crossing.*

J. J. Foley's is yet another Irish pub that's worth a visit. Blue-collar workers down their Guinness pints along with neighboring Financial District suits, shoppers from Downtown Crossing take a break with a cider or ale. The atmosphere is no-frills, no-fuss. ✉*21 Kingston St., Downtown* ☎*617/338–7713* Ⓣ*Downtown Crossing.*

MOST HISTORIC PUBS
Bell in Hand Tavern, Faneuil Hall
Doyle's, Jamaica Plain
Green Dragon Tavern, Faneuil Hall
The Last Hurrah, Downtown
Warren Tavern, Charlestown

The Kinsale by day offers lunch and a pint to the business crowds of Government Center. By night, the pub comes alive with revelers from nearby Faneuil Hall. The pub was reassembled here, piece by piece, after being constructed in Ireland, and has live music several nights a week. ✉*2 Center Plaza, Downtown* ⊕*www.classicirish.com* ☎*617/742–5577* Ⓣ*Government Center.*

Last Hurrah, at the Omni Parker House, might make you feel like a Brahmin, even if just for a drink or two. The historic setting and location right on the Freedom Trail makes it an easy stop for those hitting the main sites Downtown. ✉*60 School St., Downtown* ☎*617/227–8600* ⊕*www.omnihotels.com* Ⓣ*Downtown Crossing, Park Street.*

News is one of Boston's few late-night eating options that isn't simply a diner. Though required to stop serving liquor at 2 AM, it continues dishing out everything from sushi to omelets to steak tips until 4. Flat-screen TVs and a see-and-be-seen vibe attract out-of-towners and clubbers not ready for the drive home. Wednesday is Ladies' Night, when women get a free three-course meal. Valet parking is free until 10. ✉*150 Kneeland St., Downtown* ☎*617/426–6397* ⊕*www.newsboston. com* Ⓣ*South Station.*

RumBa, in the InterContinental hotel, highlights two distinctive spirits: rum and champagne. Vintage rums are available for sampling; the champagne lounge area has a more-secluded atmosphere for quieter celebrations. ✉*510 Atlantic Ave., Downtown* ☎*617/451–2622* ⊕*www. intercontinentalboston.com/dining* Ⓣ*South Station, Aquarium.*

FANEUIL HALL

★ **Bell in Hand Tavern** is the country's oldest continuously operating pub. It's on the perimeter of Faneuil Hall and has live music every night of the week. If you're brave, you can join the Tuesday-night karaoke. ✉*45-55 Union St., Faneuil Hall* ☎*617/227–2098* ⊕*www.bellinhand. com* Ⓣ*Haymarket.*

The Black Rose is decorated with family crests, pictures of Ireland, and portraits of the likes of Samuel Beckett, Lady Gregory, and James Joyce—just like a Dublin pub. Its Faneuil Hall location draws as many tourists as locals, but nightly performances by traditional Irish and contemporary performers make it worth braving the crowds. ✉*160 State St., Faneuil Hall* ☎*617/742–2286* ⊕*www.irishconnection.com/index.* Ⓣ*Government Center, Haymarket, State.*

Cheers is the result of popular demand to replicate the TV set from the show. The owners of the former Bull & Finch in Beacon Hill, which was the inspiration for the show, created an exact reproduction of

5

the TV set, complete with Sam's Red Sox jacket and the photo of the Indian chief behind the bar. Despite overpriced burgers and seafood, tourists and students are frequent customers. ✉*Faneuil Hall Marketplace, Government Center* ☎*617/227–0150* ⊕*www.cheers boston.com* Ⓣ*Government Center, Haymarket.*

Green Dragon Tavern is a less-rowdy pub than its Faneuil Hall neighbors. It has cover bands a few nights a week, regular lunch specials, and very friendly waitstaff. ✉*11 Marshall St., Faneuil Hall* ☎*617/367–0055* Ⓣ*Haymarket, Government Center.*

Hennessy's claims to be the best Irish pub in town, although it has plenty of competition in that category, not

> **SARAH'S TOP 5**
>
> ■ Have a refined evening at the **Boston Symphony Orchestra**, or **Boston Ballet**.
>
> ■ Rock out at the **Paradise**, the **Middle East**, **T.T.** the **Bear's Place**, and **Great Scott**.
>
> ■ Toss back a pint (or two) at an authentic Irish pub such as the **Burren**, **Doyle's**, or the **Kinsale**.
>
> ■ Indulge your sweet tooth at **Finale** or the **Four Seasons'** dessert buffet.
>
> ■ Check out the hot salsa scene at **Ryles**, the **Havana Club**, El **Bembe**.

least from its neighboring watering holes of Faneuil Hall. Expect a rowdy crowd on weekends, and a quieter scene during the workweek. ✉*25 Union St., Faneuil Hall* ☎*617/742–2121* Ⓣ*Haymarket, Government Center.*

The Hong Kong may not be Faneuil Hall's rowdiest bar, but it comes close. Packed with bachelorette parties, fraternity boys thirsty for a famous Scorpion Bowl, and those ready to hit the dance floor, the Hong Kong is often a first or last stop on a bar crawl. Even if you don't plan to stay, sampling a beef teriyaki stick is worth the trip. ✉*65 Chatham St., Faneuil Hall* ☎*617/227–2226* ⊕*www.hongkongboston. com* Ⓣ*Aquarium, State, Government Center.*

Jose McIntyre's, an Irish-Mexican bar, satisfies your double craving for a margarita and a Guinness—each expertly poured. The eclecticism continues with a dance floor, several big-screen TVs, and a pool table. ✉*160 Milk St., Faneuil Hall* ☎*617/451–9460* ⊕*www.irishconnection.com/index.php?id=42* Ⓣ*Aquarium.*

Kitty O'Shea's, on the outskirts of Faneuil Hall in the Financial District, is a sister pub to the original in Dublin. The bar, the fireplace, the stained-glass windows, and even some of the staffers have been imported from the Emerald Isle, giving the impression of a dyed-in-the-wool Irish establishment. ✉*131 State St., Downtown* ☎*617/725–0100* ⊕*www.kittyosheas.com/boston.asp* Ⓣ*Aquarium, State.*

THE FENS

Boston Beer Works is a "naked brewery," with all the works exposed—the tanks, pipes, and gleaming stainless-steel and copper kettles used in producing beer. Seasonal brews, in addition to a regular selection, are the draw for students, young adults, and tourists. It's too crowded and noisy for intimate chats. ✉*61 Brookline Ave., Fens* ☎*617/536–2337* Ⓣ*Kenmore.*

Jake Ivory's, on the always lively Lansdowne Street, is a bar known for its dueling piano players. Each night is a competition as the two pianists attempt to outperform the other. Bring a few extra dollars to put in requests, and expect a raucous crowd. ⊠*9 Lansdowne St., Fens* ☎*617/247–1222* ⊕*www. jakeivorys.com* Ⓣ*Kenmore.*

Jillian's, a sprawling nightspot, with multiple bars, pool tables, a bowling alley, and a nightclub is like

> **BOSTON'S BEST IRISH PUBS**
>
> ■ **The Burren,** Somerville
> ■ **Doyle's,** Jamaica Plain
> ■ **The Druid,** Cambridge
> ■ **The Kinsale,** Downtown
> ■ **Kitty O'Shea's,** Downtown

Chuck E Cheese for adults. If you're just going for drinks and pool, you can kick back with ease; expect to wait for a lane if you want to bowl. ⊠*145 Ipswich St., Fens* ☎*617/437–0300* ⊕*www.jilliansboston.com* Ⓣ*Kenmore.*

The Modern favors cocktails and designer black over beer and T-shirts. Though it's connected to the Embassy megaclub, this place is a cool departure from the loud Lansdowne scene. There's seldom live music; young professionals come to talk, sip martinis, and lock gazes among the mirrors and backlighting. ⊠*36 Lansdowne St., Fens* ☎*617/536–2100* ⊕*www.shuttavac.com/themodern/* Ⓣ*Kenmore.*

JAMAICA PLAIN

Fodor'sChoice
★ **Doyle's Café,** truly an institution, is a friendly, crowded, neighborhood Irish pub that opened in 1882 and has been a Boston political landmark ever since. Candidates for everything from Boston City Council to the U.S. Senate drop by to eat corned beef and cabbage, sample one of the 32 brews on tap or 60 single-malt Scotches, and, of course, make speeches and shake hands. ⊠*3484 Washington St., Jamaica Plain* ☎*617/524–2345* ▤*No credit cards* Ⓣ*Green St., Forest Hills.*

OLD WEST END

Boston Beer Works near the TD Banknorth Garden is nearly identical to its sister location outside Fenway Park, but this one is naturally frequented by more Celtics and Bruins fans. ⊠*110 Canal St., Old West End* ☎*617/896–2337* Ⓣ*North Station.*

The Ruby Room, in the Onyx Hotel, is true to its name, with every shade of red imaginable. It's a sexy and comfortable spot to sip a designer cocktail and nosh on appetizers. Upstairs in the hotel, the Britney Spears Foundation Room was designed by the pop star's mother, but don't expect to see celebrities here. ⊠*Onyx Hotel, 155 Portland St., Old West End* ☎*617/557–9950* ⊕*www.rubyroomboston.com* Ⓣ*North Station.*

Sports Grille Boston is a heavyweight sports bar with 140 televisions tuned to every contest in the country and then some. A quick tour of Boston's more-glorious moments is evident from the memorabilia on the walls. Pack the Pepto for an overstuffed bar menu of burgers and fried foods. ⊠*132 Canal St., Old West End* ☎*617/367–9302* Ⓣ*North Station.*

Blue-Law Blues

Why do Boston bars close so early? Something of the old Puritan ethic of the Massachusetts Bay Colony lingers in the so-called "blue laws" that prohibit sales of alcoholic drinks at bars and restaurants after 1 AM on weekdays and 2 AM on weekends. The state remains of two minds when it comes to social leniency. The first state to legalize gay marriage was also one of the last states to allow liquor sales on Sunday. (Both became legal in 2004.)

Historians surmise that the origin of the blue laws goes back to colonial times when special laws were actually written on blue paper. In 17th-century Boston, it was forbidden to walk on the street on Sunday, or to sing, dance, fiddle, pipe, or use a musical instrument at night. Most of these laws have been repealed (though it's still technically illegal to sit on the grass on Boston Common without a proclamation from the mayor). But periodic attempts to push back closing time still meet with heavy opposition from conservative neighborhood groups.

Late-night revelers party on in other ways. Asking for "cold tea" at certain Chinatown restaurants might get you a beer, and at certain Irish bars around town, the lights are off but somebody's home. A modern trend has been to form "private clubs" such as Rise, on Stuart Street, where members pay yearly fees for the privilege of partying (although not drinking) all night. Thankfully, it's no longer illegal to dance until dawn.

SOUTH BOSTON

Lucky's Lounge is a subterranean spot with live jazz on weekends, perfect martinis, and a mixed yuppie/artist crowd. The Rat Pack vibe is a lot of fun, and the salads, pizzas, and homemade meat loaf are first-rate. ✉ *355 Congress St., Fort Point, South Boston* ☎ *617/357–5825* ⊕ *www.luckyslounge.com* Ⓣ *South Station.*

SOUTH END

★ **Club Café** is among the smartest spots in town for gay men and lesbians—even when they're dining or partying with their straight friends. Behind stylish restaurant 209, the two-room "video lounge" is a relaxed vibe to dance to current- and classic-music videos, watch cult movies and TV shows, or bust out with weekly karaoke. There's never a cover charge. ✉ *209 Columbus Ave., South End* ☎ *617/536–0966* ⊕ *www. clubcafe.com* Ⓣ *Back Bay/South End.*

Delux Café & Lounge is a great spot to mix with twentysomething hipsters or to grab creative, affordable comfort food that always includes a grilled-cheese sandwich worth trying. Yellowing posters and postcards on the wall give the place a retro vibe. The quesadillas are generally worth the wait for a table. ✉ *100 Chandler St., South End* ☎ *617/338–5258* Ⓣ *Back Bay/South End.*

The Fours is all about sports. Located just outside the TD Banknorth Garden, it's packed with fans on game and concert nights. Visit during lunch on a weekday for a quieter atmosphere. ✉ *166 Canal St., Old West End* ☎ *617/720–4455* ⊕ *www.thefours.com* Ⓣ *North Station.*

Franklin Cafe is a neighborhood institution known for great martinis, microbrews on tap, and upscale pub food. There's no placard bearing its name, just look for the martini sign (or the crowd waiting for a dinner table) to know you're there. ⊠*278 Shawmut St., South End* ☎*617/350–0010* ⊕*www.franklincafe.com* Ⓣ*Back Bay/South End.*

Fritz Lounge is a gay sports bar popular with the local after-work crowd. Casually dressed patrons sip brew from the large beer list or drop in for steak and eggs during the hopping weekend brunch. ⊠*26 Chandler St., South End* ☎*617/482–4428* ⊕*www.fritzboston.com* ▬*No credit cards* Ⓣ*Back Bay/South End.*

Harp is the place for a crowded, rollicking atmosphere, just outside North Station and the TD Banknorth Garden. Although technically an Irish pub, the Harp is a three-story megabar that serves postgame or concert crowds, sports fans, and ticketless night owls wanting to be close to the action. ⊠*85 Causeway St., Old West End* ☎*617/742– 1010* ⊕*www.harpboston.com/harpboston* Ⓣ*North Station.*

The Living Room, on the outskirts of the North End, has killer martinis and tasty appetizers in an upscale setting modeled after its name— feel free to stretch out on the lounge's many elegant love seats and armchairs, or pull up a seat at the bar. On weeknights, the bar is quieter, with friends meeting for drinks or watching the game; on weekends, expect a packed house, a DJ, and dancing. ⊠*101 Atlantic Ave., Waterfront* ☎*617/723–5101* ⊕*www.thelivingroomboston.com* Ⓣ*Haymarket, Aquarium.*

The Purple Shamrock is a tourist favorite. Just off Faneuil Hall, the bar has live music (including karaoke some nights), standard pub grub, and a chance to mingle with your fellow travelers. Be prepared to wait in line on weekends. ⊠*1 Union St., Faneuil Hall* ☎*617/227–2060* Ⓣ*Haymarket, Government Center.*

CAMBRIDGE & SOMERVILLE

FodorśChoice **The Burren** pulls in a devoted local, mostly student, crowd. It's got all the
★ elements of a great Irish bar—expertly poured Guinness on tap, comfort food such as fish-and-chips, bangers and mash, and shepherd's pie, and live Irish music nightly—all in a warm, friendly environment. ⊠*247 Elm St., Somerville* ☎*617/776–6896* ⊕*www.burren.com* Ⓣ*Davis.*

Cambridge Brewing Company is a cheerful, collegial, cavernous microbrewery that's a favorite among MIT students and techies. Try a pint of the company's Cambridge Amber or Charles River porter. If you've got a group, order a "tower" (83 ounces). In warm weather you can sit outside on the patio. ⊠*1 Kendall Sq., Bldg. 100, at Hampshire St. and Broadway, Cambridge* ☎*617/494–1994* ⊕*www.cambrew.com* Ⓣ*Kendall/MIT.*

Casablanca has a Moroccan interior replete with wicker chairs and ceiling fans. The bar serves fantastic martinis and rich, North African–influenced appetizers. It's the cool place to be, especially with a date: rattan love seats and Bogey's aura make it an ideal spot for two. ⊠*40 Brattle St., Cambridge* ☎*617/876–0999* ⊕*www.casablanca-restaurant.com* Ⓣ*Harvard.*

★ **Chez Henri,** a French-Cuban restaurant equidistant from Harvard and Porter squares, has a hip after-work bar scene. There you'll find the best Cuban sandwiches north of Miami, and mojitos *muy fuertes* with which to wash them down. ⊠*1 Shepard St., midway between Harvard and*

Porter Sqs., Cambridge ☎*617/354–8980* Ⓣ*Harvard, Porter.*

Druid makes you feel like you're in Dublin with well-poured pints, a dusky atmosphere, and black-and-white pudding on the menu. Its location in residential Inman Square gives you a chance to get to know the locals. ⊠*1357 Cambridge St., Cambridge* ☎*617/497–0965* Ⓣ*Lechmere, Harvard; then Bus 69.*

★ **Enormous Room,** somewhat whimsically named, is tucked into a tiny space above a restaurant in Central Square. Cambridge hipsters line up on weekends in front of the door, which is coolly unmarked. Inside, they nosh on Middle Eastern appetizers, including the "enormous platter" full of chicken skewers, olives, pita wedges, and other bites perfect for sharing. Instead of tables or booths, you'll find luxurious rugs and oversize throw pillows for stretching out, drinking, and people-watching. ⊠*567 Massachusetts Ave., Cambridge* ☎*617/491–5550* Ⓣ*Central.*

Grendel's Den is low lighted and brick walled, the quintessential grad-student hangout. During happy hour (5–7:30 daily and 9 PM–11:30 PM Sunday through Thursday), spinach, artichoke, clam dip, littleneck clams, and other tasty entrées go for half price with a $3-per-person drink purchase. ⊠*89 Winthrop St., Cambridge* ☎*617/491–1160* ⊕*www.grendelsden.com* Ⓣ*Harvard.*

John Harvard's Brew House dispenses—from behind its long, dark bar—ales, lagers, pilsners, and stouts brewed on the premises. It even smells like a real English pub. The food is no-frills and hearty. On Monday, college students get selected appetizers at half price. ⊠*33 Dunster St., Cambridge* ☎*617/868–3585* ⊕*www.johnharvards.com* Ⓣ*Harvard.*

Middlesex Lounge combines the minimalist design of a New York lounge with the laid-back friendliness of a Cambridge pub to create one of the hottest scenes on this side of the river. Rolling settees lend themselves to a variety of seating configurations, or can be cleared at night for dancing to crowd-pleasing electronic and indie music. ⊠*315 Massachusetts Ave., Cambridge* ☎*617/868–6739* ⊕*www.middlesexlounge.com* Ⓣ*Central.*

★ **Noir** is a sexy nightspot in the Charles Hotel where Cary Grant and Katharine Hepburn would feel right at home. Sink into a wraparound black-leather couch, order a martini (try the strawberry-basil), and perfect your best air of mystery. ⊠*Charles Hotel, 1 Bennett St., Cambridge* ☎*617/661–8010* ⊕*www.noir-bar.com* Ⓣ*Harvard.*

Orleans brings a cool Back Bay vibe to Somerville's Davis Square. It has live music on Friday nights, a lounge full of comfy couches and settees, and a large-projector screen playing the night's game. Try the bar's mango mojito or peach martini for a sweet buzz. ⊠*65 Holland St., Somerville* ☎*617/591–2100* Ⓣ*Davis.*

River Gods, a popular bar outside Central Square, is true to its name, cluttered with frequently changing decorations of the pub's namesake gods on every surface. It's also known for a variety of great meals (Irish, Thai, American, and more) done on the cheap. ⊠*125 River St., Cambridge* ☎*617/576–1881* ⊤*Central.*

Temple Bar is a classy place to enjoy a cocktail after a long day exploring, with signature drinks including espresso and chocolate martinis. If

<table>
<tr><td colspan="2">BEST FOR BEER CONNOISSEURS</td></tr>
<tr><td>■</td><td>**Boston Beer Works,** The Fens</td></tr>
<tr><td>■</td><td>**Bukowski Tavern,** Back Bay</td></tr>
<tr><td>■</td><td>**Cambridge Brewing Company,** Cambridge</td></tr>
<tr><td>■</td><td>**John Harvard's,** Cambridge</td></tr>
<tr><td>■</td><td>**Sunset Grill & Tap,** Allston</td></tr>
</table>

you're hungry, be sure to sample executive chef Tom Berry's latest seasonal creations. ⊠*1688 Massachusetts Ave., Cambridge* ☎*617/547–5055* ⊕*www.templebarcambridge.com* ⊤*Porter, Harvard.*

West Side Lounge tempts cool cats and hipsters with comfort food, a comprehensive list of martinis and cocktails, and late-night lounging. Try the white ginger cosmo or prickly-pear margarita. ⊠*1680 Massachusetts Ave., Cambridge* ☎*617/441–5566* ⊕*www.westsidelounge. com* ⊤*Porter, Harvard.*

BOWLING ALLEYS & POOL HALLS

Pool halls in Boston make a popular winter refuge for teens and university students. Forget Paul Newman and smoky interiors: Boston likes its billiards halls swanky and well lighted, with plenty of polished brass and dark wood. Many of them do double duty as bowling alleys. Be forewarned, however, that in New England bowling is often "candlepin," with smaller balls and different rules. Some pool halls have age requirements (either over-18 or -21); call for details.

★ **Boston Billiard Club,** a comfortable and roomy space, has 55 tables and some private rooms. It feels like a classic billiards hall, but with waitresses in sexy outfits and everyone drinking designer cocktails. ⊠*126 Brookline Ave., Fens* ☎*617/536–7665* ⊕*www.bostonbilliardclub. com* ⊤*Kenmore.*

Felt is decked out so stylishly with chrome furnishings, cushy lounge chairs, and space-age light fixtures that it's easy to forget that it's a pool hall. Sports stars and other minor celebrities mingle among young professionals and businesspeople on a night out to impress. Upstairs are 16 billiards tables covered with dark-blue felt, and a fourth-floor dance club. ⊠*533 Washington St., Downtown* ☎*617/350–5555* ⊕*www. feltclubboston.com* ⊤*Chinatown, Downtown Crossing, Boylston, Park Street.*

Flat Top Johnny's is the hippest billiards hall around. Alternative rock, chosen by the tattooed and pierced staff, blares from behind the bar. Artwork by local painters hangs on the exposed-brick walls; the tables are covered in crimson instead of green. The bartender pours one of the best selections of draft beers in the city. Members of Boston's cooler

SWEET NIGHTSPOTS

The Viennese Dessert Buffet at the Four Seasons' **Bristol Lounge** is a scrumptious array of pastries, dessert crepes, and chocolates, accompanied by live jazz. The drinks menu includes chai tea and a pomegranate martini. ✉ *200 Boylston St., Back Bay* ☎ *617/338–4400* ⊕ *www.fourseasons.com* Ⓣ *Arlington, Boylston.*

Finale is all about desserts, and with creative ingredients and immaculate presentations, it's hard to pick just one. Possibilities include a molten chocolate cake, an updated Boston cream pie, and crème brûlée. Tasting plates for sharing and sampling make decision making easy. ✉ *1 Columbus Ave., Theater District* ☎ *617/423–3184* ⊕ *www.finaledesserts.com* Ⓣ *Arlington* ✉ *30 Dunster St., Cambridge* ☎ *617/441–9797* Ⓣ *Harvard* ✉ *1306 Beacon St., Brookline* ☎ *617/232–3233* Ⓣ *Coolidge Corner.*

local bands often hang out here on their nights off. ✉ *1 Kendall Sq., Bldg. 200, Cambridge* ☎ *617/494–9565* ⊕ *www.flattopjohnnys.com* Ⓣ *Kendall/MIT.*

Jillian's Boston is often called the city's best playground for grown-ups. The multistory complex on the corner of club-hopping Lansdowne Street has more than 30 pool tables and each floor has a lively bar. On the third level, Lucky Strike Lanes has 16 bowling lanes and an 80-foot video wall blasting sports and music videos, and the ground floor is home to Tequila Rain, "where it's Spring Break 52 weeks a year." Everything's open until 2 AM. ✉ *145 Ipswich St., Fens* ☎ *617/437–0300* ⊕ *www.jilliansboston.com* Ⓣ *Kenmore.*

Milky Way Lounge & Lanes has classic New England candlepin bowling souped up with dancing, live music, DJ acts, cabaret shows, or karaoke. Particularly popular is Tuesday night "live karaoke," where you can live out your rock-and-roll fantasies in front of your own backup band. It draws a hip urban crowd of twenty- and thirtysomethings, as well as families with children. ✉ *403–405 Centre St., Jamaica Plain* ☎ *617/524–3740* ⊕ *www.milkywayjp.com* Ⓣ *Stony Brook.*

CAFÉS & COFFEEHOUSES

Boston has a great nighttime coffeehouse scene. If you just want a cup of coffee, you can find plenty of Starbucks cafés and Dunkin' Donuts. But beyond the cookie-cutter establishments, a more-interesting set of independent cafés pump out the espresso. A few of them feel like true old-fashioned coffeehouses, complete with live folk music. Others are perfect to recaffeinate your spirits during a busy day of sightseeing. To eavesdrop on the liveliest conversations—some in Italian—head to one of the many espresso bars on Hanover Street in the North End.

BOSTON

Café Graffiti has a modern European feel, with Italian espresso drinks, liqueurs, and desserts on the menu, soccer on the television, and leather- and Dolce & Gabbana–clad patrons gossiping in Italian.

Owner Luigi has a smile for all who enter. ⊠*307 Hanover St., North End* ☎*617/367–3016* ⊕*www.caffegraffiti.com* Ⓣ*Haymarket.*

Fodor'sChoice **Caffé Vittoria** is the biggest of the cafés in the North End, with gleaming
★ espresso machines going nonstop. This is a good place to stop for dessert—think tiramisu, cannoli, and gelati—and coffee after a meal in one of the nearby restaurants. ⊠*296 Hanover St., North End* ☎*617/227–7606* ⊕*www.vittoriacaffe.com* Ⓣ*Haymarket.*

Solstice Café is an ambient and often noisy spot that serves coffee, tea, wine, beer, and a selection of wraps, soups, pastas, salads, and sandwiches. At night a full menu is offered, sometimes together with live folk or Latin music; on other evenings DJs mix dance music, or a film or sports match is shown on the projection-screen TV. ⊠*1625 Tremont St., Mission Hill* ☎*617/566–5958* Ⓣ*Brigham Circle, on the Green Line's E train.*

Tealuxe is the downtown branch of the popular "tea bar," which serves 70 kinds of tea and not a single type of coffee. Faux-antique Chinese tea bins behind the counter clash with more-modern steel-and-copper decor. In summer, Newbury Street window-shoppers fill the outdoor patio, enjoying tea and chai of the iced variety. ⊠*108 Newbury St., Back Bay* ☎*617/927–0400* ⊕*www.tealuxe.com* Ⓣ*Copley.*

★ **Trident Booksellers & Café** stocks esoteric books and magazines, and serves coffee and teas. This is a nice spot for a light meal with a date, solo journal writing or reading, or surfing the Web with free wireless access. The windows facing Newbury Street are great for people-watching. It's open daily until midnight. ⊠*338 Newbury St., Back Bay* ☎*617/267–8688* ⊕*www.tridentbookscafe.com* Ⓣ*Hynes/ICA.*

CAMBRIDGE & SOMERVILLE

Café Algiers is a genuine Middle Eastern café serving pita-bread lunches, teas, and strong coffee. Small, tightly clustered tables fill both floors. Upstairs you can peer at the soaring, wood-panel cathedral ceiling. Service is sluggish; visit when in the mood to linger over conversation or a novel. ⊠*40 Brattle St., Cambridge* ☎*617/492–1557* Ⓣ*Harvard.*

★ **Club Passim** has seen Joan Baez, Bob Dylan, Suzanne Vega, and many other folkies on their way up. It's one of the country's first and most famous venues for live folk music. In the basement room, where the seating is pressed close together, there's table service and a counter where you can buy prepared food—Middle Eastern vegetarian items are especially good. If you travel with your guitar, call about one of the club's many open-mike nights. ⊠*47 Palmer St., Cambridge* ☎*617/492–5300, 617/492–7679 box office* ⊕*www.clubpassim.org* Ⓣ*Harvard.*

Dado Tea has a new-age feel, with an extensive listing of teas, multigrain meals, and a few sweet options, too. The Harvard Square location is a bit roomier than other cafés in the area, and if it's not too crowded, you can linger without interruption. ⊠*50 Church St., Cambridge* ☎*617/547–0950* ⊕*www.dadotea.com* Ⓣ*Harvard* ⊠*955 Massachusetts Ave., Cambridge* ☎*617/497–9061* Ⓣ*Harvard, Central.*

★ **Diesel Cafe** is a bright and sunny spot with bold local artwork and spacious booths. In addition to drawing Davis Square hipsters and Tufts students, it's a favorite hangout for lesbians and their friends, who congregate around the pool tables in back. Wireless is available for $5 an hour. ⊠*257 Elm St., Somerville* ☎*617/629–8717* ⊕*www.diesel-cafe.com* Ⓣ*Davis.*

Tealuxe is a "tea bar" with Bombay flair, more than 70 different herbal and traditional blends, an assortment of teatime snacks—and no coffee. It's a favorite hangout for students, who huddle over textbooks as they savor a cup of Earl Grey or ginseng chai at one of the copper-top tables. ⊠*0 Brattle St., Cambridge* ☎*617/441–0077* ⊕*www.tealuxe.com* Ⓣ*Harvard.*

COMEDY CLUBS

Comedy Connection, which has been called the best comedy club in the country, has a mix of local and nationally known acts seven nights a week, with two shows Friday and Saturday. The cover is $12–$24. ⊠*Faneuil Hall Marketplace, Quincy Market Bldg., 2nd fl., Faneuil Hall* ☎*617/248–9700* ⊕*www.comedyconnectionboston.com* Ⓣ*Government Center, Haymarket, State.*

★ **ImprovAsylum** features comedians who weave audience suggestions into seven weekly shows blending topical sketches with improv in shows such as "Lost in Boston" and "New Kids on the Blog." Tickets are $20; at the $10 midnight show on Saturday expect raunchier material. ⊠*216 Hanover St., North End* ☎*617/263–6887* ⊕*www.improvasylum.com* Ⓣ*Haymarket, North Station.*

ImprovBoston turns audience suggestions into a situation comedy, complete with theme song and commercials. Be careful when you go to the restroom; you might be pulled onstage. On some nights, performers face off in improv competitions judged by audiences. Shows, which run Wednesday through Sunday, are $5 to $15. There's no alcohol. ⊠*Back Alley Theater, 1253 Cambridge St., Cambridge* ☎*617/576–1253* ⊕*www.improvboston.com* Ⓣ*Central, Kendall/MIT.*

Jimmy Tingle's Off-Broadway was founded in funky Davis Square in 2002 as a venue for this Boston-native comedian's sharp brand of political humor. It regularly features other established and up-and-coming local comics, music, and farcical theater productions. Tickets are $15–$35. ⊠*255 Elm St., Somerville* ☎*617/591–1616* ⊕*www.jimmytingle.com* Ⓣ*Davis.*

Nick's Comedy Stop presents local comics Thursday through Saturday night. Well-known comedians occasionally pop in. Local boy Jay Leno reportedly got his start here. Reservations are advised on weekends. Tickets are $22. ⊠*100 Warrenton St., Theater District* ☎*617/423–2900* ⊕*www.nickscomedystop.com* Ⓣ*Boylston.*

DANCE CLUBS

★ **Aria** fills up with the young, the beautiful, and the hopelessly chic Thursday through Saturday. Doors at this cozy space below the Wilbur Theatre usually open after 10:30. The DJs spin everything from house to reggae to international, but if the dancing gets too steamy, you can revive by sipping a cocktail on one of the plush, red sofas. This is as exclusive as it gets in Boston. ⊠*246 Tremont St., Theater District* ☎*617/338–7080* Ⓣ*Boylston, Chinatown.*

Buzz is Boston's most popular, and arguably sweatiest, gay party ground. Well known for its grinding dance floor and chic martini lounge, it's most famous for its hot bartenders. ✉ *246 Tremont St., Theater District* ☎*617/267–8969* ⊕*www.buzzboston.com* Ⓣ*Boylston, Chinatown.*

Gypsy Bar half calls to mind the decadence of a dark European castle, with rich red velvet and crystal chandeliers. Its rows of video screens broadcasting the Fashion

Network, however, add a sexier, more-modern touch. Thirtysomething revelers and European students snack on lime-and-ginger-marinated tiger shrimp and sip "See You in Church" martinis (vodka with fresh marmalade) while the trendy dance floor throbs to Top 40 and house music. ✉ *116 Boylston St., Theater District* ☎*617/482–7799* ⊕*www.gypsybarboston.com* Ⓣ*Boylston.*

★ **The Roxy** has a spacious interior that resembles an early-20th-century ballroom, but this club is hardly sedate. It throws theme nights such as "Sexy Fridays," as well as Chippendales male reviews. Watch for occasional rock concerts with bands such as The Killers. ✉ *279 Tremont St., Theater District* ☎*617/338–7699* ⊕*www.roxyboston.com* Ⓣ*Boylston.*

Umbria in the Financial District, attracts a mature, upscale crowd that ranges from mid-20s to over 40. Dress accordingly: no sneakers or caps. Wander among the five floors for formal Italian or informal dining, an "ultralounge," and a nightclub featuring R&B, techno, and international tunes. ✉ *295 Franklin St., Downtown* ☎*617/338–1000* ⊕*www.umbriaristorante.com* Ⓣ*South Station.*

Venu brings Miami's South Beach to Boston. A warm energy distinguishes this club from the city's other dark, techno-industrial spots. The crowd is diverse—stylish international students mix with young downtown suits cutting loose on their off-hours. Local DJs spin Top 40 and international tunes. Sunday is Brazilian night, and Saturday is Asian night. ✉ *100 Warrenton St., Theater District* ☎*617/338–8061* ⊕*www.venuboston.com* Ⓣ*Boylston, Arlington.*

MUSIC CLUBS

BLUES & R&B CLUBS

★ **The Cantab Lounge/Third Rail** hums every night with live Motown, rhythm and blues, folk, or bluegrass. The Third Rail bar, downstairs, holds poetry slams, open-mike readings, local DJ Turn Ta Bill, and improv comedy. It's friendly and informal, with a diverse under-40 crowd. ✉ *738 Massachusetts Ave., Cambridge* ☎*617/354–2685* ⊕*www.cantab-lounge.com* ⊟*No credit cards* Ⓣ*Central.*

Harpers Ferry, noisy and crowded, is known for its live rock and blues acts and has played host to the likes of Bo Diddley and BB King. If music's not your thing, turn to the pool tables or darts. ✉ *158 Brigh-*

ton Ave., Allston ☎*617/254–9743* ⊕*www.harpersferryboston.com* Ⓣ*Harvard Ave. on the Green Line's B train.*

Johnny D's Uptown is a restaurant–cum–music hall where every seat is a good seat. It lines up Cajun, country, Latin, jazz, blues, and more. Come early for Southern and Mediterranean bistro food. On weekends it hosts a popular jazz brunch. ✉*17 Holland St., Somerville* ☎*617/776–9667 recorded info, 617/776–2004* ⊕*www.johnnydsuptown.com* Ⓣ*Davis.*

JAZZ CLUBS
Clubs often alternate jazz with other kinds of music; always call ahead for program information and times.

Atrium Lounge, which overlooks Faneuil Hall Marketplace, is a fern-filled lounge with piano, jazz, or cabaret-style music Thursday through Saturday. A buttoned-up clientele has no problem with the collared-shirt-required dress code. ✉*Millennium Bostonian Hotel, 26 North St., Faneuil Hall* ☎*617/523–3600* ⊕*www.millenniumhotels.com* Ⓣ*Haymarket, Government Center, or State.*

Bob's Southern Bistro has been serving up live jazz and authentic Southern cuisine for more than 50 years in the South End. The club-restaurant books live acts Thursday through Saturday nights and also hosts a popular Sunday jazz brunch. ✉*604 Columbus Ave., South End* ☎*617/536–6204* ⊕*www.bobthechefs.com* Ⓣ*Massachusetts Ave.*

Regattabar is host to some of the top names in jazz, including Sonny Rollins and Herbie Hancock. Tickets for shows are $15–$30. Even when there's no entertainment, the large, low-ceiling club is a pleasant (if expensive) place for a drink. ✉*Charles Hotel, 1 Bennett St., Cambridge* ☎*617/661–5000 or 617/395–7757* ⊕*www.regattabarjazz.com* Ⓣ*Harvard.*

★ **Ryles Jazz Club** uses soft lights, mirrors, and greenery to set the mood for first-rate jazz. The first-floor stage is one of the best places for new music and musicians. Upstairs is a dance hall staging regular tango, salsa, and merengue nights, often with lessons before the dancing starts. Ryles also holds occasional open-mike poetry slams and a Sunday jazz brunch (call for reservations). It's open nightly, with a cover charge. ✉*212 Hampshire St., Cambridge* ☎*617/876–9330* ⊕*www.ryles.com* Ⓣ*Bus 69, 83, or 91.*

Scullers Jazz Club hosts well-known acts such as Wynton Marsalis, Diana Krall, and Harry Connick Jr. Shows are Tuesday through Thursday nights at 8 and 10, Friday and Saturday at 8 and 10:30. Tickets are $20–$50 per show, more with dinner included; advance tickets are advised. ✉*Doubletree Guest Suites hotel, 400 Soldiers Field Rd., Allston* ☎*617/562–4111* ⊕*www.scullersjazz.com* Ⓣ*BU West, Bus 47, or CT2.*

Fodor'sChoice **Wally's Café** is a rare gem for blues and jazz fans. Founded in 1947, the ★ club continues to play host to big names such as Branford Marsalis and Chick Corea but is still best known for performances by local bands. Wally's has a more-diverse crowd than most other Boston clubs, and brings in both South End and Roxbury locals and lots of college students, especially those from Berklee College of Music. It's open every night of the year and there is no cover—but get there early if you want a seat. ✉*427 Massachusetts Ave., South End* ☎*617/424–1408* ⊕*www.wallyscafe.com* Ⓣ*Massachusetts Ave.*

ROCK CLUBS

Great Scott books an impressive lineup of local and visiting indie rock bands, with live music nearly every night of the week. The crowd typically consists of Allston hipsters, Boston University students, and the lonely sports fan. ✉*1222 Commonwealth Ave., Allston* ☎*617/566–9014* ⊕*www.greatscottboston.com* Ⓣ*Harvard Ave.*

Green Street is the place for both a meal and music. Start with spicy Caribbean food, then stick around for the night's show, which might be jazz, Latin, folk, or serious rock. There's usually no cover charge. ✉*280 Green St., Cambridge* ☎*617/876–1655* Ⓣ*Central.*

> **MADE IN BOSTON**
>
> Musicians from Boston include:
>
> Aerosmith
> Aimee Mann
> Boston (go figure ...)
> Dresden Dolls
> Juliana Hatfield
> Patty Larkin
> The Lemonheads
> Mighty, Mighty Bosstones
> Mission of Burma
> Morphine
> The Pixies

Harpers Ferry is a rock and blues club where not only local rock bands take the stage, but also legends like Steven Tyler and Joe Perry. Also ⇨ *see Blues & R&B Clubs, above.* ✉*158 Brighton Ave., Allston* ☎*617/254–9743* ⊕*www.harpersferryboston.com* Ⓣ*Harvard Ave.*

Lizard Lounge is a low-key nightspot that often features more-experimental and local cult bands. Seven nights a week see folk, rock, acid jazz, and pop, sometimes mixed with cabaret, burlesque shows, or poetry readings. Martinis are a house specialty; upstairs, the Cambridge Common restaurant serves excellent burgers and comfort food (chicken potpies, curly fries). ✉*1667 Massachusetts Ave., between Harvard and Porter Sqs., Cambridge* ☎*617/547–0759* ⊕*www.lizardloungeclub. com* Ⓣ*Harvard, Porter.*

★ **The Middle East Restaurant & Nightclub** manages to be both a Middle Eastern restaurant and one of the area's most eclectic rock clubs, with three rooms showcasing live local and national acts. Local phenoms the Mighty Mighty Bosstones got their start here and still perform regularly. Music-world celebs often drop in when they're in town. There's also belly dancing, folk, jazz, and even the occasional country-tinged rock band. ✉*472–480 Massachusetts Ave., Cambridge* ☎*617/497–0576 or 617/864–3278* ⊕*www.mideastclub.com* Ⓣ*Central.*

Midway Café, in Jamaica Plain, books a mix of live rock bands, DJs, and hip-hop artists for an eclectic set any night of the week. There's also a lesbian dance party and "queeraoke" each Thursday night. ✉*3496 Washington St., Jamaica Plain* ☎*617/524–9038* ⊕*www.midwaycafe. com* Ⓣ*Green Street, Forest Hills.*

Fodor's Choice
★ **Paradise Rock Club** is a small place known for hosting big-name talent like U2, Coldplay, and local stars such as the Dresden Dolls. Two tiers of booths provide good sight lines anywhere in the club, as well as some intimate and out-of-the-way corners, and four bars quench the crowd's thirst. The 18-plus crowd varies with the shows. The newer Paradise Lounge, next door, is a more-intimate space to experience local, often acoustic songsters, as well as literary readings and other artistic events.

It serves dinner. ⊠*967–969 Commonwealth Ave., Allston* ✦*Near Boston University* ☎*617/562–8800 or 617/562–8814* ⊕*www.thedise. com* Ⓣ*Pleasant St.*

T.T. the Bear's Place schedules live rock nightly, showcasing the hottest local bands and on-the-rise alternative bands such as Dear Leader and the Rudds. Separate rooms make it easy to concentrate on the music, chat around the bar, or relax over a game of pool. Monday night is usually acoustic night. It closes at 1 AM. ⊠*10 Brookline St., Cambridge* ☎*617/492–2327* ⊕*www.ttthebears.com* Ⓣ*Central.*

SALSA CLUBS

An Tua Nua is an Irish pub that, however improbably, hosts one of the city's most popular salsa nights each Wednesday. Arrive early for a lesson with local experts Johnny and Kelly, then put your new moves to the test on the packed dance floor. ⊠*835 Beacon St., Boston University* ☎*617/262–2121* ⊕*www.tuanuaboston.com* Ⓣ*BU Central, Fenway, St. Mary St.*

Havana Club at the Greek American Political Club in Central Square has a 5,400-square foot ballroom dance floor, a rotating cast of DJs and live bands, and (usually) free food such as burritos or nachos. Typically, 400 people show up to dance, creating a lively scene for dancers at any level. The club is open for salsa on Friday and Saturday (open for private functions other nights). ⊠*288 Green St., Cambridge* ☎*617/312–5550* ⊕*www.havanaclubsalsa.com* Ⓣ*Central.*

Ryles is home to one of the city's friendliest salsa scenes, **Temporada Latina.** It's held Thursday nights with newcomers and experts dancing the night away (often together). Dancing starts at 9:30; arrive at 8 for the lesson. ⊠*212 Hampshire St., Cambridge* ☎*617/876–9330* ⊕*www.ryles.com/dancing.cfm* Ⓣ*Bus 68 or 69.*

THE ARTS

DANCE

Boston Dance Alliance serves as a clearinghouse for local dance information. Visit its Web site for upcoming performances and details about Boston dance companies and venues. ⊠*19 Clarendon St., South End* ☎*617/456–6295* ⊕*www.bostondancealliance.org.*

BALLET

★ **Boston Ballet,** the city's premier dance company, performs at the Citi Performing Arts Center (the former Wang Center) from October through May. In addition to a world-class repertory of classical and high-spirited modern works, it presents an elaborate signature *Nutcracker* during the holidays at the restored downtown Opera House. ⊠*19 Clarendon St., South End* ☎*617/695–6950* ⊕*www.bostonballet.org.*

José Mateo's Ballet Theatre is a young troupe building an exciting, contemporary repertory under Cuban-born José Mateo, the resident artistic director-choreographer. The troupe's performances include an original *Nutcracker,* and take place October through May at the **Sanc-**

tuary Theatre, a beautifully converted former church at Massachusetts Avenue and Harvard Street in Harvard Square. ✉ *400 Harvard St., Cambridge* ☎ *617/354–7467* ⊕ *www.ballettheatre.org.*

CONTEMPORARY

Dance Complex presents varied dance styles by local and visiting choreographers at Odd Fellows Hall, an intimate space that draws a multicultural crowd. Works range from classical ballet to contemporary and world dance. Recent performances have included video and spoken word. ✉ *536 Massachusetts Ave., Central Sq., Cambridge* ☎ *617/547–9363* ⊕ *www.dancecomplex.org* Ⓣ *Central.*

FOLK/MULTICULTURAL

★ **Art of Black Dance and Music** performs the music and dance of Africa, the Caribbean, and the Americas at venues including the **Strand Theatre**, at Columbia Road and Stoughton Street in Dorchester, and local area universities. ☎ *617/666–1859* ⊕ *www.abdm.net.*

Cambridge Multicultural Arts Center presents local and visiting arts programs, ethnic music, and dance performances. Two galleries showcase the visual arts. ✉ *41 2nd St., Cambridge* ☎ *617/577–1400* ⊕ *www.cmacusa.org* Ⓣ *Lechmere.*

Folk Arts Center of New England promotes participatory international folk dancing and music for adults and children, as well as traditional New England contra dancing at locations throughout the greater Boston area. ✉ *42 W. Foster St., Melrose* ☎ *781/862–7476 recorded info, 781/662–7475* ⊕ *www.facone.org.*

World Music presents the biggest names in traditional dance and music from around the globe; regular performers include Africa's Ladysmith Black Mambazo and Ireland's Mary Black, and January's Boston Flamenco Festival has become a winter highlight. Its CRASHArts series offers more-daring, contemporary fare. Performances take place at the Sanders Theatre in Cambridge, Berklee Performance Center, and other venues around Boston. ✉ *720 Massachusetts Ave., Cambridge* ☎ *617/876–4275* ⊕ *www.worldmusic.org* Ⓣ *Central.*

FILM

With its large population of academics and intellectuals, Boston has its share of discerning moviegoers and movie houses, especially in Cambridge. Theaters at suburban malls, downtown, and at Fenway have better screens, if less-adventurous fare. The *Boston Globe* has daily listings in the "Living/Arts" and "Sidekick" sections, and both the *Boston Herald* Friday "Scene" section and the *Boston Phoenix* "Arts" section list films for the week. Movies cost $8–$11. Many theaters have half-price matinees, but theaters sometimes suspend bargain admissions during the first week or two of a major film opening.

★ **Boston Public Library** regularly screens free family, foreign, classic, and documentary films in the Rabb Lecture Hall, usually on Monday evenings. ✉ *700 Boylston St., Copley Sq., Back Bay* ☎ *617/536–5400 Ext. 2317* ⊕ *www.bpl.org* Ⓣ *Copley.*

Brattle Theatre shows classic movies, new foreign and independent films, themed series, and directors' cuts. Tickets sell out every year for its acclaimed Bogart festival, scheduled around Harvard's exam period; the Bugs Bunny Film Festival in February; and *Trailer Treats,* an annual fund-raiser featuring an hour or two of classic and modern movie previews in July. It also has holiday screenings such as *It's a Wonderful Life* at Christmas. ⌧*40 Brattle St., Harvard Sq., Cambridge* ☎*617/876–6837* ⊕*www.brattlefilm.org* Ⓣ*Harvard.*

The Coolidge Corner Theatre has an eclectic and frequently updated bill of art films, foreign films, animation festivals, and classics, as well as an intimate 45-seat video-screening room for more-experimental offerings. It also holds book readings, concerts, and popular midnight cult movies. ⌧*290 Harvard St., Brookline* ☎*617/734–2501, 617/734–2500 recorded info* ⊕*www.coolidge.org* Ⓣ*Coolidge Corner.*

Harvard Film Archive screens works from its vast collection of classics and foreign films that are not usually shown at commercial cinemas. Actors and directors frequently appear to introduce newer work. The theater was created for student and faculty use, but the general public may attend regular screenings for $8 per person. ⌧*Carpenter Center for the Visual Arts, 24 Quincy St., Cambridge* ☎*617/495–4700 or 617/496–6046* ⊕*www.harvardfilmarchive.org* Ⓣ*Harvard.*

The Institute of Contemporary Art, Boston screens art films, foreign-film award winners, experimental movies, and documentaries. ⌧*100 Northern Ave., Waterfront* ☎*617/478–3100* ⊕*www.icaboston.org/ programs/film/* Ⓣ*South Station, Courthouse.*

Kendall Square Cinema is devoted to first-run independent and foreign films. There are nine screens and a concession stand with choices such as cappuccino and homemade cookies. Note that 1 Kendall Square stands where Hampshire runs into Broadway, not near the Kendall Square T stop. The free Galleria Mall shuttle runs directly from the T stop to the theater continually Monday–Saturday 9–6, and Sunday noon–6. ⌧*1 Kendall Sq., Cambridge* ☎*617/499–1996* ⊕*www.landmarktheatres. com* Ⓣ*Kendall/MIT.*

The Museum of Fine Arts screens international and avant-garde films, works by local filmmakers, and films connected to museum exhibitions in Remis Auditorium. ⌧*465 Huntington Ave., Fens* ☎*617/369–3306 box office, 617/369–3300 recorded info* ⊕*www.mfa.org/film* Ⓣ*Museum of Fine Arts, Ruggles.*

MUSIC

For its size, Boston has a great diversity and variety of live music choices. New York has more events, but 10 times the population. Most of the year the music calendar is crammed with classical and pop events. Jazz, blues, folk, and world-music fans have plenty to keep them busy as well. *(See also Music Clubs in Nightlife, above.)* Supplementing appearances by nationally known artists are performers from the area's many colleges and conservatories, which also provide music series, performing spaces, and audiences.

The jewel in Boston's musical crown is the multifaceted Boston Symphony Orchestra, which performs at Symphony Hall September through April and at Tanglewood Music Center in Lenox, Massachusetts, in July and August. A favorite of television audiences, the Boston Pops presents concerts of "lighter music" from May to July and during December.

But pop orchestral arrangements and the warhorses of the 19th-century symphonic repertoire aren't Boston's only classical-musical offerings today. The city has emerged as the nation's capital of early-music performance. Dozens of small groups, often made up of performers who have one foot in the university and another on the concert stage, are rediscovering pre-18th-century composers, whose works they play on period instruments, often in small churches where the acoustics resemble the venues in which some of this music was first performed. **The Cambridge Society for Early Music** (☎617/489–2062 ⊕*www.csem. org*) helps promote early-music performances and deserves much of the credit for early music's preeminence in Boston's musical scene.

If you're a die-hard early-music devotee, plan to visit Boston in odd-number years, when the biennial **Boston Early Music Festival** (☎617/661–1812 ⊕*www.bemf.org*) takes over the city for a week in June.

CONCERT HALLS

★ **Bank of America Pavilion** gathers up to 5,000 people on the city's waterfront for summertime concerts. National pop, folk, and country acts play the tentlike pavilion from about mid-June to mid-September. ⊠*290 Northern Ave., South Boston* ☎617/728–1600 ⊕*www.bankofamericapavilion.com* Ⓣ*South Station.*

Berklee Performance Center, associated with Berklee College of Music, is best known for its jazz programs, but it also is host to folk performers such as Joan Baez and pop and rock stars such as Aimee Mann and Henry Rollins. ⊠*136 Massachusetts Ave., Back Bay* ☎617/747–2261 box office, 617/747–8890 recorded info ⊕*www.berkleebpc.com* Ⓣ*Hynes/ICA.*

The Boston Opera House hosts plays, musicals, and traveling Broadway shows, but also has booked musical performers such as Ricky Martin, BB King, and Pat Metheny. ⊠ *539 Washington St., Downtown* ☎617/259–3400 ⊕*www.broadwayacrossamerica.com* Ⓣ*Boylston, Chinatown, Downtown Crossing, Park Street.*

★ **Hatch Memorial Shell,** on the bank of the Charles River, is a wonderful acoustic shell where the Boston Pops perform their famous free summer concerts (including their traditional Fourth of July show, broadcast live nationwide on TV). Local radio stations also put on music shows and festivals here April through October. ⊠*Off Storrow Dr. at the embankment, Beacon Hill* ☎617/626–1470 ⊕*www.mass.gov/dcr/ hatch_events.htm* Ⓣ*Charles/MGH, Arlington.*

Fodor'sChoice **The Isabella Stewart Gardner Museum** holds concerts in its beautiful Tap-
★ estry Room—jazz on the first Saturday of every month, and chamber music every Sunday—both at 1:30 PM. It also hosts a "composer portrait series," which highlights the work of a particular composer, and the warmer months see the enchanting "Vivaldi in the Courtyard" concerts

in the museum's stunning garden courtyard. The charge is in addition to the museum admission. ✉*280 The Fenway, Fens* ☎*617/278–5156 box office, 617/566–1401 recorded info* ⊕*www.gardnermuseum.org* Ⓣ*Museum of Fine Arts.*

The Institute of Contemporary Art, Boston hosts experimental musicians, with some performances in partnership with World Music/CRASHArts. Expect the unexpected—concerts here could contain a mix of disparate instruments, fusions of melody and spoken word, or electronica mashups. ✉*100 Northern Ave., Waterfront* ☎*617/478–3100* ⊕*www. icaboston.org/programs/performance* Ⓣ*South Station, Courthouse.*

The Museum of Fine Arts has jazz, blues, and folk concerts in its outdoor courtyard every Wednesday evening from late June through August (bring a blanket and a picnic). During the rest of the year, the action moves inside to the Remis Auditorium on various nights of the week. ✉*465 Huntington Ave., Fens* ☎*617/369–3300* ⊕*www.mfa.org/concerts* Ⓣ*Museum of Fine Arts.*

★ **New England Conservatory's Jordan Hall** is one of the world's acoustic treasures, and is ideal for chamber music yet large enough to accommodate a full orchestra. The Boston Philharmonic often performs at the relatively intimate 1,000-seat hall. ✉*30 Gainsborough St., Back Bay* ☎*617/585–1260 box office* ⊕*www.newenglandconservatory. edu/concerts* Ⓣ*Symphony.*

Sanders Theatre provides a jewel box of a stage for local and visiting classical, folk, and world-music performers. "The Christmas Revels," a traditional, participatory Yule celebration, delights families here each December. ✉*Harvard University, 45 Quincy St., Cambridge* ☎*617/496–2222* ⊕*www.fas.harvard.edu/tickets* Ⓣ*Harvard.*

Fodor'sChoice **Symphony Hall,** one of the world's best acoustical settings—if not *the*
★ best—is home to the Boston Symphony Orchestra (BSO) and the Boston Pops. The BSO is led by the incomparable James Levine, who's known for commissioning special works by contemporary composers, as well as for presenting innovative programs such as his two-year Beethoven/Schoenberg series. The Pops concerts, led by conductor Keith Lockhart, take place in May and June and around the winter holidays. The hall is also used by visiting orchestras, chamber groups, soloists, and many local performers. Rehearsals are sometimes open to the public, with tickets sold at a discount. ✉*301 Massachusetts Ave., Back Bay* ☎*617/266–1492, 617/266–2378 recorded info* ⊕*www.bostonsymphonyhall.org* Ⓣ*Symphony.*

TD Banknorth Garden, formerly known as the FleetCenter, hosts concerts by big-name artists from Bob Dylan to U2, ice shows, and, of course, Bruins and Celtics games. ✉*100 Legends Way, Old West End* ☎*617/624–1000* ⊕*www.tdbanknorthgarden.com* Ⓣ*North Station.*

Tsai Performance Center, associated with Boston University, presents many free classical concerts by both student and professional groups. The New England Philharmonic and Boston Musica Viva are regular guests in the 500-seat theater. More recently, the center has played host to tapings of *Late Night with David Letterman* and *The Daily Show with Jon Stewart.* ✉*685 Commonwealth Ave., Fens* ☎*617/353–6467, 617/353–8725 box office* ⊕*www.bu.edu/tsai* Ⓣ*Boston University East.*

CHORAL GROUPS

It's hard to imagine another city with more-active choral groups than Boston. Many outstanding choruses are associated with Boston schools and churches.

The Boston Cecilia, which dates from 1876, holds regular concerts at Jordan Hall and other venues, and is especially noted for its period-instrument performances of Handel. ☎*617/232–4540 ⊕www.boston cecilia.org.*

Boston Gay Men's Chorus seeks to "create a more-tolerant society through the power of music." Their repertoire ranges from holiday favorites to show tunes, chamber selections to pop hits. They perform at Symphony Hall, the Cutler Majestic Theatre, and other venues around town. ☎*617/542–7464 ⊕www.bgmc.org.*

Boston Secession is a professional vocal ensemble that's trying to modernize the choral experience with both virtuoso singing and creative, thematic programs such as "Berlin on the Charles" and the annual anti-Valentine "(un)Lucky in Love." ☎*617/499–4860 ⊕www. bostonsecession.org.*

Cantata Singers perform music dating from the 17th century to the present, with a special emphasis on Bach's cantatas, at various venues in Boston. ☎*617/868–5885 ⊕www.cantatasingers.org.*

CHURCH CONCERTS

Boston's churches have outstanding music programs. The Saturday *Boston Globe* and the Friday *Boston Herald* list performance schedules.

★ **Emmanuel Music** holds concerts at Emmanuel Church, known as "the Bach church" for its Holy Eucharist services on Sunday at 10 AM. The concert series, which is performed by a professional chamber orchestra and chorus, is one of Boston's hidden gems, and runs weekly from September to May. ✉*15 Newbury St., Back Bay* ☎*617/536–3356 ⊕www.emmanuelmusic.org* Ⓣ*Arlington.*

Trinity Boston presents a free half-hour organ or choir recital Friday at 12:15, as well as seasonal choral concerts, in the vaulted neo-Romanesque interior of Copley Square's Trinity Church. ✉*Trinity Church, 206 Clarendon St., Copley Sq., Back Bay* ☎*617/536–0944 ⊕www. trinityboston.org* Ⓣ*Back Bay/South End, Copley.*

CONCERT SERIES

The Bank of America Celebrity Series presents about 50 events annually—renowned orchestras, chamber groups, recitalists, vocalists, and dance companies—often at Symphony Hall or Jordan Hall. Regulars include Yo-Yo Ma and the Alvin Ailey American Dance Theater. ✉*20 Park Plaza, Suite 1032, Downtown* ☎*617/482–2595, 617/482–6661 box office ⊕www.celebrityseries.org.*

EARLY-MUSIC GROUPS

Boston Camerata, founded in 1954, has become a worldwide favorite thanks to its popular recordings. It performs a series of medieval, Renaissance, and baroque concerts at various venues. ☎*617/262–2092 ⊕www.bostoncamerata.org.*

Frugal Fun

The nightlife and arts options we list are worth their weight in gold. Yet if you're feeling the pinch, you can be entertained without dropping a dime.

Nosh on gratis appetizers at the **Fritz Lounge** during happy hour on weekdays.

See a film at the **Boston Public Library.**

Go baroque—not broke—with classical concerts at the **Tsai Performance Center.**

Head to **Trinity Church** for free Friday organ or choir recitals at 12:15 PM.

Groove to DJ-dispersed hip-hop, house, and more at stylish dance club **Q.**

Get down to blues and jazz at **Wally's Café** jazz club.

Ladies, head to **News** on Wednesday night for a free three-course meal.

Buy a coffee or smoothie, and surf wireless Internet for free at **Trident Booksellers & Café.**

See art in the making: check out one of the weekend **Boston Open Studios** (⊕ www.bostonopenstudios. org) in neighborhoods throughout the city. Summer brings even more free activities:

Bop along with the **Boston Pops** (☎ 617/266–1200 or 888/266–1200 ⊕ www.bso.org) at the Hatch Memorial Shell.

In July and August, the Commonwealth Shakespeare Company brings you **Shakespeare in the Park** (⊕ www.freeshakespeare.org) in Boston Common.

From April to September, the Hatch Shell on the Esplanade is busy with free concerts, movie showings, and more, all part of the **Esplanade Summer Events** (☎ 617/626–1250 ⊕ www.mass.gov/dcr/hatch_events. htm). Perennial favorites include the Boston Pops' Fourth of July concert and "Free Friday Flicks" outdoor movie screenings.

Cinephiles can catch "Movies by Moonlight": classic films shown waterside as part of the Boston Harbor Hotel's outdoor **Summer in the City Series** (☎ 617/439–7000 ⊕ www. bhh.com). Other weekly offerings include swing dancing, soul singing, and blues concerts staged on a barge anchored behind the hotel.

Boston Early Music Festival focuses on medieval, baroque, and Renaissance music. Throughout the year, concerts, master classes, and lectures take place at churches and concert halls throughout Boston. Every other year in June, a fully staged opera is performed. Past productions have included Conradi's *Ariadne* (1691) and Mattheson's 1710 opera *Boris Goudenow.* ☎ 617/661–1812 ⊕ www.bemf.org.

★ **Handel & Haydn Society,** America's oldest music organization, has a history of performances that dates from 1815. It presents instrumental and choral performances at Symphony Hall. The group's holiday-season performances of Handel's *Messiah* are especially popular. ☎ 617/266–3605 or 617/262–1815 ⊕ www.handelandhaydn.org.

ORCHESTRAS

★ **Boston Philharmonic** is headed by the charismatic Benjamin Zander, whose informal preconcert talks help audiences better understand what they're about to hear. Most performances take place at Harvard's Sanders Theatre or the New England Conservatory's Jordan Hall. ☎617/236–0999 ⊕*www.bostonphil.org.*

Boston Pops perform a mix of American standards, movie themes, and contemporary vocal numbers during May and June at Symphony Hall, followed by outdoor concerts at the Hatch Memorial Shell throughout July. The extremely popular outdoor concerts are free. ☎617/266–1200, 888/266–1200 *box office* ⊕*www.bostonpops.org.*

Boston Symphony Orchestra presents more than 250 concerts annually. The season at Symphony Hall runs from late September to late April. In July and August, the activity shifts to the orchestra's beautiful summer home at the Tanglewood Music Center in Lenox, Massachusetts. ☎617/266–1200, 888/266–1200 *box office* ⊕*www.bso.org.*

OPERA

Boston Lyric Opera stages four full productions each season at Citi Performing Arts Center (formerly the Shubert Theatre), which usually include one 20th-century work. Recent highlights have included Puccini's *Madama Butterfly* and Mozart's *Le Nozze di Figaro.* ☎617/542–4912, 617/542–6772 *box office* ⊕*www.blo.org.*

Opera Boston draws a connoisseur crowd with its fully staged performances of little-known or rarely seen works such as Handel's *Semele* or Verdi's *Ernani*. Shows are at the Cutler Majestic Theatre at Emerson College. ☎617/451–3388 ⊕*www.operaboston.org.*

THEATER

In the 1930s Boston had no fewer than 50 performing-arts theaters; by the 1980s, the city's downtown Theater District had all but vanished. Happily, in the late 1990s several historic theaters saw major restoration, opening to host pre-Broadway shows, visiting artists, and local troupes. More recently, the long-awaited renovation of the Opera House in 2004 has added new light to the district. Meanwhile, established companies such as the Huntington Theatre Company, near Northeastern University, and the American Repertory Theatre, in Cambridge, continue to offer premieres of works by major writers, including David Mamet, August Wilson, and Don DeLillo.

MAJOR THEATERS

The Charles Playhouse was formerly a church, a YWCA, a Prohibition-era speakeasy, and a nightclub. These days it plays host to the long-running *Shear Madness,* a pun-packed whodunit set in a hair salon, and the *Blue Man Group,* a loud, messy, exhilarating trio of playful performance artists painted vivid cobalt. (Warning: don't dress up, especially if you're sitting close to the stage.) ✉*74 Warrenton St., Theater District* ☎*617/426–5225 Shear Madness, 617/426–6912 Blue Man Group* ⊕*www.broadwayacrossamerica.com* Ⓣ*Boylston.*

Citi Performing Arts Center, formerly the Wang Center for the Performing Arts and the Shubert Theatre, is a performance space complex dedicated to both large-scale productions (at the former Wang) and more-intimate shows (at the former Shubert). Expect names such as *Riverdance* and other nationally touring Broadway shows, popular comedians, and the occasional ballet. ⊠ *270 Tremont St., Theater District* ☎ *617/482–9393* ⊕ *www.citicenter.org* Ⓣ *Boylston.*

The Colonial Theatre has ornate red wallpaper, intricately carved balconies, and stately marble columns that evoke its turn-of-the-20th-century glamour. Visiting stars from W. C. Fields to Fanny Brice to Katharine Hepburn have trod its boards. More recently, the theater welcomed Broadway productions *The Producers* and *Spamalot.* ⊠ *106 Boylston St., Back Bay* ☎ *617/880–2495 day, 617/880–2410 evening* ⊕ *www.broadwayacrossamerica.com* Ⓣ *Boylston.*

The Huntington Theatre Company, Boston's largest resident theater company, consistently performs a high-quality mix of 20th-century plays, new works, and classics under the leadership of dynamic artistic director Nicholas Martin, and commissions artists to produce original dramas. ⊠ *Boston University Theatre, 264 Huntington Ave., Back Bay* ☎ *617/266–0800 box office* ⊕ *www.huntingtontheatre.org* Ⓣ *Symphony* ⊠ *Calderwood Theatre Pavilion, Boston Center for the Arts, 527 Tremont St., South End* ☎ *617/426–5000* ⊕ *www.bcaonline.org* Ⓣ *Back Bay/South End.*

★ **The Opera House** features lavish musical productions such as *The Lion King* and Boston Ballet's *The Nutcracker.* The meticulously renovated 2,500-seat, beaux arts building has $35 million worth of gold leaf, lush carpeting, and rococo ornamentation. ⊠ *539 Washington St., Downtown Crossing, Chinatown* ☎ *617/880–2495 or 617/259–3400* ⊕ *www.broadwayinboston.com* Ⓣ *Boylston, Chinatown, Downtown Crossing, Park Street.*

Stuart Street Playhouse regularly books traveling productions such as *I Love You, You're Perfect, Now Change* and *Menopause, The Musical* for long-running engagements. Originally a movie theater, the reconstituted performance space has been showing live performances since 1996. ⊠ *200 Stuart St., in Radisson Hotel Boston, Theater District* ☎ *617/426–4499* ⊕ *www.stuartstreetplayhouse.com* Ⓣ *Boylston.*

The Wilbur Theatre, a small traditional house, was in and out of foreclosure a few years back. It has made a comeback with off-Broadway hits such as *Stomp* and *The Vagina Monologues.* ⊠ *246 Tremont St., Theater District* ☎ *617/426–1083* ⊕ *www.broadwayinboston.com* Ⓣ *Boylston.*

SMALL THEATERS & COMPANIES

American Repertory stages experimental, classic, and contemporary plays, often with unusual lighting, stage design, or multimedia effects. Its home at the Loeb Drama Center has two theaters; the smaller also holds productions by the Harvard-Radcliffe Drama Club. A modern theater space down the street, called the Zero Arrow Theatre, has a more-flexible stage design for electrifying contemporary productions. ⊠ *64 Brattle St., Harvard Sq., Cambridge* ☎ *617/547–8300* ⊕ *www. amrep.org* Ⓣ *Harvard.*

★ **Boston Center for the Arts** houses more than a dozen quirky, low-budget troupes in six performance areas, including the 300-seat Stanford Calderwood Pavilion, two black box theaters, and the massive Cyclorama, built to hold a 360-degree mural of the Battle of Gettysburg (the painting is now in a building at the battlefield). The experimental Pilgrim Theater, multiracial Company One, gay/lesbian Theatre Offensive, Irish-American Súgan Theatre troupe, and contemporary SpeakEasy Stage Company put on shows here year-round. ✉*539 Tremont St., South End* ☎*617/426–5000, 617/933–8600 box office* ⊕*www.bcaonline.org* Ⓣ*Back Bay/South End.*

> **BEST ALFRESCO ARTS EVENTS**
>
> ■ The Boston Pops at the Hatch Memorial Shell
>
> ■ Summer rock shows at the Bank of America Pavilion
>
> ■ Shakespeare in the Park on the Boston Common
>
> ■ Summer concerts at the Museum of Fine Arts' Calderwood Courtyard
>
> ■ Live music on summer evenings in Copley Square

Harvard's Hasty Pudding Theatricals at Harvard University calls itself the "oldest collegiate theatrical company in the United States." It produces one show annually, which plays in Boston in February and March and then goes on tour. The troupe also honors a famous actor and actress each year with an awards ceremony and a parade (in drag) through Cambridge. Recent honorees include Scarlett Johanssen and Ben Stiller. ✉*Zero Arrow Theatre, 0 Arrow St., at Massachusetts Ave., Cambridge* ☎*617/495–5205* ⊕*www.hastypudding.org* Ⓣ*Harvard.*

Sports & the Outdoors

6

WORD OF MOUTH

"Red Sox tickets are tough to come by. Most games are already sold out. But check www.redsox.com to be sure. If you can't get tickets there you'll have to use a ticket broker such as StubHub. Also consider taking a tour of Fenway—very reasonable and lots of fun."

—bennnie

"If the kid is young, a whale-watching trip is just a long boring sit on a boat. There is no guarantee you'll see a whale. For grown-ups, the boat trip itself can be a pleasure. Bring a sweater. The Fenway Park tour is good if you admire baseball. It's a beautiful field. If you don't, it's just a bunch of walking around."

—capxxx

Updated
by Sarah
Pascarella

EVERYTHING YOU'VE HEARD ABOUT THE zeal of Boston fans is true; here, you root for the home team. You cheer, and you pray, and you root some more. Who cares that the Celtics last hung up a banner in 1986, and the Bruins haven't brought home a Stanley Cup since 1972? "Red Sox Nation" witnessed a miracle in 2004, with the reverse of the curse and the first World Series victory since 1918. Now the Patriots' recent Super Bowl victories aren't the only thing to cheer about.

Bostonians' long-standing fervor for sport is equally evident in their leisure-time activities. Harsh winters keep locals wrapped up for months, only to emerge at the earliest sign of oncoming spring, striving to push back the February blues through feverish exercise. Once the

SARAH'S TOP 5

■ Taking in a Red Sox game at Fenway Park, the nation's oldest ballpark—the experience can't be duplicated.

■ Running or biking along the Charles River or, better yet, sailing on it with Community Boating.

■ Seeing magnificent whales and their young close-up on a whale-watch boat tour.

■ Exploring the quiet, awe-inspiring trails and shorelines of the Boston Harbor Islands.

■ Strolling through the parks and gardens of the Emerald Necklace (including the Boston Common and Public Garden).

mercury tops freezing and the snows begin to thaw, Boston's extensive parks, paths, woods, and waterways teem with sun worshippers and athletes—until the bitter winds bite again in November, and that energy becomes redirected once again toward white slopes, frozen rinks, and sheltered gyms and pools.

Most public recreational facilities, including skating rinks and tennis courts, are operated by the **Department of Conservation & Recreation** (*DCR* ✉*251 Causeway St., Suite 600, North End* ☎*617/626–1250* ⊕*www.mass.gov/dcr*). The DCR provides information about recreational activities in its facilities and promotes the conservation of Massachusetts parks and wilderness areas.

The **Appalachian Mountain Club** (✉*5 Joy St., Beacon Hill* ☎*617/523–0655* ⊕*www.outdoors.org* Ⓣ*Park St.*) makes a helpful first stop for anyone with questions about the great outdoors. Its bookstore has maps and guides about hiking and other active pursuits in the Northeast and Mid-Atlantic. The club also runs workshops and organized hiking, paddling, biking, and skiing trips throughout New England. Programs fill up fast, so advance reservations are essential. Fees are higher for nonmembers. A one-year individual membership starts at $50; discounted family, youth, and senior memberships are available. The club is open weekdays 8:30–5.

BEACHES

Although nearly 20 years of massive cleanup efforts have made the water in Boston Harbor safe for swimming, many locals and visitors still find city beaches unappealing since much better beaches are a short drive or train ride away.

If you're using public transportation to get around, you have several choices. Just north of the city, **Revere Beach** (⊠ *Revere*), the oldest public beach in America, has faded somewhat since its glory days in the early 20th century when it was a Coney Island–type playground, but it still remains a good spot to people-watch and catch some rays. The sand and water are less than pristine, but on hot summer days the waterfront is still packed with colorful local characters and Bostonians looking for an easy city escape. Most of the beach's former amusements are gone, but you can still catch concerts on the bandstand in summer. Take the Blue Line to the Revere Beach Station; one-way fares are $1.70.

'WHICH WAY TO THE BEACH?

The huge, juicy roast beef sandwiches served at Kelly's Roast Beef (⊠ *410 Revere Beach Blvd., Revere* ☎ *781/284–9129* ⊕ *www.kellysroastbeef.com*), a local institution since 1951, is the sole reason some Bostonians make the trek to Revere. Other menu favorites include the fried clams and hand-breaded onion rings. It's open from 5 AM to 2:30 AM Sunday through Thursday, and until 3 AM Friday and Saturday.

Singing Beach (⊠ *Beach St., Manchester-by-the-Sea*), 32 mi north of Boston in a quiet Cape Ann town, gets its name from the musical squeaking sound its gold-color sand makes when you step on it. The beach is popular with both locals and out-of-towners in summer. It's also worth a visit in fall, when the crowds have gone home and you'll have the splendid shores all to yourself. There's a snack bar at the beach, but it's worth taking a 10-minute stroll up Beach Street into town to get a cone at Captain Dusty's Ice Cream (60 Beach Street). Because there is no public parking at the beach, the easiest way to get here is by Rockport commuter rail train from North Station to the Manchester stop, which is a 15-minute walk from the beach. From downtown Boston, the train takes 45 minutes and costs $6.75 each way.

Sandy Cape Cod and the rocky North Shore are studded with New England beach towns, each with its favorite swimming spot. **Nantasket Beach** (⊠ *Hull*), a 45-minute drive from downtown Boston, has cleaner sand and warmer water than most local beaches. Take Route 3A South to Washington Boulevard, Hingham, and follow signs to Nantasket Avenue. Part of the 1,200-acre Crane Wildlife Refuge, **Crane Beach** (⊠ *Ipswich* ☎ *978/356–4354*), an hour's drive to the north of Boston in the 17th-century village of Ipswich, has 4 mi of sparkling white sand that serves as a nesting ground for the threatened piping plover. From Route 128 North (toward Gloucester), follow signs

Thar She Blows

Ships depart regularly for whale-watching excursions from April or May through October, from coastal towns all along the bay. Humpbacks, fin-backs, and minkes feed locally in season, so you're sure to see a few—and on a good day you may see dozens. Bring warm clothing, as the ocean breezes can be brisk; rubber-soled shoes are a good idea.

The ☾ **New England Aquarium** (✉ *Central Wharf at end of Central St., Downtown* ☏ *617/973-5200* ⊕ *www.neaq.org*) runs daily whale-watching cruises from Central Wharf. The trip, with an aquarium staff whale expert on board, lasts three to four hours. The high-speed catamarans of **Boston Harbor Cruises** (✉ *Long Wharf next to aquarium, Downtown* ☏ *877/733-9425* ⊕ *www.bostonharborcruises.com*) glide to the whaling banks in half the time of some other

cruises, allowing nearly as much whale time in only a three-hour tour.

The old fishing port of Gloucester is Massachusetts Bay's hot spot for whale-sighting trips. **Cape Ann Whale Watch** (✉ *Rose's Wharf, 415 Main St., Gloucester* ☏ *800/877-5110* ⊕ *www.caww.com*) has run whale-watch tours since 1979. Tours with **Captain Bill's Deep Sea Fishing/Whale Watch** (✉ *24 Harbor Loop, Gloucester* ☏ *978/283-6995 or 800/339-4253* ⊕ *www.captbillandsons.com*) make use of knowledgeable naturalists from the Whale Center of New England.

South of Boston, whale-watch trips leave from Plymouth and locations around Cape Cod. **Capt. John Boats** (✉ *10 Town Wharf, Plymouth* ☏ *508/746-2643 or 800/242-2469* ⊕ *www.captjohn.com*) sends out several daily whale-watch cruises from Plymouth Town Wharf.

for Route 1A North, 8 mi to Ipswich. The well-groomed beaches of **Plum Island** (✉ *Plum Island Blvd., Newburyport*) are worth the effort to find a parking space. The water is clear and blue, but quite cold. From I–95 follow Route 113 East (becomes Route 1A South) 3½ mi to Newbury. Then, take a left on Rolfe's Lane and a right on to the Plum Island Turnpike.

PARKS

☾
Fodor'sChoice
★

Comprising 34 islands, the **Boston Harbor Islands National Park Area** is somewhat of a hidden gem for nature lovers and history buffs, with miles of lightly traveled trails and shoreline and several little-visited historic sites to explore. The focal point of the national park is 39-acre Georges Island, where you'll find the partially restored pre–Civil War Fort Warren that once held Confederate prisoners. Other islands worth visiting include Peddocks Island, which holds the remains of Fort Andrews, and Lovells Island, a popular destination for campers. Lovells, Peddocks, Grape, and Bumpkin islands allow camping with a permit from late June through Labor Day. There are swimming areas at Lovells, Grape, and Bumpkin islands, but only Lovells has lifeguards. Pets and alcohol are not allowed on the Harbor Islands. The **National**

Park Service (☎617/223–8666 ⊕*www.bostonislands.com*) is a good source for information about camping, transportation, and the like. To reach the islands, take the **Harbor Express** (☎617/222–6999 ⊕*www.harborexpress.com*) from Long Wharf (Downtown) or Weymouth to Georges Island. High-speed catamarans run daily from May through mid-October and cost $10–$12. Other islands can be reached by the free interisland water shuttles that depart from Georges Island.

As soon as the snow begins to recede, Bostonians emerge from hibernation. Runners, bikers, and in-line skaters crowd the **Charles River Reservation** (⊕*www.mass.gov/dcr*) at the Esplanade along Storrow Drive, the Memorial Drive Embankment in Cambridge, or any of the smaller and less-busy parks farther upriver. Here you can cheer a crew race, rent a canoe or a kayak, or simply sit on the grass, sharing the shore with packs of hard-jogging university athletes, in-line skaters, moms with strollers, dreamily entwined couples, and intense academics, often talking to themselves as they sort out their intellectual—or perhaps personal—dilemmas.

The **Hatch Memorial Shell** (☎617/626–1250 Ⓣ*Charles/MGH*) on the Esplanade holds free concerts and outdoor events all summer.

☾ ★ The six large public parks known as Boston's **Emerald Necklace** stretch
FodorśChoice 5 mi from the Back Bay Fens through Franklin Park, in Dorchester.
★ Frederick Law Olmsted's design heightened the natural beauty of the Emerald Necklace, which remains a well-groomed urban masterpiece. Locals take pride in and happily make use of its open spaces and its pathways and bridges connecting rivers and ponds. The **Emerald Necklace Conservancy** (☎617/232–5374 ⊕*www.emeraldnecklace.org*) maintains a regular calendar of nature walks and other events in the parks. Rangers with the **Boston Parks & Recreation Department** (✉*1010 Massachusetts Ave.* ☎617/635–7383 ⊕*www.cityofboston.gov/parks/parkrangers*) lead tours highlighting the area's historic sites and surprising ecological diversity. The sumptuously landscaped **Arnold Arboretum** (✉*125 Arborway, Jamaica Plain* ☎617/524–1718 ⊕*www.arboretum.harvard.edu* Ⓣ*Forest Hills*) is open all year to joggers and in-line skaters. Volunteer docents give free walking tours in spring, summer, and fall.

Cambridge's historic **Mt. Auburn Cemetery** (✉*580 Mt. Auburn St., Mt. Auburn, Cambridge* ☎617/547–7105 ⊕*www.mountauburn.org* Ⓣ*Harvard, then Bus 71 or 73 to Mount Auburn St. at Aberdeen Ave. stop*) is known as one of the best birding spots in the area, and also has walking paths, gardens, and unique architecture. You can also see the graves of distinguished New Englanders such as Oliver Wendell Holmes, Henry Wadsworth Longfellow, and Mary Baker Eddy, among many others.

SPORTS

BASEBALL

Fodor's Choice ★ Hide your Yankees cap and practice pronouncing "Fenway Pahk." Boston is a baseball town, where the crucible of media scrutiny burns hot, fans regard myth and superstition as seriously as player statistics, and grudges are never forgotten. The **Boston Red Sox** (⊠ *Fenway Park, The Fenway* ☎ 617/482–4769 ⊕ *www.bostonredsox.com*) made history in 2004, crushing the Yankees in the American League Championship after a three-game deficit and then sweeping the Cardinals in the World Series for their first title since 1918. More than 3 million fans from "Red Sox Nation" celebrated the championship team and the reversal of the "Curse of the Bambino" with a victory parade through the streets of Boston and down the Charles River. Although losses and the departure of key players in 2005 turned BoSox fans' elation to disappointment again, the pilgrimage of fans from all over New England to Fenway Park shows no signs of letting up. The Red Sox ownership has committed to staying in the once-threatened Fenway Park for the long term, so you can still watch a game in the country's oldest active ballpark and see the fabled "Green Monster" (the park's 37-foot-high left-field wall) and one of the last hand-operated scoreboards in the major leagues. Baseball season runs from early April to early October. The play-offs continue several more weeks, and postseason buzz about contracts, trades, and injuries lasts all winter long.

DID YOU KNOW?

The longest measurable home run hit inside Fenway Park—502 feet—was batted by legendary Red Sox slugger Ted Williams on June 9, 1946. A lone red seat in the right-field bleachers marks the spot where the ball landed.

BASKETBALL

★ The **Boston Celtics** (⊠ *TD Banknorth Garden, Old West End* ☎ 617/624–1000, 617/931–2222 *Ticketmaster* ⊕ *www.celtics.com*) have won the National Basketball Association (NBA) championship 16 times since 1957, more than any other franchise in the NBA. Even though the team hasn't added to that number since 1986, the mystique of the Celtics' former glory days keeps fans coming back year after year in hopes that a championship banner might again be hoisted above the court. Basketball season runs from October to April, and play-offs last until mid-June.

BICYCLING

★ It's common to see suited-up doctors, lawyers, and businessmen commuting on two wheels through Downtown; unfortunately, bike lanes are few and far between. Boston's dedicated bike paths are well used, as much by joggers and in-line skaters as by bicyclists. The **Dr. Paul Dudley White Bike Path,** about 17 mi long, follows both banks of the Charles River as it winds from Watertown Square to the Museum of Science.

6

The **Pierre Lallement Bike Path** winds 4 mi through the South End and Roxbury, from Copley Place to Franklin Park. The tranquil **Minuteman Bikeway** courses 11 mi from the Alewife Red Line T station in Cambridge through Arlington, Lexington, and Bedford. The trail, in the bed of an old rail line, cuts through a few busy intersections—be particularly careful in Arlington Center.

For other path locations, consult the **Department of Conservation & Recreation** (*DCR* ⊕*www.mass.gov/dcr*) Web site.

The **Massachusetts Bicycle Coalition** (*MassBike* ⊠*171 Milk St., Suite 33, Downtown* ☎*617/542-2453* ⊕*www.massbike.org*), an advocacy group working to improve conditions for area cyclists, has information on organized rides and sells good bike maps of Boston and the state. Thanks to MassBike's lobbying efforts, the MBTA now allows bicycles on subway and commuter-rail trains during nonpeak hours. **Community Bicycle Supply** (⊠*496 Tremont St., at E. Berkeley St., South End* ☎*617/542-8623* ⊕*www.communitybicycle.com*) rents cycles from April through October, at rates of $25 for 24 hours. **Back Bay Bicycles** (⊠*366 Commonwealth Ave., Back Bay* ☎*617/247-2336* ⊕*www.backbaybicycles.com*) has mountain bike rentals for $25 per day and road bikes for $35 per day. Staff members also lead group mountain bike rides on nearby trails.

> ## ON YER BIKE!
>
> Boston may be dubbed America's Walking City, but it's a fine place for pedal-pushing, too. **Boston Bike Tours** (☎*617/308–5902* ⊕ *www.bostonbiketours.com*) offers a variety of themed excursions on weekends from spring through fall. Most outings cover about 10–12 mi. It costs about $25 a person. No reservations needed: just show up at the Visitor Information Center on the Boston Common at 11 AM Saturday or Sunday. You bring the adrenaline, they bring the bikes, helmets, and water.

BOATING

Except when frozen over, the waterways coursing through the city serve as a playground for boaters of all stripes. All types of pleasure craft, with the exception of inflatables, are allowed from the Charles River and Inner Harbor to North Washington Street on the waters of Boston Harbor, Dorchester inner and outer bays, and the Neponset River from the Granite Avenue Bridge to Dorchester Bay.

Sailboats can be rented from one of the many boathouses or docks along the Charles. Downtown, public landings and float docks are available at the **Christopher Columbus Waterfront Park** (⊠*Commercial St., Boston Harbor, North End* ☎*617/635–4505*) with a permit from the Boston harbormaster. Along the Charles, **boat drop sites** are at Clarendon Street (⊠*Back Bay*); the **Hatch Shell** (⊠*Embankment Rd., Back Bay*); **Pinckney Street Landing** (⊠*Back Bay*); **Brooks Street** (⊠*Nonantum Rd., Brighton*); **Richard T. Artesani Playground** (⊠*Off Soldiers Field Rd., Brighton*); the **Monsignor William J. Daly Recreation Center** (⊠*Nonantum Rd., Brighton*); **Cambridge Parkway** (⊠*Near Longfellow Bridge,*

Cambridge); **Charles River Dam, Museum of Science** (✉ *Cambridge*); and **Memorial Drive** (✉ *Off Magazine St., Cambridge*).

The **Charles River Watershed Association** (☎ *781/788–0007* ⊕ *www. charlesriver.org*) publishes a 32-page canoe and kayaking guide with detailed boating information.

LESSONS & EQUIPMENT

★ From May to September, **Boston University** (✉ *Soldier's Field Rd.* ☎ *617/353–2748* ⊕ *www.bu.edu/fitrec*) offers beginner to advanced rowing and sailing programs. From May through mid-November, you can rent a canoe, kayak, paddleboat, rowboat, or rowing shell from **Charles River Canoe & Kayak Center** (✉ *2401 Commonwealth Ave., Newton* ☎ *617/965–5110* ⊕ *www.paddleboston.com*). May through September, it has Learn to Row sessions. The Canoe & Kayak Center's **kiosk** (✉ *Soldiers' Field Rd. near the Eliot Bridge, Allston*) rents canoes and kayaks and is open Thursday evening, Friday afternoon, and weekends early May through early October. It's open weekdays only for group appointments. **Community Boating** (✉ *21 David Mugar Way, Beacon Hill* ☎ *617/523–1038* ⊕ *www.community-boating.org*), near the Charles Street footbridge on the Esplanade, is the host of America's oldest public sailing program. From April through October, $80 nets you a 30-day introductory membership, beginner-level classes, and use of sailboats and kayaks. Full memberships grant unlimited use of all facilities; splash around for 60 days for $135 or all season long for $190. Experienced sailors short on time can opt for a two-day sailboat rental for $100.

Community Rowing (✉ *Daly Memorial Skating Rink, Nonantum Rd., Newton* ☎ *617/923–7557* ⊕ *www.communityrowing.org*) teaches introductory to competitive adult and youth rowing courses. Free rowing orientations are offered on the first and third Tuesday of each month between late April and August. From April to October, the **Jamaica Pond Boat House** (✉ *Jamaica Way and Pond St., Jamaica Plain* ☎ *617/635–7383*) provides lessons and equipment for rowing and sailing on its namesake pond.

EVENTS

In mid-October more than 7,500 male and female athletes from
★ all over the world compete in the annual **Head of the Charles Regatta** (☎ *617/868–6200* ⊕ *www.hocr.org*). Thousands of spectators line the banks of the Charles River with blankets and beer (although the police disapprove of the latter), cheering on their favorite teams and generally using the weekend as an excuse to party. Limited free parking is available, but the chances of finding an open space close to the race route are slim, so take public transportation if you can. During the event, free shuttles run between the start and end point of the race route on both sides of the river.

FISHING

Efforts to clean up the city's waterways have heightened the popularity of recreational fishing in and around Boston. For saltwater fishing, locals cast their lines from the **John J. McCorkle Fishing Pier** on Castle Island off Day Boulevard in South Boston and **Tenean Beach** and **Victory Road Park** off Morrissey Boulevard in Dorchester. The **Boston Harbor Islands National Park Area** (☎*617/727–5290* ⊕*www.bostonislands. com*) is also known for great fishing, although note no public piers are available.

You can try to catch freshwater fish in **Jamaica Pond** (⊠*Jamaica Way and Pond St., Jamaica Plain*); Turtle Pond in **Stony Brook Reservation** (⊠*Turtle Pond Pkwy., Hyde Park*); Quarter Mile Pond and Dark Hollow Pond in **Middlesex Fells Reservation** (⊠*Off Rte. 93, Stoneham*); or Houghton's Pond in **Blue Hills Reservation** (⊠*Off Rte. 128, Milton*).

Nonresidents can purchase a three-day Massachusetts fishing license for $27.50 at the **MassWildlife Boston Office** (⊠*251 Causeway St., North End* ☎*617/626–1590* ⊕*www.mass.gov/dfwele*), Brookline Town Hall, and some sporting-goods stores around the city. No license is required for recreational ocean angling.

FOOTBALL

Although this has long been a baseball and basketball town, Boston has begun to change its tune—and for good reason. The Patriots' dynamo coach Bill Belichick and heartthrob quarterback Tom Brady have brought the formerly abysmal team three Super Bowl wins since 2002 and awakened football zeal in sports fans across New England.

In 2002 the **New England Patriots** (⊠*Gillette Stadium, Rte. 1, off I–95 Exit 9, Foxborough* ☎*800/543–1776* ⊕*www.patriots.com*) amazed their fans by recovering from a sluggish start to win the first Super Bowl in the team's history. The team's subsequent wins in 2004 and 2005 were less surprising, but no less celebrated. Exhibition football games begin in August, and the season runs through the play-offs in January. The state-of-the-art Gillette Stadium is in Foxborough, 30 mi southwest of Boston.

DID YOU KNOW?

The New England Patriots, formerly the Boston Patriots, played in Fenway Park from 1963 to 1968 before moving to Foxborough.

With the only Division 1A football program in town, the **Boston College Eagles** (⊠*Alumni Stadium, Chestnut Hill* ☎*617/552–3000*) play against some of the top teams in the country.

Built in 1903, Harvard Stadium is the oldest concrete stadium in the country and the home of the **Harvard University Crimson** (⊠*Harvard Stadium, N. Harvard St. and Soldiers Field Rd., Allston* ☎*617/495–2211*), who went undefeated in 2001 and 2004. The halftime shows of the Harvard Band make any game worth the trip.

GOLF

Although you'll need to know someone who knows someone who *is* someone to play at Brookline's **Country Club,** one of the nation's top-rated private courses, anyone can use the public courses in Boston, which are among the best in the country.

Donald Ross crafted the 6,009-yard, par-70 **Franklin Park Golf Course** (⊠ *1 Circuit Dr., Dorchester* ☎ *617/265–4084*) in the early 1900s. It's open year-round, weather permitting. Greens fees are $14 for 9 holes and $23 for 18 holes on weekdays, and $16 and $29, respectively, on weekends. (You can play 9 holes only after 1 PM on weekends.) If you're not a Boston resident, the course ups the ante by $2 to $5. Club rentals run $10 for 9 holes and $12 for 18 holes. The course is part of a delightful city park with picnic facilities and jogging courses. Festivals and other outdoor activities take place all year.

The hilly **George Wright Golf Course** (⊠ *420 West St., Hyde Park* ☎ *617/364–2300*) is more challenging than the other Donald Ross–designed course at Franklin Park. The par-70, 6,096-yard course is open for the season starting in April each year. Weekend 18-hole greens fees are $40; weekday fees are $28. Tee times are necessary on weekends.

The **Massachusetts Golf Association** (⊠ *300 Arnold Palmer Blvd., Norton* ☎ *800/356–2201* ⊕ *www.mgalinks.org*) represents 400 clubs in the state and has information on courses that are open to the public.

HIKING

With the Appalachian Trail just two hours' drive from Downtown and thousands of acres of parkland and trails encircling the city, hikers will not lack for options in and around Boston.

☾ ★ A 20-minute drive south of Boston, the **Blue Hills Reservation** (⊠ *695 Hillside St., Milton* ☎ *617/698–1802*) encompasses 7,000 acres of woodland with about 125 mi of trails, some ideal for cross-country skiing in winter, some designated for mountain biking the rest of the year. Although only 635 feet high, Great Blue Hill, the tallest hill in the reservation, has a spectacular view of the entire Boston metro area. It's open daily, and maps are available for purchase at the reservation headquarters or the Blue Hills Trailside Museum. To get there, take Route 128 South to Exit 3, Houghton's Pond.

☾ The **Blue Hills Trailside Museum** (⊠ *1904 Canton Ave., Milton* ☎ *617/333–0690*), which is managed by the Massachusetts Audubon Society, organizes hikes and nature walks. Open Wednesday through Sunday 10–5, the museum has natural-history exhibits and live animals. Admission is $3. Take Route 93 South to Exit 2B and Route 138 North.

Just a few miles north of Boston, the 2,575-acre **Middlesex Fells Reservation** (☎ *781/662–2340*) has well-maintained hiking trails that pass over rocky hills, across meadows, and through wetland areas. Trails range from the quarter-mile Bear Hill Trail to the 6.9-mi Skyline Trail.

Mountain bikers can ride along the reservation's fire roads and on a designated loop trail. This sprawling reservation covers area in Malden, Medford, Stoneham, Melrose, and Winchester. To get to the western side of the reservation from Boston, take Route 93 North to Exit 33, and then take South Border Road off the rotary.

Easily accessible from downtown Boston, the **Boston Harbor Islands National Park Area** is seldom crowded. The park maintains walking trails through diverse terrain and ecosystems (⇨ *Parks, above*).

Rangers with the **Boston Parks & Recreation Department** (⊠ *1010 Massachusetts Ave.* ☎ *617/635–7383* ⊕ *www.cityofboston.gov/parks/ parkrangers*) lead walks through the Emerald Necklace parks.

Excellent hiking footpaths crisscross the 475-acre **Stony Brook Reservation** (⊠ *Turtle Pond Pkwy.* ☎ *617/333–7404*), which spans Hyde Park and West Roxbury.

HOCKEY

Boston hockey fans are informed, vocal, and extremely loyal. Despite frequent trades of star players, disappointing losses, high ticket prices, and the complete lockout of the 2004–05 season, the stands are still packed at Bruins games. That said, local college hockey teams tend to give spectators more to celebrate at a much more reasonable price.

The **Boston Bruins** (⊠ *TD Banknorth Garden, 100 Legends Way, Old West End* ☎ *617/624–1000, 617/931–2222 Ticketmaster* ⊕ *www. bostonbruins.com*) are on the ice from September until April, frequently on Thursday and Saturday evenings. Play-offs last through early June.

Boston College, Boston University, Harvard, and Northeastern teams face off every February in the **Beanpot Hockey Tournament** (☎ *617/624–1000*) at the TD Banknorth Garden. The colleges in this fiercely contested tournament traditionally yield some of the finest squads in the country.

ICE SKATING

The Department of Conservation & Recreation operates more than 20 **public ice-skating rinks** (☎ *617/626–1250* ⊕ *www.mass.gov/dcr*); hours and season vary by location. Call for a complete list of rinks and their hours of operation.

Thanks to a refrigerated surface, the **Boston Common Frog Pond** (⊠ *Beacon Hill* ☎ *617/635–2120* ⊕ *www.bostoncommonfrogpond.org*) transforms into a skating park from November to mid-March, complete with a warming hut and concession stand. Admission is $4 for adults; kids 13 and under skate free. Skate rentals cost $8 and lockers are $1. Frog Pond hours are Monday 10–5, Tuesday through Thursday and Sunday 10–9, and Friday and Saturday 10–10.

Skaters flock to the frozen waters of the lagoon at **Boston Public Garden.** Ice on one side of the bridge is theoretically reserved for figure skating and the other for faster-paced ice hockey, though most ignore the rule during slow times.

Outside the city, try the skating rink in **Larz Anderson Park** (⊠ *23 Newton St., Brookline* ☎ *617/739–7518*), at the top of a wooded hill. Admission for Brookline residents is $4; nonresidents pay $7. Skate rentals are $5. The rink is open from December through February.

SKATE RENTALS

Beacon Hill Skate Shop (⊠ *135 Charles St., off Tremont St., near Wang Center for the Performing Arts, South End* ☎ *617/482–7400*) rents skates for use in the Frog Pond and Public Garden for $10 per hour or $15 per day. A credit card is required; call in advance and they'll have the skates sharpened and ready for you.

RUNNING & JOGGING

Boston's parks and riverside pathways almost never lack for joggers, even in the worst weather. Paths on both sides of the Charles River are the most crowded and best maintained, particularly along the **Esplanade.** Watch out for in-line skaters and bikers. At **Castle Island** in South Boston, skaters and joggers zip past strolling lovebirds and parents pushing jogging strollers. The wooded 1½-mi-long loop around **Jamaica Pond** is a slightly less-crowded option.

For equipment and information on local running routes, contact the **Bill Rodgers Running Center** (⊠ *Faneuil Hall Marketplace, Government Center* ☎ *617/723–5612* ⊕ *www.billrodgers.com*).

EVENTS

Fodor'sChoice
★

Every Patriots' Day (the third Monday in April), fans gather along the Hopkinton–to–Boston route of the **Boston Marathon** (⇨ *see box p. 84*) to cheer on more than 20,000 runners from all over the world. The race ends near Copley Square in the Back Bay. For information, call the **Boston Athletic Association** (☎ *617/236–1652* ⊕ *www.bostonmarathon.org*).

In October, women runners take the spotlight on Columbus Day for the **Tufts Health Plan 10K for Women** (☎ *617/439–7700* ⊕ *www.tufts-health-plan.com/tufts10k*), which attracts 7,000 participants and 20,000 spectators. Four American records have been set at this race since it began in 1977.

SKIING

CROSS-COUNTRY

From mid-December to March, the **Weston Ski Track** (⊠ *200 Park Rd., Weston* ☎ *781/891–6575* ⊕ *www.skiboston.com*) provides cross-country skiers and snowshoers with 9 mi of groomed, natural trails and a snowmaking area with a lighted 1-mi ski track. Rentals and basic instruction are available.

DOWNHILL

The closest downhill skiing to Boston is at the **Blue Hills Ski Area** (✉ *Blue Hills Reservation, 4001 Washington St., Canton* ☎ *781/828–5070* ⊕ *www.thenewbluehills.com*). It has more than 220 acres of skiing area and 55 trails to choose from. There's a large ski school, equipment rentals, and a restaurant. Off-peak and group rates are available. Take Route 93 South to Exit 2B and Route 138 North.

On weekends and holidays, serious skiers and snowboarders head north to the mountain resorts along I–93 in New Hampshire. The first big resort off the interstate, **Waterville Valley Resort** (✉ *Rte. 49, off I–93 Exit 28, Waterville Valley, NH* ☎ *603/236–8311 or 800/468–2553*), is one of the state's most popular ski destinations with 52 trails and a terrain park with a 400-foot half pipe.

Nearby **Loon Mountain Resort** (✉ *Off I–93 Exit 32, Lincoln, NH* ☎ *603/745–8111 or 800/229–5666* ⊕ *www.loonmtn.com*) has 45 trails spanning more than 2,100 vertical feet and five terrain parks. Farther north in Franconia Notch, the historic **Cannon Mountain Resort** (✉ *Off I–93 N Exit 34A, B, or C, Franconia, NH* ☎ *603/823–8800* ⊕ *www.cannonmt.com*) is the site of North America's first aerial tramway and home to the New England Ski Museum. There are 55 trails and nine lifts. **Ski NH** (☎ *603/745–9396 or 800/887–5464* ⊕ *www. skinh.com*) is a good source for local ski information.

The **Berkshires** (✉ *135 mi west of Boston along I–90 and Rte. 2* ⊕ *www. berkshires.org*) region in western Massachusetts offers a little bit of Aspen on the East Coast, with tony ski resorts, fine dining, and an upscale atmosphere for those able to take a daylong or weekend ski trip. For details on the various resorts in the Berkshires, go to www. berkshireskiing.com.

SOCCER

⟳ New England's major-league soccer team, **New England Revolution** (✉ *Gillette Stadium, Foxborough* ☎ *800/543–1776, 617/931–2222 Ticketmaster* ⊕ *www.nerevolution.com*), plays from April to November.

On any clear weekend morning, pickup games at most of Boston's parks, especially the fields at the western end of **Back Bay Fens Park** and at **Mayor Thomas W. Danehy Park** near the Alewife transit center in Cambridge, become meeting places for amateur soccer players and fans.

TENNIS

The **Department of Conservation & Recreation** (☎ *617/626–1250* ⊕ *www. mass.gov/dcr*) maintains public tennis courts throughout Boston. These operate on a first-come, first-served basis. Lighted courts are open from dawn to 10 PM; other courts are open from dawn to dusk.

Some of Boston's most popular lighted courts are those at **Charlesbank Park** (✉ *Storrow Dr. opposite Charles St., Beacon Hill*); **Marine Park** (✉ *Day Blvd., South Boston*); and **Weider Playground** (✉ *Dale St., Hyde Park*).

Shopping

WORD OF MOUTH

"Harvard Square, like many other places, has been transformed into a chain-store area—not just bookstores. There are still some small funky shops but it's not the destination it once was. Head down Mass Ave., to Central Square, and you'll find non-chain shops."

—gail

"All of the good shopping is on Newbury St. It could take the whole day to walk from one end to the other stopping in all the stores. A good mix of boutiques and high end stuff. Charles St. in Beacon Hill is also very nice. All boutiques and a lot of antique stores. The Copley Mall is very nice if you're looking for Gucci type of shopping."

—wyatt92

Updated by
Erin Byers
Murray

SHOPPING IN BOSTON IS A lot like the city itself: a mix of classic and cutting-edge, the high-end and the handmade, and international and local sensibilities. Though many Bostonians think too many chain stores have begun to clog their distinctive avenues, there remains a strong network of idiosyncratic gift stores, handicrafts shops, galleries, and a growing number of savvy, independent fashion boutiques. For the well-heeled, there are also plenty of glossy international designer shops.

Boston's shops are generally open Monday through Saturday from 10 or 11 until 6 or 7 and Sunday noon to 5. Many stay open until 8 PM one night a week, usually Thursday. Malls are open Monday through Saturday from 9 or 10 until 8 or 9 and Sunday noon to 6. Most stores accept major credit cards and traveler's checks. There's no state sales tax on clothing. However, there's a 5% luxury tax on clothes priced higher than $175 per item; the tax is levied on the amount in excess of $175.

ERIN'S TOP 5

■ Head to **Louis Boston** for exquisitely made clothing and personalized attention.

■ Pick up a Red Sox hat at the T-shirt stand outside Fenway Park on a game day.

■ Make an appointment with designer Daniela Corte to buy one of her signature custom-made wrap dresses.

■ Pick up a slew of Danish-designed tableware and home decor (that no one else will have!) at **Lekker** in the South End.

■ Hit **Charles Street** to troll through the dozens of antiques shops.

MAJOR SHOPPING DISTRICTS

Boston's shops and department stores are concentrated in the area bounded by Quincy Market, the Back Bay, and Downtown. There are plenty of bargains in the Downtown Crossing area. The South End's gentrification creates its own kind of consumerist milieus, from housewares shops to avant-garde art galleries. In Cambridge you can find lots of shopping around Harvard and Central squares, with independent boutiques migrating west along Massachusetts Avenue (or Mass Ave., as the locals and almost everyone else calls it) toward Porter Square and beyond.

BOSTON

Pretty **Charles Street** is crammed beginning to end with top-notch antiques stores such as Judith Dowling Asian Art, Eugene Galleries, and Devonia as well as a handful of independently owned fashion boutiques whose prices reflect their high Beacon Hill rents. River Street, parallel to Charles Street, is also an excellent source for antiques. Both are easy walks from the Charles Street T stop on the Red Line.

BLITZ TOURS

Study the T map (see inside back cover) before plunging into one of the following shopping tours. You're almost always better off leaving your car behind than trying to navigate congested city streets and puzzle out parking arcana.

ANTIQUES

Avid antiques shoppers have their work happily cut out for them. Plan to spend at least three hours on Charles Street, which has more than 30 stores on five blocks. Start at the north end of the street, in Beacon Hill right over the walking bridge from the Charles/MGH T stop. Bargain hunters should check out **Reruns Antiques** and the jumble of dealers inside the **Boston Antique Co-op.** Other favorite stops include **Tierney Trading, Eugene Galleries, Marika's,** a tangle of American and European objets d'art, and furniture with a smattering of Japanese prints. At the corner of Mt. Vernon Street, turn right and then left onto River Street—some small but intriguing galleries are on this block. Turn left on Chestnut Street to return to Charles Street; on the corner, up a flight of stairs, is the engrossing **Devonia: Antiques for Dining.** From here, continue along Charles Street to Beacon Street and cut through the Public Garden to Newbury Street to reach **Autrefois Antiques** and the **Brodney Gallery.** For more reasonably priced choices, hop on the Green Line to the **Cambridge Antique Market,** near the Lechmere stop.

BEANTOWN BAHGAINS

Thriftiness is considered one of the highest moral virtues in New England—even when buying luxury items. At **DSW** you can always find high-end designer shoes for both sexes at decent prices. Several shops full of watches and jewelry at reduced prices (some barely above wholesale) are found along Washington Street. If vintage is your thing, Newbury Street is dotted with consignment shops lined with gently worn Prada, Gucci, Burberry, and their ilk. Look first in **Second Time Around,** or try across the river in Harvard Square at **Oona's.** Both are also known to carry more-daring labels such as Chloé and Catherine Malandrino for women, and Ermenegildo Zegna for men.

BOOKS

Boston is a bibliophile's dream. For rare, antique, or just plain unusual books, start at **Ars Libri Ltd.** in the South End, a few blocks away from the Back Bay T stop. From here, head to Newbury Street (turn right on Waltham Street, walk three blocks, and cross Tremont Street, then pick up Clarendon Street to Newbury Street) for a break at the **Trident Booksellers & Café,** one of the city's first bookstore-cafés, almost directly across the street. Alternatively, from Ars Libri follow Waltham to Tremont Street, make a right, and head over the turnpike to reach West Street and the **Brattle Bookshop.** From here catch the Red Line T into Harvard Square to browse through the **Harvard Book Store** and, just around the corner, **Grolier Poetry Bookshop.**

7

Copley Place (⊠ *100 Huntington Ave., Back Bay* ☎*617/369–5000* ⊤*Copley*), an indoor shopping mall in the Back Bay, includes such high-end shops as Christian Dior, Louis Vuitton, and Gucci, anchored by the pricey but dependable Neiman Marcus and the flashy, over-priced Barneys. A skywalk connects Copley Place to the **Prudential Center** (⊠ *800 Boylston St., Back Bay* ☎*800/746–7778* ⊤*Copley, Prudential Center*). The Pru, as it's often called, contains moderately priced chain stores such as Ann Taylor and the Body Shop.

Downtown Crossing (⊠ *Washington St. from Amory St. to about Milk St., Downtown* ⊤*Downtown Crossing, Park St.*) is a pedestrian mall with a Macy's and a handful of decent outlets. Millennium Place, a 1.8-million-square-foot complex with a Ritz-Carlton Hotel, condos, a massive sports club, a 19-screen Loews Cineplex, and a few upscale retail stores, seems to be transforming the area, as promised, from a slightly seedy hangout to the newest happening spot.

Faneuil Hall Marketplace (⊠ *Bounded by Congress St., Atlantic Ave., the Waterfront, and Government Center, Downtown* ☎*617/338–2323* ⊤*Government Center*) is a huge complex that's also hugely popular, even though most of its independent shops have given way to Banana Republic, the Disney Store, and other chains. The place has plenty of history, one of the area's great à la carte casual dining experiences (Quincy Market), and carnival-like trappings: pushcarts sell everything from silver jewelry to Peruvian sweaters, and buskers carry out crowd-pleasing feats such as balancing wheelbarrows on their heads.

★ **Newbury Street** (⊤*Arlington, Copley, Hynes/ICA*) is Boston's version of New York's 5th Avenue. The entire street is a shoppers' paradise, from high-end names such as Brooks Brothers to tiny specialty boutiques such as Diptyque. Upscale clothing stores, up-to-the-minute art galleries, and dazzling jewelers line the street near the Public Garden. As you head toward Mass Ave., Newbury gets funkier and the cacophony builds, with skateboarders zipping through traffic and garbage-pail drummers burning licks outside the hip boutiques. The best stores run from Arlington Street to the Prudential Center. Parallel to Newbury Street is **Boylston Street,** where a few standouts, such as Shreve, Crump & Low, are tucked among the other chains and restaurants.

South End (⊤*Back Bay/South End*) merchants are benefiting from the ongoing gentrification that has brought high real-estate prices and trendy restaurants to the area. Explore the chic home-furnishings and gift shops that line Tremont Street, starting at Berkeley Street. The MBTA's Silver Line bus runs through the South End.

CAMBRIDGE

CambridgeSide Galleria (⊠ *100 CambridgeSide Pl., Kendall Sq.* ☎*617/621–8666* ⊤*Lechmere, Kendall/MIT via shuttle*) is a basic three-story mall with a food court. Macy's makes it a good stop for appliances and other basics; it's a big draw for local high-school kids.

Central Square (⊠ *East of Harvard Sq.* ⊤*Central*) has an eclectic mix of furniture stores, used-record shops, ethnic restaurants, and small, hip performance venues.

Harvard Square (⊤*Harvard*) takes up just a few blocks but holds more than 150 stores selling clothes, books, records, furnishings, and specialty items.

The Galleria (⊠*57 JFK St.* ⊤*Harvard*) has various boutiques and a few decent, independently owned restaurants. A handful of chains and independent boutiques are clustered in **Brattle Square** (⊠*Behind Harvard Sq.* ⊤*Harvard*).

Porter Square (⊠ *West on Mass Ave. from Harvard Sq.* ⊤*Porter*) has distinctive clothing stores, as well as crafts shops, coffee shops, natural-food stores, restaurants, and bars with live music.

DEPARTMENT STORES

★ **Barneys New York.** The hoopla (not to mention the party) generated by this store's arrival was surprising in a city where everything new is viewed with trepidation. But clearly Boston's denizens have embraced the lofty, two-story space because it's filled with cutting-edge lines like Comme des Garçons and Nina Ricci, as well as a few bargains in the second-level Co-op section. ⊠*100 Huntington Ave., Back Bay* ☎*617/385–3300* ⊤*Copley.*

Lord & Taylor. This is a reliable, if somewhat overstuffed with merchandise, stop for classic clothing by such designers as Anne Klein and Ralph Lauren, along with accessories, cosmetics, and jewelry. ⊠*760 Boylston St., Back Bay* ☎*617/262–6000* ⊤*Prudential Center.*

Macy's. Three floors offer men's and women's clothing and shoes, housewares, and cosmetics. Although top designers and a fur salon are part of the mix, Macy's doesn't feel exclusive; instead, it's a popular source for family basics. ⊠*450 Washington St., Downtown* ☎*617/357–3000* ⊤*Downtown Crossing.*

Neiman Marcus. The flashy Texas-based retailer known to many as "Needless Markup" has three levels of swank designers such as Gaultier, Gucci, Ferragamo, and Calvin Klein, as well as cosmetics and housewares. ⊠*5 Copley Pl., Back Bay* ☎*617/536–3660* ⊤*Back Bay/ South End.*

Saks Fifth Avenue. The clothing and accessories at Saks runs from the traditional to the flamboyant. It's a little pricey, but an excellent place to find high-quality merchandise, including shoes and cosmetics. ⊠*Prudential Center, 1 Ring Rd., Back Bay* ☎*617/262–8500* ⊤*Prudential Center.*

SPECIALTY STORES

ANTIQUES

Newbury Street and the South End have some excellent (and expensive) antiques stores, but Charles Street—coincidentally, one of the city's oldest streets—is the place to go for a concentrated selection.

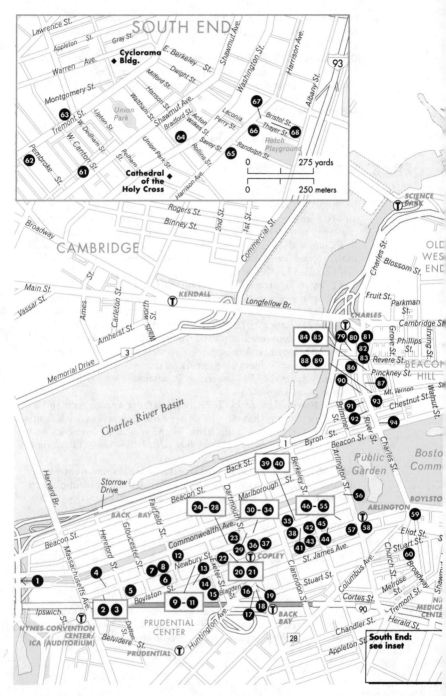

Boston Shopping

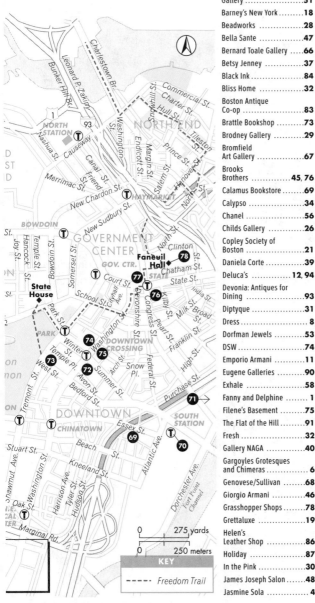

7

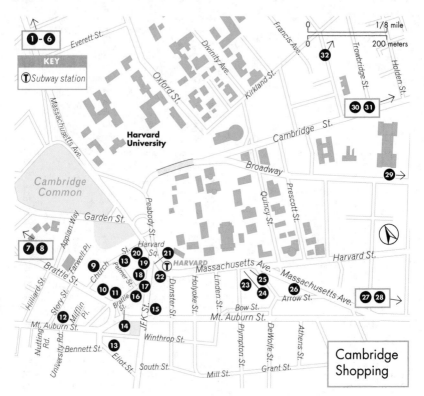

Cambridge Shopping

Autrefois Antiques. Come here to find French country and Italian 18th-, 19th-, and 20th-century furniture, mirrors, and lighting. ✉*130 Harvard St., Brookline* ☎*617/566–0113* Ⓣ*Coolidge Corner.*

Boston Antique Co-op. This flea market–style collection of dealers occupies two floors, containing everything from vintage photos and paintings to porcelain, silver, bronzes, and furniture. ✉*119 Charles St., Beacon Hill* ☎*617/227–9810 or 617/227–9811* Ⓣ*Charles/MGH.*

Brodney Gallery. In addition to plenty of porcelain and silver, Brodney claims to have the biggest selection of estate jewelry in New England. ✉*145 Newbury St., Back Bay* ☎*617/536–0500* Ⓣ*Copley.*

Cambridge Antique Market. Off the beaten track this may be, but it has a selection bordering on overwhelming: five floors of goods ranging from 19th-century furniture to vintage clothing, much of it reasonably priced. There are two parking lots next to the building. ✉*201 Monsignor O'Brien Hwy., Cambridge* ☎*617/868–9655* Ⓣ*Lechmere.*

Devonia: Antiques for Dining. Some of the fabulous china sets here are fit for a queen—some really were designed for royalty. Feast your eyes on tens of thousands of pieces of tableware, including, perhaps, the custom-made set of Baccarat once owned by the Sultan of Brunei. ✉*43 Charles St., Beacon Hill* ☎*617/523–8313* Ⓣ*Charles/MGH.*

★ **Eugene Galleries.** This store is chockablock with prints, etchings, old maps, and books; a 19th-century print of a Boston landmark, for instance, makes for a unique and lasting souvenir. ✉*76 Charles St., Beacon Hill* ☎*617/227–3062* Ⓣ*Charles/MGH.*

Judith Dowling Asian Art. Judith Dowling's sophistication results from spareness and restraint. High-end Asian artifacts range from Japanese pottery to scrolls, Buddha figures, painted screens, cabinets, and other furnishings. ✉*133 Charles St., Beacon Hill* ☎*617/523–5211* ☉*Closed Sept.–June.*

Marika's. Every available inch of space in this jam-packed store, including the walls, is used to display wares. That silver chafing dish might need a polish, and the telephone table may be slightly scratched, but such imperfections keep the prices reasonable. ✉*130 Charles St., Beacon Hill* ☎*617/523–4520* Ⓣ*Charles/MGH.*

Reruns Antiques. Don't let its low prices and jumble-shop aspect fool you. Poke around Reruns and you may come up with a Hiroshige print, a 19th-century Moroccan lamp, or an Asmat ancestral figure. If you're in the mood for a history or an anthropology lesson, owner Tom Armstrong is glad to oblige. ✉*125 Charles St., Beacon Hill* ☎*No phone* Ⓣ*Charles/MGH.*

ART GALLERIES

Although Newbury Street has the highest concentration of galleries in the city, a neighborhood in the South End, discordantly dubbed SoWa (for South of Washington), has emerged as a hot spot for contemporary artists.

★ **Alpha Gallery.** This gallery specializes in 20th-century and contemporary American and European painting, sculpture, and master prints. ✉*38 Newbury St., Back Bay* ☎*617/536–4465* Ⓣ*Arlington.*

Barbara Krakow Gallery. Krakow shows contemporary paintings, photographs, drawings, prints, and sculptures by emerging and established regional and international artists. ✉ *10 Newbury St., 5th fl., Back Bay* ☎ *617/262–4490* Ⓣ*Arlington.*

Bernard Toale Gallery. Toale's contemporary tastes tend toward more-experimental pieces, including sculpture, paintings, photographs, and works on paper. ✉ *450 Harrison Ave., South End* ☎ *617/482–2477* Ⓣ*New England Medical Center.*

Bromfield Art Gallery. A small, cooperative operation, Bromfield mounts monthlong shows of its members' work, including oil and acrylic paintings, charcoals, and pastels. ✉ *450 Harrison Ave., South End* ☎ *617/451–3605* Ⓣ*New England Medical Center.*

Childs Gallery. Childs carries paintings, prints, drawings, watercolors, and sculpture from the 1500s to the present. ✉ *169 Newbury St., Back Bay* ☎ *617/266–1108* Ⓣ*Copley.*

Copley Society of Boston. After more than a century, this nonprofit membership organization continues to present the works of well-known and aspiring New England artists. ✉ *158 Newbury St., Back Bay* ☎ *617/536–5049* Ⓣ*Copley.*

Gallery NAGA. Here are contemporary paintings, sculpture, and furniture displayed in a striking space: the Church of the Covenant. ✉ *67 Newbury St., Back Bay* ☎ *617/267–9060* Ⓣ*Arlington.*

Genovese/Sullivan. One of the pioneers of the SoWa neighborhood, Genovese shows paintings, sculpture, prints, photography, and installations by nationally known contemporary artists. ✉ *450 Harrison Ave., South End* ☎ *617/426–9738* Ⓣ*New England Medical Center.*

Nielsen Gallery. Both established and aspiring artists show their representational and abstract paintings and prints. ✉ *179 Newbury St., Back Bay* ☎ *617/266–4835* Ⓣ*Copley.*

Rolly-Michaux. You'll find only the highest quality works here, from the likes of Moore, Calder, Picasso, Chagall, Miró, and Matisse. ✉ *290 Dartmouth St., Back Bay* ☎ *617/536–9898* Ⓣ*Copley.*

Sampson Projects. A truly cross-cultural blend of exhibits, this gallery shows the experimental works of young contemporary artists. ✉ *450 Harrison Ave., South End* ☎ *617/357–7177* Ⓣ*New England Medical Center.*

Vose Galleries. Established in 1841, Vose specializes in 19th- and 20th-century American art, including the Hudson River School, Boston School, and American impressionists. The addition of works of contemporary American realism recognizes an area that is often overlooked by the trendier set. ✉ *238 Newbury St., Back Bay* ☎ *617/536–6176* Ⓣ*Copley, Hynes/ICA.*

BEAUTY

Beauty & Main. Cosmetics boutiques are supposed to be intimidating, right? Not this one. The informed, helpful staff at Beauty & Main preside over lines both popular (Laura Mercier) and lesser known (Darphin), encouraging customers to sample the wares. ✉ *30 Brattle St., Cambridge* ☎ *617/868–7171* Ⓣ*Harvard.*

Bella Sante. As pristine as it is serene, the beautifully designed Bella Sante is well stocked with high-end products and staffed by a well-trained crew. The locker room is stocked with thoughtful amenities such as body creams and just about any hair product you might need. ⊠*38 Newbury St., Back Bay* ☎*617/424–9930* T*Arlington.*

Exhale. This Zen-like sanctuary is deceptively bigger than it appears since the subterranean lower level houses a first-rate spa and yoga studio. Upstairs, you'll find holistic body and skin-care products. ⊠*28 Arlington St., Back Bay* ☎*617/532–7095* T*Arlington.*

James Joseph Salon. Sleek and modern yet utterly free of pretense, James Joseph has a fun, talented staff that gives customers exactly the cuts, color, and treatments they ask for. ⊠*30 Newbury St., Back Bay* ☎*617/266–7222* T*Arlington.*

Mario Russo Salon. It may be the most coveted cut in town, but Mario Russo and his expert staff retain a down-to-earth attitude as they provide excellent styling and color services. The manicures are equally good. ⊠*9 Newbury St., Back Bay* ☎*617/424–6676* T*Arlington.*

Michaud Cosmedix. Makeup artist Julie Michaud and her staff have worked hard to become Boston's go-to studio for natural-looking makeup application, brow grooming, waxing, and facials. ⊠*69 Newbury St., Back Bay* ☎*617/262–1607* T*Arlington, Copley.*

BOOKS

If Boston and Cambridge have bragging rights to anything, it's their independent bookstores, many of which stay open late and sponsor author readings and literary programs.

Inside the Prudential Center is **Barnes & Noble** (⊠*800 Boylston St., Back Bay* ☎*617/247–6959* T*Prudential Center* ⊠*660 Beacon St., Kenmore Sq.* ☎*617/267–8484* T*Kenmore*). The company now runs the Harvard Coop. **Borders** (⊠*10–24 School St., Downtown* ☎*617/557–7188* T*Government Center* ⊠*511 Boylston St., Back Bay* ☎*617/236–1444*) is also prominent.

SPECIALTY

Ars Libri Ltd. The rare and wonderful books on display here make it easy to be drawn in. The airy space is filled with books on photography and architecture, out-of-print art books, monographs, and exhibition catalogs. ⊠*500 Harrison Ave., South End* ☎*617/357–5212* T*New England Medical Center.*

Fodor'sChoice ★
ۍ **Barefoot Books.** Don't come looking for the same old kids' books; Barefoot is full of beautifully illustrated, creatively told reading for kids of all ages. These are the kind of books that kids remember and keep as adults. ⊠*1771 Massachusetts Ave., Cambridge* ☎*617/349–1610* T*Porter.*

Brattle Bookshop. The late George Gloss built this into Boston's best used- and rare-book shop. Today, his son Kenneth fields queries from passionate book lovers. If the book you want is out of print, Brattle has it or can probably find it. ⊠*9 West St., Downtown* ☎*617/542–0210 or 800/447–9595* T*Downtown Crossing.*

Calamus Bookstore. This friendly, informal store carries not only books, but also videos, music, and gifts for the gay, lesbian, bisexual, or transgender shopper. ⊠*92B South St., Leather District* ☎*617/338–1931* T*South Station.*

Globe Corner Bookstore. Hands down, this is the best source for domestic and international travel books and maps. The store also has very good selections of books about New England and by New England authors. ⊠*90 Mt. Auburn St., Cambridge* ☎*617/497–6277 or 800/358–6013* T*Harvard.*

Grolier Poetry Bookshop. Proprietor Louisa Solano is an outspoken proponent of all things poetic—and her dog, Jessie, is one of the friendliest shopkeepers in Harvard Square. The store, founded in 1927, carries in-print poetry from all eras and from all over the world. ⊠*6 Plympton St., Cambridge* ☎*617/547–4648 or 800/234–7636* T*Harvard.*

★ **Harvard Book Store.** The intellectual community is well served here, with a slew of new titles upstairs and used and remaindered books downstairs. The collection's diversity has made the store a frequent destination for academics. ⊠*1256 Massachusetts Ave., Cambridge* ☎*617/661–1515* T*Harvard.*

Harvard Coop Society. Begun in 1882 as a nonprofit service for students and faculty, the Coop is now managed by Barnes & Noble. In addition to books and textbooks (many discounted), school supplies, clothes, and accessories plastered with the Harvard emblem are sold here, as well as basic housewares geared toward dorm dwellers. ⊠*1400 Massachusetts Ave., Cambridge* ☎*617/499–2000* T*Harvard.*

Kate's Mystery Books. A favorite Cambridge haunt, Kate's is a good place to track down mysteries by local writers; look for authors in the flesh at the shop's frequent readings and events. ⊠*2211 Massachusetts Ave., Cambridge* ☎*617/491–2660* T*Porter.*

Trident Booksellers & Café. Browse through an eclectic collection of books, tapes, and magazines; then settle in with a snack. It's open until midnight daily, making it a favorite with students. ⊠*338 Newbury St., Back Bay* ☎*617/267–8688* T*Hynes/ICA.*

WordsWorth. One of the biggest bookstores in Harvard Square, Words-Worth has about 100,000 titles, most of them discounted. It's easy to get lost among the narrow stacks. ⊠*30 Brattle St., Cambridge* ☎*617/354–5201* T*Harvard.*

CLOTHING & SHOES

The terminally chic shop on Newbury Street, the hip hang in Harvard Square, and everyone goes Downtown for the real bargains.

★ **Alan Bilzerian.** Satisfying the Euro crowd, this store sells luxe men's and women's clothing by such fashion darlings as Yohji Yamamoto and Ann Demeulemeester. ⊠*34 Newbury St., Back Bay* ☎*617/536–1001* T*Arlington.*

Anne Fontaine. You can never have too many white shirts—especially if they're designed by this Parisienne. The simple, sophisticated designs are mostly executed in cotton and priced around $160. ⊠*318 Boylston St., Back Bay* ☎*617/423–0366* T*Arlington, Boylston.*

Betsy Jenney. Ms. Jenney herself is likely to wait on you in this small, personal store, where the well-made, comfortable lines are for women who cannot walk into a fitted size-4 suit—in other words, most of the female population. The designers found here, such as Philippe Adec, Teenflo, and Nicole Miller, are fashionable yet forgiving. ⊠*114 Newbury St., Back Bay* ☎*617/536–2610* Ⓣ*Copley.*

Brooks Brothers. Founded in 1818, Brooks still carries the classically modern styles that made them famous—old faithfuls for men such as navy blazers, seersucker in summer, and crisp oxford shirts. Its Newbury Street store offers a similar vibe for women as well. ⊠*46 Newbury St., Back Bay* ☎*617/267–2600* Ⓣ*Arlington* ⊠*75 State St., Government Center* ☎*617/261–9990* Ⓣ*Government Center.*

Calypso. The women's and children's clothing here bursts with bright colors, beautiful fabrics, and styles so fresh you might need a fashion editor to help you choose. ⊠*115 Newbury St., Back Bay* ☎*617/421–1887* Ⓣ*Copley.*

Chanel. Located at No. 5 in honor of its famous perfume, this branch of the Parisian couture house carries suits, separates, bags, shoes, cosmetics, and, of course, a selection of little black dresses. ⊠*5 Newbury St., Back Bay* ☎*617/859–0055* Ⓣ*Arlington.*

Fodor'sChoice **Daniela Corte.** Local designer Corte cuts women's clothes that flatter
★ from her sunny Back Bay studio. Look for gorgeous suiting, flirty halter dresses, and sophisticated formal frocks that can be bought off the rack or custom tailored. ⊠*91 Newbury St., Back Bay* ☎*617/262–2100* Ⓣ*Copley.*

Dress. True to its name, this shop owned by two young local women carries a number of great party dresses as well as flattering tees, pretty tops, and shoes from emerging designers. ⊠*221 Newbury St., Back Bay* ☎*617/424–7125* Ⓣ*Copley, Hynes/ICA.*

DSW. Major discounts on high-quality (and big-name) shoes for men and women are what draw much of Boston to DSW, also known as Designer Shoe Warehouse. Everything from Nike to Prada can be found at varying discounts—sometimes up to 90% off. ⊠*385 Washington St., Downtown* ☎*617/556–0052* Ⓣ*Downtown Crossing.*

Emporio Armani. Head here for sportier versions of the designer's classic lines. The café next door, which spills out onto the sidewalk in warm weather, is popular with the store's international clientele. ⊠*210–214 Newbury St., Back Bay* ☎*617/262–7300* Ⓣ*Copley.*

Fanny and Delphine. Inside the stately Hotel Commonwealth, this is a favorite stopping point for visitors on the lookout for up-to-the-minute trends from little-known labels like Coven and Joeffer Caoc. There's a fine collection of skirts, tops, and accessories, too. ⊠*522 Commonwealth Ave., Kenmore Sq.* ☎*617/266–2006* Ⓣ*Kenmore.*

Giorgio Armani. This top-of-the-line Italian couturier is known for his carefully shaped jackets, soft suits, and mostly neutral palette. ⊠*22 Newbury St., Back Bay* ☎*617/267–3200* Ⓣ*Arlington.*

Grettaluxe. Drop by Copley's sassy little boutique and pick up the latest "it" pieces—from velour hoodies by Juicy Couture to the must-have Stella McCartney design du moment. There's also jewelry, handbags, and other accessories. ✉ *Copley Place, 100 Huntington Ave., Back Bay* ☎ *617/266–6166* Ⓣ*Copley.*

Helen's Leather Shop. Choose from half a dozen brands of boots (Lucchese, Nocona, Dan Post, Tony Lama, Justin, and Frye); then peruse the leather sandals, jackets, briefcases, luggage, and accessories. ✉ *110 Charles St., Beacon Hill* ☎ *617/742–2077* Ⓣ*Charles/MGH.*

Holiday. A stockpile of flirty and feminine getups—from dresses to denim—are the rage here. Cult lines such as Rock and Republic, Mint, Eberjey, and Tracy Reese are in regular rotation among the fashionable racks. ✉ *53 Charles St., Beacon Hill* ☎ *617/973–9730* Ⓣ*Charles/MGH.*

In the Pink. Don't be caught dead in Palm Beach this year without your Lilly Pulitzer resort wear, available here along with shoes, home decor, and children's clothing. ✉ *133 Newbury St., Back Bay* ☎ *617/536–6423* Ⓣ*Copley.*

Jasmine Sola. Jasmine shows the work of current designers from New York and Los Angeles. The Cambridge store includes the Sola and Sola Men shoe boutiques, and is just filled with really cool stuff. The Warehouse Store in Allston carries all discontinued lines at super-low prices. ✉ *329 and 344 Newbury St., Back Bay* ☎ *617/437–8466* Ⓣ*Copley* ✉ *35–39 Brattle St., Cambridge* ☎ *617/354–6043* Ⓣ*Harvard* ✉ *965 Commonwealth Ave., Allston* ☎ *617/562–0004* Ⓣ*Pleasant St..*

John Fluevog Shoes. Many club goers have at least one pair of these oh-so-hip shoes in their closets, perhaps because of the company's claim that their Angel soles repel all kinds of nasty liquids "and Satan." ✉ *302 Newbury St., Back Bay* ☎ *617/266–1079* Ⓣ*Copley.*

Jos. A. Bank Clothiers. Like Brooks Brothers, Joseph Bank is well known to the conservatively well dressed everywhere. ✉ *399 Boylston St., Back Bay* ☎ *617/536–5050* Ⓣ*Arlington.*

Louis Boston. Impeccably tailored designs, subtly updated classics, and the latest Italian styles highlight a wide selection of imported clothing and accessories. Visiting celebrities might be trolling the racks along with you as jazz spills out into the street from the adjoining Restaurant L. ✉ *234 Berkeley St., Back Bay* ☎ *617/262–6100* Ⓣ*Arlington.*

Marc Jacobs. Only the third stateside outpost to be opened by this celebrated designer, this two-floor boutique includes both his younger, casual line and elegant (and, of course, more expensive) collection. Look, too, for a well-edited sampling of MJ's high-end home accessories. ✉ *81 Newbury St., Back Bay* ☎ *617/425–0707* Ⓣ*Copley.*

Matsu. This shop trends towards the funkier with edgy pieces from designers like Lilith and Rozae Nichols. Look for a well-edited jewelry selection as well as high-end handbags and accessories. ✉ *259 Newbury St., Back Bay* ☎ *617/266–9707* Ⓣ*Copley, Hynes/ICA.*

Mint Julep. Cute dresses, playful skirts, and form-fitting tops make up the selection here. The Cambridge location is a little larger and easier to navigate, but Brookline houses the original. ✉ *6 Church St., Cambridge* ☎ *617/576–6468* Ⓣ*Harvard* ✉ *1302 Beacon St., Brookline* ☎ *617/232–3600* Ⓣ*Coolidge Corner.*

Queen Bee. Only clothes from the hottest, most youthful lines—Mint, Tibi, Shoshana—pass through this boutique's doors. Even if you wouldn't wear most of this stuff, it's fun just to see the latest and maybe pick up an accessory. ✉*85 Newbury St., Beacon Hill* ☎*617/859–7999* Ⓣ*Arlington, Copley.*

Relic. This ultrahip subterranean shop sells designer denim such as Miss Sixty and Meltin' Pot. The interior is a work of art; a few local artists designed the space with pieces of metal culled from the city's Big Dig project and hand-painted wall murals. ✉*116 Newbury St., Back Bay* ☎*617/437–7344* Ⓣ*Copley.*

Stil. Local designers such as Daniela Corte and Elaine Perlov share rack space with cutting-edge Scandinavian labels such as Rutzou and Bruun's Bazaar—all of it at surprisingly earthly prices. ✉*170 Newbury St., Back Bay* ☎*617/859–7845* Ⓣ*Copley.*

Toppers. Nothing old hat about this place, where you can cover your head in anything from a tam-o'-shanter to a 10-gallon. ✉*230 Newbury St., Back Bay* ☎*617/859–1430* Ⓣ*Copley.*

Wish. Everything a hip young woman could wish for, from designers such as Milly, Rebecca Taylor, and Nanette Lepore, can be found in this small but comfy addition to antiques row. ✉*49 Charles St., Beacon Hill* ☎*617/227–4441* Ⓣ*Charles/MGH.*

CRAFTS

Beadworks. Find beads of every color, texture, size, and material in the tiny bins in Back Bay's do-it-yourself jewelry store. The prices are reasonable, the staff is helpful and friendly, and there's a worktable to assemble your masterpiece in the center of the shop. ✉*167 Newbury St., Back Bay* ☎*617/247–7227.*

Cambridge Artists' Cooperative. The ceramics, weavings, jewelry, and leather work here can be pricier than most, but they're all one-of-a-kind or limited edition. ✉*59A Church St., Cambridge* ☎*617/868–4434* Ⓣ*Harvard.*

Society of Arts & Crafts. More than a century old, this is the country's oldest nonprofit crafts organization. It displays a fine assortment of ceramics, jewelry, glass, woodwork, and furniture by some of the country's finest craftspeople. ✉*175 Newbury St., Back Bay* ☎*617/266–1810* Ⓣ*Copley.*

GIFTS

Black Ink. A wall full of rubber stamps stretches above unusual candles, cookie jars, and other home accessories and gift items. ✉*101 Charles St., Beacon Hill* ☎*617/723–3883* Ⓣ*Charles/MGH* ✉*5 Brattle St., Cambridge* ☎*617/497–1221* Ⓣ*Harvard.*

Buckaroo's Mercantile. It's Howdy Doody time at Buckaroo's—a great destination for the kitsch inclined. Find pink poodle skirts, lunch-box clocks, Barbie lamps, *Front Page Detective* posters, and everything Elvis. ✉*5 Brookline St., Cambridge* ☎*617/492–4792* Ⓣ*Central.*

★ **Diptyque.** The venerable Paris house has its flagship U.S. store right here on Newbury Street. The hand-poured candles, room sprays, and gender-neutral eau de toilettes are expensive, but each is like a little work of art—and just entering the calmly inviting store is like having a mini–aromatherapy session. ✉*123 Newbury St., Back Bay* ☎*617/351–2430* T*Copley.*

The Flat of the Hill. There's nothing flat about this fun collection of seasonal items, toiletries, toys, pillows, and whatever else catches the fancy of the shop's young owner. Her passion for pets is evident—pick up a Fetch & Glow ball and your dog will never again have to wait until daytime to play in the park. ✉*60 Charles St., Beacon Hill* ☎*617/619–9977* T*Charles/MGH.*

★ **Fresh.** You won't know whether to wash with these soaps or nibble on them. The shea-butter-rich bars come in such scents as clove-hazelnut and orange-cranberry. They cost $6 to $7 each, but they carry the scent to the end. ✉*121 Newbury St., Back Bay* ☎*617/421–1212* T*Copley.*

★ **Nomad.** Low prices and an enthusiastic staff are just the beginning at this imports store; it carries clothing as well as Indian good-luck *torans* (wall hangings), Mexican *milagros* (charms), mirrors to keep away the evil eye, silver jewelry, and curtains made from sari silk. In the basement you'll find kilims, hand-painted tiles, and sale items. ✉*1741 Massachusetts Ave., Cambridge* ☎*617/497–6677* T*Porter.*

Tibet Emporium. More upscale than your average imports store, Tibet Emporium goes beyond the usual masks and quilted wall hangings to offer beautifully delicate beaded silk pillowcases, pashmina wraps in every color imaginable, appliquéd and silk clothing, and finely wrought but affordable silver jewelry. ✉*103 Charles St., Beacon Hill* ☎*617/723–8035* T*Charles/MGH.*

Tokai Japanese Gifts. Chopstick rests, origami paper, Yukata cotton robes, and high-end kimonos are among the wares here. ✉*1815 Massachusetts Ave., Cambridge* ☎*617/864–5922* T*Porter.*

GROCERS

Cardullo's. This 50-year-old shop in Harvard Square purveys exotic imports, sandwiches to go, chocolates, breads, olive oils, cheeses, wines, and beer amid impressive clutter. ✉*6 Brattle St., Cambridge* ☎*617/491–8888 or 800/491–8288* T*Harvard.*

Deluca's Market. Here's one neighborhood grocer that delivers the gourmet goods: an international cheese counter, homemade pâtés, fresh produce, and a snacks section that includes a dream team of cookies. ✉*11 Charles St., Beacon Hill* ☎*617/523–4343* T*Charles/MGH* ✉*239 Newbury St., Back Bay* ☎*617/262–5990* T*Copley.*

Savenor's. If you're looking for exotic game meats, you've come to the right place. Savenor's food market, once Julia Child's favorite butcher, carries buffalo rump, alligator tail, even rattlesnake. There are plenty of tamer choices, too, as well as outstanding cheeses, breads, and treats such as foie gras and smoked salmon. ✉*160 Charles St., Beacon Hill* ☎*617/723–6328* T*Charles/MGH* ✉*92 Kirkland St., Cambridge* ☎*617/576–6328* T*Central.*

HOME FURNISHINGS

A home-furnishings hot spot has emerged in the South End, but don't overlook the choice strip on Massachusetts Avenue in Cambridge.

Abodeon. New York decorators come to town just to shop this incredible collection of 20th-century modern housewares, both newly produced classic designs and pristine-condition vintage. You might come across a mint 1963 stove, a complete set of Jetson-esque dinnerware, or a Lucite dining set from the early 1970s. As a bonus, the back room contains more than 10,000 hard-to-find records. ⊠Massachusetts Ave., Cambridge ☎617/497–0137 ⓉPorter.

★ **Bliss Home.** Funky and colorful home designs such as brightly patterned rugs by Angela Adams, gleaming barware by Alessi, gorgeous baby blankets, handmade pottery pet bowls, and beautifully sleek handbags by Ply fill this stylish shop. ⊠*121 Newbury St., Back Bay* ☎*617/421–5544* Ⓣ*Copley.*

Gargoyles Grotesques & Chimeras. The space is so dark you can hardly see the objects for sale. But once your eyes adjust, they'll be rewarded with stained glass, architectural salvage, and devotional art perfect for a Gothic revival. ⊠*262 Newbury St., Back Bay* ☎*617/536–2362* Ⓣ*Copley.*

Kitchen Arts. There are so many gadgets, gizmos, and doodads here that it makes Williams-Sonoma look like a meagerly stocked cupboard. ⊠*161 Newbury St., Back Bay* ☎*617/266–8701* Ⓣ*Copley.*

Koo de Kir. Break out of the blond-wood school with this offbeat selection of furniture, lamps, candles, wine racks, table settings, and other urban necessities. ⊠*65 Chestnut St., Beacon Hill* ☎*617/723–8111* Ⓣ*Charles/MGH.*

★ **Lekker.** Dutch design with contemporary panache pervades South Washington Street's coolest home store—the best place to pick up bright oversize pillows, china, tables, Asian cabinets, and sleek, contemporary flatware. ⊠*1317 Washington St., South End* ☎*617/542–6464* Ⓣ*Back Bay/South End.*

London Lace. You may have spotted this company in the "resources" pages of glossy home-decor magazines. At the shop, it's hard to choose from among the exquisite curtains made from 120-year-old patterns. ⊠*470 Shawmut Ave., South End* ☎*617/267–3506 or 800/926–5223* Ⓣ*Massachusetts Avenue.*

Mohr & McPherson. These stores are a visual exotic feast; cabinets, tables, chairs, and lamps from Japan, India, China, and Indonesia, as well as new and antique Oriental rugs, make up the impressive array. Also impressive are the high prices. ⊠*356 Boylston St., Back Bay* ☎*617/421–9500* Ⓣ*Arlington* ⊠*75 Moulton St., Cambridge* ☎*617/520–2000* Ⓣ*Alewife.*

Motley Home. Here you'll find home goods for the modern set. Contemporary gadgets share space with bold-color throw pillows and sleek lamps. ⊠*652 Tremont St., South End* ☎*617/266–5566* Ⓣ*Massachusetts Avenue.*

Museum of Useful Things. This sister shop of Black Ink @ Home stocks industrial-style home accessories and furniture. ⊠ *49B Brattle St., Cambridge* ☎ *617/576–3322* Ⓣ *Harvard.*

Posh on Tremont. "Where do you get this stuff?" is something the owners hear often at Posh, a shop that somehow manages to be all things to all South End nesters. A pair of sleek silver candlesticks would be perfect for a contemporary loft, for instance, and a brownstone buyer could snap up vintage end tables. ⊠ *557 Tremont Ave., South End* ☎ *617/437–1970* Ⓣ *Back Bay/South End.*

Showroom. This industrial-looking shop has some of the finest modern furniture in town. Collections from Italian lines Flexform and Cappellini are set up in roomlike designs on the floor to give shoppers an accurate visual of their future interior design. ⊠ *240 Stuart St., Back Bay* ☎ *617/482–4805* Ⓣ *Arlington.*

JEWELRY

Alpha Omega. Rarefied timepieces from such makers as Rolex, Breitling, and Chronoswiss pack these stores. ⊠ *Prudential Center, 800 Boylston St., Back Bay* ☎ *617/424–9030* Ⓣ *Prudential Center* ⊠ *1380 Massachusetts Ave., Cambridge* ☎ *617/864–1227* Ⓣ *Harvard.*

Brodney Gallery. Brodney sells the most estate jewelry in New England, and its wide selection of platinum filigree diamond rings ensures a steady stream of nervous male customers about to pop the question. ⊠ *145 Newbury St., Back Bay* ☎ *617/536–0500* Ⓣ *Copley.*

Dorfman Jewels. This elegant shop glows with first-class watches, pearls, and precious stones. ⊠ *24 Newbury St., Back Bay* ☎ *617/536–2022* Ⓣ *Arlington.*

★ **Shreve, Crump & Low.** Since 1796, Shreve has specialized in high-end treasures, including gems and handcrafted platinum rings, as well as high-quality antiques. But don't get the impression that you can't afford anything here: one of the store's best-selling items is a $25 ceramic pitcher called "The Gurgling Cod," in honor of the state fish. ⊠ *440 Boylston St., Back Bay* ☎ *617/267–9100* Ⓣ *Arlington.*

Small Pleasures. The antique and estate jewelry—from Victorian-era tourmaline cocktail rings to mint-condition pocket watches—that lines these cases should not be missed by vintage lovers. The staff is notably helpful and informed. ⊠ *Copley Place, 142 Newbury St., Back Bay* ☎ *617/267–7371* Ⓣ *Copley.*

Tiffany & Co. Fine service complements the finest in gems and precious metals as well as crystal, china, stationery, and fragrances. ⊠ *100 Huntington Ave., Copley Pl., Back Bay* ☎ *617/353–0222* Ⓣ *Copley.*

Twentieth Century Limited. Every kind of rhinestone concoction imaginable for the bauble babe in your life is here, as well as gently used 20th-century ladies' hats and pocketbooks. ⊠ *73 Charles St., Beacon Hill* ☎ *617/742–1031* Ⓣ *Charles/MGH.*

MUSIC STORES

As befitting a town with so many colleges and universities, live music of all kinds is never far away. Unfortunately, the market for recorded music has diminished over the years and CD and record stores are disappearing along with it.

★ **Newbury Comics.** These local outposts for new rock and roll carry especially good lineups of independent pressings. Frequent sales keep prices down. ✉*332 Newbury St., Back Bay* ☎*617/236–4930* Ⓣ*Hynes/ICA* ✉*36 JFK St., Cambridge* ☎*617/491–0337* Ⓣ*Harvard* ✉*1 Washington Mall, Government Center* ☎*617/248–9992* Ⓣ*Government Center.*

ODDS & ENDS

Grasshopper Shops. The souvenirs in this little collection of independently owned shops in historic Faneuil Hall are Boston-centric but not cheesy. The **Bostonian Society Museum Shop** (☎*617/720–3284*) has history books for children and adults. At **Explore Boston** (☎*617/725–1055*) you can buy saltwater taffy or a Boston-in-a-Box board game. **Out of Left Field** (☎*617/722–9401*) sells Red Sox gear. ✉*Faneuil Hall Sq., Government Center* Ⓣ*Government Center.*

Kate Spade. Trendsetters go wild for Kate's signature black satin–finish microfiber handbags, as well as her shoes, pj's, accessories, and travel and cosmetics cases. ✉*117 Newbury St., Back Bay* ☎*617/262–2632* Ⓣ*Copley.*

Lannan Ship Model Gallery. Though a sign on the door says it's open by appointment only, a simple knock almost always gains you admission to this water rat's dream store—but call ahead to be sure. The 6,000-square-foot space looks like the attic of a merchant seaman: in addition to finished 18th- and 19th-century ship models ($200 to $100,000-plus) and vintage pond yachts, you can find lanterns, navigational instruments, and marine charts, prints, and oils. ✉*99 High St., Downtown* ☎*617/451–2650* Ⓣ*South Station.*

Out-of-Town News. Smack in the middle of Harvard Square is a staggering selection of the world's newspapers and magazines. The stand is open daily 6 AM–10:30 PM. ✉*0 Harvard Sq., Cambridge* ☎*617/354–7777* Ⓣ*Harvard.*

RUNNING GEAR

★ **Marathon Sports.** Marathon is known for its personalized service and advice for choosing the perfect shoe, whether you're a beginning walker or a serious runner. Many marathon runners find their way here before the Boston race each spring. ✉*1654 Massachusetts Ave., Cambridge* ☎*617/354–4161* Ⓣ*Harvard.*

7

THRIFT SHOPS

Garment District. This warehouselike building is crammed with vintage, used, and new clothing and accessories. Students crowd the store year-round, and everyone comes at Halloween for that perfect costume. ✉*200 Broadway, Cambridge* ☎*617/876–5230 or 617/876–9795* Ⓣ*Kendall/MIT.*

Keezer's. Since 1895, this shop has been many a man's secret weapon for formal wear at an informal price. Pick up new or used suits, tuxedos, ties, shirts, and pants. ✉*140 River St., Cambridge* ☎*617/547–2455* Ⓣ*Central.*

Oona's. Crowded racks of cared-for, secondhand clothing for women and men are reason enough to browse through the multiple rooms of reasonably priced stock. A helpful staff and fun, eclectic vibe just make doing so that much more fun. ✉*1210 Massachusetts Ave., Cambridge* ☎*617/491–2654* Ⓣ*Harvard.*

Second Time Around. OK, so $700 isn't all that cheap for a used suit—but what if it's Chanel? Many of the items here, from jeans to fur coats, are new merchandise; the rest is on consignment. The staff takes periodic markdowns, ranging from 20% to 50% over a 90-day period. ✉*176 Newbury St., Back Bay* ☎*617/247–3504* Ⓣ*Copley* ✉*8 Eliot St., Cambridge* ☎*617/491–7185* Ⓣ*Harvard.*

TOYS

Ⓒ **Curious George Goes to WordsWorth.** Time can really slip away from you in this jungle of kids' books and gifts. Decorated with tropical plants, a fake hut, and tot-size chairs, and equipped with puzzles, toys, activity sets, and books of all kinds for all ages, this store is a wonderland for kids and a parent's salvation on a rainy day. ✉*1 JFK St., Harvard Sq., Cambridge* ☎*617/498–0062* Ⓣ*Harvard.*

Ⓒ **Henry Bear's Park.** The specialty at this charming neighborhood store is huggable bears and collectible dolls, although it also sells books, toys, and games. ✉*361 Huron St., Cambridge* ☎*617/547–8424* Ⓣ*Porter* ✉*19 Harvard St., Brookline* ☎*617/264–2422* Ⓣ*Brookline Village.*

Ⓒ **Stellabella.** Creative toys are the draw here—books and games to stimulate kids' imaginations and get their brains going without relying on TV or violence. No gun or weapon toys are sold. ✉*1360 Cambridge St., Cambridge* ☎*617/491–6290* Ⓣ*Central.*

Side Trips

WORD OF MOUTH

"Rockport is BEAUTIFUL. I love it there so much. It's a quaint, lovely, seaside town. It's full of history, beauty, and just a really nice place to visit. It's about an hour outside of Boston. You can get there on the commuter train, but then you'd have to walk a ways to the good stuff. What's the good stuff? Halibut Point State Park is lovely for hiking. Bearskin Neck is a cute shopping area with a great fudge place."

—JoanneTravelMom

"A day trip up to Marblehead, Swampscott, Newburyport, Salem area is certainly doable. Marblehead is a pretty little town, with small streets and some cute shops."

—wantsomesun

Updated by
Andrew Rimas

HISTORY LIES THICK ON THE ground in the towns surrounding Boston—from Pilgrims to pirates, witches to whalers, the American Revolution to the Industrial Revolution. The sights outside the city are at least as interesting as those on the Freedom Trail. People from all over the world visit Plymouth for a glimpse into the country's earliest beginnings. A visit to Plimoth Plantation re-creates the everyday life of the Pilgrims, and the *Mayflower II* gives you an idea of just how frightening that journey to the New World must have been. November in Plymouth includes special events centered on Thanksgiving. The town handles the annual influx with grace, but if you're wary of crowds, visit earlier in the year.

West of the city, Lexington and Concord embody the spirit of the American Revolution. The sprawling Minute Man National Historical Park provides a guided tour of all the important historical sites. These two quintessential New England towns are also home to several historic houses and small museums dedicated to the country's first serious writers—Ralph Waldo Emerson, Nathaniel Hawthorne, Louisa May Alcott, and Henry David Thoreau. Literary fans and history buffs can happily while away several days here. And, just 30 minutes outside the city, the National Historic Park in Lowell examines more-recent history: the textile mills, canals, and "mill girl" dormitories of the Industrial Revolution.

Stretching up the coast north of Boston, the North Shore is the perfect warm-weather side trip, with excellent beaches and world-famous fried clams, especially in Ipswich. Cape Ann—which locals call "the other cape"—includes Essex, a mecca for New England antiquing; Gloucester, the oldest seaport in the country; and charming Rockport, crammed with art galleries, crafts shops, and historic bed-and-breakfasts.

Also on the North Shore, Salem is the home of modern witches and historic witchcraft hysteria. It's still a magnet and meeting point for modern witches, so don't assume that all the people you see in costume are reliving Halloween. "Haunted Happenings," the city's Halloween festival, is a ghoulishly good time. Hotels fill up as early as April, and crowds are thick throughout October. This is a popular destination for Bostonians as well as tourists in summer, making traffic and parking particularly challenging on weekends. Go early in the day.

On the South Shore, you can take a one-day expedition back in time to Plymouth. Walk the decks of the *Mayflower II,* stand in awe of Plymouth Rock, and stroll through a recreation of a 17th-century Puritan Village. Another 10 mi takes you to New Bedford and the nation's largest museum on the history of whaling.

WEST OF BOSTON

West of Boston lies a group of historic sites known by every American schoolchild as the birthplace of the American Revolution. Associated with patriotism, daring deeds, and heroic horsemanship, the now

IF YOU LIKE

THE SEASHORE

Bostonians visit the North Shore for its beaches, especially those around Gloucester and Rockport. Others enjoy discovering the pretty New England coastal towns with colorful clapboard cottages, narrow streets, and antiques stores; these are found in greatest concentration inland around Essex, but there are plenty sprinkled elsewhere on Cape Ann as well.

Many of the area's attractions—swimming, boating, and fishing—focus on the water: deep-sea fishing trips are plentiful, and surf casting is popular, as is freshwater fishing in the Parker and Ipswich rivers. If you prefer to observe sea life rather than fish for it, take a whale-watching trip. Several breeds of whale feed locally between May and October, so you're practically guaranteed to see a few—and on a good day you may see upward of 40. Organized boat trips leave from many of the coastal towns; they usually last three to four hours, including travel time to and from the whales' feeding grounds.

LITERARY HAUNTS

The area west of Boston is particularly rich with literary landmarks. In Concord alone you may visit in one afternoon Alcott's Orchard House, Nathaniel Hawthorne's Wayside, the Ralph Waldo Emerson House, and Henry David Thoreau's Walden Pond. North of Boston, in Salem, is Hawthorne's House of the Seven Gables. And although you might not associate the Beats with this region, Jack Kerouac is buried in his hometown, Lowell.

THE SPIRIT OF 1775

To better understand the Boston Tea Party, the Battle of Bunker Hill, and the "Massacre," visit Lexington and Concord, where Boston's—and the country's—fight for freedom began in 1775. These communities quietly embody the region's character traits: charm, reserve, fierce independence, and, above all, pride in their history. Here you can explore Revolutionary battlegrounds, taverns, and houses as well as several excellent museums that emphasize both content and context.

quaint and costly residential towns of Lexington and Concord are where the Revolution's first military encounters took place.

If your interests lean more toward literature and philosophy, you'll find abundant evidence here of an intellectual revolution as well. Lofty thinkers Thoreau and Emerson, and writers Hawthorne and Alcott all hailed from Concord. These famed figures of American culture were nurtured in these unassuming small towns, now comfortable green commuter suburbs.

Sudbury has a few literary and botanical attractions, though it lacks the significance of Lexington or Concord. Lowell, farther west and north, underwent still another revolution—the Industrial Revolution—and its legacy is considerably less picturesque, though perhaps just as important. Despite its derelict mills and canals, Lowell has an imaginatively restored downtown area, including a large, compelling urban national park.

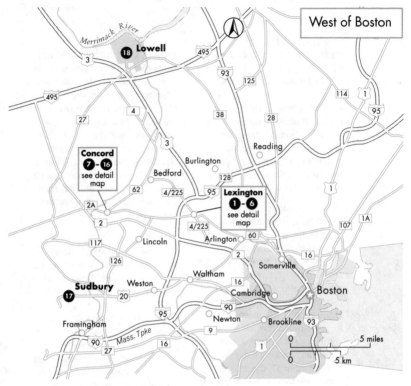

ABOUT THE RESTAURANTS

The North Shore has the most distinctive dining near Boston. Seafood restaurants big and small make it nigh impossible to pass up the lobster, clams, cod, and more that are served fried, steamed, sautéed, or stewed. Look for traditional "seafood in the rough" eating places. These seemingly low-fashion eateries serve generous (though not inexpensive) New England seafood specialties on paper plates, often at wooden picnic tables and frequently outdoors.

■ TIP→ **New Englanders can spot a visitor by the skill with which they can or can't disembowel a steamed lobster. If you don't want to give yourself away, order the classic New England clambake dinner—a cup of chowder, steamed clams, and corn on the cob.**

In many Boston-area suburbs, upscale contemporary restaurants are common; it's also possible to sample food that reflects the region's many immigrant groups, including Portuguese, Italian, Greek, and Asian.

It's always a good idea to book ahead; we mention reservations only when they're essential or are not accepted. All restaurants we list are open daily for lunch and dinner unless stated otherwise; dress is mentioned only when men are required to wear a jacket or a jacket and tie.

ABOUT THE HOTELS

New England is full of country inns and bed-and-breakfasts with delightful personal touches. The North Shore is famous for its distinctive seaside inns. Some are converted mansions of sea captains, others were once grand summer homes, and a few were built as hotels. Cedar shingles, ships' lanterns, and pineapple motifs (a pineapple on the doorstep showed that seafarers were safely returned from exotic lands) combine with patchwork quilts, shining hardwood floors, and open fireplaces to offer some outstanding accommodations. Less-expensive options—waterfront motels and B&B homes—are also widely available in summer, but be sure to make reservations early. The North Shore tourist season ends early: many lodgings are closed from late October until April or May.

> ### ANDREW'S TOP 5
>
> ■ **Plymouth Rock.** More pebble than boulder, but still you can hear the thud of the first Puritan boot to hit New England soil.
>
> ■ **The Mayflower II.** The story of the pilgrim's Atlantic crossing comes alive here.
>
> ■ **Plimoth Plantation.** The staff here hits the cadence, the world view, and the appearance of the first settlers with perfect pitch.
>
> ■ **Beaches.** Soft white sand, deep blue Atlantic—the best beaches in New England.
>
> ■ **Cranberry Bogs.** An artist's dreamscape in every season—reds, greens, golds, and blues.

The lodgings we list are the cream of the crop in each price category. We always list the facilities that are available, but we don't specify whether they cost extra: when pricing accommodations, always ask what's included and what costs extra. Properties indicated by an ✕⊡ are lodging establishments whose restaurant warrants a special trip.

Assume that all rooms have private baths, phones, cable TV, and air-conditioning unless otherwise noted and that hotels operate on the European Plan (with no meals) unless we specify that they use the Continental Plan (CP, with a Continental breakfast daily) or Breakfast Plan (BP, with full breakfast daily). Massachusetts has a statewide ban on smoking in hotel rooms, so all rooms are smoke-free.

WHAT IT COSTS					
	$$$$	$$$	$$	$	¢
RESTAURANTS	over $32	$25–$32	$15–$24	$8–$14	under $8
HOTELS	over $325	$225–$325	$150–$224	$75–$149	under $75

Restaurant prices are for a main course at dinner. Hotel prices are for two people in a standard double room in high season.

LEXINGTON

Fodor's Choice
★

16 mi northwest of Boston.

Discontent within the British-ruled American colonies burst into action in Lexington on April 19, 1775. On the previous night, patriot leader Paul Revere alerted the town that British soldiers were approaching. As the British advance troops arrived in Lexington on their march toward Concord, the minutemen were waiting to confront the Redcoats in what became the first skirmish of the Revolutionary War.

The events of the American Revolution are very much a part of present-day Lexington, a modern suburb that sprawls out from the historic sites near the town center. Although the downtown area is generally lively, with ice-cream and coffee shops, boutiques, and a great little movie theater, the town becomes especially animated each Patriots' Day (celebrated on the third Monday in April), when costume-clad groups re-create the minutemen's battle maneuvers, and "Paul Revere" rides again.

Numbers in the margin correspond to points of interest on the Lexington map.

❶ On April 18, 1775, Paul Revere went to the **Hancock-Clarke House** and roused patriots John Hancock and Sam Adams, who were in Concord to attend the Provincial Congress then in session. Revere had ridden out from Boston "to spread the alarm / Through every Middlesex village and farm," as Henry Wadsworth Longfellow's "Paul Revere's Ride" has it. After Hancock and Adams got the message, they fled to avoid capture. The house, a parsonage built in 1698, is a 10-minute walk from Lexington Common. A free 30-minute tour is offered. ⌧*36 Hancock St.* ☎*781/862-1703* ⊕*www.lexingtonhistory.org* 🎫*$5, $12 combination ticket includes Buckman Tavern and Munroe Tavern* ⊙*Mid-May–Oct., daily 11–2.*

❷ The minutemen gathered at the **Buckman Tavern** (1709) on the morning of April 19, 1775. A half-hour tour takes in the tavern's seven rooms, which have been restored to the way they looked in the 1770s. Among the objects on display is an old front door with a hole made by a British musket ball. ⌧*1 Bedford St.* ☎*781/862-1703* 🎫*$5, $12 combination ticket includes Hancock-Clarke House and Munroe Tavern* ⊙*Mid-Apr.–Oct., daily 10–4.*

❸ It was on **Battle Green**, a 2-acre triangle of land, that minuteman captain John Parker assembled his men in advance of the British soldiers, who were marching from Boston. (The minutemen were so called because they were able to prepare themselves at a minute's notice.) The British major John Pitcairn ordered his troops to surround the minutemen and disarm them but not to fire. A shot did ring out, and the rest is history. Two questions remain unanswered: Who fired that first shot? And why did Parker, a seasoned veteran of the Seven Years' War, position his men behind a two-story, barnlike meetinghouse, from which the minutemen weren't able to see the British advancing, much less make a show of resistance? Indeed, why didn't Captain Parker tell his men to take to the

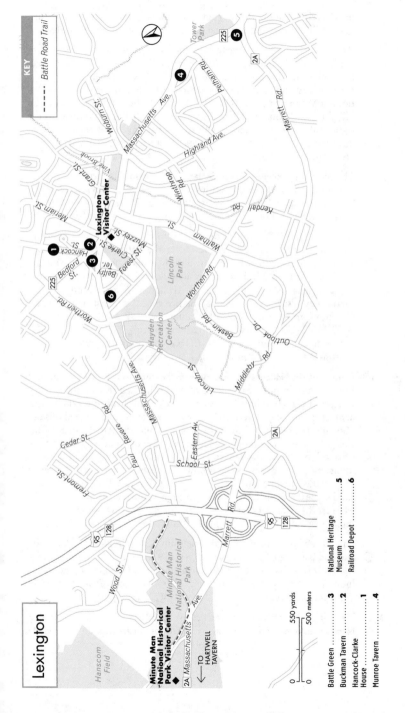

Lexington

KEY

---- Battle Road Trail

Battle Green **3**
Buckman Tavern **2**
Hancock-Clarke
House **1**
Munroe Tavern **4**
National Heritage
Museum **5**
Railroad Depot **6**

8

hills overlooking the British route? It was an absurd situation: 77 men against 700, turning it into one of history's most notorious mishaps.

Parker's role in the American Revolution is commemorated in Henry Hudson Kitson's renowned 1900 sculpture, the *Minuteman* **statue.** Facing downtown Lexington at the tip of Battle Green, the statue's in a traffic island and therefore makes for a difficult photo op. The **Revolutionary Monument,** near the statue, marks the burial site of minutemen killed in battle on April 19, 1775. The **Line of Battle boulder,** to the right of the statue, is incised with the words Captain Parker gave that morning to his 77 men: STAND YOUR GROUND, DON'T FIRE UNLESS FIRED UPON; BUT IF THEY MEAN TO HAVE WAR, LET IT BEGIN HERE.

The pleasant **Lexington Visitor Center,** across from the Battle Green, has a diorama of the 1775 clash, plus a gift shop. ⊠*Lexington Chamber of Commerce, 1875 Massachusetts Ave.* ☎781/862–1450 ⊕*www. lexingtonchamber.org* ☉*Apr.–Nov., daily 9–5; Dec.–Mar., daily 10–4.*

As April 19, 1775, dragged on, British forces met fierce resistance in Concord. Dazed and demoralized after the battle at Concord's Old ❹ North Bridge, the British regrouped at the **Munroe Tavern** (1695) while the Munroe family hid in nearby woods. The troops then retreated through what is now the town of Arlington. After a bloody battle there, they returned to Boston. The tavern is 1 mi east of Lexington Common; tours last about 30 minutes. ⊠*1332 Massachusetts Ave.* ☎781/862–1703 ⊕*www.lexingtonhistory.org* ▦*$5, $12 combination ticket includes Hancock-Clarke House and Buckman Tavern* ☉*Mid-May–Oct., 1 tour daily at 3* PM.

❺ Ironically, the **National Heritage Museum,** devoted to the nation's cultural heritage and in one of its oldest towns, is housed in a contemporary brick-and-glass building. This small but dynamic institution showcases artifacts from early American life and an evocative, ongoing exhibition, "Sowing the Seeds of Liberty: Lexington and the American Revolution," recounts the events of the Battle of Lexington through the tales of two local figures: the militia's Captain Parker and Jonas Clarke, a minister. Younger visitors can follow the exhibition under the guidance of Billy the Patriot Mouse. The museum's Courtyard Café serves soups, sandwiches, and snacks Tuesday through Saturday 11:30–2:30. ⊠*33 Marrett Rd., Rte. 2A at Massachusetts Ave.* ☎781/861–6559 ⊕*www. monh.org* ▦*Donations accepted* ☉*Mon.–Sat. 10–5, Sun. noon–5.*

One of the last remaining shed-style train depots in New England, the ❻ **Railroad Depot** has been renovated to its 1912 state. Inside, the Lexington Historical Society stages changing exhibits on Lexington, the Revolutionary War, and railroad history. ⊠*13 Depot Sq.* ☎781/862–1703 ⊕*www.lexingtonhistory.org* ▦*Free* ☉*Weekdays 8:30–4:30.*

★ ☽   West of Lexington's center stretches the 1,000-acre, 3-parcel **Minute Man National Historical Park,** which also extends into nearby Lincoln and Concord. Begin your park visit at Lexington's **Minute Man Visitor Center** to see its free multimedia presentation, "The Road to Revolution," a captivating introduction to the events of April 1775. Then, continuing along Route 2A toward Concord, you pass the point where Revere's midnight ride ended with his capture by the British; it's marked with a boulder and plaque, as well as an enclosure where rangers sometimes give educational presentations. You can also visit the 1732 **Hartwell Tavern** (open May through October daily 9:30–5), a restored drover's (driver's) tavern staffed by park employees in period costume. They frequently demonstrate musket firing or open-hearth cooking, and children are likely to enjoy the reproduction colonial toys.

The best way to see the park is along some or all of **Battle Road Trail,** a stroller- and wheelchair-accessible path through the park that roughly follows the route the British took to and from Boston during the battle of Lexington and Concord. Pick up a map at the visitor center. Because the path follows or parallels Route 2A for much of its 5-mi length, you can see much of it from the car as well. ⊠ *Rte. 2A, ¼ mi west of Rte. 128* ☎ *978/369–6993* ⊕ *www.nps.gov/mima* ☉ *May–Oct., daily 9–5; Nov.–Apr., call for times.*

OFF THE BEATEN PATH

Jason Russell House. As the Redcoats retreated from Lexington and Concord on April 19, 1775, they traveled through the town of Arlington, where minutemen peppered them with musket fire from behind stone walls and pine trees. The bullet-ridden Jason Russell House marks the site of the bloodiest fighting, where Russell, 11 minutemen, and several British soldiers were killed. Today the interior displays period kitchenware, spinning wheels, and even a Revolutionary War cannonball that once hit the house. Adjoining the Jason Russell House, a modern structure houses the George Abbott Smith History Museum, with changing exhibits on Arlington history. ⊠ *7 Jason St., at Massachusetts Ave., Arlington* ⊹ *5 mi southeast of Lexington* ☎ *781/648–4300* ⊕ *www.arlingtonhistorical.org* 🎟 *$3* ☉ *Mid-Apr.–Oct., weekends 1–4, or by appointment; call for tour schedules.*

WHERE TO EAT

$–$$ ✕**Bertucci's.** Part of a popular chain, this family-friendly Italian restaurant has good food, reasonable prices, and a large menu. Specialties include veal saltimbocca, lobster ravioli, and brick-oven pizzas. ⊠ *1777 Massachusetts Ave.* ☎ *781/860–9000* ⊕ *www.bertuccis.com* ⊟ *AE, D, DC, MC, V.*

$ ✕**Khushboo.** The steady crowd of local Indian-origin diners at this bright, second-story space on Lexington's main street testifies to the authenticity of the sophisticated Indian menu here. ⊠ *1709 Massachusetts Ave.* ☎ *781/863–2900* ⊟ *MC, V.*

CONCORD

Fodor'sChoice   *10 mi west of Lexington, 21 mi northwest of Boston.*
★
Numbers in the margin correspond to points of interest on the Concord map.

Concord today is a modern suburb with a busy town center stocked with arty shops, places to eat, and (recalling the literary history made here) old bookstores. It's a great place to start your foliage tour: from Boston, head west along Route 2 to Concord, and then continue on to find harvest stands and do-it-yourself apple picking around Harvard and Stow.

To reach Concord from Lexington, take Routes 4/225 through Bedford and Route 62 West to Concord; or pick up Route 2A West from Massachusetts Avenue (known locally as "Mass Ave.") at the National Heritage Museum or by taking Waltham Street south from Lexington Center.

★ ☉   The **Minute Man National Historical Park,** along Route 2A, is a three-parcel park with 1,000 acres. The park contains many of the sites important to Concord's role in the Revolution, including Old North Bridge, as well as two visitor centers, one each in Concord and Lexington. Although the initial Revolutionary War sorties were in Lexington, word of the American losses spread rapidly to surrounding towns: when the British marched into Concord, more than 400 minutemen were waiting. A marker set in the stone wall along Liberty Street, behind the North Bridge Visitors Center, announces, ON THIS FIELD THE MINUTEMEN AND MILITIA FORMED BEFORE MARCHING DOWN TO THE FIGHT AT THE BRIDGE. The **North Bridge Visitor Center** (✉ *174 Liberty St.* ☎978/369–6993) is open from May through October, daily 9–5. If you're visiting between November and April, call for hours. ✉ *Bounded by Monument St., Liberty St., and Lowell Rd.* ⊕*www.nps.gov/mima* ☉ *Daily dawn–dusk.*

➐   You can reach the North Bridge section of the Minute Man Park by
Fodor'sChoice   water if you rent a canoe at the **South Bridge Boat House** and paddle along
★   the Sudbury and Concord rivers. ✉*496–502 Main St.* ☎978/369–9438 ☉ *Apr.–Nov., weekdays 10–dusk, weekends and holidays 9–dusk.*

➑   At **Old North Bridge,** ½ mi north of Concord center, the Concord minutemen turned the tables on the British in the morning of April 19, 1775. The Americans didn't fire first, but when two of their own fell dead from a Redcoat volley, Major John Buttrick of Concord roared, "Fire, fellow soldiers, for God's sake, fire." The minutemen released volley after volley, and the Redcoats fled. Daniel Chester French's famous statue *The Minuteman* (1875) honors those brave rebels.

Of the confrontation, Ralph Waldo Emerson wrote in 1837: "By the rude bridge that arched the flood / Their flag to April's breeze unfurled / Here once the embattled farmers stood / And fired the shot heard round the world." (The lines are inscribed at the foot of *The Minuteman* statue). Concord claims the right to the "shot," believing that native son Emerson was, of course, referring to the North Bridge standoff.

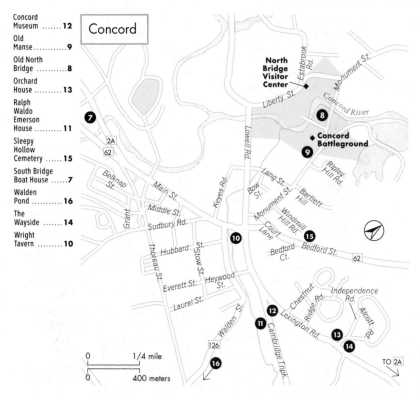

Park Service officials skirt the issue, saying the shot could refer to the battle on Lexington Green, when the very first shot rang out from an unknown source, or to Concord when minutemen held back the Redcoats in the Revolution's first major battle, or even to the Boston Massacre. ✉ *Off Liberty St. on path from North Bridge Visitor Center.*

❾ The Reverend William Emerson, grandfather of Ralph Waldo Emerson, watched rebels and Redcoats battle from behind his home, the **Old Manse,** which was within sight of Old North Bridge. The house, built in 1770, was occupied constantly by the Emerson family, except for the 3½-year period during which Nathaniel Hawthorne rented the manse. Furnishings date from the late 18th century. Tours run throughout the day and last 45 minutes, with a new tour starting within 15 minutes of when the first person signs up. ✉ *269 Monument St.* ☎ *978/369–3909* ⊕ *www.oldmanse.org* 💲 *$8* 🕐 *Mid-Apr.–Oct., Mon.–Sat. 10–5, Sun. noon–5; last tour departs at 4:30.*

❿ **Wright Tavern,** built in 1747, served as headquarters first for the minutemen, then the British, both on April 19, 1775. It's closed to the public. ✉ *2 Lexington Rd.*

⓫ The 19th-century essayist and poet Ralph Waldo Emerson lived briefly in the Old Manse in 1834–35, then moved to what is known as the

Ralph Waldo Emerson House, where he lived until his death in 1882. Here he wrote the *Essays* ("To be great is to be misunderstood"; "A foolish consistency is the hobgoblin of little minds"). Except for pieces from Emerson's study, now at the nearby Concord Museum, the Emerson House furnishings have been preserved as the writer left them. You must join one of the half-hour-long tours to see the interior. ⊠*28 Cambridge Tpke., at Lexington Rd.* ☎*978/369–2236* ⊕*www.rwe. org* ⊠*$7* ⊙*Mid-Apr.–mid Oct., Thurs.–Sat. 10–4:30, Sun. 1–4:30; call for tour schedule.*

 ⑫ The original contents of Emerson's private study, as well as the world's largest collection of Thoreau artifacts, are in the **Concord Museum.** The museum, in a 1930 Colonial Revival building just east of the town center, provides a good overview of the town's history, from its original Native American settlement to the present. Highlights include Native American artifacts, furnishings from Thoreau's Walden Pond cabin, and one of the two lanterns hung at Boston's Old North Church to signal that the British were coming by sea. If you've brought the children, ask for a free family activity pack. In summer the museum has extended hours on Sunday. ⊠*200 Lexington Rd., entrance on Cambridge Tpke.* ☎*978/369–9763* ⊕*www.concordmuseum.org* ⊠*$8* ⊙*Apr.–Dec., Mon.–Sat. 9–5, Sun. noon–5; Jan.–Mar., Mon.–Sat. 11–4, Sun. 1–4.*

⑬ The dark-brown exterior of Louisa May Alcott's family home, **Orchard House,** sharply contrasts with the light, wit, and energy so much in evidence inside. Named for the apple orchard that once surrounded it, Orchard House was the Alcott family home from 1857 to 1877. Because Orchard House had just one owner after the Alcotts left and because it became a museum in 1911, many of the original furnishings remain, including the semicircular shelf-desk where Louisa wrote *Little Women,* based on her life with her three sisters. Louisa's father, Bronson, founded his school of philosophy here; the building remains behind the house. ⊠*399 Lexington Rd.* ☎*978/369–4118* ⊕*www.louisamayalcott.org* ⊠*$8, tours free* ⊙*Apr.–Oct., Mon.–Sat. 10–4:30, Sun. 1–4:30; Nov.– Mar., weekdays 11–3, Sat. 10–4:30, Sun. 1–4:30. Half-hr tours begin every 30 mins Apr.–Oct.; call for off-season tour schedule.*

⑭ In 1852 Nathaniel Hawthorne bought a rambling structure called the **Wayside,** and lived here until his death in 1864. The subsequent owner, Margaret Sidney, wrote the children's book *Five Little Peppers and How They Grew* (1881). Before Hawthorne moved in, the Alcotts lived here, from 1845 to 1848. An exhibit center, in the former barn, provides information about the Wayside authors and links them to major events in American history. If you join one of the 35-minute tours, you can see the interior of the main house, with its displays of memorabilia. Hawthorne's tower-study is substantially as he left it, complete with his stand-up writing desk. ⊠*455 Lexington Rd.* ☎*978/369–6993* ⊠*Free, tours $4* ⊙*May–Oct., call for tour schedule.*

⑮ Each Memorial Day, Louisa May Alcott's grave in the nearby **Sleepy Hollow Cemetery** is decorated in commemoration of her death. Along with Emerson, Thoreau, and Hawthorne, Alcott is buried in a section of the cemetery known as Author's Ridge. ⊠ *Bedford St. (Rte. 62)* ☎ *978/318–3233* ⏱ *Daily dawn–dusk.*

NEED A BREAK? Locals swear by the freshly roasted turkey sandwiches at the Country Kitchen (⊠ *181 Sudbury Rd.* ☎ *978/371–0181*), a modest take-out counter in a yellow house around the corner from the Concord train station. You can get deli fare, homemade soups, and salads to go weekdays from 5 AM to 4 PM.

★ ⑯ ⏰ A trip to Concord can include a pilgrimage to **Walden Pond,** Henry David Thoreau's most famous residence. Here, in 1845, at age 28, Thoreau moved into a one-room cabin—built for $28.12½¢ Living alone for the next two years, Thoreau discovered the benefits of solitude and the beauties of nature.

The site of Thoreau's cabin—discovered only a few decades ago—is staked out in stone. A full-size, authentically furnished reproduction of the cabin stands about ½ mi from the original site, near the parking lot. Its sparseness is stirring, even if—truth be told—Thoreau was not actually that far from civilization: the railroad ran nearby and he could (and did) simply walk into town. Nevertheless, standing at the pond, particularly in cold weather when the tourist throngs are gone, you may be moved to "simplify, simplify" your life.

Now, as in Thoreau's time, the pond is a delightful summertime spot for swimming, fishing, and rowing, and there's hiking in the nearby woods. To get here from the center of Concord—a trip of only 1½ mi—take Concord's Main Street a block west from Monument Square, turn left onto Walden Street, and head for the intersection of Routes 2 and 126. Cross over Route 2 onto Route 126, heading south for ½ mi. The entrance to the state reservation is on the left. Parking is extremely tight in summer; call ahead to find out the next hour at which the lot will open again (only a certain number of visitors are allowed in at a time). The parking lot is across the road from the pond. ⊠ *95 Walden St. (Rte. 126)* ☎ *978/369–3254* ⊕ *www.magnet.state.ma.us/dcr/parks/northeast/wldn.htm* ⏎ *Free, parking $5* ⏱ *Daily 8 AM–approximately ½ hr before sunset, weather permitting.*

WHERE TO EAT

$$–$$$ ✕ **Walden Grille.** In this old brick firehouse–turned–dining-room, satisfy your appetite with tempting contemporary dishes like duck sausage with scallion potato pancakes. There are the usual pizzas, salads, and sandwiches, too, as well as entrées like bone-in flounder or veal medallions with kale and bacon. ⊠ *24 Walden St.* ☎ *978/371–2233* 🗖 *AE, D, MC, V.*

¢–$ ✕ **La Provence.** This stylish café and take-out shop has a little taste of France. It's opposite the Concord train station, and makes a good stop for a light meal. Start off the morning with a croissant or brioche, and at midday you can pick up sandwiches (perhaps pâté and cheese or French ham), quiches, or heartier fare like rotisserie chicken, beef bourguignonne, and salmon au champagne. Leave room for an éclair or a petite fruit tart. Just don't plan a late night here; the café closes at 7 PM during the week and at 5:30 on Saturday. ⊠ *105 Thoreau St.* ☎ *978/371–7428* 🗖 *D, MC, V* ⏱ *Closed Sun.*

8

SUDBURY

⑰   *20 mi west of Boston.*

Sudbury, an attractive but nondescript Boston bedroom community on Route 20, has an important literary history. Here you find **Longfellow's Wayside Inn,** which was restored, beginning in 1923, by auto titan Henry Ford. Known originally in the 1700s as How's Inn, the tavern became forever linked with the poet Henry Wadsworth Longfellow when his *Tales of a Wayside Inn* was published in 1863. The inn is far from a museum—you can still get a traditional meal and a bed for the night. The grounds include a working reproduction of an 18th-century **gristmill;** the 1798 **schoolhouse** that "Mary" and her "little lamb" reportedly attended (moved here by Ford in 1926 from Sterling, Massachusetts); and the **Martha-Mary Chapel,** which Ford built in 1940 in memory of his mother-in-law and his mother. ⊠ *Wayside Inn Rd. off Boston Post Rd. (Rte. 20)* ☎ *978/443–1776 or 800/339–1776* ⊕ *www. wayside.org.*

OFF THE BEATEN PATH

Garden in the Woods. Botanically minded Bostonians visit the garden to glimpse stunning trees, wildflowers, and shrubs from early spring until the end of foliage season. The 45-acre garden has nearly 3 mi of trails and is planted with more than 1,500 kinds of plants, all native to North America, roughly 200 of them rare or endangered. Be sure to check out the nursery, which has 500 different species for sale, the largest selection of native plants on the continent. Self-guiding booklets are available, and informal guided walks are given at 10 AM every day except Sunday, when the walks are at 2 PM. Tours for those with disabilities are provided in golf carts. The garden is about 1½ mi south of Route 20; call or check the Web site for detailed directions. ⊠ *180 Hemenway Rd., Framingham* ✛ *3½ mi south of Sudbury* ☎ *508/877-7630* ⊕ *www.newenglandwildflower.org* ⊠ *$7* ☾ *Mid-Apr.–mid-June, daily 9–7 (trails closed); mid-June–Oct., Tues.–Sun. 9–5; last admission 1 hr before closing.*

WHERE TO STAY & EAT

$–$$ ✕☷ **Longfellow's Wayside Inn.** Billed as America's oldest operating inn, the Wayside was built as a two-room homestead in 1702; owner David How expanded the building and began offering lodging in 1716. Guest rooms are furnished with colonial-style antiques. In the dining room ($$–$$$), you may want to start with a "coow woow," a rum-and-ginger concoction that's supposedly America's first cocktail, and continue with Yankee pot roast, baked stuffed fillet of sole, or other New England classics. ⊠ *72 Wayside Inn Rd., off Boston Post Rd. (Rte. 20), 01776* ☎ *978/443–1776 or 800/339–1776* ☐ *978/443–8041* ⊕ *www. wayside.org* ↩ *10 rooms* ⬙ *In-room: no TV. In-hotel: restaurant, bar* ⊟ *AE, D, DC, MC, V* ⦿ *BP.*

LOWELL

18 *30 mi northwest of Boston.*

Everyone knows that the American Revolution began in Massachusetts. But the commonwealth, and in particular the Merrimack Valley, also nurtured the Industrial Revolution. Lowell's first mill opened in 1823; by the 1850s, 40 factories employed thousands of workers and produced 2 million yards of cloth every week.

The **Lowell National Historical Park** tracks the history of a gritty era when the power loom was the symbol of economic power and progress. It encompasses several blocks in the downtown area, including former mills–turned–museums, a network of canals, and a helpful visitor center.

In summer, the Lowell Spinners, Lowell's new minor-league baseball team, plays in a ballpark just outside the town center. For all of Lowell's ties to the mainstream of American mill town history, its character also stems from its ethnic diversity, a legacy of the days when immigrants from all over North America and Europe came to work in the textile mills. Irish and French-Canadians came first, then the Greeks, but today, Cambodians and Laotians represent one of Lowell's growing ethnic enclaves.

A noted son of French-Canadian Lowell was the late Beat poet and novelist **Jack Kerouac,** born here in 1922. Kerouac's memory is honored in the **Eastern Canal Park** (⊠*Bridge St. near Boott Cotton Mills Museum*), where plaques bear quotes from his novels. Every October "Lowell Celebrates Kerouac" offers academic symposia, music, and coffeehouse poetry. Why October? "I was going home in October. Everyone goes home in October," he wrote in *On the Road*. His grave is in **Edson Cemetery,** 2 mi south of the Lowell Connector, the highway linking Lowell with Interstate 495.

The **National Park Visitor Center** in the Market Mills Complex offers a thorough introduction to the city. The 1902 Market Mills building was the headquarters of the Lowell Manufacturing Company at the height of Lowell's mill days. The visitor center has a free parking lot and makes a good starting point with the orientation film *Lowell: The Industrial Revelation*. The city's museums and historic sights spread out in three directions from here. Pick up a map for a self-guided walking tour that highlights aspects of local history, from the ubiquitous "mill girls" (young women who toiled up to 13 hours a day in factories) to the city's 5½ mi of canals. Park rangers give guided tours on foot year-round and on turn-of-the-20th-century trolleys and canal barges March through November. ⊠*246 Market St.* ☎*978/970–5000* ⊕*www.nps.gov/lowe* ⊠*Free, barge tours $10, trolley and walking tours $6* ☉*July–early Sept., daily 9–6; early Sept.–June, daily 9–5.*

The **Boott Cotton Mills Museum,** about a 10-minute walk northeast from the National Park Visitor Center, is the first major National Park Service museum devoted to industrialization. The textile worker's grueling life is shown with all its grit, noise, and dust. You know you're in for an unusual experience when you're handed earplugs—they're for the re-creation of a 1920s "weave room," authentic down to the deafening roar of 88 working power looms. Other exhibits at the complex include weaving artifacts, cloth samples, video interviews with workers, and a large, meticulous scale model of 19th-century production. The complex housing the museum also holds the **Tsongas Industrial History Center** (third floor), an educational center named for the late U.S. Senator Paul Tsongas, a Lowell legend. ⊠*115 John St.* ☎*978/970–5000* ⌨*$6* ⊙*Apr.–Nov., daily 9:30–5; Dec., daily 9:30–4:30; Jan.–Mar., Mon.–Sat. 9:30–4:30, Sun. 11–4:30.*

The **Mill Girls & Immigrants Exhibit** records the triumphs and sorrows of both mill workers and immigrants. Upstairs there's a poignant display of letters and books belonging to several mill girls; downstairs, a kitchen and parlor show how they lived; there's even a display on the food they gulped down during 30-minute breaks in their long work days. Immigrants, from the Irish to Cambodians, are celebrated with photos, video, and historical artifacts. The exhibit is housed in the Patrick J. Mogan Cultural Center, which also includes the University of Massachusetts's Center for Lowell History, an excellent resource for anyone interested in genealogy. ⊠*40 French St.* ☎*978/970–5000* ⌨*Free* ⊙*Apr.–Nov., daily 1–5; Dec., daily 1–4:30; Jan.–Mar., weekends 1–4:30.*

The small but charming **New England Quilt Museum** displays antique and contemporary examples of quilting, banishing any doubts you might have about whether quilting is an art form. The museum closes briefly several times a year to install new exhibits, so call before making a special trip. ⊠*18 Shattuck St.* ☎*978/452–4207* ⊕*www.nequiltmuseum.org* ⌨*$5* ⊙*May–Dec., Tues.–Sat. 10–4, Sun. noon–4; Jan.–Apr., Tues.–Sat. 10–4.*

The **Brush Art Gallery,** in the Market Mills Complex, mounts changing exhibitions and hosts open studios, which spotlight Lowell's cultural diversity. ⊠*256 Market St.* ☎*978/459–7819* ⊕*www.thebrush.org* ⊙*Apr.–Dec., Tues.–Sat. 11–4, Sun. noon–4; Jan.–Mar., Wed.–Sun. noon–4.*

The **American Textile History Museum,** in a former Civil War–era mill, tells the story of American textiles from 1700 to 1950 and includes an 18th-century waterwheel, a 1950s "weave room" where fabrics are still made, and hundreds of artifacts, like a gentleman's gold silk robe from the 1830s. Changing exhibits, such as a display of Hawaiian shirts, sometimes require an extra admission fee. ⊠*491 Dutton St.* ☎*978/441–0400* ⊕*www.athm.org* ⌨*$8* ⊙*Thurs. and Fri. 9–4, weekends 10–5.*

Two blocks northwest of the National Park Visitor Center is the birthplace and museum of American artist James McNeill Whistler. The Lowell Art Association purchased the gray clapboard house (built in 1823) to preserve the painter's roots in his real hometown (Whistler claimed that he was a Baltimore native). Inside, the **Whistler House Museum of Art** displays the museum's permanent collections, including a number of Whistler's etchings, as well as works by late-19th- and early-20th-century American representational artists. Hour-long tours are available. ⊠243 *Worthen St.* ☎978/452–7641 ⊕*www.whistler-house.org* ⊠*$5, tours free* ⊙ *Wed.–Sat. 11–4; call for tour schedule.*

WHERE TO EAT

$–$$ ╳**Cobblestones.** Housed within an old, brick boardinghouse in Lowell National Historical Park, this lively bar and grill is *the* place to eat, drink, and be merry in Lowell. The atmosphere is buttoned-down, the wild-game specials are worth any wait, and they've got a superlative mac and cheese on the dinner menu. A more-adult choice is the chef's garlicky fisherman's stew. On weekends, the crowds can be prohibitive. ⊠*91 Dutton St.* ☎978/970–2282 ⊟*AE, D, MC, V.*

THE NORTH SHORE

The slice of Massachusetts's Atlantic Coast known as the North Shore extends past grimy docklands, through Boston's well-to-do northern suburbs, to the picture-perfect Cape Ann region, and beyond Cape Ann to Newburyport, just south of the New Hampshire border. In addition to miles of fine beaches, the North Shore encompasses Marblehead, a picture-postcard New England sea town; Salem, which thrives on a history of witches, millionaires, and the maritime trades; Gloucester, the oldest seaport in America; colorful Rockport, crammed with crafts shops and artists' studios; and Newburyport, with its redbrick center and rows of clapboard Federal mansions. Bright and bustling in summer, the North Shore is calmer between November and June, with many restaurants, inns, and attractions operating reduced hours or closing entirely. Call ahead off-season.

MARBLEHEAD

⑲ *17 mi north of Boston.*

Numbers in the margin correspond to points of interest on the North Shore map.

Marblehead is a find. It's a miniature and manageable New England seaport village with cute shops, wonderful historic buildings, and jaw-dropping water views. Easy to reach from Boston, even without a car, its narrow and winding streets, old clapboard houses, and sea captains' mansions retain much of the character of the village founded in 1629 by fishermen from Cornwall and the Channel Islands. This is one of New England's premier sailing capitals, and Race Week (usually the last week of July) attracts boats from all along the eastern seaboard. The proud spirit of the ambitious merchant sailors who made Marblehead prosper in the 18th century can still be felt in many of the impressive Georgian mansions that line the downtown streets. ■TIP➔ **Parking in town can be difficult; try the lot at the end of Front Street, the lot on State Street by the Landing restaurant, or the metered areas on the street.** You may want to pay a call to the chamber of commerce, which has a complete visitor

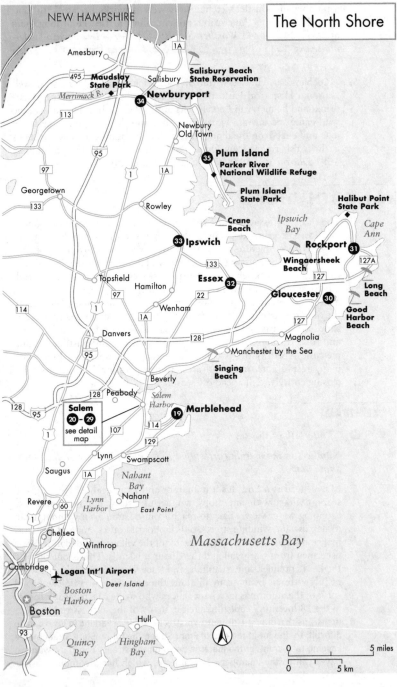

The North Shore

NEW HAMPSHIRE

Amesbury

495 Maudslay
State Park   Salisbury   Salisbury Beach
State Reservation
Merrimack R.   34 Newburyport
113

Newbury
Old Town
95
97
1   1A   35 Plum Island
Parker River
National Wildlife Refuge
Georgetown
133   Rowley   Plum Island
State Park
Halibut Point
State Park
Crane   Ipswich
Beach   Bay   Cape
Ann
33 Ipswich
Topsfield   133   Rockport 31
Wingaersheek   127A
97   Hamilton   Beach   127
Essex 32
Wenham   22   Gloucester 30   Long
114   1   Beach
1A
128   Good
Danvers   128   Magnolia   Harbor
95   127   Beach
Manchester by the Sea
Beverly   Singing
Beach
128 Peabody
Salem
Harbor
Salem   19 Marblehead
128   20 – 29
95   see detail   107   114
1   map   129
Lynn   Swampscott
Saugus   1A
Nahant
Bay
Revere 60   Lynn   Nahant
1   Harbor   East Point
Chelsea
Winthrop   Massachusetts Bay
Cambridge
Logan Int'l Airport
Boston   Deer Island
Harbor
Boston
Hull
93
Quincy   Hingham
Bay   Bay

0   5 miles
0   5 km

guide with a suggested walking tour of the city. Plaques placed on many homes note the date of construction and the original owner.

Marblehead's 18th-century high society is exemplified in the **Jeremiah Lee Mansion,** run by the town's historical society. Colonel Lee was one of the wealthiest people in the colonies in 1768, and although few furnishings original to the house remain, the rich mahogany paneling, unique hand-painted wallpaper, and other appointments, as well as a fine collection of traditional North Shore furniture, provide clues into the life of an American gentleman. The mansion is open for guided tours only. ✉ *161 Washington St.* ☎ *781/631–1768* ⊕ *www.marbleheadmuseum.org* ⊠ *Tours $5* ⏱ *June–Oct., Tues.–Sat. 10–4.*

A MARBLEHEAD MOMENT

It doesn't get more Massachusetts than this: Stop at the Selectman's Room at Abbott Hall in Marblehead to see Archibald M. Willard's painting of the *The Spirit of '76,* one of the most famous icons of Revolutionary-era art (even though it was painted a century *after* the Revolution.) The monumental painting of three patriots—a boy, a white-haired veteran, and a man in his prime—striding across a smoking battleground, with drum and fife, makes even the most cynical viewer pause for patriotic thought.

Across the street from the Jeremiah Lee Mansion, the **Marblehead Museum & Historical Society** runs two small galleries, one with changing exhibits about the area's history, the other displaying paintings of Marblehead and the surrounding seas by folk artist J.O.J. Frost (1852–1928). ✉ *170 Washington St.* ☎ *781/631–1768* ⊕ *www.marbleheadmuseum.org* ⊠ *Free* ⏱ *Tues.–Sat. 10–4.*

The town's Victorian-era municipal building, **Abbott Hall,** built in 1876, displays Archibald Willard's painting *The Spirit of '76,* one of the country's most beloved icons of patriotism. Many visitors, familiar since childhood with this image of the three Revolutionary veterans with fife, drum, and flag, are surprised to find the original

OPEN HOUSE

Several times during the year the Marblehead Historical Society runs Historic House Tours. Contact the **Marblehead Museum & Historical Society** (☎ 781/631-1768) for dates and reservations.

in an otherwise unassuming town hall. Also on-site is a small naval museum exploring Marblehead's maritime past. ✉ *188 Washington St.* ☎ *781/631–0000* ⊠ *Free* ⏱ *Mon., Tues., and Thurs. 8–5; Wed. 7:30–7:30; Fri. 8–1; weekends 10–5.*

Most of the exclusive estate-filled Marblehead Neck (a finger of land locals call "the Neck") neighborhood is privately owned, but you're free to explore it on foot. **Castle Rock** is a spectacular bit of granite that juts into the Atlantic. A well-hidden path leads to the small, rocky point and offers the views that explain why the Neck is one of the most sought-after addresses in New England. The spot got its name from the adjacent house—a large stone manor known as the Castle. ⊠*Enter through wrought-iron fence on 300 block of Ocean Ave..*

WHERE TO STAY & EAT

$$-$$$ ✕**The Landing.** Crisply outfitted in nautical blues and whites, this pleasant restaurant sits right on Marblehead Harbor, with walls of windows on two sides and a deck that's nearly afloat. The menu mixes classic New England fare (clam chowder, lobster, broiled scrod) with more-contemporary dishes like roast duck with Gran Marnier cranberry glaze. Brunch is served on Sunday. The pub area has a lighter menu of sandwiches and salads. ⊠*81 Front St.* ☎*781/639–1266* ⊕*www.thelandingrestaurant. com* ⊟*AE, D, DC, MC, V.*

$$ ✕**The Barnacle.** This is a classic
Fodor'sChoice   North Shore waterfront haunt that serves fisherman's platters and lob-
★   sters every which way. The bar and dining room bustle with locals whose faces call to mind Archibald Willard's painting *The Spirit of '76*, which hangs just up the street in the town hall. The exquisite view can be appreciated all the more from the outdoor wraparound deck seating in summer. Do not pass on the clam chowder. ⊠*141 Front St.* ☎*781/631–4236* ⊟*DC, MC, V.*

$$-$$$ ⬚**Harbor Light Inn.** Housed in a pair of adjoining 18th-century man-
Fodor'sChoice   sions, this elegant inn is handsomely appointed with Federalist antiques
★   and reproductions. Ask for a room with a brick fireplace. Many rooms have skylights and whirlpools; a soaring ceiling on the top floor reveals the original post-and-beam construction. Fresh-baked cookies served with cider (winter) or lemonade (summer) help make a stay here special. ⊠*58 Washington St., 01945* ☎*781/631–2186* ⊟*781/631–2216* ⊕*www.harborlightinn.com* ⬚*21 rooms* ⬚*In-room: VCR. In-hotel: pool, no elevator, no kids under 8* ⊟*AE, MC, V* ⊙*CP.*

$ ⬚**Harborside House.** Built in 1850 by a ship's carpenter, Marblehead's oldest B&B has a stunning view of the sailboats in the harbor from its living room. Owner Susan Livingston, a town resident since the 1960s, is a charming and considerate hostess. The simple and spacious rooms have floral wallpaper and polished wide-board floors. In warm weather, take your breakfast on the sunny garden patio. The common rooms have a working fireplace and a TV. ⊠*23 Gregory St., 01945* ☎*781/631–1032* ⊕*www.harborsidehouse.com* ⬚*2 rooms without bath* ⬚*In-room: no a/c, no TV. In-hotel: no elevator, no kids under 8* ⊟*No credit cards* ⊙*CP.*

SAILIN' SALEM

Salem's maritime history includes dastardly pirates, daring sea voyages, and whaling ships. Be sure to find an hour to tour the Peabody Essex Museum. Grab the free audio guide and register to tour the Yin Yu Tang, a reconstructed Chinese house. It's a perfect place to appreciate the history and effect of New England's seafaring trade, with its collection of maritime objects, American decorative art, and objects brought by the sailors from China, Oceania, Asia, and Europe. It's a great place for children, too—check out the Idea Center for Families in the museum.

SALEM

16 mi northeast of Boston, 4 mi west of Marblehead.

Numbers in the margin correspond to points of interest on the Salem map.

Salem unabashedly calls itself "Witch City." Witches astride broomsticks decorate the police cars; numerous witch-related attractions and shops, as well as resident witchcraft practitioners, recall the city's infamous connection with the witchcraft hysteria and trials of 1692.

The incident began in January of that year, when a couple of Salem-area girls fell ill and accused several townspeople of bewitching them. As the accusations continued and increased, more than 150 men and women were charged with practicing witchcraft, a crime punishable by death. After the resulting trials later that year, 19 innocent people were hanged, and one was pressed to death by stones for refusing a trial. The present-day commercialization—some would say trivialization—of the event led in part to the dedication of a somber, reflective monument, the Salem Witch Trials Memorial. Just a few minutes away is a large statue of the "witch" from the *Bewitched* television series, making it difficult to appreciate the core political, moral, and religious issues of the day.

Salem has much more to offer than just black arts. Its more-modern charms include the well-restored Pickering Wharf, an important museum, trendy stores and restaurants, and a classic New England common with a children's playground. Also, thanks to three centuries of maritime trade, the city has one of the richest architectural and cultural histories in New England (⇨ *"It's Not All Hocus Pocus" box, below).*

❷⓪ The best place to start a Salem tour is the large **National Park Regional Visitor Center,** where you can pick up any of a vast library of booklets and pamphlets, including a "Maritime Trail" and "Early Settlement Trail" for Essex County, and watch a free 27-minute film about the history of the region. ⊠*2 New Liberty St.* ☎*978/740–1650* ⊕*www.nps.gov/sama* ☉*Daily 9–5.*

One way to explore Salem is to follow the 1¾-mi Heritage Trail (painted in red on the sidewalk) around town.

If you don't want to walk the Heritage Trail, the **Salem Trolley** has guided tours. You may get off and back on the trolley en route. ⊠*Essex and New Liberty Sts., next to National Park Service Visitor Center* ☎*978/744–5469* ⊕*www.salemtrolley.com* ⊠*$12* ☉*Hrs vary; call for schedule.*

★ **❷⓵** **The House of the Seven Gables,** immortalized in Nathaniel Hawthorne's classic novel, should not be missed. The house tour highlights include a secret staircase, a garret containing an antique scale model of the house, and some of the finest Georgian interiors in the country. The complex of 17th-century buildings includes the small house where Hawthorne was born in 1804; it was moved from its original location elsewhere in Salem. ⊠*54 Turner St., off Derby St.* ☎*978/744–0991*

It's Not All Hocus Pocus

From police cars to souvenir shops, Salem's modern image is dominated by witches. However, the witch-trial hysteria lasted less than a year, whereas Salem's seafaring history stretches out over three centuries.

In the second half of the 17th century, Salem ships played a key role in the triangular trade (rum for slaves for molasses), bringing money to the burgeoning colonies. That same affluence attracted pirates such as the notorious Kidd and Blackbeard, who prowled the North Shore looking for plunder. **New England Pirate Museum** (⊠ *274 Derby St.* ☎ *978/741–2800* ⊙ *May–Oct., daily 10–5; Nov., weekends 10–5*) is a goofy but amusing way to explore the era, with exhibits of real pirate treasures alongside an 80-foot "pirate's cave" stocked with pirate mannequins.

Salem's merchant vessels, such as the 1797 *Friendship*, were among the first to open trade routes with the Far East. Wealthy captains built many of the mansions that still grace the city's streets and brought back cultural artifacts from distant lands.

The **Salem Maritime National Historic Site** is an excellent place to start your exploration of Salem's seafaring past. For a more-visceral experience, consider a cruise. *Fame* (⊠ *Pickering Wharf* ☎ *978/729-7600* ⊕ *www.schoonerfame.com*), a reproduction of an 1812 privateer of the same name, takes passengers on a 100-minute tour into the storied past of Salem's waters.

⊕ *www.7gables.org* ✉ *$12* ⊙ *Nov., Dec., and mid-Jan.–June, daily 10–5; July–Oct., daily 10–7.*

⊙ ㉒ Near Derby Wharf is the 9¼-acre **Salem Maritime National Historic Site,** run by the National Park Service. The site focuses on Salem's heritage as a major seaport with a thriving overseas trade. It includes an orientation center with an 18-minute film; the 1762 home of Elias Derby, America's first millionaire; the 1819 Customs House, made famous in Nathaniel Hawthorne's *The Scarlet Letter*; the 1675 Narbonne House; the 1819 Public Stores; the 1826 Scale House; the West India Goods Store; and a reproduction of *The Friendship*, a 171-foot, three-masted 1797 merchant vessel. There's also an active lighthouse dating from 1871, as well as the nation's last surviving 18th-century wharves. ⊠ *193 Derby St.* ☎ *978/740-1660* ⊕ *www.nps.gov/sama* ✉ *Free, tours $5* ⊙ *Daily 9–5.*

NEED A BREAK?   **Boston Hotdog Company** (⊠ *60 Washington St.* ☎ *978/744-2320*) has a family-friendly menu with a broad selection of—what else?—hot dogs, from classic to gourmet, all for less than $3.50. Round out your bargain meal with coleslaw, baked beans, and draft root beer.

㉓ **The Peabody Essex Museum** is a must-see for any Salem visit. The collection, with particular attention to the link between New England and Asia, includes superlative exhibits of maritime items, Chinese export art, and American decorative arts. An expansion designed by Moshe Safdie added a new wing, making the building itself a work of stream-

Fodor'sChoice ★

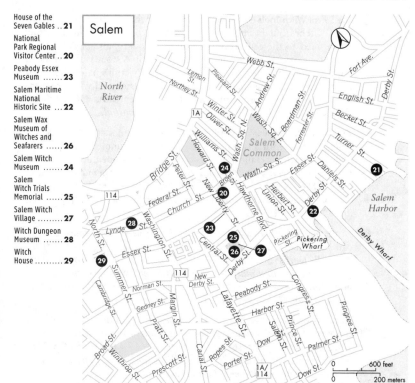

Salem

lined, glass art. Admission includes the house tour of three historic Salem mansions, which make for an interesting contrast with the Yin Yu Tang house, a 19th-century home transported from China and rebuilt in the museum's courtyard. ■**TIP→There's an additional $4 fee for viewing Yin Yu Tang, and timed tickets sell out quickly. Arrive early or order tickets online.** Be certain to look for the elaborate Japanese moon bed, the enormous wooden statue of Hawaiian god Kuka'ilimoku, and the ships' figureheads that grace the walls of the East India Marine Hall. A café in the soaring atrium is a good place for cheap snacks, but you may want to plan a meal at the elegant Garden Restaurant, which offers classic New England fare such as crab cakes or chowder, served on fine china and linen. The museum shop provides a major improvement on the typical garish witch souvenirs. ⊠ *East India Sq.* ☎*978/745–9500 or 866/745–1876* ⊕*www.pem.org* ☑*$13* ☉*Daily 10–5.*

🖐 **24** For an informative, if (extremely) hokey, introduction to the 1692 witchcraft hysteria, visit the **Salem Witch Museum.** A half-hour exhibit re-creates key scenes. A 10-minute walk-through exhibit describes witch history and witch hunts through the years. ⊠ *Washington Sq. N* ☎*978/744–1692* ⊕*www.salemwitchmuseum.com* ☑*$7.50* ☉*Sept.–June, daily 10–5; July and Aug., daily 10–7.*

㉕ **The Salem Witch Trials Memorial** honors those who died not because they
Fodor'sChoice were witches but because they refused to confess. This melancholy
★ space, next to the central burial ground, provides an antidote to the
relentless marketing of the merry-witches motif. A stone wall is studded
with 20 stone benches, each inscribed with a victim's name. Look for
the flagstones at one end of the plot that are engraved with protesta-
tions of innocence, sometimes cut off in mid-sentence. ⊠*Off Liberty
St. near Charter St.* ⊕*www.salemweb.com/memorial.*

㉖ **The Salem Wax Museum of Witches & Seafarers** presents sights and sounds
culled from a century of Salem's tragedies and triumphs. During weekends approaching Halloween, it sometimes stays open until 11 PM or
later. ⊠*288 Derby St.* ☏*978/298–2929* ⊕*www.salemwaxmuseum.
com* ⊠*$6, $10.95 combination ticket with Salem Witch Village*
☉*Nov.–Mar., daily 11–4; Apr.–June and Sept., daily 10–6; July, Aug.,
and Oct., daily 10–10.*

㉗ At the **Salem Witch Village,** across the street from the wax museum, you
can learn about historic and modern witchcraft's religious practices.
⊠*282R Derby St.* ☏*978/740–9229* ⊕*www.salemwitchvillage.net*
⊠*$6, $10.95 combination ticket with Salem Wax Museum* ☉*Nov.
and Dec., 10–5; Jan.–Mar., 11–4; Apr.–June and Sept., 10–6; July
&&and Aug., 10–9; Oct., 10–10.*

㉘ Accused witches were held in dungeons similar to those re-created at
the **Witch Dungeon Museum.** During the tour of the dungeons, a trial
is reenacted, using the 1692 transcripts. ⊠*16 Lynde St.* ☏*978/741–
3570* ⊕*www.witchdungeon.com* ⊠*$7* ☉*Apr.–Nov., daily 10–5; eve-
ning hrs around Halloween; tours every ½ hr.*

㉙ No witch ever lived at the **Witch House,** the former home of witch-
trial magistrate Jonathan Corwin, but it's the only remaining structure with direct ties to the 1692 trials; the interior is authentic to the
period. You must take a 30-minute tour to see the interior. ⊠*310½
Essex St.* ☏*978/744–8815* ⊕*www.salemweb.com/witchhouse* ⊠*$8*
☉*May–Nov., 10–5.*

**OFF THE
BEATEN
PATH**

Danvers. Not a top site for the time-crunched but for those who want
the real deal, Danvers (formerly Salem Village), several miles northwest
of present-day Salem, has the real relics of the witchcraft episode. The
home of Samuel Parris's family has long been demolished, but its founda-
tions were excavated in 1970; the Salem Village Parsonage can be viewed
behind 67 Center Street. (Park around the corner; there's no place to stop
on Center Street.) A monument to the victims was dedicated in 1992 near
178 Hobart Street.

The Rebecca Nurse Homestead (⊠*149 Pine St.* ☏*978/774-8799* ⊕*www.
rebeccanurse.org*) was the home of Rebecca, an aged and devout church-
goer. The accusation that she was a witch shocked the community. Her
trial was a mockery: she was first pronounced innocent, but the jury was
then urged to change its verdict. Nurse was hanged in 1692, and her fam-

CLOSE UP

The First Witch Trial

It was in Danvers, not Salem, that the first witch trial was born, originating with the family of Samuel Parris, a minister who moved to the area in 1680 from Barbados, bringing with him two slaves, including one named Tituba. In 1691 Samuel's daughter, Betty, and niece, Abigail, began having "fits." Tituba, who had told Betty and Abigail stories of magic and witchcraft from her homeland, baked a "witch cake" to identify the witches who were harming the girls. The girls in turn accused Tituba of witchcraft. After three days of "questioning," which included beatings from Samuel and a promise from him to free her if she cooperated, Tituba confessed to meeting the devil (in the form of a black hog or dog). She also claimed there were other witches in the village, confirming the girls' accusations against Sarah Good and Sarah Osborne, but she refused to name any others. Tituba's trial prompted the frenzy that led to the deaths of 20 accused "witches."

ily secretly buried her body somewhere on the homestead's grounds. The house has period furnishings and 17th-century vegetable and herb gardens. Admission to the house is $5; it's open mid-June–early September, noon–4:30; early September–October, weekends noon–4:30 or by appointment; and November–mid-June by appointment only.

WHERE TO STAY & EAT

$$–$$$ ✕ **The Grapevine.** Opposite Pickering Wharf is this bistro with contemporary American cuisine and northern Italian flair. The menu changes with the season and may include Basque-style seafood stew, grilled lamb with roasted garlic mashed potatoes, or a seafood stew in ginger-scallion broth, as well as vegetarian selections. ⊠ *26 Congress St.* ☎ *978/745–9335* ⊕ *www.grapevinesalem.com* ▤ *AE, D, DC, MC, V* ⊗ *No lunch.*

$–$$$ ✕ **Strega.** Italian for "witch," the name of this restaurant hints at
Fodor's Choice the Italian alchemy in the kitchen. The bar has a broad selection
★ of wines by the glass and several small plates: calamari with garlic aioli, for example, or the very popular grilled pizza. The seasonal selection of large plates might include grilled salmon with lentils or apple-cured pork chops with sweet-potato mash. ⊠ *94 Lafayette St.* ☎ *978/741–0004* ⊕ *www.stregasalem.com* ▤ *AE, D, MC, V* ⊗ *Closed Mon. No lunch.*

$$ ✕ **Finz.** Walls of windows on three sides give this contemporary seafood restaurant on Pickering Wharf prime water views (there's a spacious deck, too). Fish-and-chips, seared scallop salad, and lobster rolls highlight the lunch menu, and in the evening there's cedar plank swordfish and salmon Wellington. And you can never go wrong with a traditional steamed lobster. ⊠ *76 Wharf St.* ☎ *978/744–8485* ⊕ *www.hipfinz.com* ▤ *AE, D, DC, MC, V.*

$–$$ ✕ **Salem Beer Works.** Burgers, chicken sandwiches, and seven kinds of french fries make this place an excellent spot for lunch with the kids, and the wide selection of beer, brewed on the premises, is a grown-

up treat. ⊠*278 Derby St.* ☎*978/745–2337* ⊕*www.beerworks.net*
☰*AE, D, DC, MC, V.*

$–$$ 🏨 **Amelia Payson House.** Built in 1845, this Greek Revival house has
been elegantly restored into an airy B&B; it's near all the historic attractions. With high ceilings, floral-print wallpaper, brass canopy beds, and
marble fireplaces, the four guest rooms are delicate and feminine. ⊠*16
Winter St., 01970* ☎*978/744–8304* ⊕*www.ameliapaysonhouse.com*
🛏*4 rooms* ☦*In-hotel: no elevator, parking (no fee)* ☰*AE, D, MC, V*
🌙*Closed Nov.–Mar.* ⦿|*CP.*

$–$$ 🏨 **Salem Waterfront Hotel & Suites.** This hotel has several things going for
it: pretty water views, spacious rooms, modern facilities, and a location convenient to many of Salem's sights. ⊠*225 Derby St., 01970*
☎*978/740–8788 or 888/337–2536* ⊕*www.salemwaterfronthotel.
com* 🛏*86 rooms* ☦*In-room: Wi-Fi. In-hotel: restaurant, pool* ☰*AE,
D, MC, V* ⦿|*CP.*

NIGHTLIFE & THE ARTS

Local bands play most nights at the **Dodge Street Bar & Grill** (⊠*7 Dodge
St.* ☎*978/745–0139* ⊕*www.dodgestreet.com*); the music ranges from
blues and rock to acid jazz and folk. The **North Shore Music Theatre**
(⊠*62 Dunham Rd., Beverly* ☎*978/232–7200* ⊕*www.nsmt.org*) puts
on celebrity concerts, musicals, and children's theater from March
through December.

SHOPPING

Salem is the center for dozens of offbeat shops related to the city's
witchcraft history. The best-known supernatural store is **Crow Haven
Corner** (⊠*125 Essex St.* ☎*978/745–8763* ⊕*www.crowhaven.com*).
If you'd like to perform a little magic of your own, you can pick up
blessed candles, incense, and herbs, as well as other witchy parapher-
nalia, at the **Cat, the Crow & the Crown** (⊠*63R Wharf St.* ☎*978/744–
6274* ⊕*www.lauriecabot.com*), haunt of Laurie Cabot, the "Official
Witch of Salem." **Pyramid Books** (⊠*214 Derby St.* ☎*978/745–7171*
⊕*www.salemctr.com/pyramid.html*) stocks a wide selection of New
Age publications.

Somewhat more conventional than the witchcraft stores are the gift
and antiques shops on restored Pickering Wharf. The **Pickering Wharf
Antiques Gallery** (☎*978/741–3113*) is home to about 30 dealers. For
a different kind of antique, anyone with a sweet tooth should drop
by **Ye Olde Pepper Candy Companie** (⊠*122 Derby St.* ☎*978/745–2744*
⊕*www.yeoldepeppercandy.com*), which claims to be the oldest candy
shop in the country.

GLOUCESTER

 37 mi northeast of Boston, 17 mi northeast of Salem.

On Gloucester's fine seaside promenade is a famous statue from 1923
of a man steering a ship's wheel, his eyes searching the horizon. The
statue, which honors those "who go down to the sea in ships" was
commissioned by the town citizens in celebration of Gloucester's 300th

anniversary. The oldest seaport in the nation (and one with some of the North Shore's best beaches), this is still a major fishing port. Sebastian Junger's 1997 book, *A Perfect Storm,* was an account of the fate of the *Andrea Gail,* a Gloucester fishing boat caught in "the storm of the century" in October 1991. In 2000 the book was made into a movie, filmed on location in Gloucester.

The town's creative side thrives in the **Rocky Neck** neighborhood, the first-settled artists' colony in the United States. Its alumni include Winslow Homer, Maurice Prendergast, Jane Peter, and Cecilia Beaux. Rocky Neck is still a place that many artists call home; its galleries are usually open daily 10 to 10 during the busy summer months. From downtown, follow East Main Street.

The **Hammond Castle Museum** is a "medieval" stone castle built in 1926 by the inventor John Hays Hammond Jr., who is credited with more than 500 patents, including ones associated with the organ that bears his name. The museum contains medieval-style furnishings and paintings throughout, and the Great Hall houses an impressive 8,200-pipe organ. Walk into the serene Patio Room, with its pool and garden, and you may feel as if you've entered a 15th-century village. From the castle you can see "Norman's Woe Rock," made famous by Longfellow in his poem "The Wreck of the Hesperus." Tours led by actors portraying Hammond are given for groups of 20 or more. In addition to being closed the last two weeks of October, the museum often closes to host weddings or special events, so call ahead. ⊠ *80 Hesperus Ave., south side of Gloucester off Rte. 127* ☎ *978/283–2080 or 978/283–7673* ⊕ *www.hammondcastle.org* 🖭 *$8* ⊙ *Call for hrs, but note that the castle is frequently closed in winter.*

The **Cape Ann Historical Museum** has the nation's largest collection of paintings by the 19th-century master Fitz Hugh Lane, plus works by other artists associated with Cape Ann, including Winslow Homer and Maurice Prendergast. Also inside the furnished Federal-period house are wooden boats, fishing equipment, and other artifacts. ⊠ *27 Pleasant St., off Main St.* ☎ *978/283–0455* ⊕ *www.capeannhistoricalmuseum.org* 🖭 *$6.50* ⊙ *Tues.–Sat. 10–5, Sun. 1–4.*

WHERE TO STAY & EAT

$–$$$ ✕ **Boulevard Ocean View Restaurant.** This clam shack has a Portuguese twist. Besides fried clams, burgers, and fish-and-chips, you can try Portuguese pork-and-clam stew, grilled shrimp, and salt cod. The water view from the front deck makes it a nice place to relax. ⊠ *25 Western Ave.* ☎ *978/281–2949* ▤ *D, MC, V.*

$–$$ ✕ **Franklin Cape Ann.** Under the same ownership as the Franklin Café in Boston's South End, this funky nightspot brings hip comfort food to the North Shore. Think bistro-style chicken, roast cod, and upscale meat loaf, perfect for the late-night crowd (it's open until midnight). Tuesday evening generally brings live jazz. Look for the signature martini glass over the door. ⊠ *118 Main St.* ☎ *978/283–7888* ⊕ *www.franklincafe. com* ▤ *AE, D, MC, V* ⊙ *No lunch.*

8

$–$$$ ⊡ **Cape Ann Motor Inn.** On the sands of Long Beach, this three-story, shingled motel has no-frills rooms with balconies and ocean views. Half have well-furnished kitchenettes. The Honeymoon Suite has a full kitchen, a fireplace, a whirlpool bath, a king-size bed, and a private balcony. ⊠*33 Rockport Rd., 01930* ☎*978/281–2900 or 800/464–8439* 📠*978/281–1359* ⊕*www.capeannmotorinn.com* ⇱*30 rooms, 1 suite* ⚭*In-room: no a/c, kitchen (some). In-hotel: no elevator, some pets allowed* ⊟*AE, D, MC, V* ⦿*CP.*

$ ⊡ **Cape Ann's Marina Resort.** This year-round hostelry less than a mile from Gloucester really comes alive in summer, when two restaurants, a whale-watch boat, and deep-sea fishing excursions operate on and from the premises. The rooms all have balconies and water views; guests get a free river cruise during summer stays. The Gull restaurant is closed November–mid-April. ⊠*75 Essex Ave., 01930* ☎*978/283–2116 or 800/626–7660* 📠*978/281–4905* ⊕*www.capeannmarina.com* ⇱*53 rooms* ⚭*In-room: kitchen (some). In-hotel: 2 restaurants, pool, no elevator* ⊟*AE, D, DC, MC, V.*

SPORTS & THE OUTDOORS

BEACHES   Gloucester has some of the best beaches on the North Shore. They generally have some facilities, such as bathrooms, changing rooms, showers, and/or concessions. From Memorial Day through mid-September, parking costs $15 on weekdays and $20 on weekends, when the lots often fill by 10 AM. **Good Harbor Beach** (⊠*Signposted "S" from Rte. 127A*) is a huge, sandy, dune-backed beach with a rocky islet just offshore. For excellent sunbathing, visit **Long Beach** (⊠*Off Rte. 127A on Gloucester–Rockport town line*). Parking here is only $5. **Wingaersheek Beach** (⊠*Exit 13 off Rte. 128*) is one of New England's hidden treasures: a well-protected cove of white sand and dunes, with the white Annisquam lighthouse in the bay.

BOATING   Consider a sail along the harbor and coast aboard the 65-foot schooner *Thomas E. Lannon* (⊠*63R Rogers St., Seven Seas Wharf* ☎*978/281–6634* ⊕*www.schooner.org*), crafted in Essex in 1996 and modeled after the great boats built a century before. From mid-May through mid-October there are several two-hour sails, including those that let you enjoy the sunset or participate in a lobster bake. There's even one especially for teens. The trips are only on weekends until mid-June and then daily after that. Make advance reservations.

FISHING   Gloucester has a great fishing tradition, and many anglers in the town's busy working harbor put together fishing trips, generally May through October; gear is provided. **Captain Bill's Deep Sea Fishing** (⊠*24 Harbor Loop* ☎*978/283–6995 or 800/339–4253* ⊕*www.captainbills-whalewatch.com*) runs half-day excursions April through November for about $30. **Coastal Fishing Charters** (⊠*Rose's Wharf, 415 Main St.* ☎*978/283–5110 or 800/877–5110* ⊕*www.coastalfishingcharters.net*), under the same ownership as Cape Ann Whale Watch, operates day and evening fishing trips by private charter for up to four people. The **Yankee Fishing Fleet** (⊠*75 Essex Ave.* ☎*978/283–0313 or 800/942–5464* ⊕*www.yankeefishing.com*), at Cape Ann's Marina Resort, operates half- and full-day trips.

WHALE-
WATCHING
Gloucester is a hot spot for whale-watching tours on the North Shore. *See "Thar She Blows" box in Chapter 6 for details.*

ROCKPORT

㉛ *41 mi northeast of Boston, 4 mi northeast of Gloucester on Rte. 127.*

Rockport, at the very tip of Cape Ann, derives its name from the local granite formations, and many Boston-area structures are made of stone cut from its long-gone quarries. Today the town is a tourist center, with hilly rows of colorful clapboard houses, historic inns, and artists' studios. Rockport has refrained from going overboard with T-shirt emporia and other typical tourist-trap landmarks; shops sell good crafts, clothing, and cameras, and the restaurants serve quiche, seafood, and home-baked cookies rather than fast food. Walk out to the end of Bearskin Neck for an impressive view of the Atlantic Ocean and the old, weather-beaten lobster shack known as "Motif No. 1" because of its popularity as a subject for amateur painters.

WHERE TO STAY & EAT

$–$$ ✕ **Brackett's Ocean View.** A big bay window in this quiet, homey restaurant gives an excellent view across Sandy Bay. The menu includes baked scrod casserole, fish cakes, and other seafood dishes. ⊠ *25 Main St.* ☎ *978/546–2797* ═ *AE, D, DC, MC, V* ⊗ *Closed Nov.–Mar.*

¢–$$ ✕ **Portside Chowder House.** One of the few restaurants in Rockport open year-round, this casual seafood spot has big picture windows overlooking the harbor. Its popularity means that the wait for tables and food can be long. Chowder is the house specialty; it also serves lobster rolls, salads, burgers, and sandwiches. ⊠ *Bearskin Neck* ☎ *978/546–7045* ═ *AE, MC, V* ⊗ *No dinner Mon.–Thurs. Dec.–Mar.*

$$$–$$$$ 🏠 **Yankee Clipper Inn.** This imposing Georgian mansion sits on a rocky point jutting into the sea. Most guest rooms are spacious, with ones in the side building (the Quarterdeck) being practically in the water. (The latter do not get Wi-Fi.) Furnished with antiques, some have balconies or sitting areas, and all but one have an ocean view. Take in the seascape from the gazebo or one of the many Adirondack chairs on the grounds. ⊠ *127 Granite St., 01966* ☎ *978/546–3407 or 800/545–3699* 🖷 *978/546–9730* ⊕ *www.yankeeclipperinn.com* ➴ *16 rooms* ⚘ *In-room: Wi-Fi (some). In-hotel: pool, no elevator* ═ *AE, D, DC, MC, V* ⊗ *Closed weekdays Dec.–Feb.* ⑩ *BP.*

$$ 🏠 **Bearskin Neck Motor Lodge.** Near the end of Bearskin Neck, this small brick-and-shingle motel is in the thick of the shopping district and just a few minutes from the best local beaches. The simply appointed rooms, furnished with comfortable wooden furniture and white chenille spreads, provide the perfect backdrop for the breathtaking water views just outside your door. At night, you can go to sleep listening to the waves, and during the day, you can sun or read on the large deck. ⊠ *64 Bearskin Neck, 01966* ☎ *978/546–6677 or 877/507–6272* 🖷 *978/546–8591* ⊕ *www.rockportusa.com/bearskin* ➴ *8 rooms* ⚘ *In-room: no a/c. In-hotel: no elevator* ═ *AE, D, MC, V* ⊗ *Closed mid-Dec.–Mar.* ⑩ *CP.*

8

★ **$–$$** ⊡**Addison Choate Inn.** Just a minute's walk from the center of Rockport, this 1851 inn sits inconspicuously among private homes. The sizable and beautifully decorated rooms have their share of antiques and local seascape paintings, as well as polished pine floors and large tile bathrooms; the captain's room contains a canopy bed, handmade quilts, and Oriental rugs. In the third-floor suite, huge windows look out over the rooftops to the sea. Two comfortably appointed duplex stable-house apartments have skylights, cathedral ceilings, and exposed wood beams. Rates include afternoon tea. ⊠*49 Broadway, 01966* ☎*978/546–7543 or 800/245–7543* 🖷*978/546–7638* ⊕*www.addisonchoateinn.com* 🛏*5 rooms, 1 suite, 2 apartments* ⚘*In-room: no TV. In-hotel: restaurant, no elevator* ⊟*MC, V* ⊘*Closed Jan.–Mar.* ⏀|*CP.*

$–$$ ⊡**Inn on Cove Hill (Caleb Norwood Jr. House).** On a hillside near the town center, this Federal building dates from 1771. Its construction was reportedly paid for with gold from a pirate's booty. Some of the guest rooms are small, but all are cheerful and pretty, with wood floors, bright floral-print wallpaper, Oriental rugs, patchwork quilts, and old-fashioned beds—some brass, others canopy four-posters. ⊠*37 Mt. Pleasant St., 01966* ☎*978/546–2701 or 888/546–2701* 🖷*978/546–1095* ⊕*www.innoncovehill.com* 🛏*6 rooms, 1 suite* ⚘*In-hotel: no elevator* ⊟*MC, V* ⏀|*CP.*

★ **$** ⊡**Sally Webster Inn.** This inn was named for a member of Hannah Jumper's "hatchet gang," teetotalers who smashed up the town's liquor stores in 1856 and turned Rockport into the dry town it remains today. Sally lived in this house for much of her life, and the poshly decorated guest rooms are named for members of her family. Caleb's room is a romantic retreat with a canopy bed and floral quilts, and William's room has a crisply nautical theme. Other rooms have rocking chairs; nonworking brick fireplaces; four-poster, brass, or canopy beds; and pine wide-board floors. ⊠*34 Mt. Pleasant St., 01966* ☎*978/546–9251 or 877/546–9251* ⊕*www.sallywebster.com* 🛏*8 rooms* ⚘*In-room: no TV. In-hotel: restaurant, bar, no elevator, public Wi-Fi* ⊟*MC, V* ⊘*Closed Jan.* ⏀|*CP.*

SHOPPING

An artists' colony, Rockport has a tremendous concentration of studios and galleries selling local work. Most are on Main Street near the harbor and on Bearskin Neck. The *Rockport Fine Arts Gallery Guide,* available from the **Rockport Chamber of Commerce** (☎*978/546–6575* ⊕*www.rockportusa.com*), lists some 30 reputable galleries in town.

The **Rockport Art Association Gallery** (⊠*12 Main St.* ☎*978/546–6604* ⊕*www.rockportartassn.org*) displays the best work of local artists. Stop by to pick up a painting of the waterfront or other classic New England scenes. It's closed in January.

ESSEX

32 *30 mi northeast of Boston, 12 mi west of Rockport. Head west out of Cape Ann on Rte. 128, turning north on Rte. 133.*

The small, seafaring town of Essex, once an important shipbuilding center, is surrounded by salt marshes and is filled with antiques stores and seafood restaurants.

The **Essex Shipbuilding Museum,** still an active shipyard, traces the evolution of the American schooner, which was first created in Essex. The museum sometimes offers shipbuilding demonstrations. One-hour tours take in the museum's many buildings and boats, especially the *Evelina M. Goulart*—one of only seven remaining Essex-built schooners. ⊠*66 Main St. (Rte. 133)* ☎*978/768-7541* ⊕*www.essexshipbuildingmuseum.org* ✉*$7* ⊙*May–Columbus Day, Wed.–Sun. noon–4; Columbus Day–Apr., weekends noon–4.*

WHERE TO EAT

★ ¢–$$ ✕**Woodman's of Essex.** According to local legend, this is where Lawrence "Chubby" Woodman invented the first fried clam back in 1916. Today this sprawling wooden shack with indoor booths and outdoor picnic tables is *the* place for seafood in the rough. Besides fried clams, you can tuck into clam chowder, lobster rolls, or shellfish from the raw bar. ⊠*121 Main St. (Rte. 133)* ☎*978/768-6451 or 800/649-1773* ⊕*www.woodmans.com* ⊟*No credit cards.*

SHOPPING

Essex claims to be "America's Antiques Capital." That may be an exaggeration, but no one can deny that Route 133 (Main Street) has one of the best concentrations of antiques shops in the region. These are experienced dealers, often stocking high-end goods, so don't expect to stumble on a hidden treasure. **Chebacco Antiques** (⊠*38 Main St.* ☎*978/768-7371*) concentrates on lighting and country furniture, as well as Staffordshire plates and sterling silver. Open only on weekends, **Howard's Flying Dragon Antiques** (⊠*136 Main St.* ☎*978/768-7282*) is a general antiques shop that carries statuary and glass. The **White Elephant** (⊠*32 Main St.* ☎*978/768-6901* ⊕*www.cape-ann.com/white-elephant*) is one of the region's largest consignment shops, with furniture, china, books, records, and collectibles. For bargains, head down the street from the White Elephant to the **White Elephant Outlet Shop** (⊠*101 John Wise Ave.* ☎*978/768-3329* ⊕*www.cape-ann.com/white-elephant*). It's open only on weekends.

SPORTS & THE OUTDOORS

Explore the area's salt marshes and rivers on a 1½-hour narrated cruise on the *Essex River Queen,* run by **Essex River Cruises** (⊠*Essex Marina, 35 Dodge St.* ☎*978/768-6981 or 800/748-3706* ⊕*www.essexcruises.com*). Cruises are $23 and operate daily May–October; phone ahead for departure times.

8

IPSWICH

③③ *36 mi north of Boston, 6 mi northwest of Essex.*

Quiet little Ipswich, settled in 1633 and famous for its clams, is said to have more 17th-century houses standing and occupied than any other place in America; more than 40 were built before 1725.

Information and a booklet with a suggested walking tour are available at the **Visitor Information Center** (⊠*Hall Haskell House, 36 S. Main St.* ☎*978/356–8540* ⊙*Memorial Day–Columbus Day, Mon.–Sat. 9–5; Sun. noon–5*).

The Ipswich Historical Society offers a combined tour of two historic homes, which begins at the **John Heard House** (⊠*54 S. Main St.* ☎*978/356–2811* ⊕*www.ipswichmuseum.net*), a lovely 1800 Federalist mansion. The 1655 **John Whipple House** (⊠*1 S. Village Green*) has large fireplaces, wide-board floors, and furnishings dating back to the late 1600s. The tour costs $7 and is available May through October, Wednesday–Saturday 10–4 and Sunday 1–4.

The 59-room Stuart-style **Great House at Castle Hill,** built in 1927 for Richard Crane—of the Crane plumbing company—and his family, is part of the **Crane Estate,** a stretch of more than 2,000 acres along the Essex and Ipswich rivers, encompassing Castle Hill, Crane Beach, and the Crane Wildlife Refuge. Although the original furnishings of the mansion were sold at auction, it has been elaborately refurnished in period style; photographs in most of the rooms show their original appearance. One notable room is the library, with ornate wood carvings by 17th-century craftsman Grinling Gibbons. The Great House is open for one-hour tours and also holds concerts and other events. ⊠*Argilla Rd.* ☎*978/356–4351* ⊕*www.thetrustees.org* ⊠*Tours $8* ⊙*June–Oct., Wed. and Thurs. 10–5, Fri. 9–noon.*

ⓒ Kids can get in touch with their wild sides at **Wolf Hollow,** a nonprofit wildlife sanctuary that's home to a pack of timber wolves. The one-hour tour lets visitors see and learn the truth about wolves. After the tour, everyone gets together to howl with the pack. ⊠*114 Essex Rd.* ☎*978/356–0216* ⊕*www.wolfhollowipswich.org* ⊠*$6* ⊙*Weekends only, with formal presentation beginning at 1:30.*

WHERE TO EAT

$$–$$$ ✕**Stone Soup Café.** It may look like nothing more than a simple storefront, but this cheery café in the center of town is booked days in advance for dinner. There are two seatings of eight tables a night for lobster bisque, porcini ravioli, or whatever contemporary fare the chef is inspired to cook from the day's farm-stand finds. If you can't book ahead, stop in for breakfast or lunch. ⊠*0 Central St., off Rte. 1A* ☎*978/356–4222* ⌂*Reservations essential* ▭*No credit cards* ⊙*No dinner Sun.–Wed., no lunch Sun.*

★ **¢–$$** ✕**Clam Box.** Shaped like a giant take-out box, this small roadside stand is the best place to sample Ipswich's famous bivalves. Since 1938, locals and tourists have been lining up for clams, oysters, scallops, and onion rings. ⊠*246 High St. (Rte. 1A)* ☎*978/356–9707* ⊕*www.*

ipswichma.com/clambox ⛵*Reservations not accepted* ▭*No credit cards* ⏲*Closed mid-Dec.–Feb.*

SPORTS & THE OUTDOORS

BEACHES **Crane Beach,** one of New England's most beautiful beaches, is a sandy, ★ 4-mi-long stretch backed by dunes and a nature trail. Public parking is available, but on a nice summer weekend, it's usually full before lunch. There are lifeguards and changing rooms. Check ahead before visiting mid-July to early August, when greenhead flies terrorize sunbathers. ✉*Argilla Rd.* ☎*978/356–4354* 🌐*www.thetrustees.org* 🎫*Free; parking $10 weekdays, $20 weekends mid-May–early Sept., $5 early Sept.–mid-May* ⏲*Daily 8–sunset.*

HIKING The Massachusetts Audubon Society's **Ipswich River Wildlife Sanctuary** has trails through marshland hills, where there are remains of early colonial settlements as well as abundant wildlife. Get a trail map from the office. The Rockery Trail takes you to the perennial rock garden and the Japanese garden; the map details a further 10 mi of walking trails. You can fish in the Parker and Ipswich rivers, both of which are stocked with trout each spring. ✉*87 Perkins Row, Topsfield* ✣*southwest of Ipswich, 1 mi off Rte. 97* ☎*978/887–9264* 🌐*www.massaudubon.org* 🎫*$4* ⏲*Office: May–Oct., Tues.–Sun. 9–5; Nov.–Apr., Tues.–Fri. 9–4, weekends 10–4. Trails: Tues.–Sun. dawn–dusk.*

EN ROUTE **A good detour for children and others still engaged by toys, the Wenham Museum (✉*132 Main St. [Rte. 1A], Wenham* ☎*978/468–2377* 🌐*www.wenhammuseum.org*) has an extensive antique-doll collection and a large room full of model trains. Admission is $6.50; it's open Tuesday–Sunday 10–4.**

8

NEWBURYPORT

34 *38 mi north of Boston, 12 mi north of Ipswich.*

Newburyport's High Street is lined with some of the finest examples of Federal-period (roughly, 1790–1810) mansions in New England. The city was once a leading port and shipbuilding center; the houses were built for prosperous sea captains.

Although Newburyport's maritime significance ended with the decline of the clipper ships, the town's brick-front center is energetic once again. Inside the renovated buildings are restaurants, taverns, galleries, and shops that sell everything from nautical brasses to antique Oriental rugs. The civic improvements have been matched by private restorations of the town's houses, many of which date from the 18th century, with a scattering of 17th-century homes in some neighborhoods.

Newburyport is a good walking city, and parking is free all day down by the water.

A stroll through the **Waterfront Park & Promenade** gives a super view of the harbor and the fishing and pleasure boats that moor here.

The **Custom House Maritime Museum,** built in 1835 in Greek Revival style, contains exhibits on maritime history, ship models, tools, and paintings. ✉25 Water St. ☎978/462–8681 ⊕www.themaritimesociety.org ☞$5 ⊗Mar.–Dec., Tues.–Sat. 9–5, Sun. noon–4.

Lowell's Boat Shop, operated by the Custom House Maritime Museum, dates from 1793 and is considered to be America's oldest operating boat shop. In the shop, visitors and prospective buyers alike can observe craftspeople creating traditional flat-bottom dories, from small prams to huge ocean skiffs. ✉459 Main St., Amesbury ✛5 mi north of Newburyport ☎978/462–8681 ⊕www.themaritimesociety.org ⊗Mar.–Dec., Tues.–Sat. 9–5, Sun. noon–4.

WHERE TO STAY & EAT

$$–$$$ ✕**Glenn's Restaurant & Cool Bar.** The eclectic menu at this hip spot, a block from the waterfront parking lot, rambles from Asia to Latin America to the good ol' U.S.A. The ever-changing menu might include sesame-crusted yellowfin tuna or house-smoked baby back ribs. There's live jazz or blues on Sunday evenings. ✉44 Merrimac St. ☎978/465–3811 ⊟AE, D, DC, MC, V ⊗No dinner Mon.

★ $–$$ ▦**Clark Currier Inn.** This 1803 Federal mansion has been restored with care, taste, and imagination. It's one of the best inns on the North Shore. Guest rooms are spacious and furnished with antiques; one room has a glorious, late-19th-century sleigh bed. Rates include afternoon tea. ✉45 Green St., 01950 ☎978/465–8363 ⊕www.clarkcurrierinn.com ⬎8 rooms ⌂In-room: no TV. In-hotel: no elevator, no kids under 11 ⊟AE, D, MC, V ⏀CP.

NIGHTLIFE & THE ARTS

At the **Firehouse Center for the Arts** (✉Market Sq. ☎978/462–7336 ⊕www.firehousecenter.com), local theater productions and concerts take the stage year-round. The center also houses an art gallery, open Tuesday–Sunday noon–5. The **Grog** (✉13 Middle St. ☎978/465–8008 ⊕www.thegrog.com) hosts blues and rock bands several nights weekly.

SPORTS & THE OUTDOORS

☾ **Salisbury Beach State Reservation** (✉Rte. 1A, Salisbury ✛5 mi northeast of Newburyport ☎978/462–4481 ⊕www.state.ma.us/dcr/parks/northeast/salb.htm ☞Free, parking $7) has a long sandy beach, with an amusement area and arcades nearby. From Newburyport center, follow Bridge Road north, take a right on Beach Road, and follow it until you reach State Reservation Road.

PLUM ISLAND

③⑤ 41 mi north of Boston, 5 mi southeast of Newburyport.

A causeway leads from Newburyport to a narrow spit of land known as Plum Island, which harbors a summer colony (rapidly becoming year-round) at one end.

The **Parker River National Wildlife Refuge** has 4,662 acres of salt marsh, freshwater marsh, beaches, and dunes; it's one of the few natural barrier beach–dune–salt marsh complexes left on the northeast coast. Here you can bird-watch, fish, swim, and pick plums and cranberries. The refuge is such a popular place in summer, especially on weekends, that cars begin to line up at the gate before 7 AM. Only a limited number of cars are let in, although there's no restriction on the number of people using the beach. No pets are allowed in the refuge. ☎978/465–5753 ⊕*www.parkerriver.org* ✑*$5 per car, $2 for bicycles and walk-ins* ☉*Daily dawn–dusk. Beach usually closed during nesting season in spring and early summer.*

SPORTS & THE OUTDOORS

FISHING Surf casting is popular—bluefish, pollack, and striped bass can be taken from the ocean shores of Plum Island. If you enter the refuge with fishing equipment in the daytime from July to October, you can obtain a permit to remain on the beach after dark. You don't need a permit to fish from the public beach at Plum Island; the best spot is around the mouth of the Merrimack River.

You can rent fishing tackle at **Surfland Bait & Tackle** (✉*30 Plum Island Blvd.* ☎*978/462–4202*).

HIKING At the **Parker River National Wildlife Refuge** (☎*978/465–5753* ⊕*www.parkerriver.org*), deer and rabbits share space with thousands of birds, making it especially popular with bird-watchers in spring and fall migrating seasons. The 2-mi Hellcat Swamp Trail cuts through the marshes and sand dunes, taking in the best of the sanctuary. Trail maps are available at the office on Sunset Drive, ½ mi south of the bridge onto Plum Island. Admission is $5 per car and $2 for bicycles and walk-ins. The refuge is open from dawn to dusk.

SOUTH OF BOSTON

The towns south of Boston make an enjoyable day trip or a convenient stop on your way down to the Cape or islands. If you're a history buff or are seeking to give children an educational experience they won't soon forget, take the 40-mi trip south to Plymouth, the community locals proudly call "America's Home Town."

Here you can see the monument you've heard about since childhood—Plymouth Rock—or walk the decks of the *Mayflower II*. A couple of miles down the road at Plimoth Plantation you can stroll through a re-creation of a 17th-century Puritan village. Plimoth Plantation vividly dramatizes the everyday lives of the first English settlers: you can watch them make cheese, forge nails, and explain when and where their real-life counterparts bathed (hint: it wasn't often).

If you're more ambitious, take a drive into the seafaring towns of New Bedford, a major whaling port in the 19th century. This is where you'll find the nation's largest museum on the history of whaling. The museum houses the rare skeleton of a 66-foot blue whale, as well as the world's largest ship model.

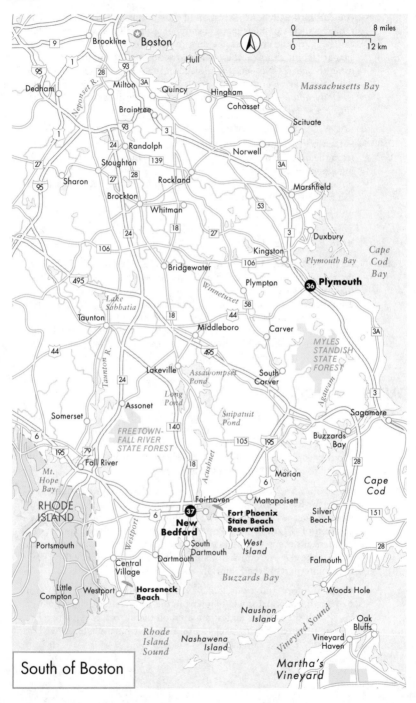

0   8 miles
0   12 km

Brookline   **Boston**

Hull

Massachusetts Bay

9

95   1

Dedham

28   93

Milton   3A   Quincy   Hingham

Braintree   Cohasset

1   93   Scituate

24   Randolph   3

Stoughton   139   Norwell   3A

27   28

95   Sharon   27   Rockland   Marshfield

Brockton

Whitman   53

24   18   27   Duxbury

106   Kingston   3   *Cape*
Cod
Bay

Bridgewater   106   *Plymouth Bay*

495   Plympton   **36 Plymouth**

Lake   *Winnetuxet*   58
Sabbatia

Taunton   18   44

Middleboro   Carver   3A

44   495   *MYLES*
STANDISH
STATE
Lakeville   *Assawompset*   South   *FOREST*
Pond   Carver

24   *Long*
Pond   *Agawam*

Somerset   Assonet   *Snipatuit*   Sagamore
Pond

6   *FREETOWN-*   140   Buzzards   3
FALL RIVER   105   195   Bay

195   79   *STATE FOREST*   28

Fall River   18   *Cape*
Cod
Mt.   *Acushnet*   Marion
Hope   6
Bay   Fairhaven   Mattapoisett   Silver   151
Beach
RHODE   **37**   **Fort Phoenix**
ISLAND   **New**   **State Beach**   28
Bedford   **Reservation**

Portsmouth   South   West   Falmouth
Dartmouth   Island   28

Dartmouth   Central
Village   *Buzzards Bay*   Woods Hole

Little   Westport   **Horseneck**
Compton   **Beach**   *Naushon*
Island   Oak
Bluffs

Rhode   Vineyard
Island   *Nashawena*   Haven
Sound   *Island*   *Vineyard Sound*

South of Boston   *Martha's*
Vineyard

PLYMOUTH

36 *40 mi south of Boston.*

Numbers in the margin correspond to points of interest on the South of Boston map.

On December 26, 1620, 102 weary men, women, and children disembarked from the *Mayflower* to found the first permanent European settlement north of Virginia. (In fact, Virginia was their intended destination, but storms pushed the ship off course.) Of the settlers, now known as the Pilgrims, a third were Separatists, members of a Puritan sect of religious reformers who wanted to establish their own church distinct from the national Church of England. This treasonous separation led the group to first flee to the city of Leyden in the Netherlands. After more than 10 years there, the group joined with other emigrants to start a new life in the New World.

Before coming ashore, the expedition's leaders drew up the Mayflower Compact, a historic agreement binding the group to the law of the majority. This compact became the basis for the colony's government. After a terrible start (half of the original settlers died during the first winter), the colony stabilized and grew under the leadership of Governor William Bradford. Two other founding fathers—military leader Myles Standish and John Alden—acquired mythical status via a poem by Longfellow, "The Courtship of Miles Standish," which recounts the fable of Alden's winning the heart of Priscilla while proposing to her on behalf of his tongue-tied friend Standish.

Today Plymouth is characterized by narrow streets, clapboard mansions, shops, and antiques stores. To mark Thanksgiving, the town holds a parade, historic-house tours, and other activities.

Historic statues dot the town, including depictions of William Bradford on Water Street, a Pilgrim maiden in Brewster Gardens, and Massasoit (chief of the local Wampanoag tribe) on Carver Street.

The largest freestanding granite statue in the United States, the allegorical **National Monument to the Forefathers** stands high on a grassy hill. Designed by Hammet Billings of Boston in 1854 and dedicated in 1889, it depicts Faith, surrounded by Liberty, Morality, Justice, Law, and Education, and includes scenes from the Pilgrims' early days in Plymouth. ⊠*Allerton St.*

Several historic houses are open for visits, including the 1640 **Sparrow House,** Plymouth's oldest structure. You can peek into a pair of rooms furnished in the spartan style of the Pilgrims' era. The contemporary-crafts gallery also on the premises seems somewhat incongruous, but the works on view are high quality. ⊠*42 Summer St.* ☎*508/747–1240* *$2, gallery free* ☉*Apr.–late Nov., Thurs.–Tues. 10–5.*

The ***Mayflower II,*** a reproduction of the 1620 *Mayflower,* was built in England through research and a bit of guesswork, then sailed across the Atlantic in 1957. As you explore the interior and exterior of the ship, sailors in modern dress answer your questions about both the reproduction and the original ship, and costumed interpreters provide a 17th-century perspective. An exhibit called "Provisioning a Ship" explores the things the Pilgrims carried with them to survive both at sea and in the New World. ✉*State Pier* ☎*508/746–1622* ⊕*www. plimoth.org* ✍*$8, $25 combination ticket with Plimoth Plantation* ⊘*Late Mar.–Nov., daily 9–5.*

A few dozen yards from the *Mayflower II* is **Plymouth Rock,** popularly believed to have been the Pilgrims' stepping-stone when they left the ship. Given the stone's unimpressive appearance—it's little more than a boulder—and dubious authenticity (as explained on a nearby plaque), the grand canopy overhead seems a trifle ostentatious.

Across the street from Plymouth Rock is **Cole's Hill,** where the company buried their dead—at night, so the Native Americans could not count the dwindling numbers of survivors. Just past the hill, on what was once called First Street, is the site of the original settlement. In 1834 the street was named Leyden Street in honor of the Dutch city that sheltered the Pilgrims. Look for plaques designating the locations of the original lots.

The **Plymouth National Wax Museum,** on the top of Cole's Hill, contains 26 scenes with 180 life-size models that tell the settlers' story. Corny? Yes, but school-age kids love it. ✉*15 Carver St.* ☎*508/746–6468* ⊕*www.capecodvisitor.com/plymouth_national_wax_museum.htm* ✍*$7* ⊘*Mar.–May, July, Aug., and Nov., daily 9–9; June, Sept., and Oct., daily 9–7.*

From the waterfront sights it's a short walk to one of the country's oldest public museums. The **Pilgrim Hall Museum,** established in 1824, transports you back to the time of the Pilgrims' landing with objects carried by those weary travelers to the New World. Included are a carved chest, a remarkably well-preserved wicker cradle, Myles Standish's sword, John Alden's Bible, Native American artifacts, and the remains of the *Sparrow Hawk,* a sailing ship that was wrecked in 1626. ✉*75 Court St. (Rte. 3A)* ☎*508/746–1620* ⊕*www.pilgrimhall.org* ✍*$6* ⊘*Feb.– Dec., daily 9:30–4:30.*

NEED A BREAK? The **Lobster Hut** (☎ *508/746–2270*), on Town Wharf at the waterfront, serves seafood in classic breaded and fried style and, of course, boiled lobsters. It's closed in January.

Over the entrance of the **Plimoth Plantation** is the caution YOU ARE NOW ENTERING 1627. Believe it. Against the backdrop of the Atlantic Ocean, a Pilgrim village has been carefully re-created, from the thatch roofs, cramped quarters, and open fireplaces to the long-horned livestock. Throw away your preconception of white collars and funny hats; through ongoing research, the Plimoth staff has developed a portrait of the Pilgrims that's more complex than the dour folk in school textbooks. Listen to the accents of the "residents," who never break out of character. You might see them plucking ducks, cooking rabbit stew, or tending garden. Feel free to engage them in conversation about their lives, but expect only curious looks if you ask about anything that

FodorsChoice
★

happened after 1627. "Thanksgiving: Memory, Myth & Meaning," an exhibit in the visitor center, offers a fresh perspective on the 1621 harvest celebration that is now known as "the first Thanksgiving."

At the **Hobbamock's Homesite,** Wampanoag Indians re-create the life of a Native American family who lived near the newcomers. In the **Carriage House Craft Center** you can see objects created using the techniques of 17th-century English craftsmanship—that is, effects the Pilgrims might have imported. (You can also buy samples.) See goats, cows, and chickens at the **Nye Barn.** Most of the animals were bred from 17th-century gene pools and are probably similar to those raised in the original plantation. The visitor center has gift shops, a cafeteria, and multimedia presentations. Dress for the weather, because many exhibits are outdoors. Admission tickets are good for two consecutive days. ⊠ *137 Warren Ave. (Rte. 3A)* 🕾 *508/746–1622* ⊕ *www. plimoth.org* 🖃 *$21, $25 combination ticket with Mayflower II* ⊙ *Late Mar.–Nov., daily 9–5.*

OFF THE BEATEN PATH

John Alden House Museum. The only standing structure in which original Pilgrims are known to have lived is about 10 mi north of Plymouth in Duxbury, a town settled in 1628 by Pilgrim colonists Myles Standish and John Alden, among others. Alden, who served as assistant governor of Plymouth colony, his wife, Priscilla, and eight or nine of their children occupied this house, which was built in 1653 and is furnished with pieces authentic to the era. ⊠ *105 Alden St., Duxbury* 🕾 *781/934–9092* ⊕ *www.alden.org* 🖃 *Guided tours $5* ⊙ *Mid-May–mid-Oct., Mon.–Sat. noon–4.*

WHERE TO STAY & EAT

¢ ✕ **All-American Diner.** The look is nostalgia—red, white, and blue, with vintage movie posters. The specialty is beloved American food—omelets and pancakes for breakfast; burgers, salads, and soups for lunch. ⊠ *60 Court St.* 🕾 *508/747–4763* ▤ *AE, MC, V* ⊙ *No dinner.*

$$–$$$ ✕▥ **John Carver Inn.** This three-story, Colonial-style redbrick building is steps from Plymouth's main attractions. The public rooms are lavish, with period furnishings and stylish drapes. The guest rooms include six "environmentally sensitive" options with filtered air and water and four-poster beds. The suites have fireplaces and whirlpool baths. There's also an indoor pool with a *Mayflower* ship model and a waterslide. The hotel's Hearth 'n Kettle Restaurant ($–$$) serves a wide selection of American favorites, including seafood and hearty sandwiches, at reasonable prices. ⊠ *25 Summer St., 02360* 🕾 *508/746–7100 or 800/274–1620* 🖷 *508/746–8299* ⊕ *www.johncarverinn.com* ⇖ *79 rooms, 6 suites* ⌂ *In-hotel: restaurant, bar, pool* ▤ *AE, D, DC, MC, V.*

$–$$ ▥ **Governor Bradford on the Harbour.** The waterfront location across from the *Mayflower II* is a big plus. Rooms are motel-basic, each with two double beds. During off-season, they're only open Friday and Saturday. ⊠ *98 Water St., 02360* 🕾 *508/746–6200 or 800/332–1620* 🖷 *508/747–3032* ⊕ *www.governorbradford.com* ⇖ *94 rooms* ⌂ *In-room: refrigerator. In-hotel: pool, no elevator* ▤ *AE, D, MC, V* ⍾ *CP.*

8

NEW BEDFORD

③⑦ *45 mi southwest of Plymouth, 50 mi south of Boston.*

In 1652 colonists from Plymouth settled in the area that now includes the city of New Bedford. The city has a long maritime tradition, beginning as a shipbuilding center and small whaling port in the late 1700s. By the mid-1800s, the city had developed into a center of North American whaling. Today New Bedford has the largest fishing fleet on the East Coast. Although much of the town is industrial, the restored historic district near the water is a delight. It was here that Herman Melville set parts of his great novel about whaling, *Moby-Dick.*

The city's whaling tradition is commemorated in the **New Bedford Whaling National Historical Park,** which takes up 13 blocks of the waterfront historic district. The park visitor center, housed in an 1853 Greek Revival house, has exhibits, maps, and information about whaling-related sites. Free walking tours of the park leave from the visitor center at 10:30, noon, and 2 in July and August. You can also view an orientation film about American whaling and the New Bedford historic sites; the film is free and is shown on the hour, daily 10–3 at the nearby New Bedford Whaling Museum. ⊠ *33 William St.* ☎ *508/996–4095* ⊕ *www.nps.gov/nebe* ⊠ *Free* ⊙ *Daily 9–5.*

Ⓒ The **New Bedford Whaling Museum,** established in 1903, is the world's largest museum of its kind. A highlight is the skeleton of a 66-foot blue whale, one of only three on view anywhere. An interactive exhibit lets you listen to the underwater sounds of whales, dolphins, and other sea life—plus the sounds of a thunderstorm and a whale-watching boat—as a whale might hear them. You can also peruse the collection of scrimshaw, visit exhibits on regional history, and climb aboard an 89-foot, half-scale model of the 1826 whaling ship *Lagoda*—the world's largest ship model. The New Bedford Whaling National Historical Park shows a film about American whaling and New Bedford history sites at the museum. Screenings are daily and on the hour 10–3 (admission is not required). ⊠ *18 Johnny Cake Hill* ☎ *508/997–0046* ⊕ *www.whaling-museum.org* ⊠ *$10* ⊙ *Daily 9–5; June–Sept., Thurs. until 9 PM.*

Seaman's Bethel, the small chapel described in *Moby-Dick,* is across the street from the New Bedford Whaling Museum. ⊠ *15 Johnny Cake Hill* ☎ *508/992–3295* ⊙ *May–Columbus Day, weekdays 10–5.*

For a glimpse of upper-class life during New Bedford's whaling heyday, head ½ mi south of downtown to the **Rotch-Jones-Duff House & Garden Museum.** This 1834 Greek Revival mansion, amid a full city block of gardens, housed three prominent families in the 1800s and is filled with elegant furnishings from the era, including a mahogany piano, a massive marble-top sideboard, and portraits of the house's occupants. A free self-guided audio tour is available. ⊠ *396 County St.* ☎ *508/997–1401* ⊕ *www.rjdmuseum.org* ⊠ *$5* ⊙ *Mon.–Sat. 10–4, Sun. noon–4.*

WHERE TO EAT

$–$$$ ✕**Davy's Locker.** A huge seafood menu is the main draw at this spot overlooking Buzzards Bay. Caloric concoctions like lobster Newburg or baked shrimp with spinach Rockefeller and seafood stuffing are balanced by simpler fare like broiled New Bedford scrod. For landlubbers, try the smothered sirloin or calf's liver with onions and bacon. ⊠*1480 E. Rodney French Blvd.* ☎*508/992–7359* ⊟*AE, D, DC, MC, V.*

¢–$$ ✕**Antonio's.** Sample the traditional fare of New Bedford's large Portuguese population at this friendly, unadorned restaurant. It serves hearty portions of pork-and-shellfish stew, *bacalau* (salt cod), and grilled sardines, often on plates piled high with crispy fried potatoes and rice. ⊠*267 Coggeshall St., near intersection of I–195 and Rte. 18* ☎*508/990–3636* ⊟*No credit cards.*

NIGHTLIFE & THE ARTS

On the second Thursday of every month from 5 to 9 PM, New Bedford holds **AHA! nights** (☎*508/264–8859* ⊕*www.ahanewbedford.org*), a downtown gallery night program that focuses on the city's art, history, and architecture. Museums and galleries, including the Whaling Museum and the New Bedford Art Museum, have extended hours and offer free admission. Concerts, lectures, shows, and other special events are often on tap.

SPORTS & THE OUTDOORS

BEACHES   The best beach in the area is **Horseneck Beach State Reservation** (⊠*Rte. 88, Westport* ✛*11 mi southwest of downtown New Bedford* ☎*508/636–8816* ⊕*www.mass.gov/dcr/parks/southeast/hbch.htm*). Thanks to a constant breeze and southern exposure, this 2-mi stretch of pristine sand is perfect for windsurfing and sunning as well as swimming. Beach access is free, but parking is $5–$7. Dogs are prohibited.

Just over the bridge from downtown is a small strip of sand at **Fort Phoenix State Beach Reservation** (⊠*End of Green St. off Rte. 6, Fairhaven* ☎*508/992–4524* ⊕*www.state.ma.us/dcr/parks/southeast/ftph.htm*), the site of the Revolutionary War's first naval battle. Parking is free, and the restrooms have showers.

SIDE TRIPS ESSENTIALS

To research prices, get advice from other travelers, and book travel arrangements, visit www.fodors.com.

TRANSPORTATION

BY BOAT

Marblehead is one of the North Shore's pleasure-sailing capitals, but the town has long waiting lists for mooring space. The harbormaster can inform you of nightly fees at public docks when space is available.

Contact **Marblehead harbormaster** (☎*781/631–2386*).

BY BUS

The Massachusetts Bay Transportation Authority, or MBTA, operates buses to Lexington from Alewife station in Cambridge. Buses 62 and 76 make the trip in 25 minutes. The Cape Ann Transportation Authority, or CATA, provides local bus service in the Gloucester, Rockport, and Essex region. The Coach Company bus line runs a commuter bus between Newburyport and Boston on weekdays. The ride takes 1–1¼ hours. MBTA buses leave for Marblehead and Salem daily from Central Square in Cambridge, and on weekdays in the early morning and evenings from Boston's Haymarket Station and Downtown Crossing. Travel time is about ½ hour from Cambridge and 1–1¼ hours from Boston. Look for numbers 441, 442, 448, or 449 for Marblehead and 455 or 459 for Salem. American Eagle Motorcoach offers service from Boston to New Bedford. Plymouth & Brockton links Plymouth and the South Shore to Boston's South Station with frequent bus service. From the Plymouth bus depot, you can take the Plymouth Area Link buses to the town center or to Plimoth Plantation.

Contacts **American Eagle Motorcoach** (☎ *800/453–5040*). **Cape Ann Transportation Authority** (☎ *978/283–7278* ⊕ *www.canntran.com*). **Coach Company** (☎ *800/874–3377* ⊕ *www.coachco.com*). **MBTA** (☎ *800/392–6100* ⊕ *www.mbta. com*). **Plymouth & Brockton** (☎ *508/746–0378* ⊕ *www.p-b.com*). **Plymouth Area Link** (☎ *508/746–0378* ⊕ *www.gatra.org/pal.htm*).

BY CAR

From Boston to Lexington, pick up Memorial Drive in Cambridge, and continue to the Fresh Pond Parkway, then to Route 2 West. Exit Route 2 at Routes 4/225 if your first stop is the National Heritage Museum; from Routes 4/225, turn left on Mass Ave. For Lexington center, take the Waltham Street–Lexington exit from Route 2. Follow Waltham Street just under 2 mi to Mass Ave.; you'll be just east of the Battle Green. The drive takes about 30 minutes. To reach Concord by car, continue west on Route 2. Or take Interstate 90 (the Massachusetts Turnpike) to Interstate 95 North, and then exit at Route 2, heading west. Driving time is 40–45 minutes.

The fastest way to reach Sudbury from Boston is the Massachusetts Turnpike westbound, then Interstate 95 North to Route 20 (head west for Sudbury). Allow about 40–50 minutes to reach Sudbury.

Lowell lies near the intersection of Interstate 495 and Route 3. From Boston, take Interstate 93 North to Interstate 495. Go south on Interstate 495 to Exit 35C, the Lowell Connector. Follow the Lowell Connector to Exit 5B, Thorndike Street. Travel time is 45 minutes to an hour.

The primary link between Boston and the North Shore is Route 128, which splits off Interstate 95 and follows the coast northeast to Gloucester. To pick up Route 128 from Boston, take Interstate 93 North to Interstate 95 North to Route 128. If you stay on Interstate 95, you'll reach Newburyport. A less-direct route is Route 1A; once you're north of Lynn, you'll pass through several pretty coastal towns. Beyond Beverly, Route 1A travels inland toward Ipswich and Essex; at this point, Route 127 follows the coast to Gloucester and Rockport.

From Boston to Salem or Marblehead, follow Route 128 to Route 114 into Salem and on to Marblehead. A word of caution: this route is confusing and poorly marked, particularly returning to Route 128. An alternative route to Marblehead: follow Route 1A North, and then pick up Route 129 North along the shore through Swampscott and into Marblehead. It's possible to take Route 1A to Salem from Boston, but it's a very slow drive, and as the road turns inland, you miss the shore views that you get along Route 129.

Driving from Boston to Salem takes about 35–40 minutes; to Gloucester or to Newburyport, about 50–60 minutes. Many of the smaller roads connecting the North Shore communities (Routes 1A, 133, 127) do double duty as the towns' main streets.

If you don't have a car, Marblehead, Salem, Rockport, and Newburyport are the most accessible of the North Shore towns; many of the historic sights, museums, and shops are within walking distance. Attractions in the other North Shore communities are more spread out and are better explored by car.

To get to Plymouth, take the Southeast Expressway Interstate 93 South to Route 3 (toward Cape Cod); Exits 6 and 4 lead to downtown Plymouth and Plimoth Plantation, respectively. To reach New Bedford from Boston, follow Interstate 93 to Route 24 South to Route 140 South, and continue to Interstate 195 East. Allow about one hour from Boston to any of these three cities, about one hour from Plymouth to New Bedford.

BY TRAIN

The MBTA's commuter rail (the Purple Line) offers service to many of the towns mentioned in this chapter. For destinations north and west of the city, trains depart from North Station, and trains to Plymouth depart from South Station. Concord is a 40-minute ride on the Fitchburg line. The station is a short walk outside the town center. Lowell is a 45-minute ride on the Lowell line—catch a Lowell Regional Transit Authority bus from the station to downtown every 30 minutes on weekdays between 5:45 AM and 7:15 PM, and every half hour Saturday between 10:05 AM and 4:35 PM. On the North Shore, you can take the Newburyport/Rockport line to Salem (25–30 minutes), Gloucester (55–60 minutes), Rockport (70 minutes), Ipswich (50–55 minutes), and Newburyport (60–65 minutes). The stations at Salem, Gloucester, Rockport, and Ipswich are within about ½ mi of the towns' historic sights. From the Newburyport station to downtown (about 1 mi), take the Merrimack Valley Regional Transit Authority Bus 51, but note that there's no Sunday service. Take the Middleborough/Lakeville line to Plymouth (50 minutes).

Contacts Lowell Regional Transit Authority (☎978/452-6161 ⊕ www.lrta. com). **MBTA** (☎800/392-6100 ⊕ www.mbta.com). **Merrimack Valley Regional Transit Authority** (☎978/469-6878 ⊕ www.mvrta.com).

BUSINESS HOURS

PHARMACIES

CVS pharmacies in Plymouth and New Bedford are open 24 hours. The CVS pharmacy in Concord is open nightly until 10, as are Walgreens pharmacies throughout the region.

Late-Night & 24-Hour Pharmacies **CVS** (⊠ *195 Sudbury Rd., Concord* ☎ *978/369–8661* ⊠ *8 Pilgrim Hill Rd., off Rte. 44, Plymouth* ☎ *508/747–1465* ⊠ *1145 Kempton St., near Rte. 140, New Bedford* ☎ *508/999–3241* ⊕ *www.cvs. com).* **Walgreens** (⊠ *201 Main St., Gloucester* ☎ *978/283–7361* ⊠ *60 Bedford St., Lexington* ☎ *781/863–1110* ⊕ *www.walgreens.com).*

CONTACTS & RESOURCES

EMERGENCIES

Police (☎ *911).*

Medical Emergencies **Emerson Hospital** (⊠ *133 Old Rd., off Rte. 2, Concord* ☎ *978/369–1400).* **Jordan Hospital** (⊠ *275 Sandwich St., Plymouth* ☎ *508/746–2000).* **Newton-Wellesley Hospital** (⊠ *2014 Washington St., Rte. 16, Newton* ☎ *617/243–6000).* **St. Luke's Hospital** (⊠ *101 Page St., New Bedford* ☎ *508/997–1515).*

TOURS

Brush Hill Tours offers daily motor-coach tours from the Transportation Building in downtown Boston (with pickups at area hotels) to Lexington's Battle Green and Concord's Old North Bridge area on weekends in May and June and then daily until November. You can also catch tours to Salem and Marblehead on Tuesday, Thursday, and Saturday from early June until late October, as well as trips to Plymouth on Monday, Wednesday, and Friday from June until October. The Concord Chamber of Commerce runs guided walking tours April through October. Tours, which last about 1½ hours, depart from the Concord Visitor Center at 11 AM Friday through Monday, with additional tours on Saturday and Sunday at 1 PM.

Essex River Cruises & Charters organizes narrated cruises of nearby salt marshes and rivers. Departure schedules often change, so call for reservations.

Colonial Lantern Tours offers guided evening tours April through November of the original Plymouth plantation site and historic district, as well as a nightly "Ghostly Haunts and Legends" tour that highlights Plymouth's more-macabre history. Call for reservations and meeting locations.

Lowell National Historical Park offers ranger-led tours on foot year-round, and canal and trolley tours in the summer months.

Contacts **Brush Hill Tours** (☎ *781/986–6100, 617/720–6342, or 800/343–1328* ⊕ *www.brushhilltours.com).* **Colonial Lantern Tours** (☎ *508/747–4161 or 800/698–5636* ⊕ *www.plimouth.com).* **Concord Chamber of Commerce** (☎ *978/369–3120* ⊕ *www.concordnhchamber.com).* **Concord Visitor Center**

(☎ *978/369–3120*). **Essex River Cruises & Charters** (☎ *978/768–6981 or 800/748–3706* ⊕ *www.essexcruises.com*). **Lowell National Historical Park** (☎ *978/970–5000* ⊕ *www.nps.gov/lowe*). **Plymouth Area Link** (☎ *508/746–0378* ⊕ *www.gatra.org/pal.htm*).

VISITOR INFORMATION

The Concord Chamber of Commerce operates a visitor information center that's open April–October, daily 9:30–4:30. The Lexington Visitor Center is open April–November, daily 9–5, and December–March, daily 10–4. The North of Boston Visitors & Convention Bureau covers the North Shore in general, but many other organizations cover more-specific local areas. The Cape Ann Chamber of Commerce is open weekdays 8–6, Saturday 10–6, and Sunday 10–4. The Rockport Chamber of Commerce is open Monday–Saturday 9–5 between Memorial Day and Columbus Day, and Monday, Wednesday, and Friday 10–2 the rest of the year. The Ipswich Visitor Information Center is open Memorial Day–Columbus Day, Monday–Saturday 9–5, Sunday noon–5. In November, it's open only on weekends. The Marblehead Chamber of Commerce Information Booth is open weekdays 1–5 and weekends 10–6. The National Park Visitor Centers in both Lowell and Salem are open daily 9–5. The Waterfront Visitor Center in New Bedford is open weekdays 8:30–4:30 and weekends 9–5. The Plymouth Visitor Center is open mid-April–November, daily 9–5, with longer hours (8–8) in summer.

Contacts **Cape Ann Chamber of Commerce** (☎ *978/283–1601* ⊕ *www.capeannvacations.com*). **Concord Chamber of Commerce** (☎ *978/369–3120* ⊕ *www.concordchamberofcommerce.org*). **Concord Visitor Center** (☎ *978/369–3120*). **Ipswich Visitor Information Center** (☎ *978/356–8540* ⊕ *www.ipswichma.com*). **Lexington Visitor Center** (☎ *781/862–2480* ⊕ *www.lexingtonchamber.org*). **Marblehead Chamber of Commerce Information Booth** (☎ *781/639–8469* ⊕ *www.visitmarblehead.com*). **National Park Visitor Center** (☎ *978/970–5000* ⊕ *www.nps.gov/lowe* ☎ *978/740–1650* ⊕ *www.nps.gov/sama*). **New Bedford Office of Tourism** (☎ *508/979–1745 or 800/508–5353* ⊕ *www.ci.new-bedford.ma.us*). **Plymouth Visitor Information Center** (☎ *508/747–7525 or 800/872–1620* ⊕ *www.visit-plymouth.com*). **Rockport Chamber of Commerce** (☎ *978/546–6575* ⊕ *www.rockportusa.com*).

8

Boston
Essentials

PLANNING TOOLS, EXPERT INSIGHT,
GREAT CONTACTS

There are planners and there are those who,
excuse the pun, fly by the seat of their pants.
We happily place ourselves among the planners.
Our writers and editors try to anticipate all the
issues you may face before and during any journey, and then they do their research. This section
is the product of their efforts. Use it to get excited
about your trip to Boston , to inform your travel
planning, or to guide you on the road should the
seat of your pants start to feel threadbare.

GETTING STARTED

We're really proud of our Web site: Fodors.com is a great place to begin any journey. Scan Travel Wire for suggested itineraries, travel deals, restaurant and hotel openings, and other up-to-the-minute info. Check out Booking to research prices and book plane tickets, hotel rooms, rental cars, and vacation packages. Head to Talk for on-the-ground pointers from travelers who frequent our message boards. You can also link to loads of other travel-related resources.

■ RESOURCES

ONLINE TRAVEL TOOLS

ALL ABOUT BOSTON

Boston.com (⊕ www.boston.com), home of the Boston Globe online, has news and feature articles, ample travel information, and links to towns throughout Massachusetts. The site for Boston's arts and entertainment weekly, the Boston Phoenix (⊕ www.bostonphoenix.com), has nightlife, movie, restaurant, and arts listings. The **Bostonian Society** (⊕ bostonhistory.org/faq.php), answers some frequently asked questions about Beantown history on their Web site. The **iBoston** (⊕ www.iboston.org) page has some wonderful photographs of buildings that are architecturally and historically important.

Safety Transportation Security Administration (TSA ⊕ www.tsa.gov).

Time Zones Timeanddate.com (⊕ www.timeanddate.com/worldclock) can help you figure out the correct time anywhere.

Weather Accuweather.com (⊕ www.accuweather.com) is an independent weather-forecasting service with good coverage of hurricanes. **Weather.com** (⊕ www.weather.com) is the Web site for the Weather Channel.

Other Resources CIA World Factbook (⊕ www.odci.gov/cia/publications/factbook/index.html) has profiles of every country in the

world. It's a good source if you need some quick facts and figures.

VISITOR INFORMATION

Contact the city and state tourism offices for general information, details about seasonal events, discount passes, trip planning, and attraction information. The National Park Service has a Boston office where you can watch an eight-minute slide show on Boston's historic sites and get maps and directions. The Welcome Center and Boston Common Visitor Information Center offer general information.

WORD OF MOUTH

After your trip, be sure to rate the places you visited and share your experiences and travel tips with us and other Fodorites in Travel Ratings and Talk on www.fodors.com.

Contacts Boston Common Visitor Information Center (⊠ Tremont St. where the Freedom Trail begins, Downtown ☎ 617/426–3115). **Boston National Historical Park Visitor Center** (⊠ 15 State St., Downtown ☎ 617/242–5642 ⊕ www.nps.gov/bost). **Cambridge Tourism Office** (⊠ 4 Brattle St., Harvard Sq., Cambridge ☎ 800/862–5678 or 617/441–2884 ⊕ www.cambridge-usa.org). **Greater Boston Convention and Visitors Bureau** (⊠ 2 Copley Pl., Suite 105, Back Ba ☎ 888/733–2678 or 617/536–4100 🖷 617/424–7664 ⊕ www.bostonusa.com). **Massachusetts Office of Travel and Tourism** (⊠ State Transportation Bldg., 10 Park Plaza, Suite 4510, Back Bay ☎ 800/227–6277 or 617/973–8500 🖷 617/973–8525 ⊕ www.massvacation.com).

■ THINGS TO CONSIDER

GEAR

The principal rule on Boston weather is that there are no rules. A cold, overcast morning can become a sunny, warm afternoon—and vice versa. Thus, the best advice on how to dress is to layer your clothing so that you can remove or add garments as needed for comfort. Rain often appears with little warning, so remember to pack a raincoat and umbrella. Because Boston is a great walking city—with some picturesque but uneven cobblestone streets—be sure to bring comfortable shoes. In all seasons, remember it's often breezier along the coast; always carry a windbreaker and fleece jacket or sweatshirt to the beach.

SHIPPING LUGGAGE AHEAD

Imagine globe-trotting with only a carry-on in tow. Shipping your luggage in advance via an air-freight service is a great way to cut down on backaches, hassles, and stress—especially if your packing list includes strollers, car seats, etc. There are some things to be aware of, though.

First, research carry-on restrictions; if you absolutely need something that isn't practical to ship and isn't allowed in carry-ons, this strategy isn't for you. Second, plan to send your bags several days in advance to U.S. destinations and as much as two weeks in advance to some international destinations. Third, plan to spend some money: it will cost least $100 to send a small piece of luggage, a golf bag, or a pair of skis to a domestic destination, much more to places overseas.

Some people use Federal Express to ship their bags, but this can cost even more than air-freight services. All these services insure your bag (for most, the limit is $1,000, but you should verify that amount); you can, however, purchase additional insurance for about $1 per $100 of value.

Contacts **Luggage Concierge** (☎800/288-9818 ⊕www.luggageconcierge.com). **Luggage Express** (☎866/744-7224 ⊕www.usxpluggageexpress.com). **Luggage Free** (☎800/361-6871 ⊕www.luggagefree.com). **Sports Express** (☎800/357-4174 ⊕www.sportsexpress.com) specializes in shipping golf clubs and other sports equipment. **Virtual Bellhop** (☎877/235-5467 ⊕www.virtualbellhop.com).

TRIP INSURANCE

What kind of coverage do you honestly need? Do you even need trip insurance at all? Take a deep breath and read on.

We believe that comprehensive trip insurance is especially valuable if you're booking a very expensive or complicated trip (particularly to an isolated region) or if you're booking far in advance. Who knows what could happen six months down the road? But whether or not you get insurance has more to do with how comfortable you are assuming all that risk yourself.

Comprehensive travel policies typically cover trip cancellation and interruption, letting you cancel or cut your trip short because of a personal emergency, illness, or, in some cases, acts of terrorism in your destination. Such policies also cover evacuation and medical care. Some also cover you for trip delays because of bad weather or mechanical problems as well as for lost or delayed baggage. Another type of coverage to look for is financial default—that is, when your trip is disrupted because a tour operator, airline, or cruise line goes out of business. Generally you must buy this when you book your trip or shortly thereafter, and it's only available to you if your operator isn't on a list of excluded companies.

If you're going abroad, consider buying medical-only coverage at the very least. Neither Medicare nor some private insurers cover medical expenses anywhere outside the United States besides Mexico and Canada (including time aboard a cruise

PACKING 101

Why do some people travel with a convoy of huge suitcases yet never have a thing to wear? How do others pack a duffle with a week's worth of outfits *and* supplies for every contingency? We realize that packing is a matter of style, but there's a lot to be said for traveling light. These tips help fight the battle of the bulging bag.

■ **Make a list.** In a recent Fodor's survey, 29% of respondents said they make lists (and often pack) a week before a trip. You can use your list to pack and to repack at the end of your trip. It can also serve as record of the contents of your suitcase—in case it disappears in transit.

■ **Think it through.** What's the weather like? Is this a business trip? A cruise? Going abroad? In some places dress may be more or less conservative than you're used to. As you create your itinerary, note outfits next to each activity (don't forget accessories).

■ **Edit your wardrobe.** Plan to wear everything twice (better yet, thrice) and to do laundry along the way. Stick to one basic look—urban chic, sporty casual, etc. Build around one or two neutrals and an accent (e.g., black, white, and olive green). Women can freshen looks by changing scarves or jewelry. For a week's trip, you can look smashing with three bottoms, four or five tops, a sweater, and a jacket.

■ **Be practical.** Put comfortable shoes atop your list. (Did we need to say this?) Pack lightweight, wrinkle-resistant, compact, washable items. (Or this?) Stack and roll clothes, so they'll wrinkle less. Unless you're on a guided tour or a cruise, select luggage you can readily carry. Porters, like good butlers, are hard to find these days.

■ **Check weight and size limitations.** In the United States you may be charged extra for checked bags weighing more than 50 pounds. Abroad, some airlines don't allow you to check bags over 60 to 70 pounds, or they charge outrageous fees for every excess pound—or bag. Carry-on size limitations can be stringent, too.

■ **Check carry-on restrictions.** Research restrictions with the TSA. Rules vary abroad, so check them with your airline if you're traveling overseas on a foreign carrier. Consider packing all but essentials (travel documents, prescription meds, wallet) in checked luggage. This leads to a "pack only what you can afford to lose" approach that might help you streamline.

■ **Rethink valuables.** On U.S. flights, airlines are liable for only about $2,800 per person for bags. On international flights, the liability limit is around $635 per bag. But items like computers, cameras, and jewelry aren't covered, and as gadgetry can go on and off the list of carry-on no-no's, you can't count on keeping things safe by keeping them close. Although comprehensive travel policies may cover luggage, the liability limit is often a pittance. Your home-owner's policy may cover you sufficiently when you travel—or not.

■ **Lock it up.** If you must pack valuables, use TSA-approved locks (about $10) that can be unlocked by all U.S. security personnel.

■ **Tag it.** Always tag your luggage; use your business address if you don't want people to know your home address. Put the same information (and a copy of your itinerary) inside your luggage, too.

■ **Report problems immediately.** If your bags—or things in them—are damaged or go astray, file a written claim with your airline *before leaving the airport.* If the airline is at fault, it may give you money for essentials until your luggage arrives. Most lost bags are found within 48 hours, so alert the airline to your whereabouts for two or three days. If your bag was opened for security reasons in the States and something is missing, file a claim with the TSA.

Trip Insurance Resources

INSURANCE COMPARISON SITES		
Insure My Trip.com	800/487–4722	www.insuremytrip.com
Square Mouth.com	800/240–0369	www.quotetravelinsurance.com
COMPREHENSIVE TRAVEL INSURERS		
Access America	866/807–3982	www.accessamerica.com
CSA Travel Protection	800/873–9855	www.csatravelprotection.com
HTH Worldwide	610/254–8700 or 888/243–2358	www.hthworldwide.com
Travelex Insurance	888/457–4602	www.travelex-insurance.com
Travel Guard International	715/345–0505 or 800/826–4919	www.travelguard.com
Travel Insured International	800/243–3174	www.travelinsured.com
MEDICAL-ONLY INSURERS		
International Medical Group	800/628–4664	www.imglobal.com
International SOS	215/942–8000 or 713/521–7611	www.internationalsos.com
Wallach & Company	800/237–6615 or 504/687–3166	www.wallach.com

ship, even if it leaves from a U.S. port). Medical-only policies typically reimburse you for medical care (excluding that related to preexisting conditions) and hospitalization abroad, and provide for evacuation. You still have to pay the bills and await reimbursement from the insurer, though.

Expect comprehensive travel insurance policies to cost about 4% to 7% of the total price of your trip (it's more like 12% if you're over age 70). A medical-only policy may or may not be cheaper than a comprehensive policy. Always read the fine print of your policy to make sure that you are covered for the risks that are of most concern to you. Compare several policies to make sure you're getting the best price and range of coverage available.

BOOKING YOUR TRIP

Unless your cousin is a travel agent, you're probably among the millions of people who make most of their travel arrangements online.

But have you ever wondered just what the differences are between an online travel agent (a Web site through which you make reservations instead of going directly to the airline, hotel, or car-rental company), a discounter (a firm that does a high volume of business with a hotel chain or airline and accordingly gets good prices), a wholesaler (one that makes cheap reservations in bulk and then resells them to people like you), and an aggregator (one that compares all the offerings so you don't have to)?

Is it truly better to book directly on an airline or hotel Web site? And when does a real live travel agent come in handy?

ONLINE
You really have to shop around. A travel wholesaler such as Hotels.com or HotelClub.net can be a source of good rates, as can discounters such as Hotwire or Priceline, particularly if you can bid for your hotel room or airfare. Indeed, such sites sometimes have deals that are unavailable elsewhere. They do, however, tend to work only with hotel chains (which makes them just plain useless for getting hotel reservations outside major cities) or big airlines (so that often leaves out upstarts like jetBlue and some foreign carriers like Air India).

Also, with discounters and wholesalers you must generally prepay, and everything is nonrefundable. Before you fork over the dough, be sure to check the terms and conditions, so you know what a given company will do for you if there's a problem and what you'll have to deal with on your own.

■ TIP→ To be absolutely sure everything was processed correctly, confirm reservations made through online travel agents, discounters, and wholesalers directly with your hotel before leaving home.

Booking engines like Expedia, Travelocity, and Orbitz are actually travel agents, albeit high-volume, online ones. And airline travel packagers like American Airlines Vacations and Virgin Vacations—well, they're travel agents, too. But they may still not work with all the world's hotels.

An aggregator site will search many sites and pull the best prices for airfares, hotels, and rental cars from them. Most aggregators compare the major travel-booking sites such as Expedia, Travelocity, and Orbitz; some also look at airline Web sites, though rarely the sites of smaller budget airlines. Some aggregators also compare other travel products, including complex packages—a good thing, as you can sometimes get the best overall deal by booking an air-and-hotel package.

WITH A TRAVEL AGENT
If you use an agent—brick-and-mortar or virtual—you'll pay a fee for the service. And know that the service you get from some online agents isn't comprehensive. For example Expedia and Travelocity don't search for prices on budget airlines like jetBlue, Southwest, or small foreign carriers. That said, some agents (online or not) *do* have access to fares that are difficult to find otherwise, and the savings can more than make up for any surcharge.

A knowledgeable brick-and-mortar travel agent can be a godsend if you're booking a cruise, a package trip that's not available to you directly, an air pass, or a complicated itinerary including several overseas flights. What's more, travel agents that specialize in a destination may have exclusive access to certain deals and insider information on things such as charter flights. Agents who specialize in types of travelers (senior citizens, gays and lesbians, naturists) or types of trips (cruises, luxury travel, safaris) can also be invaluable.

■TIP➡Remember that Expedia, Travelocity, and Orbitz are travel agents, not just booking engines. To resolve any problems with a reservation made through these companies, contact them first.

A top-notch agent planning your trip to Russia will make sure you get the correct visa application and complete it on time; the one booking your cruise may get you a cabin upgrade or arrange to have bottle of champagne chilling in your cabin when you embark. And complain about the surcharges all you like, but when things don't work out the way you'd hoped, it's nice to have an agent to put things right.

Agent Resources American Society of Travel Agents (☎703/739–2782 ⊕www.travelsense.org).

Boston Travel Agent Garber Travel (☎800/359–4272 [FLY-GARBER] ⊕www.garbertravel.com).

▌AIRLINE TICKETS

Most domestic airline tickets are electronic; international tickets may be either electronic or paper. With an e-ticket the only thing you receive is an e-mailed receipt citing your itinerary and reservation and ticket numbers.

The greatest advantage of an e-ticket is that if you lose your receipt, you can simply print out another copy or ask the airline to do it for you at check-in. You usually pay a surcharge (up to $50) to get a paper ticket, if you can get one at all.

The sole advantage of a paper ticket is that it may be easier to endorse over to another airline if your flight is canceled and the airline with which you booked can't accommodate you on another flight.

■TIP➡Discount air passes that let you travel economically in a country or region must often be purchased before you leave home. In some cases you can only get them through a travel agent.

▌RENTAL CARS

When you reserve a car, ask about cancellation penalties, taxes, drop-off charges (if you're planning to pick up the car in one city and leave it in another), and surcharges (for being under or over a certain age, for additional drivers, or for driving across state or country borders or beyond a specific distance from your point of rental). All these things can add substantially to your costs. Request car seats and extras such as GPS when you book.

> ### WORD OF MOUTH
>
> "A Boston travel tip: Unless you plan some serious side trips, a car is *not* necessary."

Rates are sometimes—but not always—better if you book in advance or reserve through a rental agency's Web site. There are other reasons to book ahead, though: for popular destinations, during busy times of the year, or to ensure that you get certain types of cars (vans, SUVs, exotic sports cars).

■TIP➡Make sure that a confirmed reservation guarantees you a car. Agencies sometimes overbook, particularly for busy weekends and holiday periods.

While having a car can be convenient in Boston if you're planning day trips outside the city limits, driving in the city can be stressful since the roads and signage are not easy to maneuver. Parking can be hard to come by, especially during major events (the Boston Marathon, Red Sox games). If you do decide to rent a car, have a detailed map handy at all times.

Rates in Boston begin at about $40 a day and $200 or more a week for an economy car with air-conditioning, automatic

Online Booking Resources

AGGREGATORS		
Kayak	www.kayak.com	also looks at cruises and vacation packages.
Mobissimo	www.mobissimo.com	
Qixo	www.qixo.com	also compares cruises, vacation packages, and even travel insurance.
Sidestep	www.sidestep.com	also compares vacation packages and lists travel deals.
Travelgrove	www.travelgrove.com	also compares cruises and packages.
BOOKING ENGINES		
Cheap Tickets	www.cheaptickets.com	a discounter.
Expedia	www.expedia.com	a large online agency that charges a booking fee for airline tickets.
Hotwire	www.hotwire.com	a discounter.
lastminute.com	www.lastminute.com	specializes in last-minute travel the main site is for the U.K., but it has a link to a U.S. site.
Luxury Link	www.luxurylink.com	has auctions (surprisingly good deals) as well as offers on the high-end side of travel.
Onetravel.com	www.onetravel.com	a discounter for hotels, car rentals, airfares, and packages.
Orbitz	www.orbitz.com	charges a booking fee for airline tickets, but gives a clear breakdown of fees and taxes before you book.
Priceline.com	www.priceline.com	a discounter that also allows bidding.
Travel.com	www.travel.com	allows you to compare its rates with those of other booking engines.
Travelocity	www.travelocity.com	charges a booking fee for airline tickets, but promises good problem resolution.
ONLINE ACCOMMODATIONS		
Hotelbook.com	www.hotelbook.com	focuses on independent hotels worldwide.
Hotel Club	www.hotelclub.net	good for major cities worldwide.
Hotels.com	www.hotels.com	a big Expedia-owned wholesaler that offers rooms in hotels all over the world.
Quikbook	www.quikbook.com	offers "pay when you stay" reservations that let you settle your bill at checkout, not when you book.
OTHER RESOURCES		
Bidding For Travel	www.biddingfortravel.com	a good place to figure out what you can get and for how much before you start bidding on, say, Priceline.

10 WAYS TO SAVE

1. Nonrefundable is best. If saving money is more important than flexibility, get nonrefundable tickets. Remember that you'll pay as much as $100 if you change your plans.

2. Comparison shop. Web sites and travel agents can have different arrangements with the airlines and offer different prices for exactly the same flights.

3. Beware those prices. Many airline Web sites—and most ads—show prices *without* taxes and surcharges. Don't buy until you know the full price.

4. Stay loyal. Stick with one or two frequent-flier programs. You'll rack up free trips faster and quickly accumulate more perks. On some airlines these include a special reservations number, early boarding, access to upgrades, and more-roomy economy-class seating.

5. Watch those ticketing fees. Surcharges are usually added when you buy your ticket anywhere but on an airline Web site. (That includes by phone—even if you call the airline directly—and paper tickets regardless of how you book).

6. Check early and often. Start looking for cheap fares up to a year in advance. Keep looking until you find a price you like.

7. Don't work alone. Some Web sites have tracking features that will e-mail you immediately when good deals are posted.

8. Jump on the good deals. Waiting even a few minutes might mean paying more.

9. Be flexible. Look for departures on Tuesday, Wednesday, and Thursday, typically the cheapest days to travel. And check on prices for departures at different times and to and from alternative airports.

10. Weigh your options. What you get can be as important as what you save. A cheaper flight might have a long layover, or it might land at a secondary airport, where your ground transportation costs might be higher.

transmission, and unlimited mileage. This doesn't include gas, insurance charges, or the 5% tax. All major agencies listed below have branches at Logan International Airport.

CAR-RENTAL INSURANCE

Everyone who rents a car wonders whether the insurance that the rental companies offer is worth the expense. No one—including us—has a simple answer. It all depends on how much regular insurance you have, how comfortable you are with risk, and whether or not money is an issue.

If you own a car and carry comprehensive car insurance for both collision and liability, your personal auto insurance will probably cover a rental, but read your policy's fine print to be sure. If you don't have auto insurance, then you should probably buy the collision- or loss-damage waiver (CDW or LDW) from the rental company. This eliminates your liability for damage to the car.

Some credit cards offer CDW coverage, but it's usually supplemental to your own insurance and rarely covers SUVs, minivans, luxury models, and the like. If your coverage is secondary, you may still be liable for loss-of-use costs from the car-rental company (again, read the fine print). But no credit-card insurance is valid unless you use that card for *all* transactions, from reserving to paying the final bill.

■TIP➔ **Diners Club offers primary CDW coverage on all rentals reserved and paid for with the card. This means that Diners Club's company—not your own car insurance—pays in case of an accident. It doesn't mean that your car-insurance company won't raise your rates once it discovers you had an accident.**

You may also be offered supplemental liability coverage; the car-rental company is required to carry a minimal level of liability coverage insuring all renters, but it's rarely enough to cover claims in a really

Car Rental Resources

AUTOMOBILE ASSOCIATIONS		
American Automobile Association	315/797–5000	www.aaa.com; most contact with the organization is through state and regional members.
National Automobile Club	650/294–7000	www.thenac.com; membership open to CA residents only.
MAJOR AGENCIES		
Alamo	800/462–5266	www.alamo.com
Avis	800/230–4898 or 0870/606–0100 in U.K.	www.avis.com
Budget	800/527–0700	www.budget.com
Hertz	800/654–3131 or 0870/844–8844 in U.K.	www.hertz.com
National Car Rental	800/227–7368	www.nationalcar.com

serious accident if you're at fault. Your own auto-insurance policy will protect you if you own a car; if you don't, you have to decide whether you are willing to take the risk.

U.S. rental companies sell CDWs and LDWs for about $15 to $25 a day; supplemental liability is usually more than $10 a day. The car-rental company may offer you all sorts of other policies, but they're rarely worth the cost. Personal accident insurance, which is basic hospitalization coverage, is an especially egregious rip-off if you already have health insurance.

■ TIP→ You can decline the insurance from the rental company and purchase it through a third-party provider such as Travel Guard (www.travelguard.com)—$9 per day for $35,000 of coverage. That's sometimes just under half the price of the CDW offered by some car-rental companies.

■ VACATION PACKAGES

Packages *are not* guided excursions. Packages combine airfare, accommodations, and perhaps a rental car or other extras (theater tickets, guided excursions, boat trips, reserved entry to popular museums,

transit passes), but they let you do your own thing. During busy periods, packages may be your only option, as flights and rooms may be sold out otherwise.

Packages will definitely save you time. They can also save you money, particularly in peak seasons, but—and this is a really big "but"—you should price each part of the package separately to be sure. And be aware that prices advertised on Web sites and in newspapers rarely include service charges or taxes, which can up your costs by hundreds of dollars.

■ TIP→ Some packages and cruises are sold only through travel agents. Don't always assume that you can get the best deal by booking everything yourself.

Each year consumers are stranded or lose their money when packagers—even large ones with excellent reputations— go out of business. How can you protect yourself?

First, always pay with a credit card; if you have a problem, your credit-card company may help you resolve it. Second, buy trip insurance that covers default. Third, choose a company that belongs to the United States Tour Operators Association, whose members must set aside

10 WAYS TO SAVE

1. Beware of cheap rates. Those great rates aren't so great when you add in taxes, surcharges, and insurance. Such extras can double or triple the initial quote.

2. Rent weekly. Weekly rates are usually better than daily ones. Even if you only want to rent for five or six days, ask for the weekly rate; it may very well be cheaper than the daily rate for that period of time.

3. Don't forget the locals. Price local companies as well as the majors.

4. Airport rentals can cost more. Airports often add surcharges, which you can sometimes avoid by renting from an agency whose office is just off airport property.

5. Wholesalers can help. Investigate wholesalers, which don't own fleets but rent in bulk from firms that do, and which frequently offer better rates (note that you must usually pay for such rentals before leaving home).

6. Look for rate guarantees. With your rate locked in, you won't pay more, even if the price goes up in the local currency.

7. Fill up farther away. Avoid hefty refueling fees by filling the tank at a station well away from where you plan to turn in the car.

8. Pump it yourself. Don't buy the tank of gas that's in the car when you rent it unless you plan to do a lot of driving.

9. Get all your discounts. Find out whether a credit card you carry or organization or frequent-renter program to which you belong has a discount program. And confirm that such discounts really are a deal. You can often do better with special weekend or weekly rates offered by a rental agency.

10. Check out packages. Adding a car rental onto your air/hotel vacation package may be cheaper than renting a car separately.

funds to cover defaults. Finally, choose a company that also participates in the Tour Operator Program of the American Society of Travel Agents (ASTA), which will act as mediator in any disputes.

You can also check on the tour operator's reputation among travelers by posting an inquiry on one of the Fodors.com forums.

Traveling to Boston on a package tour makes it quite convenient for those interested only in hitting the highlights or major historic sites such as the Freedom Trail, Faneuil Hall, the Bunker Hill Memorial, Quincy Market, and Harvard Square. If you're interested in exploring more neighborhoods, a tour will likely not give you access to these.

Organizations American Society of Travel Agents (ASTA ☎800/965-2782 or 703/739-2782 ⊕www.astanet.com). **United States Tour Operators Association** (USTOA ☎212/599-6599 ⊕www.ustoa.com). ■TIP➔ **Local tourism boards can provide information about lesser-known and small-niche operators that sell packages to only a few destinations.**

TRANSPORTATION

The best form of transportation within Boston or Cambridge/Somerville is the MBTA system, or the T, as it's known locally. Five separate lines run through the entire city and out towards the outlying suburbs. The system of underground trains, aboveground trolleys, and buses will take you to every major point of interest. A car is only necessary for getting out of town.

In most cases, address numbers are listed in even numbers on one side of the street and odd number on the opposite side.

■TIP→ **Ask the local tourist board about hotel and local transportation packages that include tickets to major museum exhibits or other special events.**

■ BY AIR

Flying to Boston takes about 1 hour from New York, 1½ hours from Washington, DC, 2¼ hours from Chicago, 3¾ hours from Dallas, 5½ hours from Los Angeles, 7½ hours from London, and 21–22 hours from Sydney (including connection time). Delta, US Airways, and jetBlue have many daily shuttle flights from New York and Washington.

■TIP→ **The Boston Convention and Visitor Bureau's Web site,** ⊕ *www.bostonusa. com,* **has direct links to 19 airlines that service the city. You can book flights here, too.**

Airlines & Airports Airline and Airport Links.com (⊕www.airlineandairportlinks.com) has links to many of the world's airlines and airports.

Airline Security Issues Transportation Security Administration (⊕www.tsa.gov) has answers for almost every question that might come up.

AIRPORTS

Boston's major airport, Logan International (BOS), is across the harbor from Downtown, about 2 mi outside the city

NAVIGATING BOSTON

■ Boston is a walkable city but since its streets were originally laid out as cow paths leading from the waterfront to spots around the city, they are sometimes tricky to navigate.

■ Head towards Boston Common or the Public Garden. It's a central spot in the city and there are maps around the park to help direct you around the city. Or, if you're near the waterfront, head towards Quincy Market where there are also maps to help you navigate.

■ The Financial District and Downtown Crossing are part of Downtown. Since the streets here are part of that circuit of former cow paths, they have no rhyme or reason and often run only one way. If you're walking through the area, be sure to bring a map.

■ In general, signage in Boston is hard to come by, especially on roadways. But the city has done a great job of posting street maps at major visitor points throughout the city. If you find yourself wandering around lost, your best bet is to ask for directions as most residents are familiar with how difficult it is to find your way around. If their directions seem complicated, ask them to write it down.

■ The public transportation system, the T, offers easy-to-read navigation guides and maps in every station. It stops at all major points of interest throughout the city and just beyond the city limits, too.

FLYING 101

Flying may not be as carefree as it once was, but there are some things you can do to make your trip smoother.

■ **Minimize the time spent standing line.** Buy an e-ticket, check in at an electronic kiosk, or—even better—check in on your airline's Web site before leaving home. Pack light and limit carry-on items to only the essentials.

■ **Arrive when you need to**. Research your airline's policy. It's usually at least an hour before domestic flights and two to three hours before international flights. But airlines at some busy airports have more stringent requirements. Check the TSA Web site for estimated security waiting times at major airports.

■ **Get to the gate**. If you aren't at the gate at least 10 minutes before your flight is scheduled to take off (sometimes earlier), you won't be allowed to board.

■ **Double-check your flight times**. Do this especially if you reserved far in advance. Schedules change, and alerts may not reach you.

■ **Don't go hungry**. Ask whether your airline offers anything to eat; even when it does, be prepared to pay.

■ **Get the seat you want**. Often, you can pick a seat when you buy your ticket on an airline Web site. But it's not guaranteed; the airline could change the plane after you book, so double-check. You can also select a seat if you check in electronically. Avoid seats on the aisle directly across from the lavatories. Frequent fliers say those are even worse than back-row seats that don't recline.

■ **Got kids? Get info**. Ask the airline about its children's menus, activities, and fares. Sometimes infants and toddlers fly free if they sit on a parent's lap, and older children fly for half price in their own seats. Also inquire about policies involving car seats; having one may limit seating options. Also ask about seat-belt extenders for car seats. And note that you can't count on a flight attendant to produce an extender; you may have to ask for one when you board.

■ **Check your scheduling**. Don't buy a ticket if there's less than an hour between connecting flights. Although schedules are padded, if anything goes wrong you might miss your connection. If you're traveling to an important function, depart a day early.

■ **Bring paper**. Even when using an e-ticket, always carry a hard copy of your receipt; you may need it to get your boarding pass, which most airports require to get past security.

■ Complain at the airport. If your baggage goes astray or your flight goes awry, complain before leaving the airport. Most carriers require this.

■ **Beware of overbooked flights**. If a flight is oversold, the gate agent will usually ask for volunteers and offer some sort of compensation for taking a different flight. If you're bumped from a flight *involuntarily*, the airline must give you some kind of compensation if an alternate flight can't be found within one hour.

■ **Know your rights**. If your flight is delayed because of something within the airline's control (bad weather doesn't count), the airline must get you to your destination on the same day, even if they have to book you on another airline and in an upgraded class. Read the Contract of Carriage, which is usually buried on the airline's Web site.

■ **Be prepared**. The Boy Scout motto is especially important if you're traveling during a stormy season. To quickly adjust your plans, program a few numbers into your cell: your airline, an airport hotel or two, your destination hotel, your car service, and/or your travel agent.

center, and can be easily reached by taxi, water taxi, or subway (called the "T") via the Silver or Blue Line. Logan has five terminals, identified by letters A through E. A free airport shuttle runs between the terminals and airport hotels. Some airlines use different terminals for international and domestic flights. Most international flights arrive at Terminal E. Most charter flights arrive at Terminal D. A visitor center in Terminal C offers tourist information. Green Airport, in Providence, Rhode Island, and the Manchester Airport in Manchester, New Hampshire, are both about an hour from Boston.

■ TIP→ If you travel frequently, look into the TSA's Registered Traveler program. The program, which is still being tested in several U.S. airports, is designed to cut down on gridlock at security checkpoints by allowing prescreened travelers to pass quickly through kiosks that scan an iris and/or a fingerprint. How sci-fi is that?

Airport Information **Green Airport** (⊠ Off I-95, Exit 13, Providence, RI ☎ 888/268–7222 or 401/737–8222 ⊕ www.pvdairport.com). **Logan International** (⊠ I-90 east to Ted Williams Tunnel ☎ 800/235–6426 ⊕ www. massport.com T Airport). **Manchester Airport** (⊠ Off I-293/Rte. 101, Exit 2, Manchester, NH ☎ 603/624–6539 ⊕ www.flymanchester.com).

TRANSFERS—BY CAR OR TAXI

For recorded information about traveling to and from Logan Airport, as well as details about parking, contact the airport's ground-transportation hotline. Traffic can be maddening; it's a good idea to take public transportation to and from the airport.

When driving from Logan to downtown Boston, the most direct route is by way of the Sumner Tunnel ($3 toll inbound; no toll outbound). On weekends and holidays and after 10 PM weekdays, you can get around Sumner Tunnel backups by using the Ted Williams Tunnel ($3 toll inbound; no toll outbound), which will steer you onto the Southeast Expressway

south of downtown Boston. Follow the signs to I-93 northbound to head back into the downtown area.

Taxis can be hired outside each terminal. Fares to and from Downtown should be about $15–$18, including tip. Taxis must pay an extra toll of $4.50 and a $2 airport fee when leaving the airport (but not going in) that will be tacked onto your bill at the end of the trip. (Major traffic jams or taking a longer route to avoid traffic will add to the fare.)

Contact **Logan Airport Customer Information Hotline** (☎ 800/235–6426).

TRANSFERS—BY SUBWAY

The Blue and Silver lines on the subway, commonly called "the T" (and operated by the MBTA), run from the airport to downtown Boston in about 20 minutes. The Blue Line is best if you're heading to North Station, Faneuil Hall, North End/Waterfront, or Back Bay (Hynes Convention Center, Prudential Center area). Take the Silver Line to South Station, Boston Convention and Exhibition Center, Seaport World Trade Center, Chinatown Theater, and South End areas. From North and South stations, you can reach the Red, Green, or Orange lines, or commuter rail. The T costs $2 for in-town travel if you're paying in cash or $1.70 if you purchase a CharlieCard (a prepaid stored-value card). *See By Subway, Train, and Trolley, below for more information.* Free 24-hour shuttle buses connect the subway station with all airline terminals. Shuttle Bus 22 runs between the subway and Terminals A and B, and Shuttle Bus 33 runs between the subway and Terminals C, D, and E.

Contact **MBTA** (☎ 800/392–6100, 617/222–3200, 617/222–5146 TTY ⊕ www.mbta.com).

TRANSFERS—BY BUS OR SHUTTLE VAN

Several companies offer shared-van service to many Boston-area destinations. J. C. Transportation, Logan/Boston Hotel

Shuttle, and Ace American provide door-to-door service to several major Back Bay and Downtown hotels. (Check their Web sites for a listing of hotels.) Reservations are not required, because vans swing by all terminals every 20 minutes to half hour. One-way fares are $14 per person. Easy Transportation is also a shared-van service which runs from the airport to the Back Bay Hilton, Radisson, and Lenox hotels from 7 AM to 10 PM. Star Shuttle operates shared vans from the airport to the Marriott Copley Place and Sheraton Copley, every hour on the half hour, from 5:30 AM to 11:30 PM. Logan Express buses travel from the airport to the suburbs of Braintree, Framingham, Peabody, and Woburn. One-way fares are $11.

Contacts **Ace American** (☎800/517–2281). **Easy Transportation** (☎617/445–1107). **J.C. Transportation** (☎800/517–2281 or 781/598–3433 ⊕www.jctransportationshuttle.com). **Logan/Boston Hotel Shuttle** (☎877/315–4700). **Logan Express** (☎800/235–6426 ⊕www. massport.com). **Star Shuttle** (☎617/230–6005).

FLIGHTS

Airline Contacts **Alaska Airlines** (☎800/252–7522 or 206/433–3100 ⊕www.alaskaair.com). **American Airlines** (☎800/433–7300 ⊕www.aa.com). **ATA** (☎800/435–9282 or 317/282–8308 ⊕www.ata.com). **Continental Airlines** (☎800/523–3273 for U.S. and Mexico reservations, 800/231–0856 for international reservations ⊕www.continental.com). **Delta Airlines** (☎800/221–1212 for U.S. reservations, 800/241–4141 for international reservations ⊕www.delta.com). **jetBlue** (☎800/538–2583 ⊕www.jetblue.com). **Northwest Airlines** (☎800/225–2525 ⊕www.nwa.com). **Southwest Airlines** (☎800/435–9792 ⊕www. southwest.com). **Spirit Airlines** (☎800/772–7117 or 586/791–7300 ⊕www.spiritair.com). **United Airlines** (☎800/864–8331 for U.S. reservations, 800/538–2929 for international reservations ⊕www.united.com). **USAirways** (☎800/428–4322 for U.S. and Canada reser-

---

COMMUTING WITH A VIEW

The Rowes Wharf Water Taxi offers a stunning glimpse of the city's skyline as it makes seven-minute trips across Boston Harbor between Logan Airport and Rowes Wharf in downtown Boston.

---

vations, 800/622–1015 for international reservations ⊕www.usairways.com).

▌ BY BOAT

Rowes Wharf Water Taxi shuttles from Logan Airport to Rowes Wharf, Downtown for $10 per person. It operates weekdays year-round and daily June through September, between 7 AM and 7 PM.

Harbor Express water taxis takes passengers from Logan Airport to Long Wharf, Downtown ($10) and to Quincy and Hull on the South Shore ($12). Boats leave approximately every 40–45 minutes 6:20 AM–10:20 PM Monday through Thursday, 6:20 AM–11 PM Friday, 8:30 AM–10:30 PM Saturday, and 8:30 AM–9 PM Sunday.

City Water Taxi has an on-call boat service between the airport and 16 downtown locations that operates from 7 AM to 10 PM Monday through Saturday and 7 AM to 8 PM on Sunday from April through November. One-way fares to or from the airport are $10, and round-trip tickets are $17.

MBTA commuter boat service operates weekdays between several downtown harbor destinations and quite a few locations on the South Shore. One-way fares range from $1.50 to $6 depending on destination. Schedules change seasonally, so call ahead.

Several boat companies make runs between the airport and downtown destinations. Take the free Shuttle Bus 66 from any terminal to the airport's ferry dock to catch Boston's water taxis.

Information **City Water Taxi** (☎617/422–0392 ⊕www.citywatertaxi.com). **Harbor Express** (☎617/376–8417 or 617/222–6999 ⊕www.harborexpress.com). **MBTA** (☎617/222–5000 ⊕www.mbta.com). **Rowes Wharf Water Taxi** (☎617/406–8584 ⊕www.roweswharfwatertaxi.com).

▌BY BUS

ARRIVING & DEPARTING

Greyhound has buses to Boston from all major cities in North America. Besides its main location at South Station, Greyhound has suburban terminals in Newton, Framingham, and Worcester. Peter Pan Bus Lines connects Boston with cities elsewhere in Massachusetts, Connecticut, New Jersey, New York, and Maryland.

Concord Trailways heads to Maine and New Hampshire. C&J Trailways sends buses up the New Hampshire coast to Dover. Vermont Transit Bus Lines travels to Vermont, New Hampshire, and Montréal. Plymouth & Brockton buses link Boston with the South Shore and Cape Cod.

All of the above-mentioned bus companies leave from South Station, which is connected to the Amtrak station. The station is clean and safe. Many bus lines also make stops at Logan Airport; check individual lines for up-to-date schedules.

The Fung Wah bus offers inexpensive (very) low-maintenance service between the Chinatown neighborhoods of Boston and New York. Bonanza leaves from the South Station bus terminal.

If you want to travel in style, the Limo-Liner provides luxury bus service (with television, movies, high-speed Internet, and food-and-drink service) between Boston's Hilton Back Bay and Manhattan's Hilton New York for $79 each way. This service is open to the general public, not just guests of the Hilton. Reservations are a good idea.

Fares and schedules for all buses except LimoLiner are posted at South Station, at many of the tourist kiosks, and online.

Major credit cards are accepted for all buses. You can usually purchase your tickets online.

Bus Information **Bonanza Bus Lines** (☎888/751–8800 ⊕www.bonanzabus.com). **C&J Trailways** (☎800/258–7111 ⊕www.cjtrailways.com). **Concord Trailways** (☎800/639–3317 ⊕www.concordtrailways.com). **Fung Wah Bus** (☎617/345–8000 ⊕www.fungwahbus.com). **Greyhound** (☎800/231–2222 ⊕www.greyhound.com). **LimoLiner** (☎888/546–5469 or 617/424–5469 ⊕www.limoliner.com). **Peter Pan** (☎800/237–8747 ⊕www.peterpanbus.com). **Plymouth & Brockton** (☎508/746–0378 ⊕www.p-b.com). **Vermont Transit Bus Lines** (☎800/552–8737 ⊕www.vermonttransit.com).

Station Information **South Station** (✉700 Atlantic Ave., at Summer St., Downtown ⊤South Station).

GETTING AROUND

Buses of the Massachusetts Bay Transportation Authority (MBTA) crisscross the metropolitan area and travel farther into suburbia than subway and trolley lines. Buses run roughly from 5:30 AM to 12:30 AM.

As of this writing, fares are $1.50 if paying in cash, $1.25 if paying with a pre-purchased CharlieCard for trips within the city; you often pay an extra fare for longer lines that run to the suburbs. The SmarTraveler information line provides service updates.

CharlieCards (prepaid stored-value fare cards), sold at all subway terminals, can be purchased with cash or with debit or credit cards. To pay the bus fare, either flash your pass or pay in cash when you enter. Drivers accept dollar bills but don't have change.

Bus Information **MBTA** (☎617/222–3200, 617/222–5146 TTY ⊕www.mbta.com).

SmarTraveler (☎617/374–1234 ⊕www. smartraveler.com).

▌BY CAR

Driving isn't easy in Boston. It's important to plan out a route in advance if you are unfamiliar with the city. There is a profusion of one-way streets, so always keep a detailed map handy. It's also a good idea to pay extra attention to other drivers. Boston drivers have a bad reputation, and you should watch out for those using the emergency breakdown lanes (illegal unless posted otherwise), passing on the right, or turning from the wrong lane.

It's best to park in lots or garages rather than on the street. You're more likely to avoid tickets, accidents, or theft. Remember that the Central Artery/Tunnel Project, a massive highway reconstruction effort in downtown Boston that's also known as the "Big Dig," continues to cause traffic snarls. The latest information on the construction is available on the project's Web site, ⊕www.masspike. com/bigdig.

GASOLINE

Gas stations are not plentiful in downtown Boston. Try Cambridge Street (behind Beacon Hill, near Massachusetts General Hospital), near the airport in East Boston, along Commonwealth Avenue or Cambridge Street in Allston/Brighton, or off the Southeast Expressway just south of downtown Boston.

Cambridge service stations can be found along Memorial Drive, Massachusetts Avenue, and Broadway. In Brookline, try Commonwealth Avenue or Boylston Street. Gas stations with 24-hour service can be found at many exits off Route 3 to Cape Cod, suburban Route 128 and Interstate 95, and at service plazas on the Massachusetts Turnpike. Many offer both full and self-service.

PARKING

Parking on Boston streets is tricky. Some neighborhoods have strictly enforced residents-only rules, with just a handful of two-hour visitors' spaces; others have meters, which usually cost 25¢ for 15 minutes, with a one- or two-hour maximum. Keep a few quarters handy, as most city meters take nothing else.

Parking-police officers are ruthless—it's not unusual to find a ticket on your windshield five minutes after your meter expires. However, most on-street parking is free after 8 PM in the city and on Sunday. Repeat offenders who don't pay fines may find the "boot" (an immovable steel clamp) secured to one of their wheels.

Major public lots are at Government Center and Quincy Market, beneath Boston Common (entrance on Charles Street), beneath Post Office Square, at the Prudential Center, at Copley Place, and off Clarendon Street near the John Hancock Tower. Smaller lots and garages are scattered throughout Downtown, especially around the Theater District and off Atlantic Avenue in the North End. Most are expensive; expect to pay up to $8 an hour or $24 to park all day. The few city garages are a bargain at about $7–$11 per day. Theaters, restaurants, stores, and tourist attractions often provide customers with one or two hours of free parking. Most downtown restaurants offer valet parking.

ROAD CONDITIONS

Bostonians tend to drive erratically. These habits, coupled with inconsistent street and traffic signs, one-way streets, and heavy congestion, make it a nerve-wracking city to navigate. Many roadways in the city are under construction or in need of repairs. Potholes and manhole covers sticking up above the street are the most common hazards. In general, err on the side of caution.

ROADSIDE EMERGENCIES

Dial 911 in an emergency to reach police, fire, or ambulance services. If you're a member of the AAA auto club, call their 24-hour help bureau.

Emergency Services AAA (☎800/222–4357).

■ BY SUBWAY, TRAIN & TROLLEY

The Massachusetts Bay Transportation Authority (MBTA)—or "T" when referring to the subway line—operates subways, elevated trains, and trolleys along five connecting lines. A 24-hour hotline and the MBTA Web site offer information on routes, schedules, fares, wheelchair access, and other matters. Free maps are available at the MBTA's Park Street Station information stand, open daily from 7 AM to 10 PM. They're also available online at ⊕*www.mbta.com.*

"Inbound" trains head into the city center and "outbound" trains head away from downtown Boston. If you get on the Red Line at South Station, the train heading toward Cambridge is inbound. But once you pass the Park Street station, the train becomes an outbound train. The best way to figure out which way to go is to know the last stop on the train, which is usually listed on the front of the train. So, from Downtown, the Red Line to Cambridge would be the Alewife train and the Green Line to Fenway would be the Boston College or Cleveland Circle train.

Trains operate from about 5:30 AM to about 12:30 AM. T fares are $2 for adults paying in cash or $1.70 with a prepurchased CharlieCard. There are CharlieCard dispensing machines at almost every subway stop. Children under age 11 ride free and senior citizens pay 60¢. An extra fare is required outbound on the most distant Red Line stops (for example, the fare each way from Braintree is $2.50). Fares on the commuter rail—the

Purple Line—vary widely; check with the MBTA.

One-day ($9) and seven-day ($15) passes are available for unlimited travel on subways, city buses, and inner-harbor ferries. You must pay a double fare if you're headed to some suburban stations such as Braintree; pay the second fare as you exit the station. Buy passes at any full-service MBTA stations. Passes are also sold at the Boston Common Visitor Information Center (⇨ *Visitor Information)* and at some hotels.

The Red Line originates at Braintree and Mattapan to the south; the routes join near South Boston and continue to suburban Arlington. The Green Line operates elevated trolleys in the suburbs that dip underground in the city center. The line originates at Cambridge's Lechmere, heads south, and divides into four routes that end at Boston College (Commonwealth Avenue), Cleveland Circle (Beacon Street), Riverside, and Heath Street (Huntington Avenue). Buses connect Heath Street to the old Arborway terminus.

The Blue Line runs weekdays from Bowdoin Square and weeknights and weekends from Government Center to the Wonderland Racetrack in Revere, north of Boston. The Orange Line runs from Oak Grove in north suburban Malden to Forest Hills near the Arnold Arboretum. The Silver Line consists of two transit lines. One connects Downtown Crossing and Boylston to Dudley Square. The other runs from South Station down the waterfront to City Point. Park Street Station (on the Common) and State Street are the major downtown transfer points.

TICKET/PASS	PRICE
Single Fare	$2
Day Pass	$9
Weekly Pass	$15
Monthly Unlimited Pass	$59

Contact **MBTA** (☎800/392-6100, 617/222-3200, 617/222-5854 TTY ⊕www.mbta.com).

▌BY TAXI

Cabs are available around the clock. You can also call for a cab or find them outside most hotels and at designated cab stands around the city which are marked by signs. Taxis generally line up in Harvard Square, around South Station, near Faneuil Hall Marketplace, at Long Wharf, near Massachusetts General Hospital, and in the Theater District. A taxi ride within the city of Boston starts at $1.75, and costs 30¢ for each 1/8 mi thereafter. Licensed cabs have meters and provide receipts. An illuminated rooftop sign indicates an available cab. If you're going to or from the airport or to the suburbs, ask about flat rates. Cabdrivers sometimes charge extra for multiple stops. One-way streets often make circuitous routes necessary and increase your cost.

Taxi Companies **Boston Cab Association** (☎617/536-3200). **Cambridge Checker Cab** (✉Cambridge ☎617/497-1500). **Green Cab Association** (☎617/625-5000). **Independent Taxi Operators Association (ITOA)** (☎617/825-4000). **Town Taxi** (☎617/536-5000).

▌BY TRAIN

Boston is served by Amtrak at North Station, South Station, and Back Bay Station, which accommodate frequent departures to and arrivals from New York, Philadelphia, and Washington, DC. Amtrak's pricey high-speed Acela train cuts the travel time between Boston and New York from 4½ hours to 3½ hours. South Station is also the eastern terminus of Amtrak's *Lake Shore Limited,* which travels daily between Boston and Chicago by way of Albany, Rochester, Buffalo, and Cleveland. An additional Amtrak station with ample

parking is just off Route 128 in suburban Westwood, southwest of Boston.

The MBTA runs commuter trains to points south, west, and north. Those bound for Worcester, Needham, Forge Park, Providence (RI), and Stoughton leave from South Station and Back Bay Station; those to Fitchburg, Lowell, Haverhill, Newburyport, and Rockport operate out of North Station.

Amtrak tickets and reservations are available at Amtrak stations, by telephone, through travel agents, or online. Amtrak schedule and fare information can be found at South Station, Back Bay Station, or the Route 128 station in suburban Westwood, as well as online. The 24-hour hotline is another good source for route, schedule, fare, and other information. Free maps are available at the MBTA's Park Street Station information stand.

Amtrak ticket offices accept all major credit cards, cash, traveler's checks, and personal checks when accompanied by a valid photo ID and a major credit card. You may pay on board with cash or a major credit card, but a surcharge may apply. MBTA commuter-rail stations generally accept only cash. You may also pay in cash on board commuter trains, but there may be a $1–$2 surcharge.

Amtrak has both reserved and unreserved trains. During peak times, such as a Friday night, get a reservation and a ticket in advance. Trains at nonpeak times are unreserved, with seats assigned on a first-come, first-served basis.

Train Information **Back Bay Station** (✉145 Dartmouth St., Back Bay). **North Station** (✉Causeway and Friend Sts., North End). **South Station** (✉Atlantic Ave. and Summer St., Downtown).

ON THE GROUND

▪ COMMUNICATIONS

INTERNET

Most downtown hotels have started offering either free or fee-based wireless in their rooms and common areas. Call your hotel before arriving to confirm.

There are also a small number of Internet cafés on Newbury Street and scattered Downtown which charge a small fee ($2 and up) depending on how many minutes you use. Most Starbucks locations and locally based coffee shops, such as Espresso Royale, have Wi-Fi service.

Contacts Cybercafes (⊕ www.cybercafes. com) lists more than 4,000 Internet cafés worldwide. **WiFi Free Spot** (⊕ www.wifi-freespot.com/mass.com) lists hundreds of spots where you can connect to free Wi-Fi around the state.

▪ DAY TOURS & GUIDES

All of Boston's excellent orientation tours stop at spots along the Freedom Trail. Bus tours, which cost around $25 and run daily from mid-March to early November, traverse the main historic neighborhoods in less than four hours. Reserve bus tours at least a day in advance. Narrated trolley tours, which usually cost $26 or so, don't require reservations and are more flexible; you can get on and off as you wish. A full trip normally lasts 1½–2 hours. All trolleys run daily, though less frequently off-season. Because they're open vehicles, be sure to dress appropriately for the weather. Boston Private Tours has customized van tours of the Greater Boston area.

RECOMMENDED TOURS/GUIDES

BOAT TOURS

Boston has many waterways that offer stunning views of the city skyline. Narrated sightseeing water tours generally run from spring through early fall,

CON OR CONCIERGE?

Good hotel concierges are invaluable—for arranging transportation, getting reservations at the hottest restaurant, and scoring tickets for a sold-out show or entrée to an exclusive nightclub. They're in the know and well connected. That said, sometimes you have to take their advice with a grain of salt.

It's not uncommon for restaurants to ply concierges with free food and drink in exchange for steering diners their way. Indeed, European concierges often receive referral *fees*. Hotel chains usually have guidelines about what their concierges can accept. The best concierges, however, are above reproach. This is particularly true of those who belong to the prestigious international society of Les Clefs d'Or.

What can you expect of a concierge? At a typical tourist-class hotel you can expect him or her to give you the basics: to show you something on a map, make a standard restaurant reservation (particularly if you don't speak the language), or help you book a tour or airport transportation.

Savvy concierges at the finest hotels and resorts can arrange for just about any good or service imaginable—and do so quickly. You should compensate them appropriately. A $10 tip is enough to show appreciation for a table at a hot restaurant. But the reward should really be much greater for tickets to that U2 concert that's been sold out for months or for those last-minute sixth-row-center seats for *The Lion King*.

daily in summer, and on weekends in the shoulder seasons. (Labor Day weekend is often the cutoff point.) These trips normally last ¾–1½ hours and cost less than $20. Many companies also offer sunset or evening cruises with music and other entertainment.

The Boston Duck Tours, which gives narrated land-water tours on a World War II amphibious vehicle, are particularly popular. After driving past several historic sights, the vehicle dips into the Charles River to offer a view of the Boston skyline. These tours, costing $25 per person, run later than most, through late November.

June through September, you can relive the Golden Age of Sail aboard the *Liberty Clipper*, a replica two-masted gaff-rigged schooner that operates midday harbor tours and romantic sunset cruises from Long Wharf.

Boston Harbor Cruises and Massachusetts Bay Lines have tours around the harbor. Trips with Boston Duck Tours and the Charles Riverboat Company are along the Charles River Basin.

Fees & Schedules Boston Duck Tours (✉ Departures from Prudential Center, Huntington Ave. in front of Shaw's supermarket, and from the Museum of Science ☎ 617/267–3825 ⊕ www.bostonducktours.com). **Boston Harbor Cruises** (✉ 1 Long Wharf ☎ 877/733–9425 or 617/227–4321 ⊕ www.bostonharborcruises.com). **Charles Riverboat Company** (✉ 100 CambridgeSide Pl., Suite 320, Cambridge ☎ 617/621–3001 ⊕ www.charlesriverboat.com). Liberty Clipper (☎ 617/742–0333 ⊕ www.libertyfleet.com).

Massachusetts Bay Lines (✉ 60 Rowes Wharf ☎ 617/542–8000 ⊕ www.massbaylines.com).

BUS TOURS

Boston Private Tours has customized tours in vans or limousines. Brush Hill has more-traditional charter bus tours

as well as smaller tours, with lots of pre-packaged options and add-ons.

Both Brush Hill and Old Town Trolley have 1½-hour narrated tours. Old Town Trolley tours focus on history.

Fees & Schedules Boston Private Tours (☎ 800/620–1136 ⊕ www.bostonprivatetours.com). **Brush Hill Tours** (✉ Transportation Bldg., 16 Charles St. S ☎ 800/343–1328 or 781/986–6100 ⊕ www.brushhilltours.com).

Old Town Trolley (✉ 380 Dorchester Ave., South Boston ☎ 800/868–7482 or 617/269–7150 ⊕ www.historictours.com/boston).

THEME TOURS

See how a brewery operates at the Boston Beer Museum & Samuel Adams Brewery; hear spine-tingling tales about Boston's famous cemeteries; or tour (for free) the offices and printing plant of the *Boston Globe*. These tours are often given a few days a week. Some organizations have special restrictions, such as an age limit for children. Many tours are free, but you'll often need to make a reservation at least a few days in advance and call ahead for schedules.

Art Tours Boston Art Tours (⊕ www.bostonarttours.com ☎ 617/732–3920).

Beer Tours Boston Beer Museum & Samuel Adams Brewery (✉ Boston Beer Company, 30 Germania St., Jamaica Plain ☎ 617/368–5080 ⊕ www.samueladams.com).

Bike Tours Boston Bike Tours (✉ Meet at Boston Common near Visitor Information Center ☎ 617/368–5902 ⊕ www.bostonbiketours.com).

Children's Tours Boston by Little Feet (✉ Meet at Samuel Adams statue in front of Faneuil Hall ☎ 617/367–2345 ⊕ www.bostonbyfoot.com).

Gardens & Parks Tours Beacon Hill Garden Club Tours (✉ Charles and Beacon Sts., Beacon Hill ☎ 617/227–4392 ⊕ www.beaconhillgardenclub.org). **Boston Park Rangers** (✉ Parks and Recreation Dept. kiosk in

Boston Common ☎617/635-7487 ⊕www.cityofboston.gov/parks).

Graveyard Tours Ghosts and Legends of Boston (☎866/311-4467 ⊕www.ghostsofboston.com).

History Tours Bay Colony Historical Tours (✉1 Cordis St., Charlestown ☎617/523-7303). The **Literary Trail of Greater Boston** (✉One Broadway, Suite 600, Cambridge ☎617/621-4020 ⊕www.lit-trail.org).

Movie Tours Boston Movie Tours (✉Meet at Shaw Memorial in front of the State House ☎866/668-4345 ⊕www.bostonmovietours.net).

WALKING TOURS

Boston is the perfect city for walking tours, to explore topics ranging from history and literature to ethnic neighborhoods. Most tours cost less than $20 and last one to two hours. Guides prefer to keep groups at fewer than 20 people, so always reserve ahead. Several organizations give tours once or twice a day spring through fall and by appointment (if at all) in winter. Others run tours a few days a week, spring through fall.

The Women's Heritage Trail, the Freedom Trail, and the Black Heritage Trail can be completed as self-guided tours. Maps for the Women's Heritage Trail are available online and at the Old State House and the National Park Service Visitor Center (⇨ Visitor Information). The Boston Common Visitor Information Center (⇨ Visitor Information) has maps of the Freedom Trail, which is indicated with a red line painted on the ground. The Freedom Trail and the Black Heritage Trail can also be completed with a ranger-led group. The Boston and Cambridge centers for Adult Education lead in-depth educational tours on many topics, most of them centered around art, architecture, and literature.

Harvard Square is the starting point for free student-led campus tours.

Fees & Schedules Black Heritage Trail (☎617/725-0022 ⊕www.afroammuseum.org). **Boston by Foot** (✉77 N. Washington St. ☎617/367-2345, 617/367-3766 recorded information ⊕www.bostonbyfoot.com). **Boston Center for Adult Education** (✉5 Commonwealth Ave. ☎617/267-4430 ⊕www.bcae.org). **Cambridge Center for Adult Education** (✉42 Brattle St., Cambridge ☎617/547-6789 ⊕www.ccae.org). **Freedom Trail** (☎617/242-5642 ⊕www.thefreedomtrail.org). **Harvard Campus Tours** (☎617/495-1573 ⊕www.harvard.edu/community/visitors.html).

Historic New England (✉141 Cambridge St. ☎617/227-3956 ⊕www.historicnewengland.org). **North End Market Tour** (✉6 Charter St. ☎617/523-6032 ⊕www.northendmarkettours.com). **Women's Heritage Trail** (☎617/522-2872 ⊕www.bwht.org).

∎ HOURS OF OPERATION

Banks are generally open weekdays 9–4 or 5, plus Saturday 9 AM–noon or 1 PM at some branches. Public buildings are open weekdays 9–5.

Although hours vary quite a bit, most museums are open Monday through Saturday 9 or 10 AM–5 or 6 PM and Sunday noon–5 PM. Many are closed one day a week, usually Monday.

The major pharmacy chains—Brooks, CVS, and Walgreens—are generally open daily between 7 or 9:30 AM and 8 or 10 PM; independently owned pharmacies usually close earlier. Several pharmacies are open 24 hours a day.

Boston stores are generally open Monday through Saturday 10 or 11 AM–6 or 7 PM, closing later during the holiday-shopping season. Mall shops often stay open until 9 or 10 PM; malls and some tourist areas may also be open Sunday noon–5 or 6 PM.

▌ MONEY

Prices are generally higher in Beacon Hill, the Back Bay, and Harvard Square than elsewhere. You're more likely to find bargains in the North End, Kenmore Square, Downtown Crossing, and Cambridge's Central Square. Many museums have one evening of free admission each week. There are no "happy hours" at any Boston bars due to a state law ("blue laws") that forbids promotions of discounted liquor.

ITEM	AVERAGE COST
Cup of Coffee	$1–$2
Glass of Wine	$6 and up
Glass of Beer	$3.50 and up
Slice of Pizza	$1.50–$2.50
One-Mile Taxi Ride	$3.50–$4
Museum Admission	$7–$15

Prices throughout this guide are given for adults. Substantially reduced fees are almost always available for children, students, and senior citizens.

CREDIT CARDS

Throughout this guide, the following abbreviations are used: **AE**, American Express; **D**, Discover; **DC**, Diners Club; **MC**, MasterCard; and **V**, Visa.

It's a good idea to inform your credit-card company before you travel, especially if you're going abroad and don't travel internationally very often. Otherwise, the credit-card company might put a hold on your card owing to unusual activity—not a good thing halfway through your trip. Record all your credit-card numbers—as well as the phone numbers to call if your cards are lost or stolen—in a safe place, so you're prepared should something go wrong. Both MasterCard and Visa have general numbers you can call (collect if you're abroad) if your card is lost, but you're better off calling the number of

your issuing bank, since MasterCard and Visa usually just transfer you to your bank; your bank's number is usually printed on your card.

Reporting Lost Cards American Express (☎800/992–3404 in the U.S., 336/393–1111 collect from abroad ⊕www.americanexpress. com). **Diners Club** (☎800/234–6377 in the U.S., 303/799–1504 collect from abroad ⊕www.dinersclub.com). **Discover** (☎800/347–2683 in the U.S., 801/902–3100 collect from abroad ⊕www.discovercard.com). **MasterCard** (☎800/622–7747 in the U.S., 636/722–7111 collect from abroad ⊕www.mastercard.com). **Visa** (☎800/847–2911 in the U.S., 410/581–9994 collect from abroad ⊕www.visa.com).

TRAVELER'S CHECKS & CARDS

Some consider this the currency of the caveman, and it's true that fewer establishments accept traveler's checks these days. Nevertheless, they're a cheap and secure way to carry extra money, particularly on trips to urban areas. Both Citibank (under the Visa brand) and American Express issue traveler's checks in the United States, but Amex is better known and more widely accepted; you can also avoid hefty surcharges by cashing Amex checks at Amex offices. Whatever you do, keep track of all the serial numbers in case the checks are lost or stolen.

American Express now offers a stored-value card called a Travelers Cheque Card, which you can use wherever American Express credit cards are accepted, including ATMs. The card can carry a minimum of $300 and a maximum of $2,700, and it's a very safe way to carry your funds. Although you can get replacement funds in 24 hours if your card is lost or stolen, it doesn't really strike us as a very good deal. In addition to a high initial cost ($14.95 to set up the card, plus $5 each time you "reload"), you still have to pay a 2% fee for each purchase in a foreign currency (similar to that of any credit card). Further, each time you use the card in an ATM you pay a transaction fee of $2.50 on top of the 2% transaction fee for the conversion—add it all up and it can be considerably more than you would pay when simply using your own ATM card. Regular traveler's checks are just as secure and cost less.

Contact **American Express** (☎888/412–6945 in the U.S., 801/945–9450 collect outside the U.S. to add value or speak to customer service ⊕www.americanexpress.com).

▌ RESTROOMS

Public restrooms outside of restaurants, hotel lobbies, and tourist attractions are rare in Boston, but you'll find clean, well-lighted facilities at South Station, Faneuil Hall Marketplace, and the Visitor Information Center on Boston Common. Quarter-operated, self-cleaning public toilets can be found at Puopolo Park in the North End, near Faneuil Hall, at Central Wharf, and near the Boston Public Library.

Find a Loo **The Bathroom Diaries** (⊕www. thebathroomdiaries.com) is flush with unsanitized info on restrooms the world over—each one located, reviewed, and rated.

▌ SAFETY

With their many charming neighborhoods, Boston and Cambridge often feel like small towns. But they're both cities, subject to the same problems plaguing other urban communities nationwide. Although violent crime is rare, residents and tourists alike sometimes fall victim to pickpockets, scam artists, and car thieves. As in any large city, use common sense, especially after dark. Stay with the crowds and walk on well-lighted, busy streets. Look alert and aware; a purposeful pace helps deter trouble wherever you go. Take cabs or park in well-lighted lots or garages.

Store valuables in a hotel safe or, better yet, leave them at home. Keep an eye

(and hand) on handbags and backpacks; do not hang them from a chair in restaurants. Carry wallets in inside or front pockets rather than back pockets. Use ATMs in daylight, preferably in a hotel, bank, or another indoor location with security guards.

Subways and trolleys tend to be safe, but it's wise to stay on your guard. Stick to routes in the main Boston and Cambridge tourist areas—generally, the downtown stops on all lines, on the Red Line in Cambridge, on the Green Line through the Back Bay, and on the Blue Line around the New England Aquarium. Know your itinerary and make sure you get on the right bus or train going in the right direction. Avoid empty subway and trolley cars and lonely station hallways and platforms, especially after 9 PM on weeknights. The MBTA has its own police officers; don't hesitate to ask them for help.

▌TIP➔ Distribute your cash, credit cards, IDs, and other valuables between a deep front pocket, an inside jacket or vest pocket, and a hidden money pouch. Don't reach for the money pouch once you're in public.

▌ TAXES

Hotel room charges in Boston and Cambridge are subject to state and local taxes of up to 12.45%.

A sales tax of 5% is added to restaurant and take-out meals and to all other goods except nonrestaurant food and clothing valued at less than $175.

▌ TIME

Boston is in the eastern time zone, 3 hours ahead of Los Angeles, 1 hour ahead of Chicago, 5 hours behind London, and 15 hours behind Sydney. Daylight saving time is observed.

▌ TIPPING

In restaurants, the standard gratuity is 15%–20% of your bill. Many restaurants automatically add a 15%–20% gratuity for groups of six or more.

Tip taxi drivers 15% of the fare and airport and hotel porters at least $1 per bag. It's also usual to tip chambermaids $1–$3 daily. Hotel room-service tips vary and may be included in the meal charge. Masseuses and masseurs, hairstylists, manicurists, and others performing personal services generally get a 15% tip. Theater ushers, museum guides, and gas-station attendants generally do not receive tips. Tour guides may be tipped a few dollars for good service. Concierges may be tipped anywhere from $5 to $20 for exceptional service, such as securing a difficult dinner reservation or helping plan a personal sightseeing itinerary.

TIPPING GUIDELINES FOR BOSTON	
Bartender	$1–$2 per drink
Bellhop	$1 to $5 per bag, depending on the level of the hotel
Hotel Concierge	$5 or more, if he or she performs a service for you
Hotel Doorman	$1–$2 if he helps you get a cab
Hotel Maid	1$–$3 a day (either daily or at the end of your stay, in cash)
Hotel Room-Service Waiter	$1 to $2 per delivery, even if a service charge has been added
Porter at Airport or Train Station	$1 per bag
Skycap at Airport	$1 to $3 per bag checked
Taxi Driver	15%–20%, but round up the fare to the next dollar amount
Tour Guide	10% of the cost of the tour
Valet Parking Attendant	$1–$2, but only when you get your car
Waiter	15%–20%, with 20% being the norm at high-end restaurants; nothing additional if a service charge is added to the bill
Other	Restroom attendants in more-expensive restaurants expect some small change or $1. Tip coat-check personnel at least $1–$2 per item checked unless there is a fee, then nothing.

INDEX